Leaving My Father's House

An abridged version of *Leaving My Father's House* is available on audio tape from Shambhala Lion Editions.

Marion Woodman

Leaving My Father's House

A JOURNEY TO
CONSCIOUS FEMININITY

with
Kate Danson
Mary Hamilton
Rita Greer Allen

S H A M B H A L A
Boston & London   *1992*

Shambhala Publications
Horticultural Hall
300 Massachusetts Avenue
Boston, Massachusetts 02115

Shambhala Publications, Inc.
Random Century House
20 Vauxhall Bridge Road
London SW1V 2SA

9 8 7 6 5 4 3 2 1

First Edition

Printed in the United States of America on acid-free paper
⊗
Distributed in the United States by Random House, Inc.,
in Canada by Random House of Canada Ltd., and
in the United Kingdom by the Random Century Group

Library of Congress Cataloging-in-Publication Data

Woodman, Marion
Leaving my father's house: a journey to conscious femininity/
Marion Woodman.—1st ed.
p. cm.
ISBN 0-87773-578-6 (cloth: acid-free paper)
1. Women—Psychology. 2. Femininity (Psychology) 3. Archetype
(Psychology) I. Title.
HQ1206.W894 1992   90-53600
155.3'33—dc20   CIP

To Sophia

Contents

Preface

The four authors of this book met for the first time in October 1991. The manuscript was already in the publisher's office. For two and a half years they had chosen not to meet together. They wanted their material to be their own.

I had been at the center of this foursome, watching and participating in a process which from the beginning was propelled by a sense of inevitability—a book that wanted to be. As each of us wrote and rewrote from our thousands of pages of journaling, I realized that our inner worlds were communicating across the seeming emptiness of time and space. Repeatedly each woman thought she had finished, then something new happened in another who was hundreds of miles away, and a new threshold opened for all four.

As the time for our meeting drew near, I, who had watched the interweaving for so long, felt immense conflict building up inside me. Part of me accepted the inevitability of publishing; part was bone cold against it. I felt the integrity of the four souls involved. I also felt their vulnerability. When we finally came face to face, I was very aware of the depth of communication each recognized in the eyes of the other.

We shared our dreams about publishing. We agreed that the feminine voice had to speak its truth in the patriarchal culture. We felt strong together. . . . We allowed a long silence. And then a part of me that had never been given utterance began her faltering story in spite of the icy fingers that clutched my throat.

Fifteen years ago when I was a student at the C. G. Jung Institute in Zurich, one of our most important assignments was our individual exploration of a fairy tale. I became totally immersed in "Allerleirauh." Just before I was to deliver my paper, I received word that my mother was ill. I returned to Canada. On my arrival, Ross, my husband, told me it was too late to go to the hospital. Mother had died.

Standing alone beside her coffin the next morning, I was shattered by grief and guilt and rage. I, her only daughter, was not there when she needed me most. No final word was said. Had I listened to my intuition, I would not have returned to Zurich that term. On our way to the airport I had said, "I don't think I should go." She had replied, "Go, Marion. If you can find freedom, go." I had become too immersed in finding that freedom through the study of "Allerleirauh" and had not been sufficiently attuned to what was happening at home.

On the bleak day after her funeral, Zurich and all it stood for became a nightmare to me. A stupid fairy tale had seduced me into betraying my own mother. No phone could reach her, not even to speak three words. Eternity was a brutal, silent wall.

Sensitive to the chaos into which I was plunged, Ross invited seventeen of my women friends to our home to hear my fairy tale paper. I was outraged. How did he expect me to pull myself together? "Allerleirauh" meant nothing to my Canadian friends and nothing now to me. But he helped me arrange flowers and food and my friends arrived, Mary among them. Surrounded by their love my bone cold began to thaw. My soul very quietly began to read and gradually everything I had written began to make more sense than I could possibly have realized when I wrote it. My friends asked genuine questions and I felt they understood what freedom meant to me.

So here I was fifteen years later still working with "Allerleirauh," still reaching for deeper levels of freedom from patriarchal values, still conscious of the feminine despair that feared she would never be heard, and if she were, what difference would it make? Here I was in this moment, telling my story, trying to pull in my own masculine strength that would say yes to publication. As I spoke I felt the love and courage of the three women around me. I saw clearly how leaving our father's house had brought our own creative masculinity to birth. I saw too that inner strength that had made possible the deeper reconciliation with our personal mothers, generations of mothers, and the Great Mother. And I felt their love for us their daughters, proud of our womanhood.

Together we decided to dedicate *Leaving My Father's House* to Sophia.

Acknowledgments

Thank you

to Marie-Louise von Franz, whose understanding of fairy tales is invaluable in illuminating the psyche

to Robert Bly, whose succinct phrase during a conference became the title of this book

to Esalen, where Sophia mirrors God's grandeur, where this book was conceived and pondered in the heart

to Emily Hilburn Sell and David O'Neal, our editors

to our fathers, our mothers,
our brothers,
our physical sisters and soul sisters

to our husbands, with whom we have danced and fought,
laughed and cried,
talked and remained silent,
lived
for a total of one hundred and thirty-two years.

Marion, Kate, Mary, Rita

Leaving My Father's House

Introduction

The epiphany of that which had hitherto been hidden requires not only an ego to which it can manifest itself, but, to an even greater degree, calls for an act of attention and devotion on the part of the ego, an aptitude for being "moved," a willingness to see what wants to appear.

—ERICH NEUMANN

The eternal feminine is thrusting her way into contemporary consciousness. Shekinah, Kwan Yin, Sophia, whatever her name, she is the manifestation of the divine in matter. Among her many faces are the Black Madonna, White Buffalo Woman, Shakti, Kali, Aphrodite. Hers are the ways of peace, compassion, reverence for life and death in the oneness of nature. Knowing her has nothing to do with blindly stumbling toward a fate we think we cannot avoid. It has everything to do with developing consciousness until it is strong enough to hold tension as a creative energy. In the turmoil of our time, we are being called to a new order of reality. Working toward that consciousness, we suffer, but our suffering opens us to the wounds of the world and the love that can heal. It is our immediate task to relate to the emerging feminine whether she comes to us in dreams, in the loss of those we love, in body disease, or in ecological distress. Each of us in our own way is being brought face to face with Her challenge.

Conscious femininity is not bound to gender. It belongs to both men and women. Although in the history of the arts, men have articulated their femininity far more than women, women are now becoming custodians of their own feminine consciousness. For centuries, men have projected their inner image of femininity, raising it to a consciousness that left women who accepted the projection separated from their own reality. They became artifacts rather than people. The consciousness attributed to them was a consciousness projected onto them. That projection was sometimes an idealized image of beauty and truth, a sphinx, or a dragon. Whatever it was, it could not be an incarnated woman. A man does not have a womb, and the embodiment of his femininity is, therefore, different from a woman's.

The fact remains, however, we are all human beings. We are all the children of patriarchy. While our culture depends upon three thousand years of cultural process focused through masculine eyes, it has been won at high cost. What began as masculine values has degenerated into lust for control. Power has bludgeoned both our femininity and our masculinity. We all function with these two different energies. As health and growth depend on both dark and light, so maturity depends on an inner balance between Yin and Yang, Shakti and Shiva, Being and Doing. I prefer to call these energies femininity and masculinity because their biological images appear in dreams and their interaction or lack of interaction reveals harmony or chaos in the psyche. For me these words are not gender-bound.

Conscious femininity, as we will be discussing it in this book, has to do with bringing the wisdom in nature to consciousness. For too long we have taken the instinctual Mother Goddess for granted. In our own bodies, in our Earth, we have assumed she would nourish and protect us. We have wallowed in sentimental images. Over centuries, we have forgotten her, reviled her, raped her. Now we will either integrate her laws into consciousness or we will die. There is an evolutionary process at work on our planet and we can only hope that out of this present death, sanity will come. Thus far in our history, the unconscious feminine has been associated with instinct; now the conscious feminine is bringing light to instinct, illuminating nature with new images that come to us in our dreams and in creative work.

The task of releasing the feminine from the tyrannical power of the driven, crazed masculine is long and arduous. The process is just as difficult inside as it is outside. Observing it abstractly is one thing; experiencing it personally is quite another.

This book looks inside. It flowered out of one specific dream (see page 71). Four years ago I was preparing a lecture on the feminine in academe. Kate, one of my analysands, was currently working on her doctoral thesis, battling with herself and her professors. I asked her if she would be willing to share that dream, which she had dreamt almost two years earlier. She agreed.

The dream became increasingly significant. Two years ago I asked her permission to include it in a book.

"I know I'm not finished with that dream yet," she said and arrived at her next session with forty pages of concentrated dreamwork. She was agitated, apprehensive. Propelled by an inner inquiry, she had begun to rethink all the dreams of that period. From her present perspective, she was able to hold a detached position that allowed her to discern an emerging pattern. Like a detective in search of herself, Kate was determined to find the thread through the labyrinth of her dreams and compulsions. The deeper she went into her associations, the more questions she asked, and the more the unconscious pattern became conscious. Eventually she submitted to the inner demand, suspended her thesis for a year, and focused on the inner work she had done during the past six years. She knew that the feminine consciousness she wanted to bring to her thesis had to be rooted in her own reality.

As I watched Kate's story taking shape, I was aware of a similar process happening in two other women. Mary and Rita were working in very different ways for very different reasons at very different stages in life. All three were in a stage of their process that demanded concentrated focus to synthesize the parts into a whole. As the roots of understanding dug deeper into their hearts, each understood more clearly with her head; gradually heart and head were becoming a whole woman immersed in finding the inner truth that could set her free. For years, each had been creating her soul story every day in her dream journal, but the time had come to step back and perceive the whole story with every cell in her body.

In this transitional time, all three were discarding stereotypes that had long since died. In their dreams they were throwing out old clothes, old tapes, old furniture. As memories resurfaced, all three relived the original pain in their bodies and noted every innuendo of body awareness. They were bringing to consciousness new images that guided them in their shifting relationships. In communicating with these inner symptoms and symbols, they made sense of themselves in a new way.

"This is femininity moving into consciousness," I thought. "These three stories are paragraphs in a bigger story—Sophia's story, Sophia making herself known. Kate, Mary, and Rita are doing all they can to free her radiance from the darkness of matter."

I know how difficult it is to uphold Sophia's values in a world that has no time for her. I know how many people are alone, suffering radical upheavals in their dreams without any support. I know also that the healing power of the dream process cannot be comprehended by looking at two or three dreams. It has to be followed over a period of years, coming directly from the dreams, in order to begin to appreciate its wisdom. So I asked Kate, Mary, and Rita if they wanted to tell part of their stories. For two years we dialogued with inner figures making sure that their mystery would not be violated. Gradually each of the three women came to her own decision to publish. For the most part their material has been edited from their journals. Many of the images are archetypal, and are shared in the hope that readers will recognize some of their own images. In that recognition, there may be a growing awareness of an immense shift that is thrusting its way out of the collective unconscious into consciousness. None of us would suggest that we have reached a goal; none of us pretends to have the answer; all of us agree that the meaning is in the process.

I regret that I do not have a contemporary man's story of his evolving femininity. Certainly if we read the meditations of the saints, study great poets, musicians, and artists, we can follow their feminine soul's journey. In fairy tales, the heroine personifies the feminine in men and women. Our psychic maps are similar. Men who are trying to live their soul values in our culture are challenged and mocked in ways that women need to contemplate. We are children of the same parents. We share the cruel and tragic shadow of patriarchal power.

I recognize that in writing we fictionalize ourselves as we do in storytelling. In telling our stories, however, if we can allow the story to move with its own momentum, we can distill our truth from our fiction. And the truth changes from day to day, sometimes from hour to hour. That's why we have to keep in close touch with our story. If our imagery becomes concretized, if it ceases to come out of the living reality of our bodies, then we are worshipping stone gods and we are on our way to becoming like our gods—petrified.

Storytelling is at the heart of life. Sometimes when I drop into reverie I can see my inner life continuing where my dream stopped when I woke up. As a child, I was never bored because I could always get on with my story. I still love to walk by the water or in the woods listening to the story that never ends. Always my imagination is creating a form that gives shape to otherwise sporadic events in everyday life. That creative fire molds my inner chaos into a reflection of the sacred order I feel in nature.

I used to be very suspicious of this activity, even ashamed of it. Then I read Jung's account of the Pueblo Indians. He knew that if they ever lost faith in their story, the mystery that held them together as a noble people would vanish. I remembered the few times in my life when I had rationally cut my story off and how my life had fallen apart in those intervals. That story continues in dreams, every night doing its healing work. Gradually I am recognizing the meaning of my existence through my own myth. More and more I understand Jung's dream of the yogi meditating in a church. When he realized the yogi had his face, he awoke in profound fright with this thought: " 'Aha, so he is the one who is meditating me. He has a dream and I am it.' I knew that when he awakened, I would no longer be."[1]

Storytellers are important individuals in a culture. They take us into a world where we are no longer chopped into the piecemeal facts of life. They hold a vision beyond the literal and physical in an imaginal world where fact is linked with possibility, where individual memories, visions, and rituals can be knit into the fabric of the group. It isn't that the numinosity of the individual vision is watered down for the group, but that the group begins to have a new vision of itself and individuals are no longer isolated. Without stories, we lack the cosmos that keeps us in touch with the universal reality. Without stories, we have no way to recollect ourselves when our personal world shatters. We cannot remember what it was to love and be loved, to be cherished in the world around us.

Since stories reflect our inner lives, women need to tell stories of what it means to be a woman. I have realized this repeatedly in analytic sessions, but it came through at a tribal level when I was working with a group of women at a conference in Orillia, Canada. One woman stood up, quietly commented on what had been said, and then, beyond her control to stop it, her story began to tell itself. It came with a clarion-clear honesty that pierced the heart of every one of the hundred women in the room. Inner and outer stories came together. We recognized ourselves and the tears flowed. Afterwards, we contained the grief in ritual movement and song.

Meanwhile, Robert Bly was working with the men. The grief of the fathers and sons erupted in their storytelling. They too had seen themselves reflected in their stories. Their faces were as transformed as ours when we came back together. We sat in concentric circles, telling the essence of what had gone on in each group. There was no bickering, no bitterness. We each recognized the anguish of the other. We re-membered our shared humanity. For a few moments at least, our patriarchal glasses were torn off. We saw. We saw the depth of the wounding. We also felt the presence of the God and Goddess coming through the wound. The love that burns the heart clean was there.

Our culture is riddled with the loss of feeling values because so many stories go on in the soul but are never heard. Many people have long since forgotten what they do value, and, if they do remember, they try to forget. They want to be successful in a competitive society. They want to be loved, whatever that means, when they are pretending to be someone they are not. They are so adolescent they dare not look at themselves. That would mean taking responsibility for who they are. They dare not reflect themselves to themselves; they dare not look at the tapestry of their lives spun every night in the images of their dreams. This is a tragic loss because these images shape our inner and outer lives. Without a conscious connection to them, life is lived unconsciously. With a conscious connection, life is connected to its creative source. And because these images are continually evolving— daily in analysis if the heat is hot enough—our close relationship to them assures a link between the conscious ego and the creative energy that keeps the story vital, whole, and holy.

In finding our own story, we assemble all the parts of ourselves. Whatever kind of mess we have made of it, we can somehow see the totality of who we are and recognize how our blunderings are related. We can own what we did and value who we are, not because of the outcome but because of the soul story that propelled us. That story is our individual myth.

Perhaps it is important to point out that throughout the Christian era much attention has been focused on the distinction between spirit and flesh. The middle ground—the soul, what Keats calls "Soul-making"—was strangely absent. In the nineteenth century, the soul found its place in the music, literature, and art of the Romantic Movement. Keats's "Ode to Psyche," written in 1819, sums up his discovery and exploration of Psyche. Psyche, he says, has never been properly acknowledged and he, therefore, will build a temple to her in "some untrodden region of [his] mind"[2]—that region ignored both by spirit and flesh, mind and matter. Psyche lives in a state not unlike that of Allerleirauh in the fairy tale we will discuss. Her invisibility is her banishment; her recognition after enormous soulmaking is her return. This book differentiates Psyche as soul and creative masculinity as spirit. It is not a religious testimonial. It is not about a new religion. It is about femininity becoming human, returning from banishment and transforming our lives.

Kate, Mary, and Rita were living ordinary lives until destiny brought each to a crisis in which her suffering distilled the question from her lips, "What is my life about?" Each believed the answer was in her unconscious and, through dreamwork and bodysoul work, established a dialogue between conscious and unconscious. That dialogue became the living water in her desert. Her wounding released her creativity.

These stories are not case studies. While each woman spent some months with me working in depth, circumstances in life—distance, illness, money—made regular visits to my office over a period of several years impossible. At times, each had to dare her own depths in her own way in her own home.

Synchronistically, these three women, unknown to each other, propelled by an inner impetus, began to write their soul stories. I was close to each. I suffered with them, while at the same time holding an objective point of view. I helped to bring to consciousness the individual stories and looked for what they shared in common. I saw with my physical eyes, perceived with my inner eye, and empathized with the new life that was desperate to be born. While watching the personal stories unfold, I felt each woman tapping into ancient feminine roots—roots that I have explored in fairy tales. To connect the personal stories to a deeper understanding of the eternal feminine, I have chosen Allerleirauh as a prototype of the feminine leaving her father's house.

This book is our contribution to Sophia's book.

Leaving My Father's House

By the roots of my hair some god got hold of me.
I sizzled in his blue volts like a desert prophet.

—Sylvia Plath[1]

The "once upon a time" world of the fairy tale is the spaceless, time-less world of the soul. The ancient stories with their stark story lines map the many inner paths toward wholeness. All the characters are parts of us. They are images that personify attributes of people we live with every day, and princes, witches, and animals that visit us in our dreams every night. While the laws of the world of matter (nature) are not the laws of the world of psyche (soul), the images apply to both worlds. They are the connectors. If we concentrate on the images in our stories and dreams until we distill their truth, we ground ourselves in the reality of our own imagery. Life lived from our inner truth is not an empty performance. It is a dynamic, moment-by-moment discovery.

Distilling the truth of the image is the work. Einstein, for example, dreamed that he was sliding along a sunbeam. Then he saw himself reflected in a mirror fastened on his feet. Immediately he realized that he was, in fact, riding the sunbeam. In other words, he was moving at the same speed as light. He was light. It took him a lifetime of reflection to distill the truth of that image. The concentration that brought him to $E = MC^2$ has changed the consciousness of the world.

As I concentrated to distill the truth in the stories of Kate, Mary, and Rita, I thought, "Now these are all father's daughters. One knew her father admired her mind; one knew her father admired her body; one adored her father from a distance. As each came into adulthood, her life energy circled around men. Each was driven to please patriarchal standards. Her motors were powered by her relationships to the outer world. The total available energy of her psyche was in the father complex. The mother complex was either destructively judgmental or

9

repressed. Each is finding her own way out by centering in her own creative matrix."

Then I thought of the Grimm's fairy tale "Allerleirauh" (pronounced *Aller-lie-row*). "There's the thread," I thought. "There's a story of the feminine releasing herself from patriarchy." By patriarchy I mean a culture whose driving force is power. Individuals within that culture are driven to seek control over others and themselves in an inhuman desire for perfection. Thus a patriarchal father is no more destructive to his child's psychological growth than is a mother who may appear in dreams as an idealistic murderous Nazi officer. Both genders carry the tragic shadow of patriarchal power.

The whole story appears in the appendix of this book. I will weave the parts into the stories of Kate, Mary, and Rita.

Here were three little princesses who, like many little girls, knew that so long as they pleased their parents, they were lovable. They strove to be the best. Part of each of them was the obedient, self-effacing daughter, forever seeking, forever powerless. Part of each of them was disconnected from her source in her female body and, like her mother and generations of grandmothers, she carried deep body memories of sexual guilt and shame.

Allerleirauh, whose name means "of many kinds of fur," is the princess in her parents' kingdom. The Queen's beauty is not to be equalled on earth and, as she is about to die, she extracts from the King the promise that he will not marry again unless he finds a woman equally as beautiful with "just such golden hair." After her death, the disconsolate King mourns alone. His councillors beg him to marry again but his messengers find no one of equal beauty with "just such golden hair."

This Queen rules the roost in popular soap operas, an image of femininity for millions of men and women. Vain and jealous, she is determined to dominate her man even after death. Dependent and sentimental, he succumbs to her evil witchery, wasting his time yearning for a paradise that never was. He cannot move his energy into the flux and spontaneity of life.

Hair comes straight from the head as ideas come straight from the head. In dreams, as in life, the coiffure, the cutting, growing, and dyeing of hair are symptomatic of significant changes in the psyche (soul) or the persona (the mask we show to the world). The analyst often appears as the hairdresser. Golden is usually associated with the

sun, immortality, spiritual numinosity. In this part of the story, however, spirit is bastardized into power, plotting what amounts to the
spiritual death of the King. The creative energy associated with gold
has turned to gilt.

Now, after a long time, the volcano of repressed energy in the King
erupts when one day he sees his daughter who is just as beautiful as her
dead mother with "just such golden hair." To the horror of his councillors and even greater horror of his daughter he falls in love with her
and determines to marry her.

Who is the King in a fairy tale? Outwardly, he is the personification
of a dominant content in the collective consciousness of the culture. As
an inner image, he usually carries godlike wholeness, solar brilliance,
and spiritual insight. In our culture, professors, evangelists, gurus, and
therapists often carry the projection of the King.

Women who have adored their fathers may project their inner King
onto a simple man, crown him with light, invest him with their own
intellectual and spiritual potential, and then wonder why he isn't big
enough to fill his royal vestments. Indeed, the very intensity of the
light they are projecting may constellate the pitch blackness of his fear
and rage. Sons of such women may be doomed to pleasing or destroying their mother or their mother surrogate. Too often they carry the
royal projection of a woman who has abdicated responsibility for her
own gifts. Because she doesn't know her own King within, she projects him out. Her husband has failed in his regal role and so her son
carries the weight of Kingship with its devouring demands.

The King in this story is contaminated with some such cultural
malaise. Outwardly, he holds the power. However, his heady Queen is
dead, that is, his feeling connection to life is not there. He is locked into
his sentimental ideal of perfect womanhood. In psychological terms,
such a man is trapped in a mother complex. Until mother is brought to
consciousness, a man does not experience her as an individual woman
with thoughts and feelings of her own. She is an archetypal image that
wields either sexual or spiritual power over him. He has not brought
his own feeling values to consciousness and, therefore, cannot relate to
his woman as a person. When the perfect image that he is projecting
onto her is threatened by her expression of her own needs and
thoughts, he may roar that she is not the nourishing, loving person he
married, and go off to look for a woman who is as unconscious as his
own inner feminine. He will often find a woman who looks just like

his wife at twenty. In other words, his inner feminine has not matured at all; his self-esteem still depends on a woman's projection of golden boy onto him.

Or he may be golden daddy to his golden-haired woman. She lives in her head, cut off from the truth of her ground in her own matter. Thus her feeling values are as unpredictable as her man's. In her fear of being rejected by her father-husband, she may flip out of mother into little princess who panders to Daddy's know-it-all. Until the feminine is firmly connected to the musculature of the body, it lacks the visceral affirmation that says, "This is of value to me. This is who I am." How many people who believe they never dream are sleepwalking in their marriage, in their job, in their church, blindly adhering to ideas they never question, with no heart in what they are doing? When the emotions that quiver in the gut are connected to the feeling values, conscious femininity is grounded in its own truth. So long as the feminine is unconscious, dependent on the masculinity that is dependent on her, the psychic constellation is incestuous—mother bound to son or daughter bound to father.

We are talking here about the big M and the big F—Mother complex and Father complex, the two biggest dynamos in our psyches. Bonding or lack of bonding to our personal parents generates these dynamos of unconscious associations that influence our future relationships with men, women, children, and society. If as daughters our umbilical cord is connected to male values (our father's or mother's or both), then in adult life we think our very survival depends upon obeisance to patriarchal standards. We have to be 36–24–36, we have to measure up, we have to have backbone. Unconsciously, we are driven to fulfill expectations that may have little to do with who we are. So unconscious is the driving voice in these complexes that our bodies may have to break down before we recognize that we are slaves to an inner dictator. The complexes are in us. Projecting our rage onto men does nothing to resolve the inner victim/tyrant constellation.

The femininity of the man who has been bullied by the patriarchal aspects of his parents is in a similar situation—perhaps worse. He may have a judgmental mother complex that reduces him to paralysis if he has to displease his woman, his corporation, or his alma mater. Or he may become the dangerous bully, out to destroy what has destroyed him. Often it takes a broken heart, literally or symbolically, to bring his femininity to consciousness.

In Jung's model of the psyche, associations with our personal parents or loss of them become complexes. They cluster around an archetype. The father complex has at its core the God archetype, the mother, the Goddess, in both their positive and negative aspects. These archetypes are energy fields that leave us "sizzled in [their] blue volts."[2] They can fill us with radiant light, or overwhelm us with destruction and despair. They are our gods within, spiritually and instinctually. Without access to them, life becomes a boring two-dimensional existence. Relating to them allows us to work at incarnating our angels and our animals.

Archetypes are energy fields innate in our psyches. They are like hidden magnets. We cannot see them, but we can see their images and we are propelled by their energy. If, for example, we go to a party and see a man who makes us tremble, we may be fairly sure that our father complex is activated. If the trembling becomes shaking, we are probably being moved into archetypal energy. If we are young and inexperienced, our unconscious fires the arrow called projection. The man it strikes then carries for us our inner Father-God image. Or our demon. If his mother complex is vibrating in our presence and the vibrations are becoming harmonics, then his unconscious fires the Mother Goddess arrow into us. Or the femme fatale. If our ego is strong enough, we can choose whether "to fall in love" or not. If it is not strong enough, we are already in the soup. These archetypal magnets attract and repel. Gods and vampires, goddesses and witches are alarmingly close in this domain. They make us or break us, depending on our conscious relationship to them.

> *How Complicate*
> *The Discipline of Man—*
> *Compelling Him to Choose Himself*
> *His Preappointed Pain.*

> —EMILY DICKINSON[3]

One tragic loophole in our culture is our failure to tell the difference between *identifying* with an archetype and *relating* to it. When addicts talk about a high or a fix, what they mean psychologically is that they want to identify with an archetype. They want to forget the realities of being human beings and escape into godlike power. They want to give over their weak ego to unconscious drives. They want to be God or Goddess. However, they have not done the hard, patient work of building a psychic container. That container, which begins as the ego, has to be flexible enough to expand with divine energy. It is the instrument through which divinity manifests. It has to know that it is the instrument of the divine; it is not the God or Goddess. It has to be humble enough to return to its human dimensions.

Shakespeare, for example, having mastered his technique, could open himself to a divine seizure and allow *Hamlet* to be born. He could then be plain Will and go to the pub for a drink.

Conscious femininity is grounded enough to relate to the divine without identifying with it; conscious masculinity is discriminating enough to cut identification with a sharp sword. Identification is unconscious; relationship is conscious.

Identification with archetypal energy breeds inflation that swings into deflation. False hope, false power, fake gods collapse in agony. Without the discipline and boundaries provided by the church, many people do not know—consciously know—whether they are gods or human beings. Wild as that statement sounds, it is the root of our being swung out of too much light into despair. An unconscious mother, male or female, identifies with the Mother Goddess and burns herself out trying to nurture all the abandoned children she finds. She feeds everyone without recognizing that her own shadow is starving her own inner child. She may project golden child-god onto her son who identifies with the projection while he is in her presence. When he leaves, he collapses into the black light of a cocaine addiction. The father who projects brilliance onto his daughter may create an overachiever who unconsciously yearns for the darkness of her own earth in an eating addiction. The very unreality of the projection activates an overcompensation that attempts to restore the human balance.

Parental projections between adult men and women boggle the mind. If there is no ego container strong enough to say, "I am not a god or goddess. I am not what you think I am," then the psychic pendulum swings too far into the light. The receiver identifies with the projection, becomes inflated, dreams of exploding hot-air balloons and the pendulum ricochets into the darkness of despair. Without firm human middle ground, there is no bodysoul container in which the inner animals can be tamed, or the spirit can be embodied. The relentless swinging simply increases in velocity, until the ego is strong enough to shout, "Stop it. I am not Luke Skywalker. I'm going to find myself." In the feminine, Luke's counterpart is Lucia. Both names are derived from the Latin *lux*, meaning "light." So is Lucifer.

In our story Allerleirauh, shocked by her father's incestuous designs, decides she will not be sizzled by her father's projection. She is a warrior. She will not carry his ectoplasmic body to her grave. She devises a plan to find herself. "Before I fulfill your wish," she says to him, "I must have three dresses, one as golden as the sun, one as silvery as the moon, and one as bright as the stars; . . ."

In this book, Kate, Mary, and Rita each came to a crisis where she had either to accept her fate in incestuous collusion with patriarchy or conquer her fear and search for her own identity. Each found her own path as we all have to do. Kate began her journey in analysis. Initially, her need for meaning attracted her to the golden dress. Mary, a professional dancer, began her journey by moving consciously into her body. There she learned to wear the silver. Rita knew something about dancing in gold and silver. At seventy-two, she was ready to contemplate the brightness of the stars.

Of course, no journey can be rigidly divided into gold, silver, and stars. Some people develop their solar consciousness until their ego is strong enough to drop into lunar consciousness. Others move through the moon to the sun. In any process, however, the two energies move like two intertwining snakes. The feminine energy may move ahead until the container is strong enough to receive the masculine; the masculine spirit glows brighter as the bodysoul grows stronger. The intertwining moves through rung after rung, like a double helix on a spiral, until the inner marriage is consummated. Again it moves into more and more delicate tuning. As energies shift inside, so relationships change outside.

In this book I have made no differentiation between lesbian, homosexual, and heterosexual relationships. In all individuals, there are two energies that strive to find a harmonious balance. Sometimes they repel; sometimes they attract. To grow to our full potential, we have to allow these energies space to grow, interact, transform. The name we give them is our own choice. I prefer feminine and masculine because I watch their intertwining personified in women and men in dreams. In addition, their biological images—uterus, breasts, menstrual blood, egg, or phallus, testes, ejaculation, sperm—are fundamental to understanding the creative process in dreams. Although no two processes are the same, the psychic maps are similar.

In the fairy tale, Allerleirauh makes one further demand, which she hopes her father cannot fulfill. ". . . I wish for a mantle of a thousand different kinds of fur and peltry joined together, and one of every kind of animal in your kingdom must give a piece of his skin for it." When the King does fulfill all her seemingly impossible demands, he sets the wedding day for tomorrow and his daughter runs away in the night. She takes three treasures—a golden ring, a tiny golden spinning wheel, and a golden reel. She places her three dresses in a nutshell, puts on her mantle of furs, blackens her face and hands with soot, commends herself to God, and leaves her father's house.

What does it feel like to leave your father's house? Or your father-husband's house? How does it feel to look into his eyes and see yourself as the betrayer of the one man who has always trusted you? How does it feel to leave the security of his love even if he never cared who you were? How does it feel to say no to a man to whom you have always said yes? What happens in your body when you stand up to a beloved professor and reject all the standards that he has never questioned? And when he calls your feminine approach rambling, lacking in clarity, coherence, and emphasis, do you wonder if you are stupid? And when you find yourself alone in your empty apartment, hearing voices inside you previously thought were outside, do you wonder if finding yourself is all it was cracked up to be? Can you be the person you have always denied?

Becoming conscious of the reality of her situation takes Allerleirauh out of her unconscious Garden of Eden. Her father's lightning bolt destroys the projection that held her in incestuous bonding. Trapped in unconscious incest, a woman may identify with her father's masculinity, and/or identify with his idea of femininity and the femininity of every man who projects onto her. She is at the mercy of male projections because her identification severs her from her authentic life.

Expelled from Eden, Allerleirauh runs to the forest and does the only thing she can do. She falls asleep in a hollow tree. Her feminine instinct tells her that her survival depends on returning to the womb of nature. To do this, she has to retire from society at the court, from the King, from all the images that were projected onto her. She covers her true identity with the soot of shame and guilt and makes herself invisible in the dead skins of her father's kingdom. Some women in the hollow tree are totally withdrawn. Others know their instincts have been deadened by the world in which they have grown up, but some conventions are still necessary in order to survive at all. They hide their reality, but find men who will not engage their deepest feelings: intellectuals who reflect their brilliance in witty conversation; faithful Joes who are still in touch with their own instincts. Many women seek the womb of nature in relationships with other women.

Allerleirauh carries her feminine treasures and symbols of sun, moon, and stars in her nutshell—the whole constellation of heaven in embryo. In the fullness of time, the patient, intricate process shapes the microcosm that magnifies the macrocosm.

Sometimes the hollow tree is literally a time to sleep, if sleep is possible. The trauma of recognizing the truth for the first time creates a veil that obliterates life outside and opens inner reality. Initially this is healing. It can become dangerous if it goes on too long; sinking into the feminine inertia of nature can be seductive. It can become an escape from fears of insanity or conflicts in the outer world. Paradoxically, the hollow tree is a tomb and a womb within the Great Mother.

Allerleirauh cannot stay in her tree forever. A neighboring king and his huntsmen sniff out "the wondrous beast" lying in the tree. The King orders that the terrified creature be taken to his palace to work in the kitchen. There the huntsmen point out a closet under the stairs where no daylight enters and say, "Hairy animal, there you can live and sleep."

Now the story takes on a very feminine tidal movement. Gradually, Allerleirauh ventures up to the King's corridors, and then retreats into her own dark den, again she moves up, and then again returns, each time venturing further with more consciousness, until the venturing and the inevitability of the outcome are one.

The den under the stairs is an advanced version of the hollow tree—a womb in which she is pregnant with herself, beneath a staircase that connects her to another level of consciousness. Like many contemporary women, Allerleirauh has to learn to mother herself. The golden-haired Queen, who bewitched her father, exacted a promise that negates the ebb and flow of life. The feminine flow in the kingdom is dead because values are focused in the head with no recognition of the human animal. They lead to compulsive sexuality, compulsive exercise, compulsive anything that destroys instinctual balance. Inside her furry coat, Allerleirauh can begin to connect back to the Paleolithic goddess. In her own body she can celebrate the round beauty of her breasts and belly, feel the life-generating Goddess that recognizes Herself in the rolling hills. She can feel Her deep anger and sense of rejection, Her immense suffering, Her incredible strength. She can honor her own blood, the passionate red that connects her to the moon above and the mud below—"the mud that may slide into the sea, the mud of the flow of Christ's empty tomb, the mud that darkens the vision of the third Eye, mud that has blood in it, mud that moves, dissolves, gently invites her to sink into it."[4] This is the Great Mother alive—the creative matrix in which death is constantly giving birth to life.

This creative matrix is closely connected to the silver dress. Reconnecting to it and holding a conscious connection is a lifetime task that begins in the early stages of finding ourselves. For most of us it takes years of concentrated effort to dare to move consciously into that matrix. We run up and down our psychic stairs, we know there's a dark hole, we frantically run around it or fall into it in our addictions. The Great Mother—creator and destroyer—is waiting there.

Some people's den begins in the analyst's office. They run out of their patriarchal world at four-thirty. Their heels click-click-click efficiently down the stairs. They arrive at the office. Down comes the hair, off come the shoes, out come the soot of jealousy and shame and the furs of sexuality, fight or flight. Gradually, the tongue slows down to soul speed, they work on their journals and dreams. For a moment at least, they are in the creative matrix, what Blake calls "a Moment in each Day that Satan cannot find."[5] Some people's den is their own living room or studio or cottage. Wherever it is, it is sacred space where they can drop deep into their own nature and connect with the divine within.

The kitchen in which Allerleirauh must do the dirty work is closely related to the den. The raw unconscious energies from outside—turkeys, cows, vegetables—are brought inside. The ego works hard to clean them, civilize them, put them into the fire where they can be transformed and made accessible to human consciousness. What we eat physically and psychically becomes us. It is our task to choose what is right for us to eat, how hot to make our own fire, and when to throw out our own ashes. The dreams will tell us. Sometimes we need red meat to sustain our masculinity, fowl to feed our feminine, fish to strengthen us spiritually. Sometimes we need the fruits and vegetables from the womb of Mother. Gradually, we gain the strength and courage to go up the stairs to the ball.

Allerleirauh asks the cook if she may go, just to place herself outside the door. "Yes, go, but you must be back here in half-an-hour to sweep the hearth." The cook who tends the alchemical fire and the transformative cooking is a magician figure. He knows that conflict makes energy. Cranky and subversive as he appears, his very negativity goads the heroine into acting from her own desire. His formidable voice telling her she is good for nothing finds echoes in herself. If she cannot find her own strength, she will set herself up as a target for anybody's boots. She is in danger of becoming a willing martyr. This is the very moment when a woman may drop the hair in the soup—the detached thought that can cut her off from herself and set up the resistance that pushes the King away. The dark side of the masculine harangues the woman, "You're not good enough. You're stupid. You're not beautiful. You haven't starved enough. Why don't you give up?" This destructive potential has to be counterbalanced by the authentic voice of the feminine, however frail it initially is. Gradually, with growing discernment, the heroine may realize that the magician-cook is providing an opening into the light of the ballroom and he is ordering the making of the soup. Moreover, his know-nothing attitude when he is questioned by the King protects her from being revealed before she finds her own strength. Superficially, the nagging cook is the last thing the suffering heroine needs, but he plays an important role in the calamity that is taking her to consciousness. Light in the darkness is a central paradox in any journey.

Allerleirauh knows she is ready for her first meeting with the King. She takes her oil lamp, goes into her den, takes off her dress of fur, washes the soot from her face and hands so that her radiance comes to light. She opens the nut and puts on the dress that shines like the sun. She goes to the ball. No one knows her. All assume that she is a king's daughter. The King dances with her and thinks in his heart, "My eyes have never yet seen anyone so beautiful." She curtsies. The King turns toward her. She has vanished. No one knows whither.

Before going further with Allerleirauh, we need to ask ourselves, "Who am I when I wear my golden dress to dance with the King?"

Part One

The
Golden
Dress

Chapter 1

The Golden Dress

The creative process, so far as we are able to follow it at all, consists in the unconscious activation of an archetypal image, and in elaborating and shaping this image into the finished work. By giving it shape, the artist translates it into the language of the present, and so makes it possible for us to find our way back to the deepest springs of life.

—C. G. JUNG

In our fairy tale, the heroine is following the archetypal motif of the heavenly journey. As in many contemporary men and women, the feminine learns to trust the sun before daring to move toward the moon. Psychologically, she needs to contact her own spirit and her own sense of inner order and discrimination (sun) before moving into the chaotic depths of her own bodysoul (moon). Having digested these depths, she will be ready to open to the cosmos of which she is a part (stars).

As Allerleirauh follows the path of feminine initiation that will release her into psychological freedom, each dress in her nutshell symbolizes a specific phase of her journey. Clothes in fairy tales, like clothes in dreams and life, create an image. They cover and reveal our naked truth. If we dream that we are wearing a golden blouse and a silver fishtail, we need to seriously consider the discrepancy between our breasts and our genitals. Color, cut, texture, period are all significant. They may create a persona we assume to impress the world; they may be an authentic expression of who we are.

In the mystery religions, initiates changed their clothes at each step of initiation. The inner transformation was symbolized in particular clothing, each garment being identified with an inner archetype.

23

When the ceremony was complete, the clothes were taken off. The person was no longer identified with a god.

Ritual clothes are still very important. Think of the hours we spend choosing our bridal gown. Think of the archetype we are relating to when we choose traditional white. Contrast that image with one in which the bride and groom both wear tuxedos, she in black, he in white. Remembering the passovers in our lives, most of us can remember every detail of our clothing. And the shifts in mood when we changed.

Halloween is a festival of archetypal dress. Certainly performers like Michael Jackson and Madonna are very aware that the "media is the message."

What then is going on in a heroine who lives in a mantle of furs in a den, and then after months of wretched work in the kitchen, ascends the staircase to the ball in a dress of gold? Many women, like Kate, have so identified with patriarchal, collective values that they are buried inside the dead skins of their father's kingdom. Whether they adore their actual father, or the image of the father they never had, or their dead or divorced father, they yearn to please their perfect daddy. In idealizing the outer king, they may become competitive, ambitious, goal-oriented, and compulsively efficient. Unconsciously they may become everything they despise. Their pseudo-masculinity ravages their femininity and castrates their creative spirit. These precious parts of themselves cower in terror before the onslaught of their driving bully.

An example from my own analysis illustrates how unconsciously willpower (pseudo-masculinity) can ravage ourselves and those we love. During the first year with my analyst, Dr. Bennet, I was totally committed to becoming conscious as quickly as possible. Suddenly, I fell into a black hole. Total chaos! I decided the only solution was to understand exactly what was going on. I read day and night for a week and, bursting with knowledge, I leapt into Dr. Bennet's office. I knew what was wrong with me and I knew how to cure it. I spent the whole hour elaborating, weaving together my profound insights. I noticed he was wilting in his chair, but the more he wilted, the faster I talked. I had to please Dad. At the end of the hour, he quietly helped me on with my coat and took me to the elevator. With a twinkle in his eighty-year-old eyes, he pushed the button and said, "If I were you, Mrs. Woodman, I would take my animus for a good drink." I was so angry I didn't even take him for a muffin.

Superficially, I had done a very creative thing. I had found my spirit and driven my despair underground. However, at the level where life matters, I had run over a man I profoundly respected with a steam-roller. Feeling between us was obliterated. Spirit without love became power. I was not related to the outer man, to my creative spirit, nor to the poor creature in the den.

What was missing in my desperate effort was the soul work in the kitchen. In those days my inflated spirit was flying; my repressed instincts were caged. Both were cut off from my soul in body. I was well *trained* in a culture that abhorred "dirty" kitchen work. I had to learn to recognize the power shadow in my masculinity, push my pause button, drop my shoulders, drop my breath into my belly, and hold still until the flying masculine was ready to listen to the forsaken feminine, both within and without.

Culturally, the kitchen work is still not being done and, therefore, furs and gowns are reduced to a masquerade—costumes that cannot hide emptiness. Without the diligence to bite off, chew, swallow, digest, and assimilate the new energy available in the kitchen, the ego is often too weak to take time to evacuate. Certainly it is too lethargic to build a fire. Without fire, no transformation can take place. No passion ignites matter. No phoenix can rise from no ashes. Even the Dionysian dance symbolized in the furs becomes a boring parody of the ecstasy the body yearns for. Striving to wear the gold without sifting the ashes becomes inflation, probably puffed up by a bottle of Scotch or a shot of cocaine. When the high is over, nothing has transformed. No one was there to transform. The infantile ego limply rests in its den until another Scotch or another fix cheats it into an archetypal high, or low. The stolen gold brings momentary escape. Too soon the gift flips into darkness—sullen, vicious, chaotic.

The kitchen work is the anchor that is missing in this kind of swinging from light to dark. Many young and old visionaries thirst for an ideal world that they do not associate with the necessity of their own hard work. When they look at the news or watch an ecological program, their dreams are shattered. They feel powerless. Their energy swings into rage or escape—sadism, sexuality, or sleep. Their patriarchal, rational thinking makes them want to dominate life, to enforce their meaning on it. Their false sense of their own phallic power sets them up as arrogant Lucifers defying a stupid God. The

feminine patience, which would put them in touch with their humanness inside their own instincts, is not there. They are too proud to
submit to life. They talk about honoring the organic world of nature
(furs) and the spiritual order (gold). But it is talk until it is lived in the
relentless kitchen work.

Life is not ordered according to our perfect schemes. When gold and
furs collide, head pulls in one direction, instincts in another. Anyone
who is compulsively in love with the wrong person knows that. Head
tries to pull out of the incestuous bonding that has been the cornerstone
of life; instincts feel life is over. They may have suspected it for a long
time but then, one day, body knows that the beloved is never, never,
never coming back, never. What was is dead; what will be is not yet
born. Holding the tension between these two worlds, bringing them
to consciousness, integrating them when they meet is the soul work in
the kitchen. It goes on for a lifetime.

The inner masculine is part of ourselves, yet feels other. As an image
in dreams, that energy may appear as a monster demanding our
adoration, even subjugation. It may personify a totally unknown force
moving in to dislodge our too rigid ego standpoint. It may appear as a
radiant hairy man living in the forest.[1] It can be so magnetic and so
terrifying that women refuse to try to dialogue with it, refuse to know
it, and therefore cannot recognize that immense potential in themselves. Moreover, the Mary Magdalene–sacred whore is often partner
to that outcast living in the woods. Thus two of the most adventurous
energies in the unconscious are being repressed. And, being repressed,
they gain strength and may become the energies of an addiction.
Energy that is not allowed to transform toward creativity too often
finds a destructive outlet.

So long as a woman accepts a man's archetypal projection, she is
trapped in a male understanding of reality. Identified either with his
ideal of spiritual perfection or his ideal of the ever ready cunt, she is cut
off from her own dark, erotic, earthy shadow in her own body. Her
fiercest energy is in that shadow as many addicts know when they
succumb to the volcanic throes of lust, greed, or gluttony.

Allerleirauh, as an image of the feminine in patriarchy, has neither
her own masculinity, nor her own femininity. As a father's daughter,
she has served the Great Father collective and functioned without
owning her own creativity or instincts. Her father's proposal of marriage is like a brick-in-the-head that releases her when she realizes she

will be stuck with him forever. Many people receive a similar brick when they realize their marriage is becoming an exact replica of their parents'. That realization propels them to seek an understanding of the unconscious dynamics that have taken over control.

The heroine's task is to break from her unconscious father complex and make her intellect and her spirit her own (sunlight), to break from her unconscious mother complex and make her body and soul her own (moonlight), and ultimately to experience herself as part of a greater reality (starlight). At the beginning of her journey, the frail feminine is partnered by an equally weak masculine. The weak feminine fears the masculine tyrant; the weak masculine fears the feminine devourer. Both have been bludgeoned by power and both are haunted by victim and bully in their unconscious. In the intimacy of relationship, sexuality then becomes an act of violation and humiliation. The opposites, which should attract, repel, until repulsion becomes a form of attraction, even a challenge.

Male sun heroes have good reason to fear being sucked into the unknown, emotional morass of unconscious femininity. A man is doomed if he falls into the tender arms of a seductive vamp(ire) who can't think beyond the personal chain that binds two people together in the name of love. If his vision and intellectual energy yearn for spirit, his rage against the woman who is emasculating him may drown him in concretized spirit (alcohol). To save his own life, he has to recognize the vampire in himself. Until he can develop his own feminine feeling values, and use his masculinity to stand up for them, he will compulsively please his mother-wife, all the while yearning for an erotic maiden who will not threaten his virility. The compulsion—alcohol, fantasy, sex, work (the furs of his father's kingdom)—masks his rage and shame.

While many people are determined to throw off the tyranny of the old world and accept the anguish of initiation into the new, many more are blind to what is happening. They are repeatedly shocked. Some men, for example, who still assume that women are incompetent and, at the same time, expect them to be capable slaves, scream out when *their* woman utters a need or a thought. They scurry away if she expresses human feeling and begins bellowing or sobbing or belly laughing. Professional men who are used to silent secretaries can become ferocious bullies if their secretary offers a criticism or even a suggestion. Too often the secretary cannot stand up to the baby boy bully because she cannot say no to her own father complex. Instead she collapses. "He won't change," she says, and finds another bully boss. In avoiding the confrontation, however, she has done nothing to transform the patriarch, outside or inside. She is outraged and enraged and wonders why her skin breaks out in a red rash. He finds another silent slave and rants about hysterical women. A failed initiation for both.

Kitchen work would have taken them right into the confrontation. Working it through—fighting, holding firm, reflecting, meditating, being patient—leads to initiation. Sifting through the ashes of our broken hopes, empty stereotypes, inflated ideals, we let the dead world go and, at the same time, attend to the new energy flowing in from life's source. This source is universally recognized as feminine. To enter the source is to enter a chthonic place of power, often a womblike cave. Its released energy is so immense and chaotic that human identity can be swallowed up, as it tended to be in the bacchantes' sacred dance. Psychologically, returning to the source can result in temporary ego loss or even psychosis—real madness rather than divine madness. The immemorial male fear of the feminine is his fear of losing his male identity in the source.

The woman too can move into the creative matrix and experience annihilation. This can happen in the very early stages of the journey when the ego is weak. It can also happen when the container is very strong and begins to surrender to its full creative power. The penetration from the unconscious can break the container. Several of our greatest female artists have been tragically overwhelmed: Emily Brontë, Virginia Woolf, Sylvia Plath, Anne Sexton. Skilled kitchen work matters. Animals, demons, and angels have to endure the transformative fire.

The psychic process repeats the terror of breaking down known boundaries. It knows the dangers of chaos. For men and women whose frail security lies in order, however artificial it may be, the first stage of the journey is to establish connection with the inner king. A child who has not been mirrored by its parents, not been permitted to think its own thoughts or feel its own feelings, has been forced to obey an outer king. What will people think? What do people expect? Destructive as that outer authority is to a child's creativity, it may be the only order that is holding the fragmented personality together, even when obeisance becomes rebellion.

If the sensitive little child was never allowed to fly with its own creative spirit, if its wings were repeatedly cut off by "should, ought, and have to," then it has no faith in itself. Its feelings, intuitions, imaginings count for nothing. Poetry, music, dance—all the creative outpourings of soul reaching for spirit—have been relegated to some kind of fluffy fun and fantasy world. In the so-called real world, creative fire is not to be tolerated unless, of course, it leads to financial success and climbing the social ladder. Several recent films have developed this theme, among them *The Dead Poets' Society*.[2]

Men and women whose creativity has been raped often keep themselves invisible in their particular soot and furs. They try to keep whatever is left of them safe and hidden. Like Allerleirauh, they sometimes feel they are "good for nothing but to have boots thrown" at their head, and seem to set themselves up as martyrs. "If I hope for nothing, I will never be betrayed," they say. Yet if they hold true to their source, their inner strength can be inviolable.

If their sensitive little body has been violated by physical rape or incest, then their self-esteem may be so undermined that they think they are "only good for fucking." Although they escape into extraordinary fantasies, the fantasies are not grounded in their body, because their body has been numbed by the trauma. Unless the images arise from the body, at least in part, the imagination cannot do its healing work.[3] They may have no respect whatsoever for either their mind or their body. Their body has been taken away from them. This is quite different from giving up the power of the body to others. Incest, whether physical or psychic, results in numbness in the body. The quality of the numbness, however, is not the same. Nor is the degree of resistance to breath bringing feeling into the body. One of my analysands who experienced incest as a child explained the difference well. "It's not a matter of dancing on mechanical legs," she said. "I have no legs."

When victims of incest, psychic and/or physical, come into analysis, their initial dreams may shine with golden images. The psyche tries to rebuild their faith in their own gold, and faith in their inner authority. Dreams shine with golden birds, golden people, golden castles. This faith becomes their anchor when they have to face their rage, fear, and grief in their moon world. It is an even more important anchor when the pseudo-masculinity (the willpower) that has been their key to survival begins to break down and they feel themselves turning into "mush." Sometimes they become so enamored of their images that they try to speed up the process. But the psyche is wise. It knows they cannot yet integrate their illuminations into their experience. Then they find themselves sun-scorched in their dreams, or wearing sunglasses or blindfolds. Too much consciousness too fast can result in temporary blinding. The inner journey establishes its own balance in its own exact time.

The ball happens at the exact time. Allerleirauh is ready for the challenge. "Can I throw off my cloak of furs, wash off my soot of shame and fear? Can I be present in my golden dress? Will I look like a hairy animal dressed up in gold or will I be a princess wearing the gown that is mine?" We've all asked ourselves these questions. We've all worked hard on ourselves and then searched the eyes of others to see if they perceive any change. When we are coming out of concentrated introversion, we need the mirroring of the outer world to test our perception of ourselves. We need the moment of recognition from our inner King. The moment may come in a dream. It may come in knowing that we have tested ourselves to the utmost and we have been true to who we are. We look in the mirror and we are radiant.

Allerleirauh cannot sustain the unveiling. She returns to her matrix and again covers her face with soot and puts on her furs. The cook orders her to make supper for the King. This she does, making "bread soup the best she could, and when it was ready, she fetched her golden ring from her little den and put it in the bowl in which the soup was served." Having danced with the King, the heroine is determined to maintain a connection with him. The golden ring seals a covenant she makes with him although he is seemingly unaware of her identity. The ring in the soup is like an intuitive knowing that she and the King belong together—a magic circle that is and will be.

The image of sacred bonding is discovered in a bowl of bread soup. Bread is a powerful image of feminine transformation. The seed that died has become the new grain, which is winnowed and ground into flour. The spirit of the yeast is added and hopefully the miracle happens. If it doesn't, the bread is dense, like matter without imagination. Allerleirauh makes the bread into soup. The soup is taken up the stairs from the kitchen to the King; it is a connecting link. In the Catholic mass, physical bread through the mystery of sacrifice becomes spiritual bread. In the transformative process, something of immense value is sacrificed to something of even higher value. The bread as a symbol of the incarnation of spirit *in matter* embodies both the physical and the spiritual.

After the ball, most of us make bread soup for the King. We have reached a threshold. We have been through a rite of passage. We have lived what once seemed only possibility. We have experienced archetypal energy. God and goddess have been present in us. We want to capture that timeless moment in time. We reflect. We write a poem, paint a picture, or sing and dance our whole soul. We sacrifice the energy that we cannot hold onto in our corporeal existence and shape it into the form that best contains its spiritual essence. In that creative process, we relive the dance. In the new images we begin to recognize our new selves. In creating the bread soup, we are creating our own link to our own life's source.

Why is making bread soup healing? In modern society few people experience transformation through archetypal energy in the church, except perhaps on special occasions. For most, the key that opens the individual to the universal is not there. Addicts attempt to find it in their addictions. Others find it in private meditation or through the arts.

Without that link to our own inner depths, how can we have any idea who we are or where we are going? If we leave our father's house, we have to make ourselves self-reliant. Otherwise, we just fall into another father's house. Patriarchy has very little respect and no time for imagery and the inner world—the soul. However, it is beginning to feel the cracks in its edifice. Its power is being challenged in universities, law courts, hospitals, corporations. Men and women who are fearful of losing their power exercise it ruthlessly, because their identity is in their power. Who are they if they can't control someone else? The terror of being nobody and the rage against those who refuse to be slaves is being acted out in many homes, on our streets, in our own governments, in chaotic upheavals in the whole world. Women fear reprisal. They know that aggression that arises out of fear, impotency, and loss of identity is lethal. As women become stronger, male reprisal is being acted out increasingly against defenseless children. To strengthen ourselves to deal with the backlash, we have to be our authentic self. Unless we take time to make bread soup—to be in connection with the new imagery that is rising up in our own bodies— most of us have no way to connect to ourselves. Nor can we connect to the divine energy that is transforming us and this planet into a totally new order—love instead of power.

Preparing to wear the gold dress means dismantling central control and beginning the arduous process of pulling back projections and owning our own light and darkness. Yes, the world seems bleak, lonely, disconnected. Connections that trapped us in obsolete control systems are broken; connections that release us are opened. Gradually we find our own King in speaking the truth that allows our femininity to flower.

How does contemporary femininity prepare to wear the golden dress? What is her mantle of a thousand different kinds of fur, one of every kind of animal in her father's kingdom? What is her soot? What does she suffer in leaving her father's house? Every separation story has its own pain and every story delves deeper into hidden crannies in our own dens. Kate's story that follows is one woman's story of sifting ashes as she moves into her full stature.

> We never know how high we are
> Till we are asked to rise.
> And then if we are true to plan
> Our statures touch the skies—
>
> The Heroism we recite
> Would be a normal thing
> Did not ourselves the Cubits warp
> For fear to be a King—
>
> —EMILY DICKINSON[4]

Chapter 2

Kate

In the North American Indian tradition, the one who is to tell the story is invested with the talking stick. Like the royal scepter, it is a symbol of empowerment. For a brief period, the storyteller becomes queen over the domain that she is creating through her story. The group, in handing her the stick, accepts her invitation to enter her domain.

Our first storyteller is Kate. She is forty-seven years old. For fifteen years her domain was her home. Her husband was establishing himself in his professional career. She was putting all her energies into supporting him, supporting their two children in school, music, dance, supporting her two aging parents who lived close by. Kate's organizing skills kept things running smoothly in the household and in the church activities in which the family participated.

In 1981, Kate entered analysis shortly after she had an abortion on the advice of her doctor, and with the encouragement of her husband. Although the decision had ultimately been her own, she felt ambivalent about terminating her pregnancy. She had felt all along that the decision was being taken out of her hands by people who "knew better than I what was good for me. I knew their values were not supporting me as a woman, but I was in quicksand. I was not in touch with my own body sufficiently to know what it wanted." She seemed to emerge from the experience without any apparent difficulty and threw herself with renewed vigor into various volunteer activities. However, she soon found herself becoming more and more dissatisfied with her "peripheral existence." She felt she had somehow missed out on life. She experienced herself as aborted.

Kate was the youngest child of central European parents who

33

immigrated to Canada. In discovering her own story, she has had to come to terms with her parents' failure to nurture her. She has also had to acknowledge that, from the age of four to fifteen, she was sexually abused by an older brother.

In the first three drafts of her story, she had to write about herself in third person in order to distance herself from her early pain. Then she put her manuscript away for a year while she concentrated on her teaching and thesis. When she returned to it to make final changes, she realized she wanted to speak her own truth. She had found her own voice. She rewrote the whole manuscript in first person, writing from her own life blood.

"Telling my story is an important step in freeing my creativity," she says. "I could write without telling my childhood experiences, but so long as I felt I must not write about them, I ended up not writing about anything meaningful to me. There was always that prohibition lying between me and my creative impulse. I can't write out of lies. I can only write out of truth. I have given myself permission to delve as deeply as I must in order that the truth be told. I'm like a lot of other women who have lived part of their lives in opposition to their inner needs—a duplicity against themselves. We need courage to change that."

In her delving Kate found a picture of herself at the age of four. Her little body stands in a garden, her hands clutch the flowers she was told to hold. Her blond head is turned sideways from the camera so sharply that the veins in her neck protrude. Her eyes are closed; her mouth smiles in a smile that is close to a cry. Part of her tries desperately to please; part cowers from the lens that will betray her pain.

Describing herself as a child, Kate says, "I thought I was slow, unintelligent. I almost had to be told what to feel, what people ordinarily feel. Because my body was invaded so early, I built up defenses so strong there was a numbness in my body. Even now I can experience in ideas what I cannot experience in feeling, so there is a long delay between intellectually understanding and emotional acceptance. But I need to feel the truth of things before I can trust them, so I have to wait until the mind and heart organization comes together in order to feel whole. It takes a long time."

Kate realizes that the split between head and heart is sometimes evident in her writing style. Although she graduated with a university degree in English literature and continued in post-graduate studies, she lost confidence when she tried to finish her doctorate. She found writing impossible. She withdrew from the academic world and put all her energies into her family. As her children began to find their own world, Kate could no longer find her identity in mothering. Again her own intellectual gifts and unfinished Ph.D. came back to haunt her. Still she could not find permission within herself to write from her own heart. Nor could she speak or act from her own truth.

Her creative spirit began to leap out when she wrote down her dreams. Writing in her journal she was free of the system that had silenced her. She began to realize that what she had assumed was her shadow was, in fact, her unlived ego. The woman who was struggling to make life meaningful in the outside world was a pale shadow of the high-spirited, violently angry, and rebelliously beautiful adolescent who appeared in her dreams. Her real ego had been buried years ago under layers of duty and responsibility.

She now saw her birth family as strange figures in a wax museum. "I killed them by outgrowing them," she says. "Now my writing is killing them all over again. I thought I was transcending my family situation when I married. I thought I could be myself. I married into the same stupid soup. Now I have tremendous fear of moving into the world. It feels for me like a forbidden room that I am not supposed to enter. In stepping into my own shoes, I feel I am killing my parents. I can't be both independent and free and the person I was in relation to them. My own life is against all the family values they instilled in me. I am aware of their sacrifice for me. Writing my truth is like bloodletting. That's why writing is so miraculous."

Even into her forties, Kate still projected archetypal power onto her parents. Simple folk that they were, they were god and goddess in her life, robbing her of her own energy. When she was able to break that infantile projection and chose to live her own life, she was consumed with guilt. She hated herself for going where they could not go. Yet guilt seems necessary for maturity. When the parental figures are consciously differentiated, the god and goddess within lose their contamination. They are then free to become creative guides.

Eventually, Kate decided to return to university. Writing papers was still agony. Free and high-spirited and angry as she was in her analytic sessions, the world out there was where she had to live that spirit. She needed the high grades; she knew how to get them; she knew what she was betraying in herself by warping both her content and her style in writing. She had learned that being aggressive was not feminine; she knew that displeasing her professors could lead to rejection. Therefore, to use the passive voice, to distance herself from action even in her grammar shielded her examiner from the directness which might be perceived as an attack. If a female writer is subliminally saying, "Don't attack me, I am only guessing. I am only trying to tell the truth. Please don't hurt me for it," her muted undertone is probably masking her real passion and her real creativity.

Kate recognizes the echoes of an academic style in her writing. She knows that the style works against the heart-wrenching story that she tells. She also knows she had to begin by objectifying herself in order to speak at all. This is characteristic of the golden dress—distancing from the terror of the real feelings by describing them, rather than experiencing them. As she moves closer to breaking out of her paralysis, her style changes. She has chosen to let the transitional phases remain since they are part of her process.

Kate is now finishing her doctoral thesis. She is teaching at a university. She is still working at subduing the driving willpower that made her a mere construct of the patriarchal world. Even more important, her femininity is strong enough to open to the penetrating fire that comes through from her unconscious.

Reading her story we can watch her gradually giving up unconscious mothering. Her husband and children are no longer forced to carry the responsibility of her unlived life. She has owned her own power in so far as she is conscious of it now. That empowerment allows her to choose when and whom she will nourish and creates boundaries strong enough to protect and nurture herself. Bodysoul work does not come easily to Kate. Still she knows if she holds that connection to her *mater* (the Latin word for mother), her body weight is steady and she is secure in her own ground.

Reading Kate's story, we can be with her quietly in her den under the stairs, carefully sorting out what belongs to her and what was projected onto her. We can see her brushing her animal furs, patiently bringing her instincts to consciousness. Gradually, she sorts out the paralyzing golden gilt from the gold of her own reality. There she encounters her genuine masculinity. She knows she is not yet strong enough to sustain the full energy of that creative and spiritual power. Sometimes she returns to her soot and furs in the kitchen. Still, she knows at least what the dance can one day be.

And now we hand the talking stick to Kate.

Chapter 3

Turning Blood to Ink

KATE DANSON

Life can only be understood backwards but it must be lived forwards.

—SØREN KIERKEGAARD

What I am about to describe is a process which has yet to be completed. In fact, I have come to accept the idea that the process is ongoing and lifelong. Because I have had to do later in life what would have been much more appropriate and natural to have accomplished in childhood, the process has been painful to initiate. But events in early childhood made normal development impossible, for I was a victim of childhood sexual abuse.

The trauma resulting from sexual abuse is nothing short of disabling. That I tried to block out the memory of assault first by a man who was a family acquaintance and then, repeatedly, by my brother is understandable; in part, I succeeded. I chose to live in a special world of the imagination whose entrance was an unused room just above the family kitchen; it is to this private world I escaped whenever I could. In a large family like mine, no one really noticed my sudden reclusiveness. I was too insignificant to be useful to anyone in the family workforce; I was the youngest, a mere infant.

Transforming myself into a princess helped me to survive. But princesses must live in what the rest of the world calls "reality." I thought I knew what the "real" world was; in that world, I was my brother's plaything. Later I found other dangers in that world; it was a place where I had to measure myself constantly against other people while knowing, the whole time, that I would always come up short of the mark. Then, too, I felt like a plaything of fate because, having very little ego, I was swept away by events rather than consciously shaping them.

What started my journey toward wholeness was an unfortunate collision with fate that occurred long after I thought myself past all danger. In spite of myself, I had become the perfect success story, a kind of family showpiece. I grew up, to all appearances a sensitive, caring, and intelligent person; I married well; I had two model, well-disciplined, and clever children. And because I could function adequately as such, I continued being a princess. In fact, in my husband and children, it seemed as though I had managed to invite three other people to play at my fantasy with me. All was more or less idyllic for a time. Then, fate caught up with me at my third and final pregnancy.

What happened was simply this: I had encountered a medical complication in the initial months of an unplanned pregnancy; and I was warned that, not only would my chances of bearing a healthy child be minimal, but my own life was at risk. Under the joint pressure of doctor and husband, I agreed to terminate the pregnancy. As both had evaluated the situation in highly rational terms, they assumed that the matter would end there and that life afterwards would continue as though nothing had happened. Fortunately for me, they were wrong.

I went into analysis shortly after I had the abortion. While I had obviously been concerned about the ethical dilemma in which I had been placed, my post-op convictions were being attacked by emotional rather than intellectual considerations.

For one thing, my body had seemed to want to have a say in the whole matter. My body had wanted the child. Now it wanted to grieve, but I didn't know how to let grief happen. For another, I felt terribly ashamed, as though I had finally been "arrested" for a crime I had committed years earlier. Much later on, I was able to recognize these feelings as connected to my earlier experience of abuse.

The crisis was literally a form of "arrest" for it stopped me in my tracks. I was confronted with a "real" vision of myself; suddenly, I was like my vision of my own mother who, in not wanting me, seemed bent on destroying her child. But symbolically, I was both mother and child, both destroyer and destroyed. And one way or another, a death was being demanded. Whether I wished it or not, I, the princess, had to descend to Earth and face my trial.

Because so many unresolved issues were bound up for me in this event, it was inevitable that I would encounter it as a conflict. Paradoxically, and I see that now, the experience confronted me with life as well as death. The abortion gave me a second chance; it provided an opportunity for giving birth to myself.

My early childhood sexual experience had taught me that survival lay in being submissive; and I had, as a consequence, been submissive all my life except for periods when I would erratically break out of the mold by some radical, even rebellious act. In fact, it was a kind of act of rebellion that sent me into analysis. It was a way of showing my husband that I was deeply hurt.

Yet, if anything, I had seemed, for a time, to emerge even more resilient from the experience of abortion; my defenses were even more fully in place, and, without any apparent difficulty, I had thrown myself with renewed vigor into various volunteer activities involving children and the church. However, I had found myself becoming more and more dissatisfied with my "peripheral existence." It was as though, having entered the shadow of death and having reemerged partial and diminished, I was at last permitted to question the rules by which my life was governed. So, I continued to serve, to be for others what I could not be for myself. But, for the first time, I had begun to question how my world worked.

I began by questioning the volunteer work I was doing. While I had acquired some ability at organizing and leading groups, I found myself increasingly at odds with the authoritarian nature of several of the organizations whose aims I was ironically helping to forward through my time, effort, and skill. I had begun to feel that my work either went unappreciated, or worse, was claimed as the success of the persons who were paid to head the organization.

This was especially the case in the church whose priests, like my doctor and my husband, had a tendency to enunciate exactly what was good for me; more importantly, I was beginning to question the process whereby things got done and who got rewarded. I noticed, for example, that a great many women, very like myself, gave generously to the church of the skills they had developed in their workplace or homes; yet the feminine principle went unacknowledged in church sermons, dogma, and hierarchy.

In one of my volunteer positions, I was myself the head of a group (unpaid, of course); here I had an opportunity to shape policy, interact with people, and make enough public appearances to satisfy a growing desire for personal recognition. Observing how well the organization functioned through team effort, I wrote, printed, and distributed a newsletter that featured, on a rotating basis, the achievements of specific individuals in the organization. I could see that my power as "head" came from the energy of the various members of the "body"/organization that I represented. Without the energy of the group effort, I was powerless. The head was not greater than any individual part, let alone the sum of its parts. All the more reason for my growing unease with the situation in my church where the unacknowledged services of hardworking women were being used to forward the careers of its male power brokers.

By experiencing, at first hand, another kind of organizational strategy, one that emphasized nonlinearity and decentralization, one where equal sharing of a task was emphasized over mindless adherence to a central authority, I had found a basis from which to begin my critique. Thus began what was to be an ongoing dialogue between the head and the body. It had finally become clear to me that patriarchal structures like the church were demeaning, especially toward women. Soon I began to see my position in the church as a paradigm of my life. Increasingly, I began to feel the constraints of being a wife and mother. I knew that something vital was missing but I didn't know what it was.

What surprised me most was the way in which the patriarchal structures I had accepted and even supported had influenced my own psychological development to its detriment. By accepting the patriarchal, that is, the hierarchical model in which the individual gives up some or all responsibility to a head person, I had learned to play the patriarchal game of secret manipulator. I began to perceive that the power I was not permitted to exercise openly, I was nevertheless using unconsciously.

On my first visit to Marion Woodman, I diagnosed my problem as one of failed creativity. This turned out to be truer than I could have realized, with ramifications I could not have foreseen. It was shortly after entering analysis, for example, that I became aware how vicariously I was living through my talented children, supporting and even, on occasion, stage-managing their triumphs. I began to see that the more successful they seemed to be, the more I was being left with the sense of a life wasted and futile because my own talents were being neglected. My moods began to reflect a growing frustration and anger. A few weeks into analysis, I had the following dream:

I am in the basement of a cathedral moving along a passage. The canon of the cathedral is walking just ahead of me. He squeezes his way through a narrow, round opening. I follow. Behind me trails a crowd of children, all of whom squeeze through the opening. I emerge into a large, well-lit room. In the center, a woman is preparing some kind of entertainment for the children. There is an enormous basin in the middle of the floor. The woman is tossing something into the pot—it seems to be a powder of some kind. In the pot itself is a viscous, almost gelatinous liquid. Where the powder is dropped into the pot, there appear swirls of many extremely vivid, beautiful colors, which merge together into a muddy brown as they are whirled away from the center of the pot and toward the periphery. The woman keeps on adding powder, keeps on creating color as I wake up. [April 30, 1981]

I was both excited and troubled by this dream. What troubled me was the way in which the lovely colors seemed to turn to dull, drab nothing after their initial glory. What excited me was the sense of being reborn, as suggested by the movement through the dark, narrow opening into the large, well-lit room, which is to say, into consciousness. At first I was puzzled by the fact that I was following in the wake of a church official rather than initiating the rebirthing process by my own efforts. With Marion's help, I was able to realize that my disaffection with church hierarchy had, in fact, been the catalyst by which I was made aware of my own creative gifts and of the way in which they were being wasted. I was being given some painful home truths about the pitfalls of living vicariously through others. My work in the church was dazzling for a short time, but ultimately amounted to very little.

At about this time, I also dreamt about receiving a phone call from a long-deceased neighbor informing me that my mother was dying. Marion suggested that I was beginning to think more about my own needs and less about the opinions of others. The status quo (Mother Church and my Victorian ideal of motherhood) was losing its grip on my life; indeed, it was dying. The dying mother was releasing me from the expectations that others (like Mother) had of me and into expectations I had of myself. The energy I had formerly drawn from my adherence to conventional modes of thinking was disappearing, leaving me temporarily with a sense of helplessness.

The old man in the dream, whom I recognized as a highly support-ive neighbor and grandfather figure, was the bearer of the news that the values upon which I had built my life were now invalid. This man, and indeed his whole family, had encouraged my gifts of imagination and had showered kindness and affection upon me as a child. The dream seemed to be suggesting that, by returning to positive aspects of my early childhood, I would eventually reconnect myself to creative energy that had been blocked very early by an indifferent and unconsciously callous upbringing.

The principal difficulty in this early part of analysis was in convincing myself that I, in my own right, had creative gifts that needed nurturing. Marion encouraged me to make a place for myself in my house, and in my life, in which to nurture them. Slowly, I began to give up all those time-consuming activities, one by one, in order to "work on myself," something I had, until then, dismissed as self-indulgence. As a woman who had been brought up to serve, one who had early been deprived of a sense of self, I needed to be given permission to strive for personal development and growth.

I began to realize how patriarchal and narrow my understanding of Christianity was. For example, it had never occurred to me before that Christ, in his parable of the talents, might have had women in mind as well as men. It is consequently not surprising that my spirituality, too, was quite blinkered; it showed in the way I accepted a "nothing-but" role as wife and mother. Slowly, I began to focus more on the significance of the radical, free-spirited Mary in Christ's life and less on the domesticated Martha. Slowly, my attitude to myself in particular and womankind in general began to change. In the process, I began to give my children freedom to develop in the directions they chose, or neglected to choose. In short, I allowed myself to become less demanding of others, less critical of myself.

A dream I had at this time indicated the path I would take in order to realize my new goals. I dreamt of a burning warehouse. The fire department was on hand to rescue its occupants. An initial attempt to gain entrance from the top story met with no success. A fireman who tried to smash a window with an object he had clenched in his teeth also failed. Finally, I got in through a coal-cellar door. The dream confirmed that there was a crisis to be faced in my life; the dream also seemed to be underlining the need for me to proceed to the rescue of the disintegrating personality (the burning warehouse), not through the intellect or head (the top story), not through sheer force of hard-driving will (clenched teeth), but through the unconscious—by way of the dream (the basement window). By taking time to write down my dreams, my thoughts about their possible meaning, and my feelings about daily occurrences, I began to become acquainted with myself. It is as though I were building a friendship with myself and with it, a stronger sense of my own self-worth. I was rewarded with the following dream:

> I dream about a very beautiful woman. Her beauty comes not from her face—for I do not see her face clearly—but from an immense warmth and love she exudes. I feel incredibly drawn to her. She is almost a symbol of beauty, so intensely does she express this quality. I want this dream not to end. I am haunted by her long after I wake up. [May 13, 1981]

Much of our sense of trust we derive from our earliest contact with our primary caregivers. I feared my mother more than I trusted her. It is not surprising, therefore, that I had great difficulty forming deep relationships with other women, although, in looking back upon my life, I acknowledge the significance of several female teachers who proved to be valuable guides; still, until I met Marion, a woman to whom I developed a profound, positive transference, I had never known unconditional trust and encouragement. In a very real sense, Marion spoke to the feminine buried deep within me. The dream of the beautiful woman I just now cited indicated the potential for that beautiful inner feminine to radiate outwards, which I had never thought possible. Until I was strong enough to confirm the validity of my own feminine being, Marion served as my mentor, giving me support, encouragement, understanding, and a mother-love which I had never before trusted.

While I basked in my newfound trust for another person, I was nevertheless an adult woman who needed to rely on myself; indeed, in some measure, I had always done so. I was, in any case, not really sure that another person could understand the nature of my pain. For these reasons, the powerful, positive feminine dream image came just in time to offer solace at this particularly frightening time; it offered a kind of protection against what the unconscious was gradually to begin to reveal to me over the next several months.

During the months that followed, my nights were troubled by terrible nightmares. The dreams all followed a similar pattern: a terrifying male figure was attempting to gain entrance to my house in order to kill sometimes me, sometimes my daughter. Night after night, I killed this assassin. Sometimes I hit him repeatedly on the head; sometimes I killed him with a gun or stabbed him with a knife. Frequently, I woke up in unspeakable terror, horrified at my own murderous rage. Because I had not come to terms, at this point, with the sexual abuse I had suffered in the past, it did not occur to me to associate the man in the dream with my brother and so, initially, I could make no sense of these dreams.

Then one night, a dream warned me to pay closer attention to what was happening. I dreamt of a beautiful woman dying of a persistent heart condition. Marion, whose experience with dreams was uncovering the truth of the situation in my unconscious, expressed concern that my beautiful woman, so recently discovered, was dying of feelings so intense that they were consuming her life-energy. Paradoxically then, while I was venting violent rage upon a masculine figure, it was my own feminine that was taking the punishment. The two were inextricably intertwined. Thus, while defending myself against an assassin who seemed to be out to kill my budding femininity, I was destroying the very feminine I was trying to protect. An important piece of disquieting news provided a clue and vividly clarified the situation in the unconscious.

The news concerned my abusing brother, whom I had seen hardly at all over the years. His life had all the outer trappings of happiness and success. Then, all of a sudden, news had leaked out that he had recently been estranged from his wife and children. Furthermore, after a series of bizarre accidents, he had become severely physically disabled. The news had a devastating effect on me. My feelings were similar to those I had had about the abortion: I felt guilt and shame as though I were personally responsible for my brother's fate.

Whom had I been battering in my dreams night after night? I now understood why I was feeling such guilt. As the truth of this most bizarre coincidence dawned on me, outer reality and inner life came together, releasing a flood of memories connected with my childhood abuse. I began to realize that the assassins of my dreams were images of my brother. My terrible disquiet upon hearing of his misfortunes was resulting from my unconscious fear that my actions in my dreams were having a real effect on him. This fear must have had very deep roots in the abuse itself. As a child, I had loved and trusted my brother; but I had also come to hate him for what he was doing to me. I felt a murderous rage for him so great that I had to hide it for fear that I might actually kill the one whom I also loved. As an adult, the feelings of rage were being released in dream images and my worst long-standing fears (and, perhaps, desires?) seemed actually to be realized.

Until very recently, I have continued suffering guilt toward my brother. Now at last I can truly say I am letting the guilt and blame go. I have let my brother go too; I have let him be responsible for himself; the person he represented to me is dead and what remains is something else: a kind of stranger, a person I realize I never really knew. But then, in a very real sense my hatred of my abuser very nearly destroyed my capacity for love. And while my deep rage at my brother has died, I am aware that I have been left a distinctive legacy: I have long recognized that my feelings are not easily stirred and when they are, they come with such an intensity that I am terrified they will overwhelm me. This delayed response in feeling I attribute to the trauma of sexual abuse.

Once I consciously realized how absurd it was for me to take the blame for my brother's present plight, I could begin to understand how much I had always blamed myself for what had happened in my childhood. Just as my birth family, without examining the evidence, blamed my brother's wife for abandoning him, so I blamed myself for not preventing the abuse. Yet, for a time during analysis, I really believed that my act of consciousness, of rebellion, of self-assertion was killing my brother. And I was very nearly ready to sacrifice myself, once again, on the altar of family.

My inner dream-maker was my best guide through these difficult deliberations. Like a trusty guide moving, ever moving, just far enough ahead of me to beckon me on while keeping me in sight, each dream urged me forward in uncovering the truth of who I am. The unconscious prepared this dreamer as gently as possible, alternating violent nightmares, with their terrifying insights into early life, with dreams of great beauty that offered hope. I dreamt about the beautiful, loving, nurturing woman whenever the difficulty of confronting painful truths became almost unbearable.

After I had become accustomed to the language of images, my dream-maker sent me this dream, which not only forced me to reexamine previously held assumptions but provided a context for the terrifying nightmares. Again, this dream bears within itself the kernel of the entire analysis. Again, the dream begins in a church building.

I am with a priest and several church school teachers. I feel a tremendous attraction to the priest, a tremendous sense of wanting to be with him. He goes ahead down a slide; it is the only way to go down and the others follow him. I very much want to go down too, but I am frightened. I think of a cunning way that will give me less fright; I sit on a book by C. G. Jung and slide down easily. The priest encourages me from the bottom of the slide by smiling up at me. Again, I feel a powerful attraction to him. He moves away, leaving me with a sense of longing.

The setting changes somewhat. I am in a room in a bed. There is a pool of water in the bed. It is night. My daughter and I are floating in a liquid more viscous than water—and warm—like amniotic fluid in a womb. My daughter playfully throws fishes at me; there seem to be many varieties of fish in this sea-womb. Then the water drains out from the bed. I get up with a sense of anxiety. I must change the sheets before the room's official occupants arrive. I see that this bed belongs to my [abusing] brother and that, in this room, there is another large bed. I decide to take the sheets from the other bed and put them on this one. I begin to pull blankets and sheets off the womb-wet bed. Since only the bottom sheet is wet, I think I can replace it with the dry sheet from the other bed. When I do so, I find that the sheets don't match. I shall have to wash and dry the bottom sheet. When I pull off the sheet, bits of seaweed and dead fish shake off. Around the bed, right to the walls, are perfume bottles of ornate cut glass, jars for unguents, and jewelry boxes.

My [abusing] brother comes in wearing a dark suit. I shake his hand very formally. Behind him is an ugly, obese woman, heavily corseted and made up to look younger than she is; she has in tow several beautiful children. The youngest is rather sullen, but the oldest is about twelve and has the loveliest smile I have ever seen. I find myself mirroring back to him his wonderful smile. The woman seems to be trying to pass these children off as her own but only succeeds in emphasizing the unlikelihood of such a situation. In fact, it is likely that these children are her daughter's, born out of wedlock and taken over by this woman in order to "hide her daughter's shame." I think to myself that this woman is at least twenty years too old to have borne these children. [June 11, 1981]

As before, it was a priest who stimulated the action of the scene, perhaps underlining the archetypal numinosity and Divine Love that lies behind the worldly structure of the church. The dream made me realize that I must not tar with the same brush all priests and ministers of the church. Not without significance is the fact that the priest was a very dear friend who had recently confided in me that he was gay. I felt very safe with this man because I knew his love for me was devoid of sexuality, and thus constituted no threat to my growing but still infantile consciousness. In fact, he was the very priest who had introduced me to Marion and encouraged me to pursue, by this means, my inner journey; he has always been a great support to me.

The presence of the priest, then, celebrated the existence both of this loving priest (as distinct from those by whom I had felt used) and my inner priest or spiritual guide who was offering me the necessary support to cope with the unpleasant truths which were to emerge from the primordial layers of early memory. In the dream, I was an adult moving down a child's slide. The dream was telling me that my conscious viewpoint was childish but that in order to develop a more mature outlook, I had to return to the "playground" of my childhood memories.

I identified the book that gave me the courage to make the descent into the unconscious as one by Jung. However, in the dream I was not reading the book, but sitting on it. The dream seemed to be reminding me, as did the burning building dream, that head knowledge would be of little use. Reading about Jungian psychology is not the *via regia* to the unconscious; one has to experience the unconscious directly and, as it were, fly by the seat of one's pants. The intellectual approach may be more elegant, but ultimately, the humbling, undignified, and alarming way of personal experience was the one that would actually work for me.

In the dream I was at first floating in a kind of womb playing happily with my young feminine, but this air of unconscious innocence changed abruptly. The bed, at first mine, was suddenly my brother's. What remained after the water drained from the sea of bliss was death and detritus. What drove me out of my innocent Arcadia and separated me from my feminine playmate can be spoken in a word: incest. But behind that word lies a much more frightening reality: sexual abuse.

Much hangs, in my story, upon language. The word incest is a case in point. I had lived for many years believing that I was a wicked person because I had had an incestuous relationship with my brother. While I later realized that our relationship was a perversion of normal sibling love, I had, at its inception, no better paradigm. Yet, it never occurred to me that what I was doing was unconsciously to continue living the child's passive role on into adulthood; what I was also prolonging was the belief that I had entered into a complicitous arrangement with my brother when the fact was that I had been held captive by a form of violence and hate so seductive, so mixed up with tenderness and love, as to constitute a sophisticated form of indoctrination.

The antidote that I found to this unconscious brainwashing was the dream, which, using its own unique language of pictorial images with the potential for feeling and symbolic interpretation, was and continues to be crucial in teaching me my own reality. Many of those initial dreams showed me the child's world through the contemporary adult's perspective; it spoke to me of how things had been and where and how I began making my first erroneous assumptions.

The bed in the dream felt familiar to me; I was playing there with my own daughter, my own young feminine self; the activity and the playmate conveyed a strong sense of feminine identity. Around the bed, the room was filled with feminine articles, womblike containers and unguents, again, a positive feminine identity. But suddenly, the feeling-tone changed. The bed *had* been my own; suddenly I assumed it belonged to my brother.

When I reported the dream to Marion, I felt shame as though I were confessing to a crime: that of dirtying my brother's bed. In the dream I, in fear, attempted to make amends, to placate him, by exchanging sheets with the other bed, and so on, but my efforts were constantly thwarted, for example, by the mismatched sheets.

Marion understood my anguish as I reported the dream; but she was astonished at my arrogating to myself so much blame as I attempted to interpret it. My initial interpretation simply made no sense to her. Her puzzlement at my interpreting the dream with so powerful a sense of guilt led us both to realize, with sudden and forceful clarity, the self-humiliation that surrounds incest. Jung refers to this kind of self-loathing as *negative inflation*.

It was suddenly obvious to me that both the bed and the room in the dream are my own and it is my brother who is the usurper. It takes just a few words to make this statement but it was to take me approximately seven years fully to assimilate the knowledge that I had been a victim of abuse and not an initiator of infantile sexuality. The dreamer's frantic attempt to make everything look good reflects my own shouldering of the guilt for what happened to me as a child.

The rest of the dream confirmed this reading. The woman who accompanied my brother was clearly misrepresenting herself for the purpose of "hiding her daughter's shame." At the heart of the dream was the attempt at cover-up. The woman claimed her daughter's children as her own because she was convinced that they had been born out of wedlock and, therefore, in sin and shame. Who were these figures? Surely they were aspects of myself. In the dream I was mother, daughter, and daughter's children. Thus the young male child reflected back my own smile and confirmed his connection to me. These children represent my potential creativity blocked by my attitude of guilt and shame toward the past. No wonder the youngest child is sullen. She is my new awareness that things are not as they should be. She is the neglected feminine and has every reason to be angry.

Complicity versus violence. Incest or sexual abuse? Why had I clung all these years to the notion that incest implied complicity when it was so obvious, and my dreams suggested this over and over again, that incest was sexual abuse within the family? The answer lies in the child's absolute need to feel loved at the expense of logic, personal identity, and self-worth. I could not bear to think that my brother wanted to hurt me. If my brother loved me, would he hurt me? For me, the logic had been certain: I was the bad one. I made him want to hurt me because I took his bed. Thus the dream spoke to me of how the child thought, and how the adult followed in the footsteps of the child. But the dream tried to correct the mistake the child made by bringing to light another relationship, that between the ugly woman and the abusing brother, and showed that therein lay the true complicity. Eventually I recognized in the ugly woman not only my childhood fear of my mother but also a part of myself.

My mother, in forming an alliance with her son (unconscious psychic incest), effectively shut me out. That made me feel in the wrong, sinful. Incest between mother and son was lived unconsciously, to be redirected by the son as violence against the helpless youngest child, the family pet, me. But, by internalizing as an adult both my brother's behavior (in my sense of shame and guilt) and my mother's negativity (in my need to repress what I considered to be shameful), I allowed these aspects of myself to work in collusion against myself, undermining my very ego.

The dream indicated that I could reach my creative feminine (imaged in jars and bottles) only by passing through and beyond my brother and the ugly woman. Marion warned me to strengthen my feminine container. But these words conveyed little meaning to me at the time; later, however, nudged by the images in my dreams, I was able to integrate her words into consciousness and to give them meaning and expression. And much later still, I came to recognize that marriage, family, even my own body, all could be viewed as "containers" in that they could, if sound and strong, hold and support my ego in its struggle to develop normally.

My dream provided assurance that I could take encouragement from the young masculine (the boy of twelve who stood on the threshold of his masculine awakening) and act on the dis-ease of the young feminine (the sullen child) to put things right. The dream powerfully emphasized that violence had indeed been done. For me to have remained passive in the face of such potent new knowledge would have meant engaging in complicitous behavior. I had to free these children. They were innocent victims just as I once had been.

Words and images, I was discovering, are powerful instruments. When interpreted correctly, they have the power to free. Thus, once I began to equate incest with rape, I was able to recognize how I had been victimized not only by my brother but, ultimately, by a word. Only when I had considered this dream in the context of other dreams, were its images able to speak to me.

I had always accepted the truth of incest intellectually, while denying its lasting pain. Slowly, and one must emphasize that the process was so gradual that it took several years to make its impact, slowly I began to face the reality of my childhood marred by my brother. Slowly I began to understand what feelings of guilt and what a sense of possible complicity I had been harboring. The painful process of the next several years of analysis involved realizing that as a growing person, I had blamed the child I had once been for not crying out, or striking out against my aggressor. I was born too early for Alice Miller's assertion, and the dream's assertion, that "the child is always innocent."[1]

My task was formidable: I had to learn to forgive myself, to learn to realize that the child I was had been numbed with confusion and terror; I had to learn to grieve for this abandoned child that I carry inside me to this day. The process of accepting my own innocent child has taken a very long time; it includes acknowledging my sense of victimization and my anger at my family, who made it impossible for me to ask for help. It has involved the painful process of recognizing my love/hate relationship both with men and with my own inner masculine, the latter representing a potentially potent aspect of my creativity.

The woman in the dream is both ugly and frightening. She carries for me the negative qualities of my own mother who taught her family not to complain, not to bother her about their troubles. It was soon apparent to all of us, that whatever happened, "mother was not to know." Perfectly consistent with this attitude was another: however much criticism one levelled against what went on in the outside world, it was not a good idea to criticize family; keeping everything "in the family," and of making things look respectable even when they were not, was considered a virtue.

The negative mother figure in this dream is very much a contrast to the image of the beautiful woman of the dream cited earlier. As a child, I felt little by way of the archetypal positive mother in my own mother. I have discovered more of her as a result of my dreamwork, but, in the tough economic times of my childhood, my mother consistently showed a side of herself that was hard-driving, self-absorbed, and ungentle. I have often wondered if she herself might not have been a victim of abuse. From the little she has related to me of her childhood, I recognize in the atmosphere she describes a close copy of my own. The ugly woman of the dream had perhaps been passed on from mother to daughter for who knows how many generations. The dream made it clear that something of her nature existed in me.

Yet the two figures represent the opposing faces of the same archetypal energy: as a healing archetype from the collective unconscious, the positive feminine figure was providing a compensation for the lack of a nurturing mother in my childhood; the negative image represents its flip side, its other face: the devouring, destructive energy that I experienced frequently as a child in times of family crises. But what the dream was plainly telling me was that the negative figure, too, lived within me as my shadow; for, the ugly woman was an aspect of myself I would rather not acknowledge but, in fairness, must. The dream told me that I was hiding, and have been hiding all my life, a sense of shame too deep to be reckoned with until now. The ugly woman not only lived in me but was doing battle with my soul child; what's more, she appeared to be winning. But she was also working in a complicitous relationship with my own wounded masculine. No wonder I was having problems with creativity! My self-esteem was constantly being undermined from within.

As the past reemerged in the light of dawning consciousness, I grew more aware of what I had experienced as a child and to what I had submitted. I took note of every pain-stirring dream because each one nudged me toward memories which I had long ago blocked out and forgotten. At last I had a context, a new container for these experiences that was not tinged with shame and guilt. At long last the past was coming toward me, resurrected like Lazarus in his stinking grave-clothes led by a new, healing attitude in which I could believe and trust.

Mercifully, my dreams, Marion, my study of Jung, and the growing awareness by society of child abuse have helped me take my painful memories and integrate them into a clearer perspective. The dream of the ugly woman, which is typical of many of this period, took me back to the past and re-created the emotional situation as it was: the ugly woman and the brother approached together. Both were threatening figures; neither offered me any consolation in my expulsion from childhood innocence, from my own Garden of Eden. Although the dream I am speaking of did not include my father, I am not ignoring the part he has played in this dysfunctional family dynamic.

I adored my father. He dandled me on his knee and petted me and accorded me such a special position that it was easy for me to be a princess. I could see no wrong in him. I adored him as much as I feared my mother. He was the perfect father to a princess and I was the perfect king's daughter. I think I might have felt some gratification in being his favorite child. That my father could demand obedience and subservience from everyone may have been a source of vicarious power for me. What he thought, all were to think; what he demanded, all were to carry out. But, despite my special status, I was never able to tell him what was happening to me. It was too risky: to tell all might mean I could lose all and it was the most important thing in the world for me to be special in his eyes.

It took me so long to be able to feel critical of my father. Every step in that direction has brought me anguish. Now I recognize that my cherished father never offered any of us real emotional security. The unexpected, uncontrollable rages that marked my father as a weak, though not physically violent man, soon made me wary of him. The man I loved, I also feared. From him, I gained a dangerous perception: that tenderness comes with a price tag of pain.

Because my child-self did not have the necessary skills to deal with my frightening world, I tuned it out and numbed myself against what was too unpleasant to face. Through my imagination, I created a happier world for myself; in the solitude of my hiding place, I communicated with imaginary playmates who lent me courage to face the terrors of family life. What I, by degrees, succeeded in doing was to merge fantasy and reality into an amalgam that provided me with a viable way of existing.

As a result of my family situation, I grew up with a number of specific problems ranging from an eating disorder to sexual difficulties. I suffered from a chronic respiratory condition that finally began to disappear, as though by magic, during the course of analysis. I was later to recognize my problems with breathing as connected to the trauma and fear of early physical abuse. While I fought a constant battle with crippling shyness, over the years I succeeded in developing a persona that permitted me to appear in public as a competent and confident woman. But, I have always had an enormous problem with self-esteem.

Because I felt betrayed by my body, as I grew older I continued to dissociate myself from it. I did this by throwing myself into academic studies, perhaps hoping for a kind of permanent residence in the world of the mind. To my way of thinking, the life of the head was surely to be preferred to the life of the body. That the two were closely intertwined was something I was soon called upon to reckon with.

I don't think it actually occurred to me, to connect the panic attacks I began to suffer when I was a college student with my childhood experience of incest. Yet, the incest colored my attitude toward myself: what it did was to make me feel somehow unclean so that I was unable to express my feelings of fear to close friends who, I realize now, would have been very sympathetic. Then too, in a situation of crisis, I had a tendency to hold my breath which, in turn, caused me to panic; I was literally denying myself the breath of life by refusing to speak to other people about my deepest sense of shame and guilt. I had so little bodily awareness that I did not realize that, by cutting off my breathing, I was also cutting myself off from my sensations and feelings.

Now, with each dream, particularly those dreams that confronted me with my worst fears, I touched a central pain center. Feelings began to be released in me as I experienced literally months of nightmares in which my apartment was broken into by a man so brutal, I was impelled to attack him viciously with whatever weapon came to hand. These dreams forced me to reexperience the terror I must have felt as a child but could not let myself express. In most of these dreams, I bludgeoned my attacker viciously about the head. The dreams were really hitting me over the head, telling me to wake up and *feel* the terror directly and not just think it. Eventually, I began to realize who it was I had been hurting by keeping silent about my past. The following dream indicated that some kind of change was taking place in my attitude as a result of my encounters with the attacker:

I have entered an unfamiliar apartment. I am looking for something that has been stolen by the person who lives here. This "something" is very precious to me and I want it back. I walk through the cluttered dining room where the furniture is too large for it and enter the bedroom. Here, I find what I want. In the corner of the room is a small cage. I lift the lid and take out a small, brown, furry animal. It is very happy to see me. In the blink of an eye, the animal becomes my young daughter. Sooner or later, I have to confront the man who stole her. Suddenly, he is there, a big, ugly man with a large round head. Seizing a broom standing in the corner, I attempt to hit him and miss. He laughs. He does not take my attempts at striking him at all seriously and makes no attempt to wrench the broom from my grasp. I strike him on the back of the head as hard as I can. My blows begin to connect more and more often. He gives me a look, almost of appeal, as if to say: "One more blow and you could knock me dead. Hit me again." I do hit him again and he sinks to the floor. My daughter and I run out of the apartment to freedom. [August 1, 1981]

This dream illustrates something of the way in which the dream works in healing the psyche. The masculine figure who had terrorized me, the dreamer, for months, suddenly seemed to be willing his own death. As I assimilated the material from the unconscious, I began to have a change in attitude toward my inner masculine. This change in conscious attitude was reflected in the change in my unconscious as manifested by the dream. While my brother, in a kind of unconscious complicity with my family, did much to destroy my self-confidence, it was I who continued to act out a role long overdue for change. Slowly, I began to recognize that the dream figure I was "murdering" was not just my abusing brother, but also my own inner masculine whom I had learned to distrust, fear, and even hate. This insight was an important turning point for me.

My violent dreams forced me to acknowledge that I had been a victim; but in my action of killing a male figure I also recognized the rage locked away inside me at the hurt done to me, first by a virtual stranger, then by my brother. My unconscious forced me to bring this material to my conscious recognition, to feel it directly as emotional pain. To have remained in such an attitude, however, would have forced me into a state of helpless self-pity. The dream was pushing me to new awareness. The male figure was, as it were, asking to die. It was time for the old attitude that I was nothing but a victim to be superseded by the new, lest I continue to act as my own victimizer. The task at hand, then, was to free my inner masculine. For the first time in many years, I contemplated a return to university studies.

These violent dreams appeared within the first two years of the analytic process. Nearly fifteen years earlier, I had accompanied my husband, Michael, to Europe and embarked on my doctorate. There I was, ready to make a fresh start when, suddenly, I felt inadequate and unable to continue. It was the sixties, but I was dropping out without tuning in or turning on! Still, my decision to terminate academic studies was not without its positive side, for, with a continent separating me from my birth family, I was able to countenance the idea of having a family of my own, something my husband clearly wanted, something that I had, until then, adamantly opposed. It seems that only when I was physically distanced from my birth family could I listen to the needs of my own instinctual nature. For the first time I had a little of the courage required to trust my own body and its needs.

So, I abandoned my university studies and put the needs of my body ahead of the demands of my head. Everywhere, progressive women were attempting to juggle family and career and I had desperately wanted to do the same. Yet, something had held me back from continuing my academic studies; my psyche, at this point, was too fragile to learn the difficult balance of head and body. Thus, while I had always fiercely believed in the right of a woman to carry on a career while at the same time functioning as nurturer, I lacked the self-confidence to attempt both at once.

I had always recoiled from the idea of having a family of my own; always I had a sense that I would have to exert all the force of my being against some unknown terror trying to invade me. And the terror was real to me even though I could have given it neither name nor substance. Even to entertain the idea of giving birth was something of a triumph for me. That I responded eagerly to the idea of motherhood came as a great surprise to me. Giving birth to a child meant doing something "normal," something quite acceptable to the whole social order; it was something I didn't need to feel ashamed of, something ordinary, something people were doing every day. (Even princesses had babies.) It was a very important step in the process of my healing, and it helped me legitimize myself openly as a woman like any other.

But no sooner had we returned to our home country than my old fears returned. I was aware of an overwhelming need to protect the child I was carrying in my womb. In my birth family I recognized a palpable enemy to my child's well-being. Nevertheless, I scrupulously honored every demand made upon me by family members no matter how unreasonable. The members of my birth family were like gods that had to be expiated. I simply could not say no to them and yet I knew that I always had to have energy in reserve to hold them at bay. My protective instincts increased with the birth of our second child so that I, who had once felt powerless, was now forced to exert myself fully to protect my young family.

As our two children were growing up, I slowly began to recognize the part my new family played in my healing process; in giving them the nurturing I had been denied, and in watching them develop their spontaneous, assertive individuality, I was preparing the groundwork for my own creativity and healing. I was able to recognize how important a container for the growing ego a nurturant family situation can be.

But the children were well into their school years before I was ready to begin the process of restoring my ego container to a condition strong enough to permit intellectual creativity to take place through me. Childbirth had helped to connect me to my body which I had, until then, all but ignored. My years of volunteer activities kept me physically and mentally active during the children's developing years. But my frustration with what I felt to be my wasted life became apparent. The agony of abortion was the crisis that threatened to sever me in two; it was this that ultimately pushed me into Jungian analysis and the exploration of my dreams.

The act of discovering my dreams was like coming upon a world that all along had been an important but hidden part of me. Dreams represented new possibilities for and new means of searching for being and growing. They helped give me the courage to reenter the world that lay outside the protected circle of husband, children, and friends.

My story resumes with my recognition of the need to take up, once more, the earlier task I had abandoned, my doctoral degree. The last dream I described made it clear that I had undergone a radical change in attitude toward my inner masculine. However, the following dream preceded by nearly a year my decision to return to full time academic studies. This dream also suggested the kind of work that remained to be done.

I am in an unfamiliar place where a man that I value is being hunted. The town is on the Niagara River, which divides Canada from the United States. I go to a house in a pioneer village from where I know he began his escape. Two rather unfeeling people, a man and a youth, are discussing how they are going to capture him. They want him dead or alive. The unusual thing is that, although the townspeople are dressed in the Puritan garb of America's settlers, the man being pursued is encumbered with a full suit of medieval armor. I follow the trail left by the bits of armor he has been casting off as he runs. Eventually, I know that he will be able to cast off enough armor to dive into the Niagara River and to swim safely to freedom. In the meantime, I find evidence that he has been filing away at a band of iron across his mouth, presumably in order to remove his headgear. Then, suddenly, I see the mouthpiece itself thrown down on the rocks. I have already come across a thigh piece, a gauntlet, and an elbow joint, which has fallen into a crack in the stone and has therefore gone unnoticed by his enemies. I see these objects because I am running close to the water's edge, whereas the enemy has taken the higher ground. [September 3, 1981]

What was unusual about this dream was that I, as the dreamer, was no longer treating the unknown man as an enemy, but as someone whom I wanted to rescue but could not. The "knight" was being pursued by men who appeared to be Puritans. The dream told me that before my inner masculine could be free to reach consciousness, imaged in the dream as making the border crossing, a lot of "armor" had to be dropped. I associated the armor with all the outdated attitudes I had accumulated over the years, which, while they made me in some sense invulnerable, also weighed me down and restricted my creative movement. In psychological terms, defenses cut me off from feelings and from my instinctual side. They kept me from answering the question "What do I really want?"

I had built up defenses in order to avoid the pain of life; these defenses were now slowly cutting me off both from reality and from creative action. The man in the dream could not run in his armor; he was a prey to every enemy. I sensed that the armor represented my resistance to feelings, all those barriers I had constructed in my life to keep myself intact, a survivor, a well-defended fortress. But I had to gain access to my feelings and to my sense of self-worth in order to avoid the blows of self-doubt, my own inner enemy.

It is interesting that the enemy was Puritan; those outdated values constituted the "high moral ground" that prevented them from seeing what I saw lying by the water's edge, close to the unconscious. In many ways, they resembled the ugly woman of the earlier dream, with her morality of expediency; corseted to make herself look other than what she was she was also related to the armored knight in this dream.

The men in Puritan garb fascinated me and I soon discovered why. What I describe next is a process that Jung called "active imagination" and that others have described as "waking dream." It is a process by which one meditates upon a specific image from the unconscious until it comes to life; one then observes it in action, and may even enter into dialogue with it, focusing on holding ego-consciousness. What follows is a description of my experience of active imagination, which helped me clarify the image of the Puritans in my dream.

I had been lying ill in bed with the flu when suddenly I found myself confronted with an image of myself, as a child of five, climbing the cold, dark stairs that led from the kitchen, which was kept warm by the slow-burning log in the woodstove. Above the kitchen of the old wintry-cold farmhouse, abandoned most days except for me, little Kate, had been a tiny pantry warmed by a stovepipe connected to the woodstove in the kitchen directly below. Every day I would go to that little room; I thought of it as my own special place where I could play, uninterrupted, all day long. It was a safe place; but getting there was very dangerous. Mostly, little Kate dreaded that climb because of the voices and the vague ghostly shapes that seemed to flit about her. The trick was never to look to the left or the right but to keep her eyes fixed on the step ahead. I knew that if, even once, I saw what was there, I would never want to climb those stairs by myself again.

I, the grown-up Kate, lying in bed with the flu, climbed the stairs in my mind's eye but I knew I did not need to be afraid because I was grown up and skeptical about ghosts. So, I dared to look at the specter from which my younger self had so carefully averted her gaze. The cold chill that flew up my spine was real. What I saw was a man dressed in black clothes walking beside me, step matching step. He gave me a look of such malevolent hatred, such diabolical evil, that I ran all the way up the rest of the stairs, and gaining the safety of the little pantry, slammed the door shut.

That day, I, the grown-up Kate, came a little closer not only to an understanding of the Puritan image in the dream above, but also to an admiration of the bravery and cunning of the little child I had once been. The glimpse of the demonic Puritan figure helped me to feel her suffering. It was the beginning of compassion for her, the child I had been.

My encounter with my childhood demon helped me accept the validity of my scathing analysis of the family and its value system. Eventually I was able to identify the enemy in the dream as my inner censor who had condemned me as evil, incestuous, worthless. The dream attempted to overturn conscious attitudes and pictured the moralist as the enemy, and my beleaguered innocence as the struggling hero. Yet, so fixed was my attitude toward myself at that time as sinful, I was not immediately able to grasp, let alone experience, the truth of the dream's message.

Subsequent dreams assessed the situation with greater and greater pointedness, zeroing in on how I had been playing into the unconscious demands made upon me by family to the detriment of my own needs and abilities. For example, the following dream traces the way I had severed head from body (in psychological terms), and thereby inhibited my creativity.

I have, a certain time ago, written a letter to a convent telling the people there that I am a sister (nun); now I am being sent for and I do not know whether to admit I lied, or to continue maintaining the illusion. I contemplate trying to obtain a nun's habit and realize that, not only do I not know where to get one, but even if I did, I wouldn't have the faintest idea of how to wear it. There seems to have been some reason why I wrote the letter I did, but I cannot remember the reason now. Still, I go to the convent and am received. However, there is a sense in which I haven't been forgiven for my duplicity and that I must endure punishment for it. I am sent upstairs to spend the night in the library. The library is the topmost room of a high, circular tower with windows all around. It somehow resembles a lighthouse minus the light. Except where the tower is joined to the main building, and presumably to the mainland, it is completely surrounded by water. During the night, there is a fearsome storm during which the tower is so sorely buffeted and sways so wildly that I think it will snap off its foundations. However, it holds firm. I want no more punishment and so I decide to escape. I find a crescent-shaped object, a little like a boomerang, and by putting this against my body I am rendered invisible. So, I creep out unnoticed, passing by people who turn at the unexpected current of air but, seeing nothing, carry on with their tasks. Near the open door, a man stares right through me.

I run out into a courtyard nearly colliding with a well-dressed woman walking up the path. Noticing her car parked behind a low wall, I climb in and drive off. At this point, I panic. Surely an apparently driverless car will draw attention to itself. I do not want to become involved in a car chase, so I stop the car and take off on foot across an open field toward a small copse of trees.

I climb up one of the trees and hide in the leafy branches up high. There are other people about, some of them up in the trees. My husband seems to be one of these climbers and I decide to throw in my lot with him. Now that my escape has been discovered and the stolen car found, my pursuers are running across the field toward the copse. I climb up on my husband's back and tell him that if he concentrates very hard, he shall be able to fly. My words inspire him to try, and he succeeds. I seem to need this man either to show me the way or to give me the courage to take the journey I am afraid to make alone.

My husband alights several times: at an apartment building, at a remote farmhouse, and finally at a university where he is directed up a set of stairs that eventually takes us into an attic with wide casement windows overlooking a vast sea. We are on the final leg of our journey now; there remains only for us to cross this sea. [November 10, 1981]

Like so many others recorded here, I had this dream in the first year of analysis; yet it was a dream I went back to again and again for several years. Only after I had returned to university and experienced anew some of my old doubts and insecurities, and fought successful daily battles with shyness at facing new people and new situations, could I begin to grasp its message. From my present perspective, the dream seems to encapsulate my whole life to that time; it both articulated the problem and offered a solution. I had to unravel its meaning step by step.

Why a convent? By then I knew enough about the language of

dreams to appreciate how frequently puns were employed. Thus a nun sounds like "none," which is to say, a nonentity, a nothing, which is precisely how my life of self-imposed service was making me feel. A nun is spoken of as a "sister" who wears a "habit." I had donned, like a garment, the "habit" of denying that anything was amiss in my family; I became a "good sister" in order to survive in a difficult sibling relationship; more than that, my "habit" had helped to create in my developing years the facade of a normal, stable domestic life. By dissociating myself from my brother's abuse of me, I was able to create an illusion of normality in front of family and friends. I remember how family, friends, and neighbors would often comment on how close the relationship was between us as brother and sister. How refreshing! How lovely to see! No one ever seemed to suspect that anything unnatural lay beneath the "closeness." And it was all too easy to go on satisfying these well-meaning people with the fantasy that met the sentimental expectations of so many. But at what price?

I had simultaneously created dual fantasies quite compatible with one another: one that helped me to deny that my family situation was in any way destructive; the other, the invention of my imagination, that restored to me a world I would later strive to achieve for myself. In a sense, the former fantasy was destructive; the latter, constructive. Yet, at the base of each was a sad reality: both worlds could exist only if I was willing to be satisfied with a kind of partial existence. But full access to my creativity seemed possible only through my acceptance of the truth of sexual abuse and how it had crippled me. Only by breaking through the fantasy of denial might I hope to begin to heal myself, not as a stopgap measure, but for all time.

The convent was a particularly striking image of what was going on in my unconscious; it helped me make an intellectual and emotional breakthrough. The steps are given here of what proved to be an interpretation most helpful to me in coming to terms with my past: the monastic nun accepts certain constraints upon her behavior when she takes the vows of chastity, silence, and service. My behavior toward my brother showed a similar fidelity to such vows, but in an unconscious, perverse parody. Whereas the nun sees in her vocation an earthly image of the heavenly marriage of the soul with God and wears her veil as a token that she is the bride of Christ, I saw my incestuous self as married to my brother, committed in silent service to fulfilling whatever he asked of me, never daring to speak about the past.

The dream seemed to be telling me that, on an unconscious level, I had become the bride of a demon lover; it was here that I was leading an incestuous life and unless I examined my unconscious assumptions, henceforth I would live as though tied to my brother by the bonds of unconscious necessity. My fidelity would always be to him, and by extension, to my birth family. No wonder I spent so many troubled nights killing an unknown man. I had lived my whole life keeping silent about my brother's abuse of me; and now, breaking so ominous a bond seemed tantamount to murder. Here in the unconscious lay the root of my fantasy.

What I had to do was to bring the ideas suggested by these images out into the open and consciously come to terms with the extent to which I had assumed these vows. Only then would I be able to stop taking responsibility for my brother's life, thereby freeing myself to be responsible for my own. Only then would I be able to separate the figure of my brother from the image of my own inner masculine.

In my dream, I was shut up in the tower library (the ivory towers of academe) as a punishment. Behind my attitude was an extraordinarily high degree of self-contempt. I eventually recognized the tower on its thin stem joined to the main building as my own head, neck, and body. In order to fight my bouts of panic, I would neglect my physical being; I would push myself to work late into the night at the very brink of a deadline. My health suffered; my work suffered. To do anything creative seemed to involve pain so acute and was so short-lived that it scarcely merited the agony of preparation. But I continued to punish my body in order to allow my head to function.

However, the tower was described as a lighthouse minus the light; it housed a library. But of what use is a lighthouse or a library without a light? Cut off from my instinctual nature, my feelings, and my values, I was not able to connect to the light of wisdom. My head without this light was a mere repository of books. During the storm, the tower swayed so wildly that I thought it would snap off. I recognized the image of wind as belonging to states of terror I had experienced initially as a child during and after abuse, and later as a student at university. My dream ego panicked at the thought of continuing to act as a "sister"; yet, she also believed that she deserved to be punished if she stopped. She was living, the dream said, in a state of mutilation; unless she destroyed from within the power her brother continued to hold over her, every attempt at a creative act would end in partial failure.

The convent of this dream bore a resemblance to the high moral tone of the enemy in the previous one; the wearing of monastic habit was a little like the donning of armor; the frailty (read sinful frailty in the case of the nun) of the body had to be acknowledged, its affirmative power and value denied at all costs. Yet time spent in the mind (tower) was viewed as punishment by the dreamer. In fact, both dreams seemed to describe outmoded attitudes that are part of medieval history: the previous one relates to chivalry; the latter, to the submissive service of the convent. (In this interpretation, I am not disparaging the women who choose the monastic life as their true vocation, but rather I am commenting on the way in which I had fooled myself into living a lie.)

It was now clear to me that I had been living by a very strict code of honor that had all but stifled my natural imaginative spontaneity. Nor was it mere chance that the image of the tower/library was a lighthouse minus the light: in cutting myself off from the creativity of my own being, I was struggling unsuccessfully to derive energy from what was, after all, a mere repository of books of whose wisdom I could not avail myself. No wonder I tried to escape.

I had chivalrously, and at the expense of my own psychic health, accepted the blame which was due my persecutor; I had devoted myself to the service of others, principally to my birth family, to the very people who denied my right to a childhood. But I had done so not out of a Christian ideal, for I cannot remember why I wrote to the convent, but rather as a means of survival. By hiding the true facts, by not making an issue of my torment, by not creating a disturbance in the family, I had been able to achieve a measure of invisibility that was no longer appropriate.

The dream described very effectively my panic attacks as a wind that threatened to sever the tower from its foundations, my head from my heart. But while the wind can be seen as an image of the panic I felt, it can also be seen as an archetypal symbol of the holy spirit "whose power working within us can do infinitely more than we can ask or imagine,"[2] that is, if we are sufficiently able to withstand its force, if the container of our being is sufficiently strong. Unless I could connect myself to the ground of my being, I would not be able to withstand either the negative power of my childhood bogeyman or the

Rubbing of a typical English resurrection brass of the fifteenth century.

In the Resurrection Brass, the Christ steps out of the tomb while the soldiers sleep. In his hand he holds the cross, proof visible that he has held the opposites in tension. He is the Christ-energy; as an archetype of the transcendent function and an important part of the culture of Western civilization, the figure of Christ is still a powerful image for many of us. The figure steps easily from the tomb that confined him. He is thin but powerfully muscled. The artist has caught him in the act of freeing himself. This Christ's eyes are enormous, wide open, full of awareness; he is a person fully conscious.

Around him the guards sleep. The old guard (the status quo) is incapable of preventing the bursting forth of this new energy. The old defenses cannot hold back the newly emergent attitudes.

Jesus Christ lived a life that was often at odds with group structures, including that of the family. He spoke of individual enlightenment which, although it initially divided the individual from the group, ultimately benefited others. The process of dividing, of separation from collective values, was as painful for Christ as it is for each one of us. Christ crucified is always described as temporarily divided both from God and the human order. Yet Christ resurrected conveys this clear message: out of such a separation comes rebirth, a new life from a redefined center propelled by divine energy.

I call this energy Christ-energy, but its presence is found in every religion that celebrates transformation as an integral part of the lives of men and women. We are not the creators of Christ-energy; we are its containers. It is there in us as creativity, which is an expression of love. To love is the essence of the divine within us.

positive creative force of the Holy Spirit, the wind that bloweth where it listeth. The dream thus connected my body to my spiritual needs; it was essentially religious in its scope.

I was reminded of a myth, very special to me, which spoke to the terror of the lonely night-vigil: the tale of Cupid and Psyche.

Psyche had angered the goddess Aphrodite. People were not only worshiping Psyche, a mere mortal, because of her great beauty but they were neglecting the shrines of the goddess Aphrodite herself! Psyche, without any effort on her part, was superseding Aphrodite as an object of devotion. Eros, the divine son of Aphrodite, was sent by his mother to punish Psyche; but as he too was overcome by Psyche's beauty, he married her instead.

The marriage, for all its strange hush of secrecy was, for a time, a happy one. Eros, coming to his wife only under cover of night, had strictly forbidden her to see him in the flesh. By day she wandered through the great palace, a lonely, solitary figure. It was not too long before Psyche was begging her husband for permission to visit her sisters. With deep regret, Eros agreed.

Her two sisters were very jealous of the great wealth that had been bestowed upon Psyche. When they were told that she had never laid eyes on her husband, they convinced her that he must be a terrifying, serpentine monster. Poor, frightened, bewildered Psyche was certain that she must have a glimpse of him. So one night, she timorously took her lamp and was soon gazing in awe, not at a monster, but at the magnificence of a god. A drop of oil from her lamp wakened Eros and he, more in sadness than anger, informed her that, because of Aphrodite's anger, the two of them must part.

Psyche journeyed to Aphrodite's palace and begged her forgiveness. Instead, Aphrodite set her a number of seemingly impossible tasks, among them the task of separating into distinct piles a veritable mountain of tiny seed-grains that the goddess threw down in a heap before her. Psyche had until morning to carry out her hopeless task.

I noted that my dream and Psyche's story both involved a lonely night-vigil as punishment that carried within it a reward. But the way the two stories diverge, at that point, is significant. Psyche did what any normal mortal would do; she broke down and cried wet tears. And to her aid came the tiny ants who carefully divided the seeds into their distinct types. To cry tears was precisely what I had never felt permitted to do when I was severed from my creative masculine and forced to perform unwelcome tasks. Even to this day, although I give myself permission to cry, I find weeping difficult. I have remained dry-eyed all my life. Tears had been of no avail in softening my family's hardness. All too soon my heart hardened against myself with no tears to soften, pity, or condone. The process of uncovering my past through dreams required of me the shedding of tears; required of me submission to my unconscious instinctual nature, an instinctual nature of whose gifts I had too long deprived myself. Tears spring to my eyes now and catch me unawares at the plight of another; and then I realize that some of the tears are shed on my own behalf. Only through such subterfuge can I weep for myself.

In the story of Eros and Psyche, I see the ants as symbols of this instinctual nature, inhabiting the dark places of the earth, coming to the surface into the light, and mediating between earth and heaven, between the unconscious and consciousness. I identify the insignificant-seeming, helpful ants as the power of relatedness, the true servants of Eros, principle of relatedness. I see in the tears, and in the ants, feelings, instincts, and intuition to which I have needed to reconnect myself; I see in them a source of power of which I had not availed myself because I had neglected to take into consideration the energy of the body as a vital part of the totality of the Self. I had also failed to take into account powerful emotions such as anger, hatred, and revenge, which I had bottled up in my body and which had to be released before I could hope to invoke their more creative opposites: compassion, love, and forgiveness.

Thus, I see in my dream a way of connecting myself to my own story, which, while it provided no helpful ants, showed me instead the problematic image of the crescent-shaped boomerang of invisibility. Not only was the story a reminder of what I was doing to myself, but it suggested connections and possibilities that would nudge me toward a union of thought and feeling to make me whole again.

Unlike the Psyche story, my dream did not proceed directly toward resolution, but rather toward conflict. In a sense, I was rewarded for my ability to withstand the terrors of the night: I was given the object that conferred upon the bearer invisibility.

However, while the "invisibility" permitted escape, it did not appear to resolve the real problem. If you are "not there" (without an identity), how can you begin to create something that *is*? While the boomerang may have offered itself as a protective device, it kept me from being recognized for my own unique gifts. The dream seemed to suggest that it was time that I got rid of it. The boomerang was also described by the dreamer as a crescent-shaped object associated with the moon, the archetypal image of the feminine. Boomerangs are meant to be thrown, not held. By tossing away the boomerang, I would lose my invisibility and thus draw attention to myself; this I feared because to be noticed was to risk self-exposure. But perhaps the promise was this: a boomerang is designed to return to the hand that threw it and perhaps this one would return to me as feminine energy. Certainly the dream seemed to be urging me to take risks rather than simply to suffer the storm. Only by strengthening the container of my body through bodywork would I learn to walk proudly through the storm rather than cowering from it in the uncertain refuge of mental fantasies. While I had succeeded in avoiding conflicts with family (hiding my true creative power from them), I had also cut myself off from real creative enterprise by settling for something of a fantasy existence.

Why did the dream show me flying about? Because the real creative work happens when both feet are planted firmly on the ground. In stealing the well-dressed woman's car, I was taking on the persona of the respectable woman. In convincing my husband that he could fly and carry me about, I placed a burden upon him that said: "You are responsible for my destiny." Thus, I succeeded in drawing my husband into this fantasy! However, as long as I was perched in the attic of a university building, I would not achieve anything; I had to "come down to earth" as a real, vulnerable, mature woman, in short, as myself. I would not achieve wholeness through pipe dreams, through fantasy, through the magic of invisibility. This was perhaps the most difficult task for me, for it meant accepting my flawed humanity, my flesh-and-blood reality. It meant giving up my status as a princess. The danger would be in wanting to escape into my head rather than in rediscovering the ground of my being, my body, from which I dissociated myself long ago but was forced to make truce with during my years as a nurturing parent.

There is a strange little detail in the dream: as a result of my invisibility, a man stares right through me. Up until this point, the closest I had come to meeting my inner masculine was the armor-shedding fugitive. My invisibility, this dream suggested, may have been the reason for this. My inner masculine was as cut off from me as

my bodily feelings and instincts. No wonder I had never
positive bearer of Eros. At this point, he was either a great
the paramount block to my feminine creativity or an
insignificant figure powerless to help me. However, as I noted in
speaking of an earlier dream, he had the potential for being the strongest link to my creative self. Thus, Jung speaks of the marriage between
the masculine and feminine in the individual as the foundation for
wholeness and the fountain of creativity. But at this point, my feminine had not even been lovingly approached by the man in my dreams
because he could not see, let alone reach me.

I began to grasp the situation described by the dream only after I
reentered the university as a mature student. The dream seemed to be
warning me about what could happen unless I came to terms with my
past. Before I could expect to succeed at my doctorate on my second
time round, I had to make sure that I had become a more conscious
being.

It is for this reason that Marion prescribed a good deal of bodywork
during this period. I worked with a body therapist who helped me
gain some much needed body awareness; I also gathered about me a
group of people who were interested in a form of meditation through
dance. For a time I even considered developing this new interest into a
working venture with another person from my group—a man with
some previous dance-therapy training. However, I soon found that
what he had in mind for himself was a principal role, relegating me to
supplying financial capital and organizing the venture. I quickly realized that I had, once again, found myself in the role of "anima
woman." What's more, the man envisaged me as part of a hierarchical
organization of which he was head, assigning me a by-now-familiar
role: "serving" to advance another's career. This time, I was not taken
in for long. But it was partly my feeling of anger upon recognizing
how easily I could still be duped, how prone I still was to projecting
onto an actual man my unconscious inner masculine, that gave me the
necessary push to face the university officials.

I successfully enrolled in a program that would determine whether I
could continue as a full-time doctoral candidate. The time had come to
free the slaves. September of that year found me attending classes, as
nervous as a young school girl; I found it almost impossible to put pen
to paper in a coherent, logical way. Hadn't I achieved anything from
nearly a year of analysis? Thus I berated myself.

Just before Christmas, I had this dream. It offered me some sorely-
needed encouragement; at last I seemed to be headed in the correct
direction.

> I am taking part in a dance. We are tracing the pattern of a star—treading
> out the shape with our feet, weaving outward and inward as we trace out
> the points of the star, always in a circle, always from left to right. I
> concentrate very hard because the star shape is very important to me.
> [December 20, 1982]

The image of the star suggested to me that I was finally beginning to
work out my own destiny. A star connotes, among other things, an
individual's uniqueness. Marie-Louise von Franz speaks of following
your star as accepting isolation; it means "not knowing where to go,
having to find out a completely new way for yourself instead of just
going on the trodden path everybody else runs along."[3] The movement from left to right indicated that I was moving from unconsciousness to consciousness and that this was the correct (right) action to be
taken at that time.

While I was frequently discouraged by my dual roles of homemaker
and student, I began to realize that there were treasures to be gleaned.
Until then my dreams had seemed to be warning me about living too
much in the head; they were urging me away from a one-sided attitude
and toward balance. I needed to learn to juggle the demands of both
head and heart. The following dream came after a spirited discussion I
had with one of my professors. I had stormed into his office after
doing rather poorly on a paper for him; although I didn't tell him so, I
felt he was deprecating my intellect. What I did tell him was this: I had
tried to please him and failed; now I was going to please myself. If I
was going to be shot down, I was going down in flames, in a blaze of
glory. My professor seemed astonished but made no comment.

My attitude and behavior changed at that point; I became confident
and outspoken. In turn, the professor's attitude to me changed. What I
had been doing was projecting my infantile value system onto him.
Unconsciously I had been turning him into "father" so that I could
play the role of "good daughter." Luckily, he had been too psychologically together to participate; he was simply incapable of playing
my game. And my woman's anger, once I had been caught playing the
game of patriarchy yet again, had come to my rescue and urged me to

action; rather than getting embarrassed (thereby replicating the abused child's sense of shame), I had stood up for myself. To be forced upon my own resources at this time was the best thing that could have happened to me. I surprised myself into taking an independent stand and the payoff was newfound energy and confidence. The following dream, which introduced me to the feisty masculine aspect of myself, indicates how profound a change was at work in my outlook.

I am waiting at a bus stop in front of the public library when I see a youth who appears to be vandalizing a sign in front of an old, abandoned barn I never noticed before. I look at him sternly and he stops. He then invites me over to explore the barn, on top of which sits, rather precariously, a small attic room. We climb the rickety stairs and see, lying in the straw of the attic, a clay head or mask of primitive man, many thousands of years old. It is very beautiful. At first I think it is a death mask but I soon revise my opinion: it clearly has a vital, ritual significance because the chin, from the lower lip down, has been ornately patterned with rows of crisscross and other designs. By contrast, the eye sockets and eyelids have been very naturalistically worked. The face is long and shows that there must have been beautiful bones under the tight skin. The skull does not show the deformities of the earlier stages of man's evolution for it is very handsome; yet, it has a feeling of great age and even something of the aura of a religious relic. We see that it is tucked safely back among the straw for it seems as safe here as anywhere. [January 30, 1983]

In this dream, I finally met my young masculine, a rather feisty rebel. While he was a bit of a troublemaker on the surface, underneath he was amenable to discipline if handled courteously but firmly. I had found it difficult accepting the new academic discipline, principally because I needed encouragement badly and had no means of receiving it. In fact, I found the encouragement I needed from the very professor who seemed to underrate my efforts until I stood up for myself. What I had done by asserting myself was to waken my pugnacious young masculine who rewarded my interest in him by showing me the ancient, numinous mask. The dream indicated that there was an important treasure hidden away in the most abandoned of places—the straw of a barn. Like the birth of Christ in the stable, wondrous transformations and rebirths can be experienced in the humblest of instinctual settings. I tended to undervalue my intellectual abilities at this point; frequent bouts of panic and depression, a replication of those endured by me as a young undergraduate, attested to this. The dream seemed to be telling me that while my top story did not seem to be the most auspicious place for discovering important truths, I must have faith in myself because a treasure lay there. However, the building in which the "treasure" was housed was in a vulnerable state. An old barn in the middle of an urban setting is just a firetrap asking to be pulled down. I needed to work at restoring the building; the dream was telling me that I was still not being receptive to the needs of my body.

By the following spring, I had succeeded in meeting the criteria for entrance into the doctoral program; I received both a scholarship and a teaching position as a tutor. During the summer, before beginning the program as a full-time student, I had this dream:

> I am coming out of a university classroom when I meet a prominent woman academic who is talking to a very famous male scholar who is her mentor. He invites me into his office where he has before him a large number of documents representing my past education. He picks up a shorter document, a typed report that represents a more personal estimate of my ability. He hands me the fat dossier, warning me not to read it because a more accurate, and favorable estimation of my ability lies in the short report which he does not give me. He seems pleased with me and tells me that he has something to show me. Taking me through another door, he leads me out to a large field. There sits a large toy, a motorized airplane he often plays with. It has a cord with which the hobbyist can guide this apparatus that actually "flies." He sets the plane in motion and it takes off. Because of its large size (much bigger than one would normally expect of a toy), it makes enormous circuits round and round the field; he follows its movement by riding in a cart pulled by a mare. Somehow, he resembles Father Christmas, such anticipation, joy, and excitement does he generate. Eventually, the mare unhitches herself and comes over and talks to me. I also notice that the woman academic has returned but my attention is all on the mare. This is not only a magical talking animal, but also an incredibly sprightly, spirit-raising creature. In the end, it is the mare that fills me with lasting joy and excitement. [July 21, 1983]

At this point, the dream was showing me the split that I would have to face over the years that I remained a student at the university. This split was between my inflated respect for academic authority (the woman academic and the famous scholar) and my attraction to the instinctual, playful, and highly personal gifts (the mare). Initially, the dream suggested an apparently ideal relationship between masculine and feminine: with the masculine mentor initiating and guiding the feminine disciple. But while the masculine figure started up the motorized airplane, it turned out to be too big for him to handle on his own; he had to harness feminine energy (the mare) to empower him. At first, my attention was drawn only to the benevolent-looking man as he sat in the cart exuding considerable energy; only later did I notice that the real power was coming from the animal who pulled the carriage on which the man rode. What first struck me as an ideal arrangement of male mentor and female disciple now seemed to be a replication of the old patriarchal model I found abhorrent in church hierarchy. But the dream was offering an alternative in the freewheeling mare. If the mare was feminine energy, there was an indication that the old paradigm of subservience was giving way to new possibilities for me; if the horse was willing to be led by me, why shouldn't I bypass the outlandish old man and fly the plane myself?

Notice that the dreamer did not ask Parsifal's important question: whom does the object, in this case an airplane and not the Holy Grail, serve? Nor did she ask where the energy from the plane was coming from or who was really guiding that energy. Was it the male figure or the mare? In the dream, I was still too mesmerized by the academic patriarchy to pose such questions. Nevertheless, the unconscious, in dreams such as this, was pushing me to pose this very question.

The dream, with its initial buildup around the famous scholar and his assistant, suggested that I was attracted to the patriarchal model that makes the feminine energy subservient to the masculine. However, after I discovered the mare, this initial, patriarchal, male-female configuration seemed less reliable, less desirable, even less truthful. While it was true that the scholar held the reins, it was the mare who could abruptly stop and unhitch herself; in short, she could break the connection. What seemed clear was that both the scholar and the mare were equal partners in mediating between earth and heaven. The two energies that connected insight with instinct were masculine and feminine energies moving toward equal partnership within me. Without them, the airplane would simply run around in circles for a time and then crash-land.

The fact is, I had been projecting my own abilities onto my professors. The danger is obvious: as long as I attributed my success to their efforts on my behalf, I would not be able to have the necessary self-confidence to become a professor in my own right. The dream was warning me not to put my trust in Santa Claus fantasies that emphasize gifts given by others. In truth, the gifts lie within myself or nowhere. The dream was reminding me that my newly emergent masculine potency and the highly vulnerable area of the feminine, my own instinctual fire that I had worked so hard to ignite in the first few years of analysis, had to experience contact with the earth. The positive aspect of the dream lay in the dreamer's attraction to the little mare; however, there was a danger in the dreamer's inability, at this stage, to assess the value of the mare's talking to her.

At the time of this dream, I was following my instincts, but unconsciously rather than consciously. The fact that I had this dream in the summer break and not in the thick of the academic year provides the key to an interpretation. During this particular summer, I was taking an academic course for fun, that is, as an unofficial student. I was neither to be assigned a grade for my work nor was I obliged to contribute anything at all. So, when I was invited to present a seminar to the class, I felt free to follow my own interests. Once embarked upon the "serious business" of graduate courses, I would find such "self-indulgence" inappropriate; later, I thought, it would be necessary to work within certain fixed parameters governed by my professor's interest, not my own; after all, I would be ranked according to the professor's criteria of what was significant.

Thus, my movement toward the little horse was a luxury I permitted myself in presenting the kind of seminar that interested me in the nonserious, unofficial environment of summer studies rather than the kind I would later feel myself obliged to do, the kind I thought my professors would expect of me. It is obvious that, at this point, I was still internalizing a set of standards that were at odds with my own desires and abilities. Academic work, as defined by my actions at this time, was something acceptable to the status quo. I was unlikely to produce anything original as long as I continued to force my creativity along such prescribed channels. Nor was I at all swayed from my rigid adherence to my internally-determined patriarchal scholarship by the fact that my summer seminar was deemed a success; I assumed that the professor's praise was just words. Without a grade, what did the whole exercise matter anyway?

The following dream, which occurred a month later, in the fall term, shows how far I had strayed from my own interests and from the instinctual paradigm of that summer seminar. Once again, I had begun to try hard to follow the pattern set by the professor; the result was that I was making things harder for myself than they needed to be. I was suffering acute stress because I felt I wasn't getting anywhere. Not only was I not satisfying my own intellectual needs but I was expending far too much effort for too little gain; *and* I was working long hours sitting at a desk, all of which was putting a strain on my body. I was seriously neglecting my body, my feminine container; this dream warned me, in no uncertain terms, to mend my ways.

> I want to ask my young daughter to come with me to pick apples at the bottom of the field but I am afraid to leave my even younger son. A nurse comes in at that point holding a very sturdy-looking brown baby, approximately a year old. The doctor appears and tells me that my son is extremely healthy; my daughter, however, is not looking at all well. He thinks it would be an excellent idea if I took her apple-picking. My daughter comes in and I see that she looks unenthusiastic and depressed. She looks as though she may be suffering from a psychological disorder and immediately I feel real concern and distress for her. [October 9, 1983]

In fact, I had begun to suffer from dizzy spells as though the burden of other people's supposed expectations was beginning to take its toll. Slowly I recognized the need to reconcile opposing aspects of myself. I began to realize that my body would no longer be entirely ruled by the dictates of the head. The young son (my most recent intellectual work) must not take precedence over the ailing daughter (my feminine values). On New Year's night, I had this dream:

> I am at a seminar conducted by my favorite male professor. It suddenly occurs to me that I shall soon be called upon to give a paper and I feel panicky because all I have is a few sketchy notes. However, I soon become absorbed in the discussion about a particular author and I make the point that in this person's writing, the ink gradually turns to blood. "Do you mean the feminine?" I am asked by a fellow student. "Yes," I say. "I am bothered by the idea of succession," says the professor and to my surprise I see that a woman now heads the seminar. My male professor has become a scholarly old woman. [January 1, 1984]

I interpreted this dream as an admonition not to feel ashamed of my feminine feeling. It occurred to me that creative persons, certainly the writers I was studying, had created out of an area of themselves that was imbued with feeling (blood) even though the actual creation had become the logos of print on a page. A legitimate process of the student of literature might be to retrace that pattern of feeling in oneself. This I was now striving to do. Moreover, vital, active interpretation entails examining the way in which the structure of words conveys that process. I was aware that words themselves send out messages to the reader, both consciously and unconsciously. In order to be as objective a reader as possible, I knew I had to examine my own assumptions, as well as those disclosed in the work, in order to try to discover a context, another container as it were, for interpretation.

When it came my turn to give a paper, I presented it in a way that honored my feminine side. What did that entail? It meant, for one thing, ignoring the way that previous material had been presented. That would be pleasing father, listening to the rigid conformity of the head, taking the tried and true path to a solid passing grade. Instead, I listened to the way in which I heard the material asking to be presented, and enlisted my body to help give me the energy and courage to present it that way. I found that the members of the seminar, mainly women, found my paper particularly lively and exciting.

In my dream, the masculine outline of the figure at the head of the class blurred and took on the features of what may well be ancient feminine wisdom. I felt somehow that the dream was cheering on my efforts. Nevertheless, I was to continue backsliding, to continue mistrusting my feminine intuition. The following dream presented the situation of danger to the psyche in a fresh and amusing way.

I am climbing up stairs, story by story, and slowly reach the top of a house. Once I get up there, I become frightened, for I cannot seem to find the way down. I am with my husband and he seems equally unable to help. I look out through a window and see how incredibly far down is ground level; the only way down is through this window. I look out again and see that the firemen are below with a huge safety net. All I have to do is jump. But I am also terrified of jumping; still, I finally force myself. I land safely. To my surprise, I see a woman on a large trampoline jumping playfully, reaching higher and higher with each jump. She easily reaches higher than the window I have just vacated and she seems to be having a lot of fun while doing so. [December 18, 1985]

The dream seemed to be saying that I was in danger of being trapped in my head. An easier, and happier way of gaining the same result would be to approach my work as play. This would involve humility—literally, being down-to-earth. (The Latin root of humility is also the word for earth.) It would also mean giving the body its rightful place, because the body is the container for the creative process. The dream was also saying that individuals lost in the head waste time and energy and panic easily, especially if they are afraid of heights.

The dreams were continually leading me toward a reliance on my own feminine so I could reach my own authentic masculinity. The dreams seemed to be telling me that my masculine energy emanated from the bedrock of my feminine power. But they were also illustrating my propensity for projecting my masculine either on my own husband or on a favorite male professor. It was a difficult process for me to begin withdrawing the projection because it meant taking a leap into the unknown and trusting my own resources, my own feminine being. Yet in this dream, I finally made the leap of faith; and I landed safely. Once I successfully accomplished this, I then saw that I could leap from the solid ground of my own being rather than relying on the well-worn stairs that led up, up, up but gave no assurance of reaching a satisfactory goal.

Relying on myself felt like risky business for me at this time. Having been seriously betrayed by male figures early in my life, it is hardly surprising that I had deep misgivings about the reliability of my own inner masculinity. But, paradoxically, the less I trusted my own inner masculine, the more I either credited or blamed the men about me for my successes or shortcomings. I was overvaluing the outer and devaluing the inner. I was afraid of my creativity because I expected that my inner masculine would betray me when I least expected him to. The following dream succinctly states both the problem and its solution.

I am at the wedding anniversary party of a dear old friend and I am admiring her new china tea service when I notice a chip in the teapot just near the lid. Just then, a farmhand comes in and my friend introduces him to me. He embraces me warmly and kisses me gently on the lips. Something like love stirs within me but I think to myself: "He is only a swineherd." At this, he walks out of the house. I wait for him the whole afternoon but he doesn't return. I feel the remorse and grief of one who has lost a constant and much-loved friend. [February 1985]

This dream spoke directly to the idea of the creative container. In my dream, a feminine figure had recently accepted the teapot as a gift; the teapot was new, but already flawed. Indeed, the dream made it clear that the flaw was in me, in my failure to value my feminine energy without which the masculine power cannot be accessed. This inaccessibility was shown in my failure to recognize a potential lover in the swineherd whom I consider inferior to me.

One recalls that Christ was the cornerstone that the builders rejected; here, I was rejecting my own potential masculine power for two reasons. First of all, I was unaccustomed to thinking of it as belonging to me, as being part of me, and what I could not acknowledge, I did not "own." Secondly, the dream revealed that I had an inflated idea of what masculine power is; disappointed by the male figures in my childhood, I was unwilling to trust anything that did not measure up to my rigid notion of what was acceptable; and only the perfect need apply! In terms of the inner masculine, the best was the enemy of the good.

The dream told me that I had better put aside my inflated ideas, mere fantasy, of what constitutes creative energy no matter how enamored I was of them. Here I had the real thing within my embrace and I let it go in favor of some glamorous pipe dream! The connection between the creative feminine and the creative masculine was clear; it had to be a marriage, a union of equal partners. It was also clear that I needed to work on my feminine side, to strengthen my self-worth as a woman, before I could develop a container strong enough to accept and be impregnated by the masculine creative power.

What I remember most about this dream is the powerful feelings it stirred up in me. I remember so clearly my initial distaste of the swineherd, followed by the heartbreaking regret when he left me. The dream captured the sense of time passing as I waited, anxious and sad, for him to return. In the morning when I awoke, and for many days afterwards, I grieved for him, certain he was gone forever. Nor did the masculine figure return to my dreams in a form that my dream–ego found acceptable until nearly two years later, after I had begun to befriend my shadow (the unconscious part of a woman's femininity). That there had been a deep wounding to my feminine nature is obvious in the following dream.

I am at a dinner party of some kind. I have been having a wonderful time flirting with a man just across from me much to the amusement of my husband. We adjourn to the living room to have our coffee. Suddenly, the room becomes the kitchen of the house where I was born. A child is coming down the stairs, as children do occasionally in the middle of dinner parties in order to be, for a few minutes before being shooed back up to bed, the center of attention. The little girl who comes down seems to be just such an extrovert. I can see that she is a delightful child. I say to her equally charming mother: "Introduce us!" Immediately there appears from behind the child a second little girl, painfully shy and introverted, with the most extraordinary look of haunted terror on her face; she has the look of one who has been badly traumatized. Immediately, I realize my mistake. What was appropriate for the child I first saw, must only be a terrible ordeal for the child behind. Immediately, the child whimpers and says, "Please, no, mommy!" and the woman turns angrily to me because I am responsible for the child's present anguish. [June 21, 1986]

While I had realized something of the nature of the wound to my psyche caused by sexual and emotional abuse in childhood, I had not taken the time to come to terms with it. Nor, indeed, did I know how to go about doing this. This dream, and others like it, released in me the feelings I needed to help the process along. But I needed time for the process to happen in me; and once the feelings began to be released, they forced me to make time for them, to make me pay attention to them, by putting me in a state of depression. Soon my unconscious needs were all too poignantly brought to the fore.

It happened like this: during the period when I had successfully completed every requirement for my doctorate except the dissertation and was looking forward to beginning it, I suddenly encountered a mental block. This was a period of depression, listlessness, and a sadness for which I could find no specific cause. I persisted in this mood for well over a year. Slowly, through my dreams, I began to find the source of my grief: the hurt child I once was. In the dream, just cited, I was told that I was responsible for the child's present state; indeed, I was beginning to see how this might be possible. Had I not ignored my own abused child, the child I had been?

The dream began in a carefree state at a dinner party where I was flirting vivaciously with a man I had little interest in except as an evening's diversion. I interpreted this as my return to academic life;

there was something unreal about it, just so many hurdles to be jumped and I had, by then, learned to be quite good at hurdles. But the dream was saying that real work, the recovery of my real creative potential, had to begin in the farm kitchen of my childhood. The dream took me to that kitchen. At first the mood was light; but I was soon given a rude awakening. There was real psychic healing to be done before I could return to the task begun.

Here, at last, I began the real and very slow process of facing my early childhood. Once again my nights were filled with nightmares. In one dream, I discovered, in a cave, a child who was starved, neglected, and dying; in others, I witnessed the repeated, brutal rape of a girl. Here began the real process of the integration of my shadow. Here, I had to begin to nurture the child I was, the child my own mother seemed unable to reach.

This particular period of nightmares was similar to those experienced earlier except that, this time, the unconscious seemed to be inviting me to experience not so much the terror of being attacked as pity for the one attacked. I was being forced to confront the situation of my abuse and to nurture a potent source of creativity which had been brutally wrenched from me. This meant unblocking, at long last, the tears I was never able to shed.

Here, in the grief of my inner child, was the source of the strange sadness that overcame me whenever I attempted to write my thesis. Now that I understood the cause, I simply let the grief happen; I kept a special journal in which I poured out my love for the little child, and comforted her. I kept a picture on my desk, the only picture I had of my infant self, a picture of a child holding flowers so tightly one might have thought she was afraid someone would take them away from her.

By some mysterious process, a number of external events coincided with my inner discoveries. Jung speaks of this phenomenon as synchronicity: the mysterious conjunction of events toward a single goal or purpose. I provided examples earlier, perhaps the most significant being that of my brother's actual injuries at a time when I was dreaming of violence against him.

This time, as the dreams were taking me to the farm kitchen of my childhood, my mother was being moved to confide in me about her unhappiness as a young bride, her unending work for her large family, her sense of always feeling poor. So, curiously, during this period that I was working on loving and grieving for the child I was, I was also offering sympathy to the mother who had been unable to nurture me. Soon, it was my father's turn. He underwent a serious illness which I helped see him through. By successfully offering my help and sympathy to both my parents, I managed to rid myself, partially at least, of my sense of frustration and inadequacy with respect to them. They were only human after all and not the gods I had thought them to be when I was a child. Nurturing those who had been unable to nurture me helped to strengthen my sense of feminine power.

The following dream reports the results. Here, the goal was one of partial healing of a troubled family. I could at last accept my parents' inadequacies by accepting responsibility for my inner child. I mused on the strange paradox of events: how the child I was not destined to bear was the means of giving life and love to the child I was. At last I was ready to meet another manifestation of my inner masculinity as the following dream revealed him:

I am with a female friend and we are on a walking tour somewhere in the north of England. We have been climbing up a steep path when suddenly, at the top, we see a pair of ornately carved gates set in an ancient-looking stone wall. The gates are open and we go in. Before us is a dazzling view of a lush green valley, dotted here and there with gorse. Far below, we see rivers and stone houses. Across from us, in the distance, stand the lofty peaks of a mountain range. The glorious blue sky, touched here and there with trailing wisps of cloud, completes this picture of wild serenity. I am totally immersed in solitude and peace. My friend, however, ever restless, has begun to explore an enormous slab of stone just behind us.

The slab is at least six feet long, three or four feet deep, and four or five feet high. It is a curious piece, a bit like an altar or a tomb. My friend is examining the upper edge of the stone with her fingers and soon finds a piece she can lift; underneath, there appear to be crumbling bones and disintegrating fragments of cloth.

I am horrified both by her temerity and her insatiable curiosity and am about to chastise her when, as if on cue, a woman appears carrying a basket covered with a white cloth. The woman is white-haired but her face is unlined and sweet. She walks toward us nodding a good day, and sets out the contents of her basket, afternoon tea, on the stone table. She then collects her basket and walks out through the gates closing them firmly behind her. "I believe the gates are to be left open," I call out after her, remembering how they were when we found them. She says nothing, just shakes her head.

Behind me, I hear a pleasing male voice. I turn and see a middle-aged man, rather burly, but good-looking in a homely, rustic way. He offers us a cup of tea and a teacake from his curious tea table. I draw the man into conversation since he has been so kind, and find out that he is the owner of the land on which we stand. I soon discover that he is a farmer of means. It is he who has called for tea to be set out every day at this time. I suddenly realize that he has been patiently waiting for me to come to this place; I also realize that he will ask me to marry him and I will accept. [January 14, 1987]

The dream indicated that, for a long time, the masculine figure had been waiting patiently to be discovered. While nature had been tamed (fertile fields), the setting included both wilderness (mountain peaks) and ancient settlement (stone altar or tomb). The old woman, who seemed somehow to embody a kind of ageless youth, supplied the homely but invigorating ritual of afternoon tea. I pondered on how different this simple daily sacrament of tea was from that of the Christian ritual with its reminder of broken body and shed blood; yet a similarity lay in the celebration of each on an altar-tomb. A frankly inquisitive, even snoopy, shadow sister touched the ancient bones that set the ritual in motion.

The aged, yet eternally young woman, the bearer of the "sacrament," was a peasant. I recalled that I had always been ashamed not so much of my parents' peasant origins as of their failure to celebrate their roots with pride and dignity; this, compounded by their unpredictable outbursts of rage, convinced me that peasants were nothing better than slaves, whether of other people, or of their own passions. Yet, the peasant woman in my dream had the sweet face of a goddess, at once ancient and radiantly new. And who was right behind her? The prosperous farmer, a free man. The dream showed me that my view of the peasant was too one-sided: for it is in my deep instinctual peasant roots that I may be most successful in seeking for the ancient feminine wisdom that provides a context for masculine energy and power. To accept myself as I am, to take pride in what I have previously disparaged or hidden in shame was to be my next task. My near dismissal of the landowner as burly, homely, and rustic was dangerously close to my misjudgment of an earlier dream figure as "only a swineherd." But this time, I had my extrovert female friend on hand to get things moving. At last, I was beginning to integrate the shadow side of myself that seeks out new challenges. In the dream, I recognized the masculine principle as someone I would "marry" in order to establish a lasting foundation for my creativity.

The earlier dream, in which I had dismissed the masculine figure as "only a swineherd," began with a chip in a teapot, indicating that my feminine container needed mending. During the period in which I found myself nurturing my mother, I dreamt that my mother broke a very delicate china teapot, quite beautiful but rather impractical. At the time, I felt that the dream referred to the way in which I had been hurt as a child by my mother's neglect. But then I began to realize that I no longer felt so intensely the feelings of rage I had once had toward my mother. Nor did I any longer feel I had to meet my parents' impossible expectations of me. The teapot of the dream was part of a fantasy world I had now to leave behind. Such decorative porcelain would never stand up to everyday use, the hot water of life.

As I began to express my feelings, I came to understand the extent of my passionate nature. In the past, my emotions had been turned against myself; pent-up rage had led to a sense of futility and worthlessness. Now I began to realize that if I intended accomplishing authentic and creative work, I would have to develop toughness. In other words, before I could free my masculine, I had to find a stronger feminine container. It meant changing certain attitudes: consciously appropriating positive attitudes about my abilities as well as challenging past fantasies in a tough-minded approach. Above all, it meant continuing to trust in the need and desire of the psyche to be healed and in the power of the unconscious to heal it. The following dream indicates the work that still remained to be done and how I was being guided to proceed.

I am with a female friend and we are tourists in a European country. The people we are visiting are extremely primitive, even barbaric, so much so that we are provided with a male guide to discover their dwellings. Their houses are deep below earth level, deep, deep underground. The houses themselves are small, no more than two or three rooms barely furnished, with dirt floors. All of this indicates life reduced to subsistence level, life very low on the scale of evolution.

A young girl of about fifteen years of age lives there with her parents, real or adoptive. It is very clear that she is different from her parents, for while they are old, misshapen and rough in speech and movement like the earth from which they were formed, she is finer of feature and of form. Her skin is smooth and the color of cream; her hair is black and would probably curl if she were to let it. In fact she wears it short and spiked like the most contemporary North American street kid.

We have been talking to her—she replying in an uncouth snarl, for though she is fairly made she is not sweetly spoken—when my friend beckons me out of the room. She is certain that violence has been done in this house; perhaps the girl has murdered her parents. We decide to make our hasty departure, abandoning her to her less than promising fate because we suspect she may have a vicious, unredeemable nature. I had just been showing the girl a red lipstick when I was called from her little cubicle of a room, and I decide to leave it with her along with a little pot of face cream rather than arouse her suspicions by reclaiming them. As it turns out, these items will provide the clue she needs to track down our whereabouts.

We manage to find our way back to the surface, unguided, and journey to London, England. We have just left the Underground at Victoria Station when I realize that we are being followed. In fact, my friend has given us away by loudly reading out the address of our pied-à-terre. Although we manage to escape by cab to our destination, we know that it will be just a matter of time before we are found.

The address proves to be a tall, thin building and we are to share the top floor with another woman. The room is large and has windows on all sides. My friend calls over to me to look at the view and I am almost terrified by the sight of a great cathedral just outside our window. The little house is, as it were, nestled in its outstretched wings. However, far from feeling comforted, I am absolutely terrified, so awesome and imposing is the structure. While we are close enough to make out the pattern of its dark, gray stone, we are dwarfed by its spires and Gothic arches, its splendid intricate tracery. Certainly we are close enough to feel a kind of numinous emanation. Yet there is neither protection here, nor judgment, only a tremendous urgency to action in its unspoken message; and I am frightened by its potential anger if I do not obey.

Our landlady comes up ushering in an official looking man. After making enquiries, he leaves. Soon afterward, another male comes in, quite different from the first. This one is either drunk or very ill, for he staggers and almost immediately falls down. We get him to bed as the sun sinks behind the cathedral, suddenly blotting out the light with a black finality. We, the four of us, must now strive to heal one another in sleep. [July 28, 1987]

I and my shadow sister (a frequent companion in my dreams of this period) encountered an adolescent girl in the deepest layers of the unconscious. The girl was presented as having the potential for great beauty; yet, there was also in her a primitive savagery. Her age reminded me that I was approximately fifteen years old before my brother left home and the abuse finally stopped. The girl in the dream was full of murderous rage; the shadow sister, privy to these deep, hidden emotions, indicated as much.

I spoke earlier about my sense of guilt that prevented me from taking a firm stand against my birth family; my fear, particularly with respect to my parents, was that I would kill them. But it was not simply killer rage, locked away inside me all these years, that was at issue. The dream stated, as an allegation, that I (in that aspect of myself that appeared as the girl) had actually killed my parents. But the emphasis in the dream was not on the girl's rage, righteous or otherwise. In fact, the girl was virtually dismissed as the dregs of society. What was being communicated to me, if not the girl's rage, was the adult women's rather prim reaction of horror at her alleged actions. Releasing the feeling-tone of the dream helped me to understand its message.

To a child, parents walk as gods. And yet always, before a child can make the necessary transformation to maturity, she must cut herself off from the values and opinions of her parents, reformulating them for herself in order to live her life as an individual. To do otherwise would mean behaving like a marionette with some parental figure constantly tugging at her strings and speaking from her mouth.

The truth is that I had been afraid, all these years, of cutting my marionette strings and severing myself from my parents because they represented a link, no matter how tenuous or how brutal, for the little child I had been who feared she might otherwise be wholly abandoned. Because my siblings were so much older, I felt as though I had, not one mother and father, but many. Each one represented a formidable obstacle to my growing independence. No sooner had I cut off the head of one of these hydra monsters, but another appeared. And because my sense of identity had been profoundly battered by my brother, the task of constant battle for survival simply wore me out before I had even developed the necessary musculature to attempt real independence.

The problem was this: the child in me who had never felt secure attachment to these primal forces was now expected to make the leap to adult maturity and, wielding the sword of discretion, cut away what was inappropriate in the parent-child bond while maintaining a healthy family connection. But there was a good deal of confusion in me as to what constituted "healthy." In addition, it was as though the child, traumatized at an early stage of development, not only existed side by side with the adult, but also had a hand in the adult's decisions. Where the adult needed freedom to grow, the child I was unconscious of was screaming out for parental bonding and attachment. But the adult I had become, having lost all conscious connection with this young, demanding figure, was carrying an enormous load of guilt each time I made a burst for freedom.

The difficulty for me now was to separate my inner child from the destructive aspects of her birth family while connecting her with the vital family life I was consciously now creating for myself. The danger to consciousness would be in cutting us both off, child and adult, from the potential creativity of our deeply rooted heritage as described in the underground journey of the dream.

I recognized in the girl my own feminine potential, with its roots in a traditional Old World patriarchal culture and its visible growth in an up-to-date New World atmosphere of critical rebellion. Growing up meant thinking differently from my parents and siblings. Without being consciously aware of it, I had always felt incredible guilt in establishing my uniqueness. The dream was telling me that I had killed my parents. The adult women, my shadow and myself, were shocked and ran away. But we left something behind, some articles that belonged to the civilized, feminine world. The adolescent "murderer" had been left a trail and she successfully tracked down those who could help her make the passage into a new reality.

The dream also told me that I needed to reassess how much of myself was still imbued with this violently angry as well as rebelliously beautiful young woman. Despite my conciliatory air, bitter anger had been seething within me; it needed to be "expressed," literally to be pressed out. In my waking life, I was always terrified of hurting other people; so, rather than stand up for myself, I would give way, burying anger and resentment deep in my unconscious. Why did I always opt for a conciliatory approach? Perhaps, unconsciously, I recognized how deep my anger was; it was powerful enough to kill.

Then too, there was a terrible fear of being abandoned: to oppose others might mean killing not only others, but myself as well. Had I not thought that my dream about killing my brother could have an actual effect on his well-being in the real world? Had I not been clinging still, in an infantile way, to the very parents who had been too self-absorbed to help me? Had I not convinced myself that opposing them meant killing them?

The young woman in the dream was beautiful but savage. Before I could mollify, tame, and civilize an actively hostile feminine aspect of myself, I had to mourn the anguish and rage of my hurt child, and continue shedding the tears the child could not. The ultimate goal was wholeness, with every split-off aspect moving toward harmony and reconciliation, toward creativity. The dream was saying that, by providing my despised, hurt feminine with some encouragement (red lipstick, the color of passionate love), I might yet bring her successfully to consciousness.

In fact, the dream showed that the process was under way. The setting had moved from deep down in the unconscious and progressed upward, exploring the various levels toward consciousness (symbolized by the London Underground on upward to the tall, almost vertical brownstone house). The young woman, having followed the clues I had unwittingly left her, had perhaps arrived at our destination before us; it was she who was the unknown third occupant of our pied-à-terre. (Note that the French word, while it conveys the sense of "a lodging within walking distance" reads literally "foot on the ground"; again, I was reminded of the need for groundedness, even earthiness, in my pursuit of my feminine nature; the young girl was discovered literally under the earth and was obviously an important element in this search for grounding.) Thus, the third woman might be the feminine aspect derivable from the girl abandoned in the first part of the dream, and an important factor in the healing of the wounded masculine. If this was so, then she and the others had arrived in the nick of time: for the life of the masculine figure was clearly at risk.

At journey's end, the characters in the dream drama came together in a different sort of room, one which offered a totally different perspective on the Self. The room was dominated by the cathedral, which, both terrifying and compelling, conveyed a numinosity that suggested that a new dimension was coming to the foreground: the spiritual. Jung refers to what has been traditionally described by religions as "the god within" as the Self or Objective Psyche. Christians speak of this manifestation as the awesome presence of the Holy Spirit but the concept is found among many religions because it accords with the human experience of the numinously powerful breath of life. I recognized the image of the cathedral as the potential for enormous feminine energy which could be released in me if I were willing to take the time necessary to heal my wounded nature.

The cathedral seemed to cry out in mute but powerful appeal for help. It seemed to be neither protective nor judgmental. In other words, the Self was not dictating orders or criticizing past behavior. Nor was it saying, "Whatever you do, I'll look after you." Its compelling numinosity was urging help, action, and the taking of responsibility. The dreamer's temptation was to turn away from its demands but it was clear that the work going on within view of its stones was a healing process.

Ever present in past dreams had been this thread: I have lived in fear of either killing or being killed. Now a new thread appeared: trust and accept the burden of being trusted. The new thread said, "Trust in love."

From the dream, my mandate was clear: I needed to clear up the outer situation of conflict so that my energy would be effectively employed in carrying out the inner task. The final sentence of the dream indicated that the healing powers of the unconscious were to be entrusted with the curative task. But all the elements were in place: the totality of the Self was indicated by both the cathedral and the four people. (In Jungian psychology, four is the number of totality, of wholeness.) The task promised to move very slowly because there was much healing to be done.

During this period, I found it impossible to write my dissertation. But just after a year went by, I had the following dream which foreshadowed the removal of my creative "block."

I open my mouth, certain that I shall regurgitate something, when the head of a snake comes out of my mouth. I tamp the head gently back into my mouth, swallow, look around somewhat sheepishly, and say: "I guess I'm having a little trouble digesting this." [April 24, 1988]

The dream suggested that creative life-energy (the snake) was stirring within me, the dreamer, and was beginning to open the throat chakra. I had simply to allow the process to happen. By strengthening my feminine container and by acknowledging my own inner masculine, I was slowly beginning to find my own voice. In fact, I began to make substantial progress on my doctoral thesis at this point. The following dream suggested that I had discovered the strong feminine container I needed, one that was less delicate than the china of an earlier dream.

> I suddenly tell my husband that I am going to buy a new teapot at the potter's for $47.00. This teapot is of a specially fired pottery which is guaranteed to be heat-resistant. [January 10, 1989]

The new container was costing me every year of my life. (I was forty-seven years old at the time of the dream.) It promised to be much sturdier, if somewhat less ornately decorative, than the earlier one. A subsequent dream gave me a sense of the ongoing power of the healing process. This dream indicated that I was about to be involved in a sacred mystery whose ritual I feared but knew it was my destiny to undergo.

> I enter what I assume to be a shopping boutique. My husband waits outside. There are several women standing about whom I assume to be customers and sales clerks. I realize that this is far from the case when I notice an object on a cushion on the floor. At first I assume it to be an ornate belt or a bulky necklace. However, when I see it move, I realize that it is a large snake, black with beautiful silver white markings as iridescent as white amethysts. Then I realize, with a growing horror, why I am here. Still, I cannot accept my fate as inevitable, and when I notice that a priest has entered the room, I run to him, throwing myself in his arms and upon his mercy, sobbing and begging for his protection. But soon I calm down and let him leave as I submit to the inevitable. The women draw me to them and reassure me that all I must do is sing and allow the flickering tongue of the serpent to touch my lips. I am inwardly terrified but outwardly calm and accepting. I know I must let this happen. [January 23, 1989]

I was reminded of the words of the Psalm found in *The Book of Common Prayer*: "O Lord, open thou my lips And my mouth shall shew forth thy praise" and of lips being touched with coals of fire. Thus I associated the serpent tongue with the outpouring of the gifts of the

Holy Spirit. But I was no longer able to connect such outpourings with the institutional church. For in the dream, although I rushed toward a priest from my church, I realized that there was no help to be found there. The old patriarchal structures I used to rely on, which helped me perpetuate my fantasy world for so long a time, were to be abandoned at last. I attempted to put my trust in the new feminine way. I attempted to ground my new reality in my own being, which unified head and body, intellect and intuition, thinking and feeling. I recognized my task as both inevitable and terrifying.

In the dream, Michael's part in the ritual was to stand outside and wait because my feminine soul was about to undergo an initiatory stage of the inner marriage: the meeting of the feminine soul with the masculine spirit. The dream indicated that the dream ego could not expect to be protected from life by her outer masculine; she had to endure the process alone. The snake was a reminder both of the snake whose head emerged from my mouth in the previous dream and the reptilian beast in Psyche's story that her envious sisters warned her against. The "beast" turned out to be Psyche's husband, Eros; but Psyche had to endure various trials and develop great courage to free the masculine from the ruses of his mother, Aphrodite. My snake too had numinosity; it represented the terror I felt in surrendering to love, whether that love was physical, spiritual, or creative. These are all manifestations of the terrible and wonderful love that the Self represents.

The paradox lies in this: my Psyche/psyche was terrified of the serpent to whom she had to surrender herself; yet the serpent represented the love she needed in order truly to *be*. Perhaps this is the hardest step for those of us abused in childhood to take: the terrifying step of surrender to trust and love. We know it has the power to kill; the paradox, so difficult for us to grasp, is that it has the power to heal. Was I ready to accept this love as the basis of creativity?

A substantial period of time went by during which I was engaged in various activities, among them teaching, writing, and counseling. I had finally begun to experience the real fulfillment of the fully-lived life. The process of healing was continuing, even though I was being less scrupulous about writing down my dreams. Finally at the end of the university term, as I began to focus on the needs of my body, I had a dream that indicated to me that I was finally putting the past behind me. At last the masculine figure who had been such a threat to me in my early dreams in analysis was becoming my friend. At last the negative destructive energy he had represented was being transformed into the positive energy of creative endeavor. Here is part of that dream:

> I have just left a beautiful private house where I have been enjoying the weekend with a large number of other guests. As I must reach my destination before nightfall, I proceed at a brisk pace along a quiet country road. A young man overtakes me and proceeds to match my strides, step for step. At first I am afraid of him; while he seems bent on accompanying me, he is not particularly pleasant company. In fact, he is something of a mouthy nuisance, judging from his speech which is flippant and given to sexual innuendo; I fear he may be dangerous. But when I tell him that it is urgent that I get to a particular island in Georgian Bay before nightfall, he becomes quite serious and helpful. He offers to take me wherever I need to go; his motorboat is at my disposal. In fact, his mother is waiting at a dock nearby to pick him up; he assures me she will be happy to drop me off at my island.
>
> We soon arrive at the dock and, sure enough, there in a boat waits a pleasant woman of mature years who seems pleased to be of help to me. I suddenly realize that I am a much younger woman and that his mother is considering me as a potential wife for her son. This embarrasses me because he is so much younger than I; or is he? The years dividing us seem to be disappearing, immaterial.
>
> I now become preoccupied with getting in touch with loved ones to let them know I have arrived safely but I cannot remember their phone number. It soon dawns on me that they are not worried about me; in fact, they are aware of my well-being. I know now that I will arrive at my island; I know that I will see a great deal of this man on whose behalf his mother is so anxious a matchmaker. I suddenly relax and begin to enjoy the beauty and excitement of the moment.

This dream had echoes of many others I have described in these pages. The man of an earlier dream in which an ancient woman set out the tea things every day finds his younger counterpart here. There seems to be evidence that the marriage between the feminine and the masculine, hinted at in the earlier dream, was to be forthcoming at last.

I was at first afraid of the man; in fact, he was an image of the destructive masculine (the men I killed in earlier dreams) transformed into positive creative energy. The nurturing mother has returned as feminine wisdom who knows what the happy outcome will be. I was initially cautious every step of the way: first I mistrusted the motives of the man; later, I concerned myself over the disparity in our ages; and finally, in attempting to reassure my loved ones, I appeared to be questioning my right to take this young man as a lover.

But this dream was far from suggesting extramarital union with a younger man. Because I had been closely in touch with the evolution of this masculine figure, I recognized him as belonging to my inner life. It might have been fatal to my creative life to project him outwards now that I seemed so close to achieving some kind of union with my inner masculinity. But the "I" in the dream also drew attention to herself: suddenly she was young, much younger than the dream-ego of the beginning. The business in the dream about forgotten phone numbers, followed by my feeling of assurance that my "loved ones" knew that I was safe and doing the right thing was likely meant to reassure my conscious mind that both these young people belonged to my inner life; he had taken on the youthful figure of my masculine spirit; she, the youthful aspect of my feminine soul. The end of the dream found them sailing toward her island, a place of quiet contemplation, a place where creative life could flourish.

Just at the point where I thought that many of the conflicts that I embodied were resolving themselves, I had the following important dream, which I shall now try to unravel. The dream asked me to differentiate between the power that emanated as complexes from my personal parents and that generated by the archetypal masculine and feminine; only then could my waking ego hope to complete the quest for wholeness as symbolized by the divine marriage between archetypal spirit/soul energies and to recognize whom it is the ego is to serve.

I am at a university class reunion chatting with a woman in a silver dress when it occurs to me that I have much more in common with her now than I did when we were both students. The setting is the college gardens which are surrounded by ivy-covered stone walls. My friend's young son interrupts our pleasant reacquaintance by urgently pulling at her sleeve; he is clearly anxious to be off and doing. My friend finally acquiesces to his demands and, without apology, abruptly takes her leave.

At her departure, a few old friends join me; everyone else appears to have gone. We who remain are four in all, two men and two women.

I notice that the garden wall behind us has been transformed into a large, wooden gate of the type providing access to a farmer's field. My friends begin clambering over this gate, much to my consternation. I beg them to consider what they are doing; after all, they are entering private property. But they laugh at me in so carefree a manner that I am soon hoisting myself over the gate behind them.

What I thought was the gate to a field is in actual fact the entrance to an old and very plain wood-frame farmhouse. I am standing in the kitchen; the walls are unplastered, the floors nothing but roughly planed but well-scrubbed planks. It seems, from the lack of furniture, that no one lives here or has lived here for a very long time. My university friends seem to have disappeared; but, I am aware that my husband and daughter are somewhere in the house with me, indistinct and shadowy. I sense that my mother, too, is nearby, but she is also a vague presence.

Then, with a focused clarity, I see my father; he is utterly transformed. Far from being the man well past his eighties, he appears as youthful, handsome, and charming as the photographs portrayed him when I was a child of four or five. And I am amazed to find myself filled with emotions I have not felt since I was that child of four or five: I am surprised by reverence, respect, trust, and love.

My father acknowledges my presence with a warm, welcoming smile but does not stop what he is doing; he is setting a burglar alarm at every door and window as though he is closing up the house for some reason. Are he and my mother preparing for some extended journey? I notice a bowl of rather stale, inedible greens and, aware how my mother hates to part with anything, I toss them out the back door before she can argue for keeping them. Immediately, the alarm goes off. I grit my teeth, expecting my father to fly into a temper because, unthinkingly, I activated the alarm he set. To my surprise, he simply gives me a rather boyish smile as if to say: "See? It works!"

At this point, there is a knock at the very door whose alarm I activated. I open it and find a girl there; she is somewhere between twelve and fifteen years of age. I invite her in. Since I soon hear her chatting to my daughter and mother, I assume they were expecting her. The dream ends here, capturing this perfect moment of return and reconciliation. I sense in myself a mood of trust and love that I have not felt in a very long time.

The class reunion, with which the dream began, established its entire theme. It was likely that my current occupation of academic writing, something I was very much enjoying, was represented in the persons of my university friends. It was clear from my new appreciation of the woman in silver (which I associate with the moon, symbolic of the archetypal feminine) that I was discovering delights where I least expected to, in areas that I once found rather uninspiring. The young masculine was not interested in such musings, however. He wanted to get moving. And movement was precisely what was in store for me.

We four (a balance of masculine and feminine energies) ventured into a new area, the farmer's field. I, as the dream-ego, felt anxious about encroaching on someone else's property. In fact, in my current writing I was feeling somewhat reticent about appropriating for myself feminist criticism, a "field" of study for which I had not been specifically trained except as life had taught me. The dream presented my self-limiting tendency as an infantile return to childhood.

Thus returned to the farmhouse of my childhood, I met my father who, in checking his security system to make sure that what he had worked so hard to acquire remained intact, was defining the limits of what he owned. By following my university friends, I showed my refusal to acknowledge such boundaries. No sooner had I dared to cross the fence, than I was immediately taken back to the place and time (my childhood home) where I was first taught about limits.

But what I found there now was something very different from what I once experienced: it was empty of all furniture; even the walls and floor had been peeled back to their substructure; all of which suggested to me that much of the negative emotional content had been cleared out. The dream affirmed that the time had come for me to enter creative territory I had previously declared out of bounds for myself. Through the image of the transformed father, I could see how far I had unconsciously defined myself through the introjected patriarchal boundaries derived from my father's era. I suddenly saw the difference between recognizing one's limitations with eyes wide open and having them thrust upon one from within, from behind one's back, as it were.

This interpretation is underlined by my father's transformation to the man I had loved as a child. But where once he would have raged, here he was accepting and forgiving. The dream restored to me some of the trust I felt as a child, without mawkish sentimentality; this man was more than my father. He represented the power of the archetypal energy I had projected upon this man when I was a child. Thus his transformation went beyond the remembered father and into the realm of the archetypal Father; indeed, this transpersonal figure conveyed a numinosity that connected him to spiritual energy.

So the dream was a kind of map of my own forward movement. I was not being asked simply to overcome the limitations of my conditioning; my recent psychic gains had already transcended them. The dream was about a return to trust and love: my inner father stood at the window fixing the alarm to protect my psychic house against intruders. But the alarms were not meant to lock me in; when I opened the door he had just secured, he did not question my action in any way. The alarms were meant to protect me; they offered assurance that my ego was developing the strength to mediate between the unconscious and consciousness. The alarms were not meant to make my psychic house a prison because energy could move freely across the boundaries; the dream showed there was no obstacle to the young feminine's entry.

The image of the archetypal father freed me from the negative influence of my actual father. Like the miraculous transformation of the young man of the previous dream from dangerous, hostile male to helper and soul mate, the transformed father pointed toward the integration of the various aspects of my inner masculinity out of whose unity emanated a great healing energy.

It was true that I recognized the man in the dream to be more than my father in his openness to new ideas—not just those initiated by him, but even my ideas. But as I felt the healing power of self-acceptance, I was, for the first time, able to focus objectively on my father. I was still willing to admit that he had been an indecisive person, given to bouts of rage when confronted by situations unfamiliar to him. But now I was remembering another side to the man. He was also a dreamer, a gifted singer and storyteller; he was a man given to abstract thinking, even something of a visionary. For example, it was he who had the foresight to get his family out of Europe before his country was ravaged by war; moreover, it was he who turned a simple carpenter's craft into a lucrative business venture that turned family poverty to prosperity. But the aspect of my father that I had all too successfully introjected and was finally transcending was this: he was a true patriarch, a man given to setting down limits for others. A dreamer, yes; but he expected everyone to follow *his* dream. It simply did not occur to him that others might have dreams of their own. In trying to live my own dream, I was at last freeing myself from his deep influence on my soul; I was at last relating positively to my father complex.

But, if I was able to see my father more clearly after analyzing this dream, I was rewarded with a new and infinitely more touching understanding of my mother. The link between my feminine shadow and my personal mother was clarified as I meditated on this dream; and although the relationship is somewhat complex, I must attempt to unravel it because it is crucial to the final stages of self-discovery I relate here. For the dream traced how the mother complex was brought to consciousness, transformed into positive energy, and integrated into my personality, strengthening my feminine container.

When I first began my discourse, I described two aspects of the mother archetype, one which was benign, the other terrifying. Both aspects were reflected in this dream. The benign aspect was presented as "the moon woman" dressed in silver. The waxing and waning of the moon is the key to the moon's symbolic value: transformation. The dream was redolent of change, the most compelling example for me being, initially at least, the change in my father: his transformation made an immediate emotional impact upon me, as if it were charting the course of my long journey home to self-acceptance. It took me much longer to tease out the implications of the shadowy mother in the dream and to feel her emotional impact. The act of recognizing, in the dream, the depotentiated power of the negative mother was in itself an act of liberation from the mother complex of which I had been a prisoner.

In the dream, the act of throwing out the greens seemed a sensible, necessary, and harmless act. Necessary it was; but it once would have been anything but harmless. For if the father in this dream was now strangely benign, the mother was even more so. Where once the dream-ego would have shrunk from an action that might have constellated the negative mother complex, here the deed was done without a qualm. But, while I, as the dream's "actor," was convinced of the necessity of the act—disobedience to the mother (rejection of her values)—I did it behind my mother's back because I assumed she would oppose me. However, since the entrance of the new feminine appeared conditional upon the tossing out of the old attitudes, and since the dream stated that mother and granddaughter were expecting the young feminine who entered, it follows that the shadowy mother was perfectly aware of what was going on; indeed, what happened, happened under her auspices.

It seemed, then, that the shadowy mother in the dream was the negative mother transformed; she was also greater than my personal mother, indicating that she was an archetypal image. And once again, as my waking ego differentiated between the personal mother (the source of my mother complex) and the archetypal feminine, I was able to see my personal mother more clearly. I could now see that the origin of my terror of her power lay in her refusal to let go of me. Had she known how to forge her bonds with love, she would have elicited my willing compliance without compulsion.

But my mother had always found it difficult to part with her possessions; no matter how worn out and useless an article was, she had to keep it. She always held onto everything. Her house was full of things that ought to have been thrown out or given away long ago. Her house had been full of the children she could never let go. But in the dream, I no longer feared her. And I realized that, in the image of rotting greens, I was letting go of her obsessive hold on me. And insofar as my actual mother was introjected in my personality as my mother complex, I was helping her give me up. I was also clearing the way for my own daughter to give me up. In giving up my hold over her, I paved the way for a freer relationship between us, that is, between the current and the next generation. What was presented as a tossing out of something of no value, an action that my waking consciousness could have easily overlooked in this dream, was immensely significant. It represented a surrender of my feminine values to the unknown; it represented the sacrifice of those defenses I had held onto until then, because, for better or for worse, they were a kind of security. But the dream presented these as rotting vegetable matter. To hold onto them now would have meant introducing rot into my personality, my psychic house. Put more positively, the action of sacrificing the vestiges of dubious feminine wisdom, old wives' tales that cannot nourish my soul, and by challenging masculine authority that limits growth, I threw myself on the mercy of the unknown and opened the door to new feminine values which, to my surprise, were accepted by the father and welcomed by mother and daughter alike. What had to be sacrificed was the infantile subservience to outmoded attitudes as a bargaining point for survival. True salvation (and not merely survival) means sacrificing the old, whether it be old attitudes, old value systems, or long-standing complexes.

Again, as with the coalescence of the fragmented masculine, the healing integration of the feminine aspects of my personality caused me to redefine my personal mother; I was now able to see the deep paradox in her nature. Extraordinarily generous in many ways, she was capable of lavishing great attention and feeling upon people, a contradiction to her tight-fistedness. Rigid and limited in her views, nevertheless she could be, and often was, iconoclastic in the extreme. Particularly, in the area of work, she crossed barriers. She preferred to work with men. I suppose one could even say that she did not believe in "mens' work" as a category; to her, there was only work. She much preferred to be testing her muscle under the hot sun than working in the kitchen; but, if saddled with kitchen chores, she made short shrift of them in order to join the men outdoors with all possible speed.

My mother was thus, in some ways, quite opposite to my limit-setting father; if she wanted to hold on to the status quo, it was probably because she held on to life, embodied life lived on the run, in full vigor, without discretion, modesty, or limits. This view of my mother suggested the origin of the snooping, indiscreet, and adventuresome friend in so many of my dreams. I am very indebted to this aspect of my personal mother: for only with the arrival of the shadow friend in my dreams, did the process of integration really gain momentum; it was she who initially poked and pried into all kinds of forbidden areas, much to my consternation as dream-ego. She became the mechanism by which my ego was able to develop a more independent stand; through her efforts, masculine and feminine elements jostled one another into growth and power.

The action of throwing out the greens, impulsive and daring, shows that my ego had integrated this shadow friend at last; she and I were now one. Further evidence of my ego transformation was found in my father's nonjudgmental reaction to my tossing out the greens, which threw his security system into disarray. I expected him to explode with anger but he subverted my expectations. This masculine figure did not set limits; he responded to changing circumstances, accepting them as evidence of growth.

Getting rid of old attitudes was the means by which I unblocked the energy of my creative feminine who was literally on the threshold of her rebirth. What sacrifice meant to me was this: no more crippled clinging to values that had contributed to an ongoing self-abuse long after the abusing figures had outgrown their bogeyman status in the nursery; it meant no more hiding behind my sense of worthlessness and shame. And while I may never completely get over the degree to which I was maimed as a child, nevertheless, I think the dream was saying it was time to put these festering memories out into the garbage where they could do no more damage to my psychic house.

And because this point is so important, I must emphasize it: the significance of the father restored to youth did not imply that I had somehow miraculously returned to youthful fantasies. Far from it! Certainly, my actual father was far from returning to the man he had once seemed; he was, in point of fact, getting more and more cantankerous, judgmental, and difficult. But the dream was not speaking about my relationship to my actual father but rather was symbolic of my inner masculine spirit which has the potential of impregnating my developing feminine soul to give birth to an authentic creativity, perhaps insignificant in the world's terms, but meaningful to me. At last, by separating the parent figures from the archetypal energy emanating from the deepest layers of the collective unconscious, I could work on developing a sound basis for the divine marriage between masculine and feminine; and I trusted that such a union would provide the foundation for experiencing both creativity and a sense of self-worth.

The dream illustrated the underlying truth of my nature: I, a "father's daughter," had come full circle to the home of my childhood. As a child, I had projected my soul's archetypal image of masculinity onto my father. As a token of love, the archetypal feminine had now transformed the image which had been broken into pieces, as all such projected images must be shattered when old ideals and new realities clash. This new image of my dream father, who was so much my father and yet so different, appeared to be the foundation of my inner masculine and an important archetypal source of the young man in the previous dream. Such imagery of wholeness, brought about by feminine energy derived from the mother complex, returned me to the love of the archetypal mother and connected me to my deepest feminine self.

For my real mother was in this dream; though but a shadowy presence, she was expectantly waiting for the child on the threshold of womanhood to come through the door. She, my daughter, and the newly arrived young feminine formed an instant alliance that touched me deeply. For while my entire attention seemed focused on the transformed father at the end of the dream, the mood of return and reconciliation encompassed my whole being. In fact, when I engaged these persons in dialogue through active imagination, I discovered that an essential aspect of my well-being at the end of the dream was my sense of trust in my own body, my feminine container.

Although the mother was not sharply defined, her presence was the thread that connected the woman in silver at the dream's beginning to the young girl who entered the back door when I tossed out the greens. Initially, the mother was a shadowy figure because she was not yet fully integrated in my consciousness; as an archetypal image, she was still fragmented, still contaminated by my negative emotions surrounding my real mother. Whereas I had let my father go, a part of me still clung to my real mother. But once the old attitudes had been sacrificed (the decaying greens), the young feminine arrived and was ready to bond with my mother and my daughter.

Thus, the dream pointed to what may well have been the most important transformation of all: the restoration of my feminine being to wholeness. In the dream, my mother was the foundation of my feminine self, the pivot upon which the final act of transformation turned. What she specifically represented was my own feminine nature which included my woman's body. The dream thus represented a kind of breakthrough for me, a kind of miracle of a return home. But what, I asked myself, is home? Is it simply an acceptance of my actual mother? Just as my father in the dream was only a partial reference to my actual father, so it was with my mother. Returning home was not simply a kind of giant "love-in," where I was suddenly capable, in a flash of illumination, of understanding everyone, forgiving everyone, and entering some kind of blissful oceanic state of being like a child in a loving womb. In any case, even to the dream's end, the mother was shadowy. It was as though my acceptance of her was still very tentative, requiring the mediation of selflessly nurturing, silver ladies and innocent, adolescent girls.

The full significance of "where is home" came only after I had the following dream; what it underlines is the importance of my body in relationship to my creative feminine. In the dream, I loved my own body as the container of my feminine creative power. My desire for and acceptance of the woman's sexual relationship with me was an indication of this desire to connect with my own body. It also reflected my current and growing need to form close relationships with other women. Where once I was something of a "man's lady," I now sensed an interest in making contact "woman to woman."

I am a young woman in my twenties. It is the sixties and I am walking in front of a coffeehouse, common in those years, devoted to artists and bohemians of all types. In front of the building, spread out on the small patch of grass, are the artists' wares. A woman, also in her twenties, stands there. As soon as I see her, I fall in love with her. I cannot describe her other than to call her my soul's friend.

She takes me to her garden, where I ask her to make love to me. She begins in what I would call a uniquely feminine way. Instead of simply beginning, as a man would, with caresses, she prepares the two of us as for a ritual. Bringing out a basket that contains her soaps and unguents, she begins by washing my body, slowly and sensuously. I realize immediately that this is, for me, a proper beginning, for I am always conscious, in lovemaking, of the need first to remove the sweat of everyday activity. I find myself relaxing, ready to yield my sex to her sensitive tongue. I feel a profound love for and trust in her and in my own body.

This was a profoundly important dream for me. It spoke of the restoration of my virgin self; of my body, in innocence, returned to me. I was portrayed as a woman on the threshold of maturity, yielding to the embrace of my own creative feminine. Perhaps my lover was the girl of the previous dream now grown into maturity. At last, I was returned to my own true home: my body, the prime container of my feminine creativity. I became connected to my authentic being; I had the sense of being right at the center of "who I am," without persona, my ego surrendering to the Self.

This dream also went a long way to helping me understand the deep wounding in my relationship to my own mother. It pushed forward the message of the previous dream: returning home meant returning to my own body; it means "owning" my body. It came as a revelation to me that my creativity could be bound up with acceptance of my body. As I reflected on the lovemaking of the two women, I began to recognize how much I needed to get in closer touch with the shadowy mother in the previous dream. When I entered into dialogue with her, I found myself expressing some very negative feelings about her body and about my own body.

When I was a child, I hated my mother's body; it represented all that was ugly. I remember watching a calf being born and being told that I, too, had been born from my mother's body. I can still feel my sense of outrage; I instantly rejected the notion as repellent. I hated touching my mother or being touched by her.

Did I experience these feelings before being abused? I simply cannot remember. Perhaps I had internalized hatred for the human body even before I was abused. I certainly remember resisting physical contact with my mother very early in my infancy. On the rare occasion when she tried to cuddle me, I withdrew into myself, enduring her caresses through gritted teeth, my body tensed against her intrusion.

Releasing some of these feelings about my body helped me to understand why I had gained, and lost, in a seesaw pattern, so much weight during recent years, when sessions with Marion were few and far between. In meditating on my wounded feminine, I had constellated the negative mother complex; I had begun to *embody* the conflict and my body became filled with the rage I had repressed for so many years. Doing the "headwork" required by academe exacerbated the situation. I became a giant craving in search of a food fix at times like these. But the void I was trying to fill and the hunger I was trying to satisfy was emotional; the food I ate weighted me down without nurturing the feminine part of me that had been raped. Only now can I begin to feel how tense my body has been, how heavy it has felt. I had even stopped dancing not because, as I told myself, I had no time for such nonsense; I had stopped dancing because my soul had stopped wanting to soar. Only now could I recognize that I was literally weighed down with despair. And it was during these periods that communication with Marion for my positive feminine affirmation alleviated the suffering. Her words—"reconnect with your body"— reminded me, each time, how far I had become "stuck" in my head. When I got tense, the energy was blocked; when the tension was released, the energy flowed once more.

Now I am working at freeing my soul whose home is the body I have so long despised. The marriage of my feminine soul to my masculine spirit will take place when both have been released from their prisons—the former from her emotional pain; the latter from the confines of his preconceptions. Once freed, they will be unlikely to take their cue from the dead past with its gravely intoned NO but rather from the vital, spiritual energy of the divine YES.

Now, at last, I truly feel the importance of reclaiming my feminine container. To create, I need energy. I need my body's strength. Before, the more my dreams seemed to urge me to *know* my body, the less I experienced her. My sense of my own body had begun to slip further and further away; and the further away she slipped from my consciousness, the emptier I had felt, the less able I was to nourish her with spiritual food.

Now I am reaching out to her with all my love and sorrow and pity. Now, she weeps. In the quiet of my room, surprised and frightened by

Randolf Stanley Hewton, 1888–1960. Benedicta, c. 1935. Oil on canvas, 183 × 121 cm. McMichael Canadian Art Collection. Gift of Mr. and Mrs. H. J. Campbell, 1969.25.6.

My interpretation of this painting is very personal. The woman is dancing on the sand beside a body of water, perhaps a northern lake. She perfectly symbolizes my reborn feminine soul, once raped, but now restored to me. She exudes a kind of wise innocence. Her beauty is not that of youthful adolescence but of maturity. Unlike the women depicted by the Renaissance masters, her facial features are not perfect, nor are her bones exquisitely elongated. In fact, aesthetically speaking, she has hands and feet that are too large. They are the hands and feet of a peasant or a country woman; hands for generous, strong, creative acts, feet to tread the earth solidly yet gracefully. The woman is dancing as unselfconsciously as a child. Her eyes, like those of the Christ in the Resurrection Brass, are wide open; but although they see clearly, they show neither fear nor mistrust, only compassion and love.

We do not hear the music to which she moves; it is silent except to her ears. I believe she is not so much dancing as being danced by some invisible force that inspires her steps and her gestures, and enraptures her face in a gaze of profound blessing. She exemplifies the wisdom both of Nature and Nurture, the one upholding creation and the other sustaining creativity.

She represents to me what is deeply feminine in us all, men and women alike. I am happy to have made her acquaintance at last. She has been a long time coming.

dry sobs welling up from deep within my body, I give them utterance. Letting my body tell her story, I surrender to the moment. I open myself to a sadness that seems limitless, and afterward, to a joy that can only be expressed as coming home to a loved one. I listen to the voice of my own body and know that I am she.

I have been guilty of despising my body and the hatred can be seen in these pages. The process of healing my abused psyche would doubtless have been shortened had I been able to understand how much my body was asking to be heard. The dreams repeat the message over and over again but my very intelligence has prevented me from hearing it. Again and again, I have disobeyed my body's needs and settled for shoulds and oughts, a simpleton's litany of songs my father taught me.

What was required of me was nothing less than an act of surrender to a higher power who would demand of me an absolute trust in my own body. My former trust in myself had resided in my mental abilities alone. Going back even further, my childhood need to escape into fantasy had been the source of great intellectual empowerment. For the stories woven by my imagination were much more than childhood toys. Their archetypal images were talismans protecting me from the world's dangers. But as long as these images were active only in my head, as defenses, they were not capable of healing me. I think it is true to say that, for me, there can be no archetypal healing that isn't manifested in my body. But as I opened myself up to the images, they provided a bridge from the territory of the head to the land of the heart, connecting me to emotional wounds that I eventually felt as bodily pain.

It may even be that the stories I told myself when I was a child kept a healthy part of me alive at a time when my body, a wounded animal in retreat in its lair, could only wait passively for deliverance. A growing trust in and understanding of the power of the archetypes was the foundation for my adult act of surrender (no passive thing, this!). But the roots of that trust and understanding were nourished by the ability of the child to affirm life's beauty and harmony in her fantasy world above the farm kitchen. The strength and courage of that little child made it possible for my adult woman to reclaim her body. What is asked of me daily is a leap of faith that my body will "be there for me," that I and my body can truly be one; herein lies my greatest hope for healing and wholeness. Each day I let myself drop into the abyss of the unknown, trusting only that my body will catch me in her strong, loving arms. Thus, each day is an adventure, the stories of my childhood made flesh.

I am not entirely free of those aspects of the past which I, at long last, would like to put behind me. I look back on the interrupted years of the analytical encounter and wish that there had been some miracle cure that might have made the process work faster for me. But I recognize the wish as yet another fantasy; what I have settled for instead has been reality and the hard work of becoming conscious.

Looking back on the process, I can see the dangers I seldom avoided. My dreams always seemed just so much fodder for my intellectual ability to chew upon. My intellect was always so far ahead of my numbed feelings which needed to be stirred into life. But now, at long last, my feelings are waking up the numbed deadness of my body; Sleeping Beauty awakens limb by limb, muscle by muscle, and each cell unlocks its unique memory and surrenders its pain. This last process will perhaps be the slowest of all; but I now realize that, ultimately, I cannot release my creativity until my body is freed. As Alice Miller writes:

> The truth about our childhood is stored up in our body, and although we can repress it, we can never alter it. Our intellect can be deceived, our feelings manipulated, our perceptions confused and our bodies tricked with medication. But someday the body will present its bill, for it is as incorruptible as a child who, still whole in spirit, will accept no compromises or excuses, and it will not stop tormenting us until we stop evading the truth.[4]

Whenever I sense that I am losing touch with my bodily reality and its feelings, instincts, and intuition, I remember the ants that came to Psyche's aid and how they helped her fulfill her destiny. I have tried to take responsibility for my own fate; I strive to live my own life.

I have tried to change my attitude to my body, my prime container of life. I have begun to accept that I am part of a unity from whose center flows my breath of life; from my lungs outward to head, feet, and hands. I have begun the difficult task of moving my center from head to heart. The critique I made early on of the patriarchal institutions I deplored, I now apply to my own being; not: I think, therefore I am; but rather: I am, therefore I think. All of me is being involved in the creative process, with *Being* stressed over *Doing*. This lesson I was forced to learn during the fallow period of my year's creative block, when I had seemed incapable of either thought or action.

I have learned also to listen to my body's needs and to allow my body to dictate the agenda. I learned to say no to people who seem to be requiring of me a betrayal of my own feelings. I can feel sympathy, devoid of sentimentality and rancor alike, for my mother and father; gradually, like bits of blue sky glimpsed on a day stormy with clouds, I have begun to be more open with my parents.

On good days, I can experience feelings without being battered by them. Wary at all times, I am gradually surrendering to feelings of love without the inevitable suspicion that I will be somehow manipulated by them. I am learning to say yes, but only because I have begun to experience the power of no.

I am learning to breathe deeply and fully, savoring the sensation of the connection between body and head in daily bodywork lest there be any chance of regression, of abandonment of my feminine container. And with the change of center from the ego-dominated head to the heart has come the possibility of listening to another demand, another voice, another breath—that of the Holy Spirit, of the god-image within.

And, significantly, I am recognizing the existence of a new container, built from the structure of words. I experience a new creative energy, a kind of security and playfulness within the structure of words I create. I am rediscovering in writing, with a growing confidence and pleasure, an outlet for the outpourings of my thoughts and feelings. I write. I dance. I love. I am. Today.

Perhaps my body is both my last defence against and strongest container for the power of the spirit, symbolized in my dream of the feminine cathedral that neither judged nor protected but simply called me to take responsibility for myself; it is both my final link to a fantasy world I am ready to shut the door on forever and also the entrance to a world of dreams and of the imagination that I am just beginning to rediscover. I continue to follow the way of the dream and to face its truth.

Part Two

The
Silver
Dress

Chapter 4

The Silver Dress

*You can only be really conscious of things which you have
experienced, so individuation must be understood as life. Only
life integrates, only life and what we do in life brings out the
individual. . . . Real consciousness has to be based upon life
experienced, just talking about things is not enough.*

—C. G. JUNG

Now our fairy tale continues. Allerleirauh has danced with the King
who will one day be her bridegroom. She works in the kitchen until
there is another festival. Then, as before, she begs the cook for leave to
go and look on. "Yes," he answers, "but come back again in half-an-
hour, and make the King the bread soup which he so much likes."
Again she washes off the soot and takes out her nutshell, this time
putting on the dress that was as silvery as the moon. When she goes up
to the ball, the King rejoices to see her once more. Again they dance
together, and again she disappears so quickly the King cannot observe
where she went. She springs into her den, once more making herself
into a hairy animal, and goes into the kitchen to prepare the bread
soup. When the cook goes up to watch, Allerleirauh fetches her little
golden spinning wheel and puts it in the bottom of the bowl. Again
the King likes the soup, again the cook confesses that Allerleirauh
prepared it, again she is brought before the King in her soot and furs.
"I am good for nothing else but to have boots thrown at my head," she
says. "I know nothing at all about the little golden spinning wheel."

Repeated images, slightly transformed—these are the yarn that
holds the story together. Tiny as details are, they are the yarn that is
spun and woven, and transformed in our own soul story, whether we
know it or not. If we allow the images that arise from the organs of our

own body to shape us, we incubate our own bodysoul. If we allow ourselves to be twisted by society's images, we become sick.

Within herself, our heroine has now established a firm connection with her inner King. She knows he is in another part of the castle and that he is intrigued by her beauty and elusiveness. He stands firm. Standpoint and process, world tree and cave, together they make creativity possible.

As a woman sorts out her furs, the King in her dreams may appear in many guises. He may first appear as a phallic beetroot in the garden, a beetroot that she must tenderly cook in spite of her initial revulsion, a beetroot that will eventually transform into her heart. He may come as a hairy animal, part beast, part human, or a green man who coalesces with vines. Gradually he may turn into a radiant gypsy living outside the law. Or an artist who has no choice but to live his own truth, oblivious of patriarchal dictates. This is the figure who may transform into a shining Christ with powerful hairy legs, translucent skin, and piercing eyes. This may be the new Bridegroom.

As one energy matures, the other transforms to become an equal partner. In the fairy tale Allerleirauh's first task was to work on her own masculinity. This happens in the dream process of many people who have been brought up in a family where power was called love. To survive, they have chosen invisibility, which allows them a fantasy existence. They avoid the pain of abuse by not being there. Once they abandon their escape route, they realize the dangers of being ground-less: they are without boundaries. The rape by their unboundaried parents has left them unboundaried. They seek acceptance by serving whether they want to or not. Contact with the inner King establishes boundaries that assure space for the birth of their own soul. Once they begin to feel their own identity, they topple their old icons. In smash-ing their old images, they release energy that has been repressed in the complexes in their body.

Allerleirauh has some hard work to do before she is ready to receive her own inner King. She has inherited her mother's shadow. Her mother's energy was in her hair; she probably never knew what was in her body. Whatever it was, it did not support her in life. She left her King with no conscious ground for his feeling.

What does this look like in modern life? Generations of women have been taught that their body, their sexuality, their serpent power, and Satan are all part of the same evil. To escape hellfire, many have modeled themselves on the gentle, passive virgin and cut themselves off from their own animal. Such women can become castrators par excellence because, in cutting themselves off, they can also cut their man off from his sexuality and throw him into anger and loss of control. Sex then is being exploited for power. Their own gypsy ranges free, aggressive, threatening, outside the relationship or in erotic fantasy. Inside, the shadow of the mother becomes nagging, without phallic power and without spirit. This in turn is projected onto the man. It hooks his male shadow. He manifests his impotence in the bedroom and/or the market place. Then the problem is seen as his, not hers. Dealing with his male projection may then protect the woman from looking at her own shadow.

Woman's body has carried the man's shadow of lust, greed, and sloth. If she colludes with that shadow, she becomes unconscious mother, allurement that once assured the propagation of the race. She decorates her body, exposes it, seduces, even allows her body to be penetrated by a total stranger. Consciousness is so absent that neither recognizes the rape of the bodysoul. Neither considers it a moral issue. Neither hears the voice crying out from the dis-eased genitals. Each goes to a doctor for pills or salve.

Until we recognize the shadow, we project the problem out. What we see outside becomes an image of our own unknown energies. One way or another we come up against that shadow. The cut-off furs of our father's kingdom manifest in neurotic symptoms and physical disease. They manifest too in the heartbreak of recognizing that if we accept the old-fashioned projection, our relationship can continue. If we reject it and bring the shadow to consciousness, the relationship may break. It is painful to recognize our shadow in our mother-in-law or daughter-in-law. Most painful of all perhaps is facing our shadow in the person of our husband's mistress.

Our major task is to bring to consciousness as much of the unconscious as possible without allowing our intellect to destroy the unconscious image-making process. The unconscious is the matrix (creative source) of all life-energy. The danger in bringing unconsciousness to the conscious level is that in recognizing that we have made choices out of our unconscious instincts, we may cut ourselves off from the numinous power of our animals. In recognizing, for example, that our partner is a father surrogate, we may experience the shutdown of all sexual desire. However, the sexual energy is still in our matter in some masked form. Working on the silver dress is bringing matter to consciousness in a differentiated state.

Jung recognized that "psychic processes seem to be balances of energy flowing between spirit and instinct."[1] Having observed the dynamism that operates between these poles he concluded that "it is not only possible but fairly probable, even, that psyche and matter are two different aspects of one and the same thing."[2] To understand the dynamic of matter in a state of motion (energy) we need to look at the nature of religious need.

The processes of the psyche as it pushes toward wholeness are found in the archetypal patterns of world religions. They are also found in the inner work of individuals. For Jung, nothing was more dangerous than to worship an archetypal image that was not grounded in mythological truth. The separation of archetype from its mythological base left the individual deprived of the larger meaning without which human beings cannot live. Similarly, without bone-deep experience in the body, the archetype is lifeless. Thus the goal is not only the integration of spirit and matter, but ultimately the realization that not only does one not exist without the other, but one is the other in a different form.

Matter in a state of motion (energy) does not automatically happen in a human being, as anyone who weighs three hundred pounds and eats a thousand calories a day knows. Repressed energy blocked in concretization creates a false security base (a false mother)—physical food, physical objects, physical institutions. Until the imagery is released from the matter—in other words, until the projection of mother is pulled back from matter and claimed inside—the energy is locked in stone, adamant in addictions and compulsive behavior. Instead of the energy being free to move with the transforming imagery, it is locked into repetitive patterns. In dreams, the form that energy takes may be a great lizard lounging in mud, deigning an occasional blink. Until matter connects to spirit, mud is much easier than consciousness. Unconscious mother does not want change.

The connection takes place in soul, that eternal part of us that is embodied while we are on Earth. In dreams, soul is often imaged as a virgin. Like the virgin forest, she is full of the seeds of possibility, utterly in touch with nature. As an archetypal image she needs human cooperation and human consciousness to keep her transforming and growing. She understands cutting down a tree and planting a new one. She understands killing an animal for our own survival. She does not understand wanton destruction of animals or environment. If the bonding with nature is broken, we human beings suffer the consequences. Death involves renewal through the integration on a higher level of what has been sacrificed. Without that integration, death is murder.

The crux of the problem is need. In our so-called civilized world, few individuals know what they need. What they want and what they need are two very different issues. In nature, a mother bird's responsibility is to get her offspring out of the nest and free to survive on their own as soon as possible. There is, however, something in the unconscious human mother (or father) that would make her hold on and never let go. What causes this complication?

Jung understood religion as an instinct, and longing for eternal life as part of that instinct. He saw it as a need—the other pole of physical desire. If immortality is a need, then every instinctual act of a human being is a religious act. Every morsel of food is to give us immortal life, every building we build, every story we tell. In other words, human beings are symbol-making animals. They want to make eternal every conceivable form of behavior. The problem is that when consciousness of the religious instinct as instinct is not consciously affirmed, then behavior is concretized, fixated. Individuals become neurotically bound and their neurotic need for immortality is focused on objects or people. Then they cannot give up anything. They cannot sort out the baggage in the attic or the garage; they cannot breathe in their overladen house or overladen environment. They cannot let a relationship go even if it is destructive. They are buried in their own matter.

Even traditional religious imagery tends to encourage stultified energy—Father God and Mother Church. Such images can be used to maintain infantile behavior and incestuous bonding. "Except you become as a little child, you cannot see the kingdom of Heaven" can be sentimentally warped as an infantile way to immortality.

The virgin—often the Black Virgin—is emerging as a powerful archetypal image in our culture because our survival depends on our capacity to move with new energy into a new ethos. The transformative process is continually going on in her. In her heart, body and spirit meet in metaphor. Seemingly opposing poles come together. The magnificent chocolate-colored madonna evokes the positive earth mother who is stronger than the negative, judgmental mother. In dreams, she holds her own sexuality sacred. She cajoles a dreamer into throwing away an old persona and the dead skins of patriarchy. She delights in her own skin and the passion in her own body. She takes the feminine into the very core (Kore) of her own matter (mother), where she can never doubt the Presence of her own soul resonating in her own body. The passion of that shadow energy is not without its dangers and its agonies for it opens her to surrender to the erotic masculine. Its sacredness, however, has its own morality, which the Black Madonna upholds in no uncertain language. "There's no time for farting around," she says.

Initially, matter does not want to become conscious, nor does spirit want to be embodied. Only gradually do body and psyche push toward consciousness, and only when they are sufficiently grounded in love, can conscious matter be penetrated by the light of the spirit. The Divine Child—the new consciousness—is born of that union.

In the Black Madonna, whore and saintly virgin are reconciled. These are strong shadow figures for both men and women. Changing the unconscious depths of these images is slow work. Both sexes have to recognize that both sides are in them and then make their choices. If they decide to work their relationship through, both will hit the repressed rage that lies hidden beneath depression. Both have to suffer the tension of the opposites—sexuality and spirituality—and hold the tension, until rage is released and gradually, very gradually, transformed into love.

This is the volcano that smolders beneath many relationships. Instead of denying that volcano or erupting with it, if we can realize that the volcano contains the answer, we can deal with the problem consciously. A marriage trapped in unconscious incestuous bonding is perpetuating unconscious mother and unconscious father. The fiery, Dionysian energy is being lived elsewhere or not at all.

Men and women who are trying to live their true virgin—their essence in touch with their source—are trying to hold both sides of the feminine in consciousness. When they refuse to rape their own bodies, new images appear in their dreams. There may be a Mary Magdalene, a Shakti, a sacred prostitute—some figure that holds sexuality and spirituality together. Accepting her discipline gives the dreamer the strength to transform rage into love. Then ravishment is possible. Ravishment trajects us out of the parental complexes and empowers us in our own bodies. Feminine wisdom trapped in the underworld of the body has been maturing through centuries of patriarchy. If only we can bring that wisdom to consciousness, spirit will no longer be homesick for home.

Without that body wisdom, there is no presence between man and woman—no NOWS—where each can meet the other's truth, no sacred spaces where both are stripped to their naked fear, anger, and love. Neither has a sanctuary in which their animals can be civilized and still want to live. The feminine is not related to her core, to that deepest survival chakra.

This lack of dynamic is true intrapersonally as well so long as people are living a persona life without the heart connection that grounds them in their own body matrix. Individuals existing without that connection try to live by willpower. They try to make believe that life has meaning. Their neuroses (distorted instincts) cloak the vibrant life buried in their unconscious. They are cut off from their birthright to life.

Preparing themselves to wear the silver dress is the task of finding their own positive mother in their own body. In doing so, they will also find their true virgin—the conscious feminine who is who she is because she is grounded in her own instincts and her own imagery. She is conscious mother and virgin at the same time.

Some people learn about their own instincts by loving their own horse, or dog, or cat. They learn to tap into their own uncanny wisdom. They also learn how to discipline their animal without using a whip. Our own animal is a thoroughbred with potential few of us ever consider. In our maddest fantasies we would never starve, poison, exhaust an animal as we do our own body. It takes a lot of consciousness to recognize and feed and care for our own pedigree animal.

Silver is the metal of the moon and because woman's biology is connected to the moon, silver is associated with the feminine. The luminous glow of moonlight lacks the sharp clarity of sunlight, but its gentleness unfolds, synthesizes, brings together as one. Feelings and intuitions that remain hidden from the sun surface in moonlight. They flower into love, poetry, music.

They come in their own natural time. Sometimes the moon is dark. One night a sliver appears and, in its own time, it grows into the radiance of the full orb. It takes a strong ego to hold the darkness, wait, hold the tension, wait, waiting for we know not what. But if we can hold long enough, a tiny light is conceived in the dark unconscious, and if we can wait and hold, in its own time it will be born in its full radiance. The ego then has to be loving enough to receive the gift and nourish it with the best food. That new life may eventually transform the whole personality. This is moon consciousness. This is the light of our soul, the essence of ourselves that takes up residence in our body while we are on Earth. It knows what the conscious ego does not know. Whereas sun rhythm would rush into action, moon rhythm meditates, ponders, keeps the feeling in harmony with the thought. It brings a thinking heart to the humdrum of existence.

Understanding with the head is one thing. Allowing the thought to drop into the body is quite another. The head may say, "Divorce is the only solution." The body may continue to grieve for its beloved for years. The masculine finds the feminine slow; it can grab an illumination, pigeonhole it, and just as quickly forget it. The feminine allows light to permeate her Being before she commits to knowing.

Masculine consciousness often tries to help the feminine to speak. It jumps in and takes over. It does not wait for the body to know its truth. Nor does it wait for the right moment. Feminine consciousness senses timing. Too often by the time it is ready to speak, the masculine has long since forgotten the whole point. The feminine feels betrayed, shoved aside as if what she has to say couldn't matter less. She feels she can't be true to herself because it takes time for her to find the exact words for the new thing she is *realizing* and she has to wait for the moment of its arrival. She is waiting to *realize* what is going on right now. The discrepancy is not gender based. Many men can wait for the moment longer than women. Listening to many women's conversations we have little reason to trust their sense of the creative pause.

Feminine consciousness is rooted in the heart. The feeling comes with the thought, and as the thought is spoken, the heart opens, and feeling flows to deeper, richer levels. Femininity is silenced in our culture. There is simply no time for her. Moreover, her values and emotions are embarrassing, even to many women who love her. If we fail to speak our truth, fail to demand that others recognize our Being, we are abandoning our own soul. Standing up for femininity is saying, "Stop. Wait. What is going on here in this moment?" Talk is blather if it is outside our life situation.

The virgin makes bread soup. She sees the world with her physical eyes and perceives the essence with her inner eye. Like an image in a dream, in a picture, in a line of poetry, she distills the eternal in the transitory.

Emily Dickinson, for example, sees the whole human drama unfold in the simplest details of her home and garden. Her metaphors hold the suspension between her body and the ideal that threatened to carry her off into spirit. Describing her own heart in love, she ignites every lover's heart.

> *To my small Hearth His fire came—*
> *And all my House aglow*
> *Did fan and rock, with sudden light—*
> *'Twas Sunrise—'twas the Sky—*[3]

While she did the best she could to find her ground in her kitchen work and her garden, Dickinson knew only too well how dearly she paid for not being able to live her tiger. She had no fear of the magnificent passion that flamed from her unlived side. She knew her capacity to love but she had no way to express it in relationship. Describing the moment when she realizes she will never live her tiger, she sees herself reflected in his dead eyeballs.

> *'Twas not my blame—who sped too slow—*
> *'Twas not his blame—who died*
> *While I was reaching him—*
> *But 'twas—the fact that He was dead—*[4]

Dickinson was not to be defeated. She knew that making bread soup could keep her sane. And make bread soup she did. She surrendered to her destiny—albeit with scalding sacrifice—and transformed her instinctual tiger energy into images that resonate into our very bones. She wore the silver as triumphantly as she could in a nineteenth-century New England town.

We are moving into the twenty-first century on a sick planet. This is a new situation requiring not just an expansion of consciousness but a mutation of consciousness. The old glasses and obsolete instruments that appear in our dreams are useless because they keep us searching for ways to change the old world. We are trying to adjust to new energies finding new balances in our bodies, new energies finding new balances in the ecosystem. We cannot move into that new ethos without the wisdom of the silver dress because we are dependent on the new imagery that is constantly giving form to transforming energies. Finding our connection to the conscious feminine in the new body is crucial in our work, our play, our lovemaking. It is also crucial in our educational system.

Unknowingly, children and young adults can be seduced into believing they will climb to the top if they eradicate their femininity and with it their creativity. Their incestuous bonding with their parents—whether compliant or rebellious—hooks them into similar bonding with their teachers. Because they are unable to think or feel for themselves, they fail to recognize the power drive that has destroyed the teacher's creativity and is now destroying theirs. Under the rubric of rudeness, craziness, intransigence, histrionics, even hysteria, femininity is dismissed from young lives. Then educators wonder why students assume that school is boring. Of course, anything is boring if the feeling that gives value to the idea is massacred. The energy that would leap up and say, "What a great idea!" is not present. Nor is the energy that recognizes the word that resonates in the heart. Without the moon, the sun is not reflected. Without conscious flesh, the Word is not recognized.

Wearing the silver dress is like being a silver chalice—a sacramental wedding cup in which the mystery of new bride and new bridegroom unfolds.

Chapter 5

Mary

. . . let the moon
Shine on thee in thy solitary walk.

—WILLIAM WORDSWORTH

Mary and I were teachers together in London, Canada, twenty years ago. She taught Phys. Ed. in the gym. I taught English on the top floor.

She was not happy with her teaching because she realized that even the best athletes in her classes were absent from their bodies. Having been trained in classical ballet, at the National Ballet School of Canada, she knew from experience the pain of enforced discipline. She knew what it was to spend years trying to hold the exact alignment between ankle and thigh, trying to land with the back upright, lifted instead of dropped, trying to control every ounce she ate for fear of becoming a fat swan. Having seen her blood seeping through her pointe shoes, she knew all about torturing the body in order to achieve the perfect line. She also knew how her body yearned to embrace the air, yearned to express her soul as it melted into music. In short, she believed that in perfecting the technique, the body became the resentful slave of an inner tyrant that shouted twenty-four hours a day, "You're not good enough. You don't work hard enough. You are too fat. You'll never hear the applause. You'll never make your parents proud." That voice took over the center of her Being until her delight in the dance turned into depression in her body. The joy she once yearned to express in dance was no longer there to express.

Mary was convinced the same thing was happening in the Phys. Ed. department; excellent athletes were manipulating their exquisite machines totally disconnected from the breath of soul that would give their gestures human feeling.

Meanwhile, on the third floor, I was equally depressed listening to students mumble their way through the fiery metaphors of Blake, or the lyricism of Shelley. Shakespeare's magic never failed, but the great body of English literature was essentially dead for most of the students. Their bodies sat inert, politely listening, catching a piece of an idea here, a flying image there. Even in those distant days, I knew what the images in "Tyger, Tyger, burning bright," could create in the body. I knew if they were once injected into the bloodstream, something would happen. The brain and the body bridged by the imagination would take fire, and the power of the sounds so exquisitely orchestrated in the lines would resonate in the body cells. I knew from my own experience that poetry could change the metabolism. Finally, I could no longer endure the massacre of the poetry nor the massacre of the souls. I felt I was giving them warmed-over soup when fresh bread soup was there for the having.

Ordinarily, the Phys. Ed. department was grounded in the gym, while the English department flew on the top floor. The students were smelly bodies running and jumping downstairs, and disembodied spirits flapping and floundering upstairs, with no connection in between. Mary and I decided to try to bring body and spirit together. She brought her students upstairs to a small theater-in-the-round on the second floor. She encouraged them to concentrate inside, to breathe into their solar plexus, and allow the emotions to connect with the breath until the frozen organs felt the vibration of the genuine feeling, and then in its own time, to allow that emotion, always connected to the breath, to express itself wherever it moved in the body. Over a period of weeks, rigid, mechanical movements became the fluid expression of whatever feelings wanted to be expressed through movement. When the joy and suffering in those young bodies was unfettered, the release of energy through their dance was almost uncontrollable.

Meantime, I was bringing my students from the top story down to the same little theater-in-the-round. They lay on the floor and breathed in the breath of life until their rigid bodies were relaxed. Often we did simple yoga asanas until the energy that was focused in their heads was more balanced throughout their bodies. We did obscene tongue, lip, and jaw exercises until they could open their mouths. Then we brought the *m* and *n* sounds resonating into their skulls, and the *o* and *a* vowels resonating into whatever dark corners opened.

The students moved until the movement was spontaneous. Then we created the poetry together. The boys, for example, decided "The

Tyger" was theirs. They divided themselves into bass and tenor voices, stood in a circle and intoned the poem together. I quickly realized that I was working with young men whose energy I had never seen before. I let their poem evolve in them. Their energy driving into the center enlarged the circle and held, until they were able to work as a unit facing the audience around them. Ten solo voices took each of the ten questions. "In what distant deeps or skies / Burnt the fire of thine eyes?" crescendoed to "What dread grasp / Dare its deadly terrors clasp?"[1] Each question depended on all the previous ones, because if one student poured everything he had into his question, there was no place for those who followed to build. Daily the tyger's energy grew until his "fearful symmetry" pulsed off the walls. And daily the students asked more questions about Blake until they were ready to do parts of "The Marriage of Heaven and Hell." They had no trouble understanding, "Man has no Body distinct from his Soul, for that called Body is a portion of Soul discern'd by the five Senses, the chief inlets of Soul in this age."[2]

Our work dovetailed ever more closely when we co-led the theater arts program. Mary and I began to understand what we were, in fact, activating. Her dance training gave me insight into the unconscious blocks in a body and how to breathe and move in order to release them. My understanding of metaphor and sound and the release of energy through implanting an image in the body brought new insights to her. Body and soul came together in the programs that we and the students created in that space midway between the gym and the top floor.

In rehearsal one day I realized with some alarm that I was like the conductor of an orchestra. Sometimes I didn't seem to be doing anything, but if my concentration wavered for sixty seconds, something went wrong on the floor. The energy became lax, muffled, attenuated, an edge of fear crept in, the courageous spontaneity was lost. I suddenly understood that perceiver and perceived were one: my perception of a block in a body influenced the energy in the perceived block without one word spoken. Similarly, my lack of perception (while I thought about softening the spotlight) resulted in unconscious whorls on the stage.

Mary was also recognizing the phenomenon with her dancers. As the process evolved, we encouraged the students to hold the position of outside observer for themselves, to hold that position of conscious witness and allow themselves to drop even deeper into their own creativity. The results were astonishing within the group process. While they were each holding that double perspective, the love among them, or the energy, however you want to name it, was so open and intense that the group as one voice could initiate a long pause, which they had never taken before, and resume with every tongue exactly on the *t*. Every performance became a new performance riveting in its concentrated vitality.

My destiny took me to Zurich. My health took me deeper into the mysteries of body and soul. My wise old woman told me to take the positive images that God gave me in my dreams, plant them in my body, and allow their light to emanate through all my molecules. I did as I was directed by my dreams for four years. Then, just before I returned to Canada, I had a powerful dream in which my dark body was dismembered and when the old shell fell off, light shone from my skeleton through my translucent flesh. I knew the dream was prefiguring what I had yet to do. Even now, after further years of meditation, I am still working on missing connections.

By my third year in Zurich, I was in training to become a Jungian analyst. That February, Mary received the blow that she describes in her story that follows. Thousands of physical miles separated us, but souls that love each other have ways of dispelling distance. Because we knew each other well, we could write exactly what we felt and trust that the other could receive without misunderstanding. She sent me her dreams and, because I understood the depth of her loss, I thought best not to focus on an intellectual interpretation of what was taking place in her depths. Instead, we worked from what we had discovered watching the students transform from putting on a performance into living the authentic depths of their own Being. We concentrated on the images in her dreams, allowing them to come to life in her body, allowing her body to experience the energy of the image, until it transformed into a new image and new energy. This process Mary wrote down every day in her journal, thus reinforcing her container, the consciousness that could witness the unconscious process without falling into it. She was supported by a loving, though frightened, husband and several strong female friends.

During the summer months we live a boatride from each other on Georgian Bay. That first summer we worked almost daily, connecting her dreams with her bodysoul work. It was important to recognize the dark, evil forces that were so ready to usurp command. It was equally important to honor and live the healing power evolving from the radiant center in the Self. It was like watching an archetypal battle between good and evil with the frail but determined soul as prize.

Crucial to Mary's healing was the witness, the ego position that objectively observes what is happening in the bodysoul. We had never talked about "the witness" in our work with the students but, when we realized its importance, the witness was always there. However chaotic the theater became as the students dropped into their musculature to discover who was there, the witness was one hundred percent concentrated on what was happening, holding the conscious container. Sometimes the students witnessed each other; always one of us was witnessing the group.

When Mary was working alone, she knew that unless she held the light of the conscious witness, she would simply fall deeper into unconscious darkness. As perceiver and perceived, she was creating the container in which the healing process could evolve. Whatever happened in the unconscious was brought to consciousness as transformation slowly progressed. In fairy tales, the treasure that the hero or heroine has labored so long to obtain is often lost just as home appears on the horizon. Overconfident, the ego allows its concentration to wander, and the treasure is snatched away by the evil shadow who dwells in the unconscious. It is dangerous to work without a conscious witness, whether that witness is within or without. It is crucial to realize that even the perception of darkness is light in the darkness; it is the beginning of healing.

To further strengthen the witness position, Mary used active imagination extensively. While she allowed a complex to take over her emotions and body, she wrote everything down that the complex had to say, thus bringing unconscious material to consciousness. Giving the complexes names—Good Mary, Bad Mary, Medicine Woman, Deer—helped her to humanize and later integrate the material into her daily life.

Fifteen years ago Mary could not have articulated her revolt against the values in which she had been trained. Like Kate, she had climbed the patriarchal ladder and when she neared the top, she discovered the ladder was against the wrong wall. When I returned to Zurich, analysis was not available to her and like the heroine in the fairy tale, she summoned all her inner resources, wrapped herself in her instincts, treasured her nutshell, and took refuge in her own tree. Unlike Kate, whose first task was to wear the golden dress, Mary's primary work was with the silver. Since body language was her most direct medium of communication, she had to go down into the ashes of her own matter and fan the spark of her own feminine consciousness.

If you as a reader are unfamiliar with the cyclic movement of the feminine, your linear expectations may be thoroughly disoriented as you read Mary's journal. You may find yourself thinking, "This is naive, frightening, chaotic, crazy." And that's precisely how Mary and other initiates feel as they begin to give up the rigid thinking patterns that have protected them from the spontaneity of their inner world. Throughout the fourteen years that were distilled into thousands of journal pages and now distilled into the following seventy, Mary was very functional in the world. But this story is not focused on Mary's behavior at faculty meetings or what she and her husband fight about. The life revealed in these journal entries is her soul story beginning with a few desperate minutes snatched from her compulsions, evolving into essential time each day, and gradually infiltrating every part of her life.

It may help to remind yourself that if you have no experience of the wisdom of the conscious body, you are in unknown territory listening to your mother tongue. Its rhythms beat with the heart, with the emotions that circle and repeat and again repeat with totally new vibrations of feeling. Its vocabulary is simple; its knowing deep. This is not the language of polished English prose. It is heart language calling out to other hearts. It rings true on the breath. It fumbles at times, yes, because it prefers silence or dance or poetry or song. It is the language of dreams. To hear the feminine we have to dare to open our receptors to old words with new meanings. Love spoken from the mind is one thing; love whispered from a volcano is another. If this sounds apologetic, it is not meant to be. It is fact. People who have dared the brink to find their femininity are weary of being patted on the head with a silent, "It's all right, dear." They know they must be heard.

For most women and many men, the royal road to the unconscious is through the complexes experienced in their body. Often they arrive in my office, physically ill and psychically alienated. "What's the point of doing analysis?" they ask. "I never dream." The fact is they do dream, but when the alarm clock rapes them out of the underworld, they have no conscious container strong enough to hold the images that are creating new life. However, if they try, they catch an image each night. They write it down in their journal, or paint it along with their associations. Gradually the unconscious begins to trust that the ego does care and gradually complete dreams follow. Nuns, prostitutes, pirates, murderers, gypsies—an astonishing cast of characters begins to appear in the bourgeois living room. Allowing these complexes to talk, move, dance, sing, and draw is the beginning of releasing repressed energy from opaque, unconscious matter. If the dreamer can dialogue with these images, allow them to speak and move through the muscles and bones, the body will thaw and express the emotions it can now feel. It is crucial that the ego be strong enough to hold its own standpoint, listen to the imaginary figures, express its point of view. At the same time it must remain open to the expansion that comes through taking responsibility for these lost parts. Instead of blindly acting out the old patterns, the dreamer cooperates with the story that is going on inside. This is what Jung calls active imagination.

Mary began as a reflection of her parents' image of her. She became what Jung calls an "anima woman," a woman who instinctively knows how to be whatever men project onto her. When she was a child, her father paid little attention to her. However, at fourteen, when her older sister left home for university, she instinctively knew her developing dancer's body won his undivided attention. Throughout her years at ballet school, she was her Daddy's Darling. The psychic bonding between her and her father held her soul captive, turned her body into a feelingless machine, and her mind into a fantasy realm populated by ghostly lovers. She was a femme fatale for other men.

As she struggled to find her own identity, she dialogued for years with an inner figure called Medicine Woman, whose love cracked through the armored rage in Mary's body. Beneath the rage, she found Deer, whose gentleness released her body from Witch and Hitler, two fearsome patriarchal figures. Somehow Mary knew that if she could find Eve in herself, she would be able to connect to her own creative masculinity. This energy appeared first in Black Dog and Fish. Nellie, the wise old crone, held the still point. She was and is the mediator between darkness and light.

Mary is now teaching dance in the Faculty of Kinesiology at the University of Western Ontario in London, Canada. I am a Jungian analyst in Toronto. The roots of our relationship are in the Georgian Bay mud. We still work together in workshops with men and women committed to their own journeys. We are still working with the same concepts toward finer, more delicate tuning in the subtle or energy body. Our waterlilies are opening toward the sun through the love of the Great Mother—creation opening herself to consciousness.

And now we hand the talking stick to Mary.

Chapter 6

Redeeming Eve's Body

MARY HAMILTON

WINTER 1976
WOUNDING

"Is the baby dead?" I hear myself ask the intern.

"Well, that's one possibility we might consider," he says, avoiding my eyes. He turns quickly and leaves the room.

"Baby, don't be dead. Oh God, don't let him be dead."

I hear an inner voice say to me, "Get in control of yourself, woman. Here, read this magazine."

I wait. No one comes.

I go to the phone at the nurses' station. I phone my husband. "John, they can't find a heartbeat." I am bursting into tears. "Hang onto yourself," yells the inner voice. "Nobody wants a crying fool around here. Get control."

I go numb. I leave my body and watch myself as if I were a camera objectively filming a dramatic scene in a hospital. I see myself calmly ask the nurse where the intern has gone.

"Oh, he is very busy today, dearie," she answers, smiling sweetly at me.

Finally the intern returns. He is in a great rush. "Everything is favorable," he says and leaves again.

The inner voice knowingly says to me, "Well, that's it. The baby is dead."

I feel nothing. I am in total control. I cease to think of my beloved bump as a child. It has become a black cancerous tumor. I am going to have an operation today to have it removed.

Hours later I angrily push the tumor out. I watch the pale face of the young female intern. She keeps asking me if I am terrified by the experience. I wonder if she is there to add comic relief.

"It's a boy. Cut here."

The silence is thick.

Voices surround me. "Sign here, please." . . . "Thank you very much." . . . "Now, do you want a funeral?" . . . "Do you want to see your baby?" . . . "May we have the body for science?" . . . "Thank you very much." . . . "Your husband must go now."

Finally I am alone. For the first time in nine months I roll over onto my stomach. There is nothing there. I cry uncontrollable tears. I am afraid someone might hear me. I stop crying.

I am home. The florist keeps delivering flowers. The house looks like a funeral parlor. I wonder who died? I try to echo John's hope for another child. I am only an echo.

People arrive at the door. They talk at me. I smile. Inside my head yells a voice, "Goddamn it, woman, your child is dead. What the hell are you smiling for?" But when my smile turns to tears, the people leave. I have a disease. It is called death.

Each morning I make a list of things I must do. I rarely cry now. I am emotionally strong. My head has gone ahead and organized my life, ignoring my body that still thinks she is supporting another life. My breasts are filled with milk. Inner voices natter in my head. "The death occurred in your body. Within you is the reason he died. Your journey is to find the answer."

I go through the motions of being alive. I have no sense of time. My memory is utter blackness. I have to be very careful with myself in order to stay in control. I avoid people now. Their eyes see into my nightmare. I am terrified of falling apart as my mind flips into strange spaces.

I am disoriented with no job, no baby, no challenge, no outward place to direct my energy. It turns back inwards toward a blackness circling in my gut. I seem to be losing my sense of who I am. Every day when I dance in the studio I see a thin, agonized woman in the mirror. Pain drips off her body like tears. I do not recognize her. And my body can't contain anything. I can't eat and I have continual diarrhea. Wild dreams plague me all night; wild voices plague me all day.

I fear if the unconscious grief in me surfaces I will explode and the agony will kill me. I am afraid of the darkness of grief and yet I am driven to understand it. My dream world and my outer reality all become one. I am sinking into madness.

I go to the doctor. He doesn't understand what I am trying to say to him about the voices, so I stop talking. He prescribes tranquilizers. They work—no dreams, no voices, no visions, no terror in the body, no life in the body. I cannot even dance. I am a living corpse. My life in my madness is better than my death in drugs.

"I'll commit suicide," I think to myself.

"No," answers a voice in my head. "Death is only a short escape from life. You will return to a body and be forced to face your madness."

With no escape in life or in death I begin corresponding with Marion in Zurich.

Life is a living hell. I am driven to do anything to ease both the gnawing ache in my gut and the bizarre anguish in my head. Fearful of being seen, fearful of falling apart, and fearful of being told I am crazy, I dance alone each morning in my living room behind closed green curtains. In my old, baggy housecleaning clothes, with my scraggly hair and ugly glasses full of tears, I forget every plié, fouetté, and arabesque I have trained so long to perfect. I let my body dance the fury of my dreams. I let my body dance the ecstasy of my visions. Wild emotional outbreaks terrify my controlling persona. When in hell, however, I have nothing to lose. I allow myself to dance and dance and dance. Slowly the grief and the rage are peeled away to my core and there I find the love for my "beloved bump," the "child" I have lived for, for nine months. Now I dance my tears.

Every afternoon I discipline myself to record my feelings and insights in my journal. I am compelled to bring them to consciousness. I write and I write, trying to find meaning in my suffering. My journal is my lifeline. In the evening I get myself to the studio. I have to prove to myself that I am not crazy, that I can be normal, even though powerful visions invade my waking consciousness.

In a vision, a Raven sits on my desk as I write. He flies away and bursts of energy fill my body. The energy comes in yellow circles with brilliant red, fiery centers. Circles keep forming in front of me, then they pierce down inside my body. The light is so brilliant that I have to dance around the house to dissipate the intensity. I do not know if I am in agony or ecstasy. Finally the circles stop. I feel full. I am aware that I am ravenously hungry.

But the food I eat seems to feed the voices in my head. I seem to fall into separate pieces that are at war with each other. My one voice divides into many voices. My core disintegrates, and my sense of self falls off me like dead skin. A strong inner voice keeps saying to me, "Surrender, let the new energy reweave the tapestry of your soul-self in matter."

I do not have the energy nor the will to withstand this power. My self divides into three feminine voices, three different complexes that take over my pen as I write in my journal.

SPRING 1976
DISINTEGRATION

"I am Good Mary," writes a complex. I try to be a still life portrait of society's perfect woman on the front page of *Vogue* magazine. My thin, rigid body is a "thing" that I can starve or exercise to the point of exhaustion. I give birth to ideals of the head, but not to earthly children. Sexuality is dirty and so I have left my body and live in the head. Here my spiritual ideals reach the illusion of perfection for they are released from the darkness of matter. I know that original ideas of my own are dangerous so I fill my mind full of facts that I can quote on command. This knowledge gets me what I want in life—degrees, jobs, respect from authorities. Without a body to feel what I value in life, I value those things that are good according to society's standards. I am predictable, reliable, dependable—just what others want.

"I am a 'righteous woman,' " continues the voice of the complex. "I am determined to make it to front row center in heaven. I use my innocent sweetness as power. Unconsciously identified with the power of my dancer's beauty, I tempt men but I never deliver the goods. I lure men lovingly out of the reality of their dirty bodies, out of the reality of their lives. I use my intuition to figure out what others want of me. I know what my parents want of me, even when they don't know. Daddy wants to possess his own darling daughter so I am a femme fatale to other men; Mommy wants a popular socialite. I perform accordingly. Mommy wants to be a dancer so I am the dancer for her. I am a good person."

"Like hell you are," yells a wild woman in me. She takes over my pen with great fury. "Good Mary is a master manipulator. You are blind to her destructiveness."

"Who are you, wild woman?" I ask, trying to hold the ego position.

"I am your Eve self, your Bad Mary. I am a free spirit who knows no outer laws. I terrify you for I serve Life and not the values of society. Your Good Mary calls me a whore. My misunderstood energy has been repressed and therefore has been forced to turn against itself. Good Mary calls me a cancer in her body because I know that the vagina is a divine-smelling jewel box. That fool in your head keeps trying to scrub it clean. I know that my body is a flower opening to the Gods. I am the fire living inside the plastic face and frozen, skinny, dead body of Good Mary. Your Good Mary is a fucking saint who would rape the Earth to please the authorities. Now, release me into life so that I can teach you of feminine wisdom."

Good Mary is terrified of Eve living in her body. To get the Good Mary's attention, Eve gives me tension headaches, indigestion, diarrhea, PMS, and painful periods. Good Mary hangs on to her reality with bitten fingernails. I can no longer withstand the power of Eve. Split apart in despair, I physically collapse on the bedroom floor and weep. In the despair, another voice appears. I look into the mirror and see my agony. The agony changes into the face of an old Medicine Woman.

"Allow yourself to enter into the labyrinth of your darkness."

"But this is insane," I say. "You are an illusion."

"No," says the image of the Medicine Woman in the mirror, "you are the illusion."

I am being torn apart. That night I dream of Medicine Woman handing me bones of prehistoric animals.

"These are your animals," she says to me in the dream. "Good Mary's animals have no soul in their bones. Eve's animals have soul. If you want soul, love the animals of Eve."

Good Mary tells me to be a good girl, to listen to her God the Father, the big daddy-judge in the sky, to kill Eve's energy, for she is only an evil whore.

Eve's energy makes Good Mary's life a physical hell.

Medicine Woman tells me to dig into the earth of my body and find the healing waters. My body is knotted and twisted in pain.

I sit in my living room and try to relax my body. I close my eyes and on my inner screen Eve appears. She carries a great long whip. Suddenly I see that she is standing in my womb, and a huge green snake coils around her. Eve is calm and still. She and the snake breathe in unison. The power between them is awesome. Eve suddenly breaks into an earthy laugh that shakes my body into a terrorized state.

"I have the power of the snake. She is mine to do with as I wish. Snake and I are friends. We are to enter life together. You cannot kill us. We will kill you first."

"What do you want from me?" I ask, panic-stricken.

"LIFE! I want to be seen in the light for who I am. That stupid Good Mary in your head was going to kill us all with her guilt. She was going to give you cancer. I chose to kill the child to force you to hear me. LIVE ME! I demand it of you."

I start to feel myself sinking. I look out of my eyes, and reality seems so far away. I hear voices, but their bodies are ghosts. I see real people but I cannot respond to them. They do not hear me when I speak of these voices. I wonder who looks out of my eyes. Who is this being who writes these words?

Each morning I discipline myself to listen to the voices within. They tell me that on their battlefield is the birthplace of my feminine self. They tell me to dance their energy out of my body and to speak their voices so that I can understand how they possess my bodymind. They tell me I am on a dangerous journey but that if I have the courage to stay with them they will reveal to me the secrets of my womanhood.

One morning I have the feeling that a great presence is in the living room with me. It is a positive energy, but ruthless. I finally have the courage to visualize it. On my inner screen I see the old Medicine Woman. She is a weather-beaten, ugly old crone. Although I am terrified of her, I am irresistibly drawn to her. Intuitively, I know that if I can focus on her presence, I will not go insane. My energy reaches out to grasp her but she returns it forcefully.

"Do not give me your power," she says sternly to me. "Keep it for yourself. You need it. Listen and obey me but never cling to me. Walk by my side, but do not enter my being. The power will destroy you. I will touch you, and my touch will heal you, but you must never touch me. I am here to teach you how to accept your crucified Christ. If you respect my space, your knowing me will not destroy you."

"How can I do this? I can hardly stay sane as it is!"

"If you want life, listen to me; if you want death, don't listen to me. If you choose not to listen, then the life-force will have no reason to keep you here on this plane of reality. There is work to be done. If you listen, your myth will be manifested through your actions on planet Earth. Live your death, or die and live your life."

In dreams Medicine Woman tells me to make friends with my animal nature. She tells me to thaw the frozen soil of my body and to let spring come forth in celebration of being. She tells me to dance a fertility dance with laughter in my soul. Without knowing what a fertility dance is, I let Eve dance my body. A vision spontaneously comes to me:

> I am standing in a dark fertile swamp where luscious marsh marigolds surround me. My heart is full of life as Eve takes my hands and we dance in the dark, moist wetness. She tells me to see the pure, clean swamp between my legs and then a lotus flower will bloom from it.
>
> Medicine Woman appears and speaks to me. "Through your vessel the conscious feminine is to be born. Eve is to be brought into the sunlight."

SUMMER 1976
HEALING THE WOUND

Though I am at the island in Georgian Bay and surrounded by beauty, I am filled with grief. I am my Good Mary self with no voice and I am Eve with no way of living my creative life force. I am the woman whose son is dead, and I hurt. Grief is vomited out of me. I hear others telling me that I am not adjusting well, for it isn't right to spend my days crying. I am torn, angular, and wild with energy. There is no civilized woman in me, but there is a woman. I am that woman and in my grief I know what I value. I also know that healing for me lies in the saltwater of my tears.

As I lie on the hot Georgian Bay rocks crying silently, I see myself in a vision:

> I am lying in the fetal position, and my skin starts to fall off. I become thinner and thinner as layer after layer is removed. I see the organs inside my body no longer function. They, too, start to disappear. I see my bones covered in blood, but gradually the blood dries and disappears. Then my skeleton collapses, and the bones separate so that there is no body left.
>
> Medicine Woman appears.

"Your soul does not care if she lives or dies. The life force speaks through whatever vessel is willing to receive its energy. In this life your function is to listen and live unconditional love for all forms of life.

"You are now experiencing the peace of death, the world of soul, the world of permanence. There is no suffering here: suffering happens in the body. If you choose to return to your body, you will suffer. If you choose death you will be returned to another body to complete your soul's journey. However, if you return to your body, my wisdom will manifest through you."

I feel a huge surge of energy as I am forced back into my grieving and now terrified body. I don't want to live and yet I am terrified that I am dead. I stand on the edge of a rock cliff not knowing if I should jump into death or walk inland into life. As I wait I seem to split into two energy systems, one gold and one red. The gold energy system shoots a golden arrow into the heart of the red energy system. It hits with such force that I fall to the ground. I know that if I stand up, I will live; if I stay on the ground, I will die. My selves are connected by an outside source of infinite love. Words speak through my mouth. "I want life," I whisper to the open waters. "I don't know why and I don't care why, but I want to live."

I walk back to the center of the island. I lie down on the Earth and cry. Again I hear myself speaking, "O Mother Earth, forgive me for not loving matter, for not seeing you, for not hearing you." I feel deep sobs coming out of my gut. I do not know if I am weeping or if Mother Earth is weeping through my body. I am weeping the grief I seem to absorb from the Earth.

I roll over onto my back and the heat of the sun coming through the leaves of the trees warms my flesh. Circles of red and yellow light dance around my belly. I know that I am being healed. My womb is ready to receive new life.

That night I have the following dream.

Medicine Woman hands me the body of my dead son. I lift up my arms and raise his little nude body to the sunlight, as though I am offering him to the Gods. My long hair is filled with strawberries. Suddenly his heart is pierced with a golden dagger.

"He is the sacrifice the Gods demanded of you," says Medicine Woman. "Mother Earth demands that all is returned to her. Bury him in her soil, and she will in turn give you life. Life feeds on death."

The immense impact of the dream makes me understand the meaning of sacrifice. The son I longed for unconsciously to justify my existence as a woman, gives me my life through his death. My life has been the real stillbirth.

FALL 1976 TO SPRING 1979
MOTHERHOOD

In reflection, the timing of this dream is an act of grace. After my summer on the island in Georgian Bay, I conceive and, in the summer of 1977, give birth to a beautiful healthy daughter. Thus, released into my own life through the conscious assimilation of the dream of the sacrifice, I am free to live my life and my daughter is free to live her own life, unburdened by the projection of my unlived self.

Now my daughter is born my life is filled with the chores of mothering. However, I continue to develop tools to keep me connected to my inner world. From my correspondence with Marion I know that dialoguing with dream symbols is not madness; madness for me is repressing their energy. The inner journey seems to push onwards regardless of what is happening in my outer life.

For the next two years I work daily with journal writing and dialoguing with dream symbols. During this time I conceive again, and give birth to another beautiful little girl. My daughters teach me about the Eve I once was. Their beautiful, round, nude bodies, their total acceptance of their being, their joy in receiving physical love, become an inner support system to my own new self. I know that on the physical level I am the mother of my own children; however, on the psychic level I am also mother to my inner child. In dreams, my daughters symbolize the new life of the woman-child in me.

I begin to feel a new reality in my body that is very different from the frozen controlled stillness I have lived before my journey began. Though peaceful and controlled on the surface, I used to feel that I was a two-dimensional, frozen still point, living the illusion of control over my life. I was afraid that people would see the terrible person I was beneath my controlling persona. Now, I feel I am a multidimensional moving point beginning to live the reality of surrender into the process of living. Instead of feeling the tremendous need to have control over life, I feel the need to let life move freely through me. It is very frightening but so much better than the frozen life of controlled emotions. Whether I feel them or not, the emotions are there. I can, however, choose to feel them, to face their reality and to participate with them in the life around me and within me. I feel joy and pain, peace and fear. To others who know me I appear to be out of control, tearful, over-emotional, and not my "happy, perky, positive self." But inside me, I start to feel real, to feel alive. Though so fragile and vulnerable, the feelings of living my emotional reality give me the strength to simply be whoever I am becoming.

When the children nap, I work on my dream material. I notice the bodywork changing; it feels quiet. Although the emotions are always honored through tears of anger or joy, there are no primal outbreaks. When alone I work with a single dream symbol such as a flower, rather than with an entire dream. I choose one positive symbol that creates pleasant physical sensations in my body when I think about it. I never work alone with a negative symbol, one that arouses in me fear, anxiety, or terror. I respect the power of the dark side of a complex over my ego, over the I that knows who I am as separate from the complex. However, I know that if I hold the detached position of the witness, the position where a conscious part of me knows exactly what I am doing, I can safely work alone with a positive dream symbol. I relax my body through ten minutes of yogalike exercises and deep breathing. Lying on the floor in stillness, I recall a positive dream symbol. On the exhale of a breath, I let the symbol fall into my body and go wherever it wants to. While maintaining the objective position of witness, I experience how the energy of the symbol affects the sensations and emotions in my body. Frequently I observe one emotion transform into another and again into another and the symbol shifting with each energy change.

For example, in a dream I am given a magnificent orange tiger lily. When I work with the flower, it chooses to rest peacefully in my womb. It is delicate, radiating, beautiful, and exquisitely formed. Slowly the image rises up into my solar plexus where it transforms into swirls of powerful orange and red energy. Watching the image shift as I lie quietly on the floor, I gradually find my body moving with the changing image. It is following the energy released in my body by the symbol. My body turns around, my arms carve powerful shapes through space, my torso spins. My energy is radiant. And then the movement and swirls of color transform into a magnificent tiger that takes over my entire body. Instantly the wild swirls of energy are contained in stillness. I stand perfectly alert, poised, self-contained. I begin to walk as a tiger, slowly, with purpose, grace, power. I feel a living awareness in every muscle and bone in my body. For the first time in my life I feel connected to the power of the instincts living in my body.

When a symbol has a great deal to say, I tape our dialogues. Through listening to the tapes later, I start to recognize nuances in my voice that indicate what complex is speaking: the abandoned child, the negative animus, the negative mother, the positive feminine. Over the next years I actually hear my own voice release from the complexes that hold my muscles rigid. Medicine Woman in her practical, direct voice of positive feminine wisdom continues to teach me through active imagination, about a spirituality that is rooted in matter, in my own body.

SUMMER 1979
TEACHINGS OF MEDICINE WOMAN

During the long, warm days at the island, Medicine Woman is a powerful inner guide. One day while I am watching the energy of the waves, their rhythm transports me into an altered state of consciousness. A vision spontaneously unfolds before me.

A huge black snake with golden diamonds comes up out of the water. Angrily she whips her tongue out at me. Although she can bite me, I know that she won't kill me. I grab her behind the neck and our eyes meet. "Go back into the swamp where you belong." She wriggles her strong body and disappears.

Medicine Woman appears on the rocks beside me. "Surrender to the golden snake, to the part of you that is not you, but other; surrender to the part of you that is all-powerful and all-knowing. There lives the wisdom you are to speak of. If you perceive the snake as black, she will destroy you; if you perceive the snake as golden, she will create you. It is the same snake energy. Now, shift your perspective."

I see myself go down to the waters of the swamp. Medicine Woman hands me a flute. When I play it, the black snake comes out of the water and rears her head at me in anger. I cry out to her, "I am sorry, Snake, for what I have done to you. I do not know what your energy is but I must kill you."

I grab the black snake behind the neck and again our eyes meet. Her great strength almost knocks me over. Then her body goes limp; she totally surrenders to me. I drag her body to Medicine Woman. I see a magnificent golden snake coiled around Medicine Woman, its energy radiating blinding white light.

I return to ordinary consciousness and start to weep, not knowing if in joy or despair. As I walk back to the cottage my senses are alive. I am awed by the beauty of the birds singing, by the colors reflecting off the waters, by the wind touching my body. I become a point of consciousness between the sensations in my body and the beauty surrounding me, between personal individual life and impersonal collective life.

That night I have a dream of a spider who tells me that I am to find the berries of my feminine soul and that when I have lost everything I will be free. I hate spiders, but know I must have the courage to speak to this energy living in me.

"What do you want from me, Spider?" I ask in meditation.

"You."

"But why? You terrify me."

"I have to be aggressive because you keep trying to kill me. If you ignore me, you give me no energy and without your energy I am unlived life."

"But who are you?"

"You, a part of you that you can't see yet."

"What part?"

"Conscious, unconditional, feminine love. I won't kill you but you must listen to me. Enter the love for your own inner family. Love the Eve-child in you who lives without rules. Throw away all the books that tell you how to live. Live from your heart, forget conventions, open to the moment and express freely the energy of love. In the world of the heart there is no holding. Your wounded heart, your rejected feminine soul, will be healed if you express this energy."

"But what will people think if I live this way?"

"Start to live your own life. You were meant to love. Love is a way of seeing that pierces through illusion and sees the violence of life and accepts it. Love sees death staring in its eyes with the knowingness of pain, decay, and separation. Love accepts the darkness and the light equally."

"Spider, are you Medicine Woman?"

"Yes, I come in many different forms."

"How can I trust you, Medicine Woman, when you don't exist?"

"In your heart you know that I exist. You can now sense my energy around you. You have been conditioned to believe that the inner world is deceptive and dangerous. This perceived danger you project onto the outer world; the outer world is merely a screen for your inner state of being. People threaten you because your inner characters threaten you. The wilderness is full of dangerous animals because your inner wilderness is full of dangerous animals.

"Your mother was taught by her mother, and her mother was taught by her mother, that the feminine body contained the evil of mankind. You are terrified of your body and yet she touches you all the time; she is you. Your mother, severed from her own life-force, her own living flesh, could not teach you of your feminine instincts. Your ancestral mothers taught you that human flesh was ignorant matter. They slept in their flesh, forgetting the divine wisdom of nature.

"You have never contacted another human being, for you have been too afraid that someone will steal your body from you. Your body was stolen from you at birth; you do not know this. By repressing the consciousness in your body, your ancestors have denied your life. You beat your body through exercise, starve her, numb her feelings, so that you can prostitute her to get you what you need to survive in your society. You objectively watch the life-blood trickle out of you and feel nothing. You are bleeding to death by this wounding. Many women in your culture bleed from psychological wounds that they no longer feel.

"I will make you feel the wound; once felt, the wound will force you to take the necessary action to stop the pain. You have seen life through the eyes of a stone Witch; your culture gave you these eyes.

"Inside you, waiting, is a man whom your Eve-self calls forth. Someday they will meet each other. However, first you must find the Witch who holds both Eve and this man in bondage. Then, you must kill the Witch."

"How do I find the Witch?"

"She lives in the contracted muscles of your body and the collective values of your culture. Once you see her, you can dissolve her. When you have experienced the full terror of her energy, you will know how to deal with her. Throw hot water over her. It works in fairy tales."

"Damn you, Medicine Woman. How do I throw hot water over an illusion in my body's muscles? Sometimes you are full of it."

"No, you are the one who is full of it. Learn to shit, woman. Get the poison out of your body."

I am aware of Medicine Woman watching my pain. The grief and confusion on my face and in my body are obvious, yet she stands motionless and watches me. She doesn't try to ease the pain, nor does she try to take it away. Like the old crone that she is, she encourages me to stay with the feelings in my body.

"Sink into your body," whispers Medicine Woman. "Love the fear and the terror. Accept them; they are not your enemies. You are now a woman and the time has come for you to learn to love like a woman. This love accepts human frailty. It is the love that sees the oneness of all forms of life. It is the love that sees the divine light hiding in the fear of darkness. It is the love that heals, for it dissolves fear into forgiveness. Learn to love the fear, the rage, and the anger, and then you will experience love of the divine. Let go. Everything in life is born to die. The old must make way for the new."

"Are you telling me to let go of my perceptions of reality?"

"Yes. What you previously experienced as evil, you will experience as life unmanifesting; likewise, what you previously experienced as good, you will experience as life manifesting. Life manifesting and life unmanifesting are balanced polarities.

"You have not respected your intuitive voice. You have been taught that it was untrustworthy, for it knows without knowing why. However, intuitive knowing is the wisdom of your inner soul-self. Her mysteries are understood in silence. When you allow the mysteries to live consciously in you, you will know that your human soul and your human body are the expression of a divine spirit.

"Your intuitive voice has the seeds of your feminine soul. These seeds you must bury in the swamp of your body. Then your instinctual sexual energy living in your body will connect you to your spiritual life-force. Empowered by the mysteries of feminine wisdom, your flesh will become radiantly alive. Conscious of itself as spirit, your body will be transformed into bodysoul, where body and spirit are lived as one reality."

"How will my perception change? My understanding of feminine mysteries is my menstrual curse. Like every other woman I know, I hate it. I wish I had a man's body. I find nothing to celebrate about being in this woman's body."

"When you were a young girl, there was no wise old woman to teach you about the deep secrets sleeping in your womb. The mysteries were not revealed to you until you started to menstruate. But your society perceives menstruation as a curse, for it does not know the powers of the blood. If you had the courage to listen to your Eve-self, who celebrated at the first drop of blood, then your so-called curse could have been an initiation into your womanhood. Womanhood is the celebration of being.

"In school, you were taught to think with your head. Even your sex education was of the head and not of the heart. Your heart and your womb have been ripped out of you. Your sexual center is vacant. In your body, you know something terrible has happened to you; your menstrual cycle cries out to you in pain each month. Your feminine soul has been raped. In your heart and in your womb a great sin has occurred. You believe that your body is responsible for this raping; you feel guilty for allowing it to happen. But you are not the guilty party; you are the victim because you allowed yourself to be the victim. The intuitive voice that could have connected you to your mysteries was condemned as nonsense. If you are to fulfill your destiny, you must listen to the voices of intuition and allow them to initiate you into your womanhood. Your sexuality is not evil; it is your creative center of being. Your menstrual cycle is the door to feminine wisdom. Make friends with your blood. Listen to Eve."

"But Medicine Woman, if I start to talk like you, people will think that I am crazy. It isn't normal to talk to inner voices. At the university I studied that schizophrenics hear voices and that they believe that the voices are real. My society will drug me."

"You have been given a task to do. If you choose not to do it, the creative energy of Eve will turn against you and, like a cancer, eat you. You have a choice."

FALL 1979
BODY WISDOM

I had intended to go back to work part time, but my feet are so swollen that I can hardly walk. Some mornings my feet are so painful that I have to crawl around on my hands and feet. The doctor can find no reason for the swelling; needless to say, the drugs that he gave me don't work.

In meditation my feet call out to me, "Talk with me."

"Why should I?" I answer. I am beginning to think all this feminine unconscious stuff in my body that Medicine Woman spoke of is bullshit.

"Think what you like," continues the voice of my feet. "The fact remains that you are immobile and in great pain."

"Why do you keep doing this to me? I just get to the point where I can manage life and then you stop me."

"I am your body speaking. Your world of the head is very belligerent, arrogant, and know-it-all. The character traits you hate in others, especially in men, are the very qualities that you possess in your head. You thought that you could use the wisdom of Medicine Woman to make you appear a wise teacher. Her wisdom is not yours; it is of the divine. Since you are still ruled by the desire for personal power over life, you wanted to use her wisdom for revenge against the collective ideals that raped your Eve-self. To prevent you from abusing the wisdom, I have reduced you to an animal. You are to learn humility in the face of the divine. When you get into your body, when you become your body, when you accept your humble self, then your health will be returned to you."

"How can we work together?" I ask.

"When you understand that I am your life-force, your golden snake energy, your creative instinctual life, then you will know humility. I am your Christ-self, if you like the Christian terminology. I am the soul of the living body. Without matter, I am only energy; without soul, matter is dead. Your purpose is to be soul-infused matter radiating divine light.

"This lesson is difficult for you. If you choose to identify with the wisdom of the light, the wisdom will eventually burn you. If you become a container of the energy and let it flow through you, you will be alive in awareness of life itself."

"What can I do?"

"Die into your body. You must go into its darkness and release the light."

"How can I do that? My body is my enemy. I have to control her feelings."

"You are killing her and you don't know it. Unconsciously, you still hold the belief that your body, Eve's body, is the cause of the Fall of mankind into hell. You still believe snake energy is evil."

I start to feel the pain of my condemned and rejected body. "How can I save this thin, wounded animal?"

"Give her life," says Medicine Woman to me gently.

"I don't know if I can. I do not have the courage. I see the grief in my stone body and I haven't the love to endure the suffering."

I breathe deeply and say, "I love you, body." A rose appears in my heart. I physically gasp for air.

"Give birth to your feminine body. Receive the suffering as a gift of self-awareness."

"Why do you seem so heartless, Medicine Woman? Do you not know the pain I feel?"

"I am your soul. It is up to you as a human being living in the flesh to suffer this through. To incarnate into flesh is to suffer. I am the new myth of woman being written. I need your incarnated life. I need the birth of your feminine soul in order to bring my wisdom into conscious life. There could be so much love in the human body if only the flesh could live consciously its divine self. But your culture rejects the life of the flesh. Now let the rose in your heart transform the grief of your rejected flesh into love for its divinity."

I feel the pain in my body turn to terror.

"I am dissolving, Medicine Woman."

"Yes, there can be no you. You hold onto the safe patterns in your head, the known realities. Relax and fall apart."

"But what will hold me together?"

"I will. The food of the soul is subtle. Surrender, accept the blackness, accept yourself as you are."

All is silent. I sense breathing happening to my body; it flows effortlessly into my lungs and out again. I accept my wounding. I feel ancient, humbled, and very small. When I stand up there is no pain in my feet. They are healed. I feel as though I have disappeared and yet, whoever is still living in my body is a knowing entity.

WINTER 1980
WITCH PASSION[1]

I realize that the time has arrived for me to face the Witch in me. Although my outer life is free-flowing, my inner life is like an erupting volcano.

I am becoming conscious of my Witch destroying my family. I am grief-stricken as I see Witch unconsciously killing life around me and turning the children's spontaneity into stone.

When Witch rules my house, I am severed from the life of my body. I see children as make-work projects for me and hate the endless errands. I see men as foolish mouse-men. I become a cat with claws; I sit on men's laps and purr. I let the bastards stroke me, leer at me, for then I have sexual power over them.

I loathe other women when I look through Witch's eyes. My Witch judges them with venom as she smiles sweetly. No one knows such a demon shares my bodymind.

Witch has no joy, no love, and no laughter. Mechanically she runs the house hoping that others will see how much she has sacrificed. She is a survivor. No one can take advantage of her. She is powerful and alone, surrounded by people who are attracted to her for her talents. They do not know they are seduced by Witch. They do not see Witch's fear of losing her power, the power that holds her isolated in her stone tower.

When my Witch projects father onto my husband, I feel he owns my body and my Witch-self hates him for it. I then dream he is a Hitler who keeps my life's passions locked up. I am then an angry little girl, helpless in the concentration camp. Then Witch gets hold of my helplessness and says, "I am my own woman. I am nobody's property."

My little girl, living under Witch's skirt, knows that Daddy/men don't want strong women. They know women/mothers/Witches devour little boys, so I play little girl and let Witch devour my husband.

I witness how my little girl/Witch catches her man/Daddy/husband/Hitler in her web and she instantly becomes Mother and keeps him at her breast. Being a good girl/wife she creates a lovely home. And my man/husband/Daddy/Hitler becomes my son-lover, bewitched by Witch's magic spells. Both little girl/Witch and son-lover Daddy/husband suffocate in the marriage, while believing they are intoxicated with love.

My Witch is married to a Hitler who serves the collective values of the culture. Together they kill my inner life of Eve and prostitute my bodysoul to get in life whatever is needed for recognition and personal success.

Witch holds me captive in my body; she is the ruling power complex (yet always so loving and caring!) controlling my every move. Witch is the essence of a woman's unconscious identification with the instinctual power of the female body. Witch's motto is, "Make them want you, but never let them have you." Through unconscious manipulation of the sexual energy of my own body, I unconsciously dress her up and act in whatever manner necessary to get what I believe I need in order to be successful. I can starve my body if thin means power in beauty; I can get degrees if intelligence means power in education. I can use my various physical appearances to seduce men mentally (they, who are always in the power position) to give me what I need—a job, prestige, attention. With Witch in control I can be a man's "darling little princess," or his "bright little girl," or his "whore," or his "disembodied spiritual anima." In other words, I am an anima woman, reflecting whatever a man wants. Under the performing persona of my Good Mary dwells Witch who hates men. And "I," as conscious ego, am not there. No one is home and "i," as complexed ego, never knew it!

WINTER 1981
BODY CONSCIOUSNESS

Witch and Hitler own my body and prevent me from experiencing body wisdom. I am depressed and tired all the time. The only way I have any energy is to be driven by the power of Witch, but I can't let her drive me anymore.

"I want Witch out of my body," I cry out in meditation. "Get out of my head, my womb, my marriage bed."

"Who is this talking now?" I ask myself.

"I am me," answers another voice. "I am strong, passionate, and alive. I fight for my life. Witch and Hitler are killing me."

"If I remove them and let you live, what will you do?"

"Nothing, I don't want to do or be anything. If I die, I die, but I will live my death."

"Does death bring life?" I ask.

"Death brings a void, a nothingness that is pure. However, life is the void for me. I am the ache, the gnawing depression in your body. I am the illusion born at your birth. I am dying."

"Who will live?"

"Your body. She has not lived. You had to freeze her at birth and live in the head. No child could endure the rejection of your feminine flesh both in your family and your culture. With a frozen body, life happened in your head, in the world of ideas and fantasies. Since the body was perceived as an object, an animal to be tamed, controlled, and mistrusted, consciousness could not identify with the feelings in the body. In your culture the body is expected to function for the life the head wants, regardless of the abuse it receives. The body is the inert flesh where Eve and Satan dwell. To be alive and living joyously in the flesh is the sin. So the flesh dies. Look at the dead flesh in your society; it weeps like Mother Earth. Conscious woman of the loved flesh has not been born. This is her birth."

"Are you her?"

"Yes. I am the female child who remembers her soul song. I am connected to the snake, the instinctual life of your body. Now, release me from the spell of the Witch and the damnation of that Hitler you call God the Father."

I visualize vomiting out the blackness of Witch. My body crumbles onto the floor in grief. Medicine Woman appears on my inner screen. She is pointing to a huge cauldron.

"Jump," she demands.

Suddenly, flames leap out of the cauldron. I am terrified as I watch this vision. And then a calmness fills me. I can no longer live hating my flesh as a Witch. I choose death, knowing that death is better than perpetuating Witch's killing energy. I surrender myself to my body, and I accept whatever happens. I feel the arms of Medicine Woman lifting me up into the flames. Her arms are the energy of unconditional love, a love that I have never felt before. In the fire I watch my Witch's body burn to ashes but I feel no pain. I watch myself disintegrate. Then a new, brilliant green sprout emerges out of the ashes. It is attached to the golden snake. The snake rears its head out of the cauldron, and the fire stops. The new sprout opens into a pink rose. My whole being recognizes the pink rose as the symbolic essence of the instinctual bodysoul in my rose body.

"I have revealed to you ways in which to connect to your inner wisdom," whispers Medicine Woman, "but if you do not have the love for humanity in your heart, these tools are useless. Trust your body, trust your process, trust your old terrified flesh as she transforms into the body of the rose. The new rose body will enable you to listen to the symphony of the universe through the vibrations of her flesh."

AUTUMN 1981
CREATIVE ANIMUS

As I work through Witch and release my bodysoul from her devouring greed and her constant drive for perfection, success, and control, I dream of two hairy wild men chained in my basement. By discovering these two men I have committed a great sin against my society. I wake up from the dream terrified. When I release their energy through active imagination, one transforms into a huge black dog who, pointing his nose in the air, walks across water to follow the spirit of the winds.

"I am Black Dog," speaks the dream symbol to me in meditation. "I do not speak in words, but I penetrate your mind so that you under-   . stand my thoughts. I follow the scent carried on the winds. That is how I know the direction to go. My strong body is in tune with the spirit. I am fast, and although I am large, my body is light. I kill and I eat only what is necessary to sustain my life. I do not waste. You indulge because you have no understanding of what life of the flesh needs in order to sustain itself. You spend your life seeking pleasure and happiness and not in serving Life. You have no understanding of the purpose of life, for you hide the life in you. Secretly you eat yourself to fatness. There is no life behind indulgence; indulgence is death. The meaning of life comes from knowing the direction of the wind. Learn to listen to the winds. Be alert and knowing. This is not pleasure; it is being."

"Black Dog, stay with me, help me. Please."

"I stay with no one, only the wind. You must keep up with me. I am energy flowing. If you hesitate or doubt, I will be gone. I am movement into spiritual life."

The other wild man becomes a fish. He too speaks to me.

"I am the life of the body that is unconscious. I am the soul of the flesh, the Christ. It is time to redeem me. Take me out of your watery unconscious and bring me to the sunlight of your being."

I understand that Hitler (old patriarch) and the Witch keep these men in chains for they, like Eve, serve Life and not the self-serving values of our culture.

With the physical strength and spiritual courage of the dog and fish, I am able to release my bodysoul from the spell of Witch's drive for personal power. I begin to see that our culture, consumed with appearances—cosmetics, fashions, cars, gadgets—is a culture unconsciously held captive by the Witch, by the energy of power over our own bodies, over others' bodies, over the planet Earth. Just as Witch, unconscious in me, manipulates and rapes my bodysoul, Witch, unconscious in our culture, collectively rapes our sacred planet Earth. When we are caught in the complex of Witch, there is never enough: enough meaning in life; enough academic papers published; enough spiritual food; enough money. The complex demands to have more, just one more and that one more is never enough. Behind the aggression demanded by the Witch, which destroys the joy of simply being alive, lives a rage, a sense of impotent anger at the inability to change the hectic, driven, and unsatisfying life. When Witch dwells inside, a person is a paralyzed victim of life, driven compulsively to succeed. Our culture is dominated by "successful" victims of Witch.

While I am in meditation a Wise Old Man dressed in a monk's robe speaks to me: "I come to teach you of the feminine beauty that your culture does not understand. Vanity and appearance make up your concept of feminine beauty. However, if you allow my acceptance of Eve to penetrate your mind, you will know that the green snake of life flowing through a woman's body is feminine beauty. Send your roots into the earth where the bones of your dead parts nourish your new self-image. The secret of spiritual reality begins in the body."

I dream of a man who teaches me how to relate to my Eve's body. I am standing at the edge of a forest. An old shaman appears. He does not call forth my Witch, nor does he want my dutiful Good Girl. He calls forth Eve in me. At first Eve appears as a child, and the man relates to her as a loving father, accepting her roundness and grace. He does not direct sexual energy toward her; rather, he respectfully celebrates Eve's budding sexuality. His acceptance of her, as she is, allows her to grow into a woman who is capable of loving and respecting her feminine body that is round, fertile, and soft. The man gives Eve skills to express her own innate body wisdom. He does not tell her what she is to learn, but teaches her to trust her innate wisdom.

The relationship changes. Eve transforms into a woman who experiences her sexuality as jewels given to her by LIFE. She wears veils to cover her body, not in shame, but in order to contain and contemplate her inner creative mysteries. Her silent meditations upon her body's spiritual creative beauty calls forth a Warrior man. The father turns and leaves.

The Warrior is gentle, a man of few words, and like Eve, his presence speaks of strength. He listens to the winds; they point the way.

Then I am Eve. The Warrior hands me his spear. I know that the spear is my strength and my ability to walk into consciousness with my eyes open and focused. The spear then becomes my spine and it supports the roundness of my pelvic bowl.

I practice visualizing the Warrior's spear in my spine. After many careful observations I learn to sense the difference between being supported by the inner masculine as compared to being defeated before I even get started by the fierce negative animus. When the negative animus controls my body, my insecure and performing persona has to hold me up. It is the distinction among three postures: proper alignment with my positive masculine; a collapsed upper body with my negative masculine; an assumed rigid and inflated posture with my persona.

Later in a dream my Warrior speaks to me: "Carry this golden egg in your womb. It is your most valuable possession. Listen to Eve; she knows how to take care of her jewels."

When I visualize putting the imaginary egg into my womb, I am instantly given a vision.

Eve sits on the rocks of the island. From her vagina a water lily grows upwards through her spine and opens its face to the sun. The stem of this lily reaches into her womb, which is dark and secretive. Eve sits in quiet meditation.

Suddenly I recognize that I am Eve. I am filled with grief and joy. The grief comes from the knowledge that in my outer and inner life, I have never met a man nor a woman who has seen Eve as sacred flesh connected to her dark mysteries.

It takes all my concentration to focus on this reality, for I sense the collective energy trying to deny my vision of its existence. I know that the vision is the life-force bursting into conscious form through my flesh.

My joy comes from the knowing of the purity of the spirit when manifested in conscious flesh, my grief from the realization of the suffering women have had to endure because of the curse of the flesh of

Eve. Their bodies, like all human bodies, served Satan in hell, and their bodiless souls served the God in heaven. I know now that the reality of the life of my body gives conscious birth to the reality of the life of my soul.

SPRING 1982
REDEEMING EVE

Underneath the power of controlling Witch, I discover another layer of the wounded body of Eve. Though her sacred flesh has been falsely blamed for the evils of mankind and damned in hell for centuries, Eve, unlike raging angry Witch, feels no anger toward her masculine oppressors. Rather, her knowledge that the humanity she loves is at war with itself fills her with a profound grief that knows only forgiveness in love.

Eve loves, is love. Eve knows that sexual energy is a sacred power of a divine nature. She lives a morality of the body that honors the interconnectedness of all forms of life. Through her eyes and her unconditional love my self-image is transformed from self-loathing to self-acceptance and eventually to self-love.

"I am Eve," she says to me in meditation. "I am beautiful, for my body is created by divine energy. The sacred snake coils around my body and penetrates my being with wisdom. I know how to say 'Yes' to life. When negative energy comes toward me, I know how to say 'No.' I send the serpent out to bite when my flesh is treated without reverence. Disrespect for my flesh is a cancer to me. Women have cut off my arms so that when they prostitute my energy, I cannot tell them that they are destroying themselves.

"When you release me from your frozen body, I am joyful. I am laughter, pleasure, and movement. I am a flower with the morning dew drop, but I need the sunlight to reflect my beauty. I am creative, for I am creation; creation happens through me. I am fully aware that whatever comes through me is the expression of the Great Goddess who gives form to the formless. I know that I am a vessel for her creativity; that is why creativity brings meaning to me. And whatever is created through me must be returned to the Goddess. All creations die. That is the cycle. My menstrual cycle tells me that I am a circle, that life is a circle, that form transforms on the circle. Everything is a process; if the process is blocked, divine energy is denied its rightful expression. Each moment is an event, designed to transform into the next.

"I am the energy of the soul manifesting in matter. As Eve, I am to bring the soul into the conscious life of the body. Soul without matter is lifeless; soul in matter is the reincarnation of Christ. Christ is the living body infused with soul. But Western man has only identified with the light of the soul; he has put his doctrine into churches, and he has damned the flesh. I am the bread, the body, the earth. My earth energy is calling forth the light that I long to release.

"When you give me back my arms, my voice becomes yours. When you release me into life, I will know whom to call forth. There is nothing to fear. My arms know whom I wish to embrace in love. I call forth the divine spirit in man. I want to celebrate creating in flesh. If I am brought into your awareness, you will experience me as radiating light. I will give your life meaning. I will teach your body the sacred dance of life. Your body will become soft, mutable, and round; you will move like the wind in curves and spirals. Your womb will sing the song of creation. Your vagina will be filled with the nectar of creativity.

"It is women's responsibility to become conscious of my sacred energy. When women are connected to me, their bodies become sacred temples. They do not abuse their bodies sexually, nor do they starve and exercise their bodies for beauty and power. Instead they care for their bodies in love of divine matter, and they express their divinity without shame and without guilt. Their radiating love of matter protects them from rape and abuse.

"I am the joy of planet Earth that simultaneously expresses death and life. But I am dying, my voice is getting weaker. You fight for security against death, instead of celebrating the birth of each day. You want to use my energy to satisfy your greed, but since you are severed from your serpent you no longer know what your real needs are. Connect to the serpent; connect to life and stop killing me with your power.

"I am crying out for life; my trees want air they can breathe; my soil wants to be ploughed in love. When you connect to your divine natural self, you will connect to life. I am also the meaning in a man's life, but it is up to women to teach men that nature is divine. Women radiating my energy will teach men reverence for matter.

"If I am not given expression soon, I will die. My heart is breaking; the collective heart is breaking. When I die, life dies, for I am the life of this planet."

With Eve's energy alive in me I discover I no longer see bodily "imperfections" in myself or in others, only incredible woundings and emotional scars where the love of Eve has been denied life.

SUMMER 1982
BIRTH OF THE FEMININE BODY

Continued active imagination with Eve gives birth to another strong feminine dream symbol:

> I leave the city and go into the forest. There before me stands a deer. She is magnificent. Her eyes are soft and warm, but her spirit seems broken. We meet in silence. In my body I know that I have known her spirit for centuries.

In meditation I ask the spirit of the deer to come forth and teach me of her wisdom.

"I am the deer. I am soft, wise, and graceful. I have no voice to speak with so I cannot tell you of the feelings in my heart. You have no ears to hear me, for you are always too busy doing things to satisfy your needs in life. I am slaughtered by your frantic pace in life, the pace that keeps the terrified part of you from hearing what I am to say to you.

"I am without a voice, for I am seen only as meat, as ignorant flesh. Your Witch hates me and seeks to slaughter me. I do not hate. I take my death in silence in the hope that women will turn inwards and discover my energy. Violence does not stop violence; it perpetuates the same energy. Love transforms violence.

"My energy is the wisdom that knows that all things are in fact one, that the interrelatedness of all life is a delicate web of dependency, where all parts are equal and necessary. Each part of the planet is perfectly suited for its function in the web of life.

"Western people have claimed that some things are good and necessary and that some things are evil and unnecessary. Therefore, believing themselves to be a righteous people, they set out to destroy the evil in the world. But if they were to look into their hearts, they would discover that the things they claim are good are, in fact, those things that make them powerful over nature; the things they claim as unnecessary or evil are, in fact, the very things that could teach them that they are not all-powerful beings. They would see that there is a greater reality beyond themselves. Humans are but a link in the chain; however, they want to be the chain and to have life serve them. I am the wisdom that tells humanity that they are to serve Life. Women know of me intuitively, for their bodies produce life in the service of the life-force. Women cannot disconnect from me without losing their feminine souls. Women in your society are too busy to listen to what I have to say. When they do hear me, they drug themselves with addictions."

For a year I let the deer dance in my body until I can physically experience her strength in feelings of gentleness, love, beauty, and grace. Deer has no fear, therefore she needs no power. She is power for she transforms fear into love. Her fearless heart longs for love to stream consciously through matter.

WINTER 1983
INTEGRATION: REWEAVING THE TAPESTRY

Seven years after my son's death I have the following dream.

> I dream that my Warrior and I walk toward the stream of life. We follow the Deer. It is springtime, and the world is soft under my feet. New life bursts forth around us. I look into the eyes of the Deer, and I experience eternity, the vastness of the universe and the vastness of human suffering. Deer raises her head with great dignity. She walks toward the battlefield that is encircled by the stream of life. I experience no fear. Deer's radiance creates a stillness that resonates in shimmering white light. All the voices within me are silent, for they melt in the sunlight radiance of her presence. Deer says nothing. It is her loving being that transforms my fear. Quietly my Warrior and I sit in the meadow where the battle has occurred. We watch the setting sun. The bodies of my inner self lie slain about the field. I see that in this war I am the slaughtered and the slayer. I experience total defeat. I watch my old selves writhe in pain and die. The flesh on their bones rots away. I then stand up and collect the bones in my arms. They seem weightless, but

the grief held in them is overwhelming. My Warrior comes to me. "Take the bones to the Old Man," he says.

Deer then looks at me. She knows that I feel the full extent of the grief, and in that moment I feel her love, and love radiates from my bodysoul. I walk toward the field of the Old Man, the field that lies on the far side of the stream of life. As I walk, I hear only the voice of the One. My mind is focused. I know my destiny is to listen in absolute obedience to the One.

1983–1986
BODY AS INSTRUMENT

I continue to meditate daily and work with dream symbols. I meditate, too, on events in my outer life that are difficult. The key for me is consciousness—to know my complexes as both physical sensations resonating in my body and mental thoughts influencing my thinking and outer behavior. As my body "thaws out" from the ice of Witch, I become more and more alive with feelings. Not only can I physically experience negative resonances deadening to the spirit, but I can also receive positive ones enlivening to the spirit. Light and love begin to penetrate my body. I experience an infusion of joy, undifferentiated in my still somewhat disowned body.

Being conscious of the sensations in my body requires a disciplined vigilance that usually I am unable to maintain. However, when I do, I start to notice that I can differentiate between my own unconscious material and the unconscious material that others project onto me. For example, the other day I felt my thorax suddenly dance with life when a man projected his anima onto me. At first I thought I was really physically attracted to him, but after monitoring the feelings in my body, I realized they did not coincide with my real feelings about the man. I like him but I am not physically attracted to him. I recognize that my thorax was physically possessed by the energy of his projected positive anima. This state of physical enchantment was not mine; it was his unconscious material. I also recognize that when a woman projects onto me her inner, judging Witch lurking in her unconscious, I feel a coldness in my body, as if I were standing beside an ice statue.

As I continue to witness my bodysoul being played by my own unconscious material and the unconsciousness of others, I grow to understand that for me, consciousness has to be rooted in my body. I also know that my body is a sensitive instrument with a wisdom of its own yearning to be brought to consciousness through honoring it as a sacred instrument.

When I allow myself to experience my body as a sacred instrument capable of receiving and generating sensations, I start to notice that my attitude about my body becomes more impersonal. I am teaching myself to listen to the sensations resonating in my flesh and to differentiate between sensations originating without ("I read the body receiving sensations") and sensations originating from within ("I read the body generating sensations"). As I allow others to affect me, I have to hold more firmly onto my own center of awareness. I know that if I lose my bearings and forget my own center, I will become possessed, possessed by the unconscious emotional life of others. (I realize that for most of my life I have lived this tragic condition.)

To help me develop greater discipline in tuning to this delicate balance, I keep reminding myself that I am the listener to the sensations in the body and not the sensations themselves. I visualize the essence of my being as a laser beam of light piercing through the center of my body. It extends way above my head and deep into the Earth. I train myself to read my body as a computer printout: sounding board of thorax registering activity of fear; solar plexus resonating personal power directed to overtake body; feet registering danger: "Stay away from this projection"; sensations around head registering expansion into unknown condition of grace—safe, loving environment.

The challenge to live this way demands that I take full responsibility for my own unconscious pollution of the emotional environment around me. I witness that when my "sounding board thorax" registers Witch power from someone outside, my solar plexus from the inside automatically flips into one of two activities: if my Witch is stronger than the outer Witch, I become a fiercely powerful competitor, driven by personal power to win; if my Witch is weaker than the outer Witch, I become a helpless, weak victim, motivated to lose. (In losing, the victim can survive, making outer Witch appear all-powerful, all-wonderful, and a true savior.) I recognize that this automatic reaction has to be dealt with consciously, otherwise, as Witch or victim, I am perpetuating the collective power complex. When I am able to see this unconscious, automatic reaction I am given the choice to be neither Witch nor victim. Instead, I can attune to the laser beam that pierces through me. This allows me to choose to expand into the known condition of love. But oh, the vigilance that this requires.

I recognize that my consciousness is moving from my limited, known, personal, subjective position, centered in my body, to a more expansive, unknown, impersonal, objective position, centered outside my known body. Paradoxically, the experience of this expanding consciousness is a crystal clear point that is simultaneously everywhere. Though spacious, my consciousness is not hazy. On the contrary, it is focused with an alert clarity that, by comparison, makes normal everyday consciousness seem dull, sluggish, cluttered, judgmental, and usually possessed by a complex. In contrast, my expanded consciousness is experienced as a nonjudgmental state of being, a condition of love that delicately embraces polarities and weaves them into a celebrated whole.

Deep inside me I know that if enough people have the courage to move beyond their limited, known, personal position to allow more light and love to enter their bodysouls, our collective body, Earth, might have a better chance of surviving.

SPRING 1987

THE DREAM: DANCING THROUGH
THE OPEN MOMENT

In a dream I experience the source of Light as angelic beings surrounding a mountaintop. I am not sure if it is a dream or not; it is too real, but I remember waking up, so I must have been dreaming.

I am standing at the top of a great mountain where the space is crystal clear and still. I don't have a body; I am only a center of awareness that knows itself to be me. Without my body I feel a freedom to be more truly myself. I discover that with my bodiless self I can penetrate the stillness. The essence of the stillness is movement. It is direct, precise, fluid, playful like diamonds of light reflecting off open water. I discover that I understand this paradoxical movement of stillness because my bodiless self is living it, dancing it.

I became aware of the Light in the moment that I am the stillness in the living moment. I don't know how I know this, or how I even experience it. However, I know in the depths of my formless self that I am being penetrated by an all-encompassing condition of love that is intense Light.

The experience is a dance of great beauty that infuses my formlessness with a joy. I realize that this joyous dance is choreographed to lead me into the valley and out into the world that lies beyond. The sensation is one of being danced by a magnet that pulls me down into the world of form, human forms. To my amazement, the sensation of this pulling force is like one of falling into love. I know that I must leave the mountaintop, compelled by the dance of stillness.

Looking down from my elevated formless position I recognize my body.

"Why that's me!" I say.

"Yes," answers a formless masculine voice beside me.

"But why aren't you taking on a form?"

"It's not my time; not yet anyway. Sometime I may."

"Must I take on the form now?" I ask. "I mean, I want to be here, in this beautiful, clear, formless space. I want to live the dance of freedom, of clarity, of beauty, of Light."

"Then you will have to learn to be in both places at once."

"How?"

"That is why you are taking on a form. It is what you are to learn."

"But I don't want to be in a form anymore. I want to be with the Light, to live it, to dance it, to speak it."

"Light doesn't walk. It *is*. It is the dance. You walk because you now have a human form but you can learn to *be* the dance. And when you learn that, you will always be aware of the Light. It has been here forever and it will be here forever. Your task is to recognize it as you walk on the Earth with human legs, human thoughts, and human feelings."

I don't want to leave the mountain. But then, something happens. I am jolted into another perspective. I remember the Self who knows the Light of dancing motion living in me and that Self has a function to perform in the unfolding of humanity. I can't remember what the function is, but in the moment, I am so overwhelmed by the sensation of profound compassion for humanity that I forget my longing to remain formless. I live a commitment to alleviate the suffering within the human family, my family. I understand that I have to go into the valley of life. In total love I feel my formlessness surrender to the downward pull of the planet.

The sensation of the pulling force makes me feel confined and dense. The freedom of movement is gone but as long as I can remember mySelf as formless Light, I can endure the trapping into my body. I feel old and wise, though my body is youthful. I know that, if I live the love and commitment, I will remember mySelf and mySelf will know the truths. I also know that in this body I will be able to endure the personal suffering involved in being a human being even to the point of my physical death.

I enter my body. I have a vague memory of doing this many times before, sometimes in a man's body and sometimes in a woman's. It doesn't seem to matter; the body is a vehicle for moving about the earth where other bodies can relate to it. It is rather like getting a new car. The formless mySelf is the driver—the car just keeps being renewed. I walk down the mountain. I notice that my body is similar to other bodies of Light around me; all of us are sexless forms, like ancient monks dressed in long, hooded, earthen robes.

I become aware of the most beautiful music, which is a chorus of angels singing. I can't see the angels, nor can I hear the music with my ears. The music is radiating out through the monk's bodies. My body is living the music. It pours through me like radiant sunlight. The experience of this is of unbearable love—unbearable, that is, to the human form. It feels like a fire burning in the center of my cells.

I wake up from the dream with the words of Blake on my lips: "And we are put on earth a little space, / That we may learn to bear the beams of love."[2] Before this dream, I knew these words in my head; now I know them in the cells of my body. They live them. I understand the profound difference between the experience of knowing in the mind and living consciously in the body.

From my Jungian work I know that the Self of my dream, symbolized by the Light of profound love, is the God image within—the unfathomable mystery. I long to bring that mystery, that exquisite quality of being, into every aspect of my waking life—when making lunches for the kids to take to school, when teaching dance in the bowels of the university, when talking with students in my closet-office with no windows, when grocery shopping. Oh, if only I could feel the beauty of mySelf flowing into the movement of my life. That is the dance through the open moment.

In the dream experience, I knew the source of Light was other than my physical body. To call it God, however, doesn't seem right; for me the word God in the Judeo-Christian tradition carries negative connotations concerning the female body and the role of women in spiritual life. I choose, therefore, not to label it. I want to keep the living experience of this reality pure, uncluttered by familiar experiences and past associations.

SUMMER 1987
NELLIE

I am working in the kitchen, cleaning up the dinner dishes. As I stand at the sink, I notice a star. My body relaxes as I become absorbed by the clarity of its tiny light. I become aware that at some point my perspective shifts into a space where I can see Earth from the position of the star. As if I am the eye of the star, I ponder the beauty of Earth floating effortlessly through the darkness of eternity. In my heart I intuitively know that the essence of the planet, Earth, is love.

I weep. The contrast between the reality of what is happening to Earth and what my heart now knows fills me with grief. I cry for the humanity that I am; I cry for the suffering that humanity inflicts on itself, and I cry for Earth that cannot speak of its love for the humanity it supports.

A despair grows in me. I don't know what to do, what action to take. I can't even speak about what I know for I don't know how I know it. I just know deep in my heart that the humanity I love is destroying itself.

If anyone had told me that I would experience the living reality of the Light while doing housecleaning chores, I never would have believed them. But one morning while I am defrosting the fridge, the image of Earth floating through space imprints itself in my mind. Overwhelming grief consumes me. I feel as though a loving presence embraces my body with enormous grieving arms. And then the Light in my dream infuses my body.

"You are grieving for the state of humanity," an inner masculine voice says to me. "Your matter weeps."

The essence of this masculine voice has the same quality of love as the angelic voice in my dream. I call the voice Atman, and continue to dialogue with it.

When his words impress themselves in my consciousness I feel the unusual sensation of being thought in my body. It reminds me of the dance of stillness at the mountaintop. My physical body is still, and the words dance upon the stillness like rain upon a rooftop. All I have to do is listen to the dance and nothing else. Yet the precision and discipline of listening is physically exhausting.

"You see many people dreaming their lives," continues the voice.

"How do we wake up?" I ask the voice. "How can we ever emerge from the sleeping state we call life?"

"Detachment from all the traps that the collective mind offers you."

"Is detachment all that is needed?"

"Detachment without love kills life; detachment with love frees life from sleeping matter. Love is the essence of freedom."

"But how can I detach myself from the very forms I love?"

"Love more deeply. Your body already lives the detached love of freedom. Stop possessing her. Release her from the bondage of your personal desire to own her. Live totally in the body until you penetrate to the other side of matter. Celebrate the possibility of matter conscious of its function."

"How do I do that?"

"Go among the many who sleep. Their sleeping energy will be like a great magnet pulling you back into the dream state. Your task is to stay awake."

"How can I ever do that? I am one of them. I am a sleeping human being."

"Remember yourSelf. You cannot go back. Let yourSelf walk on the planet. She is here to serve humanity and not to serve you. YourSelf longs to live fully among humanity."

As I wipe the sticky fingerprints from around the handle of the fridge door, I become increasingly aware that the grief I feel in my solar plexus is being shifted gently into my heart by a wave of joy. I feel lighter, more expansive and I am enjoying cleaning the fridge! The task is no longer burdensome. The joy connects me to my feelings of gratitude for the food in the fridge and to the fridge that can house the wonderful food. I feel peaceful knowing that what is happening this morning as I clean is connecting me to mySelf.

Over the next months I continue to dialogue with Atman. One morning I discover that I have shifted to the position of Atman and am speaking to my small conscious self. I instantly recognize that it is possible to consciously shift my psychological position. In dreams the shift appears as staircases and elevators.

However, my demeaning animus voice continues to say to me, "You have little to offer others, for you fail by their standards. You cannot possibly live yourSelf in every moment." I then find myself looking up to the voice of Atman as though it lives in heaven. I want Atman to give me clearer direction, to tell me what to do. I also long to be with the Light Being and away from this ordinary world with its endless errands. I know that the longing is pulling me away from life and only a dream or a vision will give my life meaning. Finally I am given a dream:

> I am standing on a rocky point of land overlooking a large open space of water. I look down at my feet and I notice a beautiful rainbow bridge reaching out over the water to an isolated island. A magnificent white Dove appears before me and beckons me to climb on his back. The Dove flies me to the island.
>
> My dream ego asks, "How can I survive here on the barren rock without any food?"
>
> "Look at yourself. You have no form," says the Dove.
>
> "Why have you brought me here?"
>
> "When the form is clear of you, Mary, it will resonate with the space surrounding it; yet, it will know that it is not the space," replies the Dove.
>
> The Dove carries me gently on its back and returns me to the high cliff where I experience the rocks as being clear, open space yet very solid. The space within the rocks is made of the same formless space that I was made of.
>
> "You cannot enter the formless state in matter," an inner voice warns me, "until you live love for that form. If you enter before the love is there, it is a dangerous escape from life. When you love your personal identity, the formlessness and form will become one continuum. Then you will love humanity, and not the old spiritual image of a God in heaven. Rather than projecting onto a disembodied spirit yearning for union with a God, realize that all is within, if you can endure the opening to the Spirit."

I do not have the ego strength to relate to the power of this dream. The Holy Spirit (Dove) is providing me with a perspective on life from the formless position of the Self (barren rock island). The subtle body (rainbow bridge) consciously connects the ego to the Self. The ability to receive unconditional love and to participate with it (opening to the Spirit) is a prerequisite for living conscious divine love. As yet, however, I am incapable of receiving the profound gift of love experienced in the feeling-tone of the dream. Therefore, I am incapable of bringing divine love into my simple daily life.

In my waking hours I fluctuate between love and despair. When I remember the total experience of love shared with the Dove and the Light Being, I am infused with love for the humanity that I am part of. But when I read the newspaper in the morning, the events of the world—violence, pollution, war, sexual abuse, murder—only confirm in my mind that humanity is out to destroy the planet and eventually itself. A sense of despair and helplessness takes over.

I know I need to find a position where I can relate consciously to the wisdom in the unconscious without being inflated or depressed. In my daily meditations I ask repeatedly for help.

I am used to images floating across the inner screen of my mind when I meditate. This morning Nellie appears on the inner screen. She looks like an old bag lady, only it is instantly clear to me that Nellie has no baggage. She is a clear, free-spirited soul who lives a passionate instinct for life.

Nellie wears a moth-eaten cardigan that hangs lopsided over her green, flower-printed, cotton house dress. She is seven feet tall, with a light physical frame that reminds me of a crow about to take flight. Though tall and thin, she radiates light all around her so that my sense of her is that she is huge. Nellie is also grounded, firmly connected to the Earth by large, black oxford shoes and rolled-down ankle socks. Sometimes when I look into her soft gray-blue eyes, they seem at once to embrace the whole of me and all the space around me. Other times Nellie's eyes are points of brilliant golden light that pierce through my body like laser beams. I recognize Nellie as a seer whose compassionate wisdom will translate into a practical spirituality that I cannot question.

I know that Nellie is a more personal form of Atman. A dream tells me that she is both masculine and feminine. In this dream I see that she has a penis hanging down between her legs. I think I should tell her to keep her parts hidden, that it isn't nice for a lady to show her penis, but the direct intensity of Nellie's eyes tell me her penis is where it belongs and that she has no intentions of covering it up. The visual picture of this crone in my imagination enables me to relate to her practical wisdom with greater ease.

"Cultivate your weeds, dear," says Nellie to me in a forthright voice. "They are strong, determined parts of you waiting to be nourished."

"And what are my weeds, Nellie?"

"Your dreams and visions. You treat them like weeds. You try to pull them out of you. Give them your compost. Feed your dreams. Give them life. For you there can be no division between what you know in dreams and your waking life. For you, life is reversed. Your reality is the dream state."

As Nellie speaks, I experience a subtle shift in my consciousness. The space about me seems to be filled with meaningful symbols, as in a dream. As I listen to Nellie in this dreamlike state, her words make perfect sense to me.

"And don't forget to treat the birds with great respect. They connect you to the sky. It is important to remain connected. That is what is troubling you, dear. You have lost your connection."

"Is that why I am so depressed, Nellie?"

"You are stuck in the position of a child who is waiting to be told what to do," she answers firmly. "You are useless to yourself and to humanity in this position. Be the herSelf of your dreams and then you will know what to do."

"But how can I be that?"

"Through trusting, listening, and waiting. Be open, receptive, and alert in your body. Relax so deeply that your body opens and becomes porous, mutable, and sensitive to the impressions of the space around you. When you are ready, a radiance that warms like the sun will shine through the porousness. In the stillness of your body, the life of herSelf will drop upon the flesh enabling Her to ripple throughout you. For this to happen, though, your bodysoul must be clear. This clearness of bodysoul is a state of profound love.

"Do not look up for guidance. Your work has nothing to do with heaven and the concept of a God living there. The world is where you are to work and humanity is your teacher. You must find your own way, dear, your own path. Spirituality is not in the space above the Earth; spirituality is the Earth—is your flesh."

I love Nellie's company. Though she is ruthlessly critical, she loves me, and I can feel her love in my body.

I never question Nellie's reality. Something in me knows that Nellie's perspective is simply different from the reality of others. Nellie is an old mystic and, unlike most of humanity, she has awakened from the dreamlike state. Nellie remembers herSelf.

The integration of my positive masculine with my positive feminine ego has allowed for this transition from Medicine Woman to Nellie.

Medicine Woman is a great teacher of Goddess wisdom. Over the years she has instilled in me the ability to receive light and love into the very depths of my body. She has given me the insight that love in matter is the natural condition of being human.

Nellie on the other hand demands immediate action into life. She instills in me the knowledge that everything I am given is given to humanity and not to me personally. She demands that there be no identification with the giving, absolutely no possessiveness of the gifts. Love for Nellie is an action—an immediate action in life whenever it is required, regardless of the personal sacrifice.

FALL 1987
LOVE

"Love humanity as your own family," keeps echoing through my head. When I meditate upon the words an inner voice tells me that my family is to be lived as the microcosm of the human family.

Sometimes, when the confusing words of my inner voice repeat themselves without making sense to me, Nellie will appear in meditation.

"The heart belongs to the universe, dear," says Nellie in her usual stern, direct voice. "It is not yours to keep. It is designed to function as a small receiving unit for the very large and all-encompassing current of deep love. If your heart serves personal love and desire, your heart will break. You are designed this way. Disease will creep into it, for how can a heart function in a way it is not designed to? Work with the function of your heart. Love humanity as you would your own children."

"I cannot love humanity as I love my own children, Nellie," I snap. "You know that I can hardly endure their pains and sufferings. How can I ever endure the suffering of humanity? It will kill me."

"Shift into space," says Nellie very matter-of-factly.

"What space, Nellie?"

I breathe deeply and I feel the chair supporting me. I witness my heartbeat becoming slower and slower. I fall into a deep state of relaxation where there is no fear, only a silence until the spaces between my heartbeats are like moments suspended in timelessness.

"I love you," whispers Nellie in the space between my heartbeats.

"I love you, too," I whisper silently to myself.

Nellie remains my vigilant and silent witness. I hear my heart pulse and with each pulse I experience vibrations moving into the space around me. The vibrations expand into the space of my home. The expansion takes leaps into the space until the vibrations are a web about the Earth. I feel no physical heart in this moment; I am a sounding vibration that embraces all of human suffering in forgiveness.

I feel a release. All my life I have lived with a vague feeling of never belonging to my family, to my school, to my profession. Now I belong. I belong to the family of humankind and our shared home is planet Earth.

"Now you know," whispers Nellie. "Just live it."

I feel a great love for Nellie whose presence is always with me now. And though she is a strict teacher, her comments are given with a love that speaks to my essence—not my persona but my living core. Sometimes my persona experiences Nellie's words as harsh but my core always experiences her words as profound love.

I start to experience myself in a different way. I know I am simply a sample of a human condition. Although my experience of life is impersonal and detached, the depth of the experience is personally very deep and very moving. When I kiss the children goodnight, I am "woman kissing child." The depth of my love for the condition of mother and child often brings tears to my eyes. When I cook I am "woman providing for family." Throughout the day I have glimpses of myself as "woman teaching," "woman feeling impatient at grocery store lineup," "woman forgetting her deep feelings and thinking she is angry."

I have started to listen to the music of Chopin again. How I used to love to dance to his music! Though I can no longer dance as I once did, my bodysoul longs to be danced by the beauty of classical music. While relaxing my muscles as deeply as possible, I sit with my spine balancing in alignment and my eyes softly focusing outwards. I listen to Chopin's "Nocturnes" with every cell of my body. I am beginning to feel the beauty of the music dancing in my cells. Where once darkness and self-hatred lived, now light and beauty dance. Conscious that self-hatred can easily flip into inflation, I try to maintain the detached position: "Woman living love."

"Allow the beauty of your soul to sing your cells," suggests Nellie one morning.

I relax into her words. I start to feel an inner joy growing inside me. I know that it is mySelf living consciously within. I feel that I have a song of love to sing to humanity, not as a preacher might, but as a flower . . . in silence. I feel that the perfume of mySelf longs to be recognized through human eyes, longs to be recognized as LOVE manifesting.

I enter a state of profound reverence for life. I experience a need to sit quietly and to listen to my heart in silent contemplation. This form of contemplation is new to me, and yet, I seem to know all about it. In the morning, after I put the dirty clothes into the washing machine, get the kids off to school, and walk Gandolf, my large golden retriever, I have an hour before I have to teach. I know I ought to prepare for my lesson, but instead I sit on the couch in peaceful silence.

"Be like a Rose," says Nellie, "and in the silence of the space about you let the perfume of your Being fill the space. Become a giver of life, not a receiver, but know that what you give is not yours to give. It is Love's longing to recognize itself through human eyes. Go into your world and let Love recognize itself in others. Be of service to Love. Take responsibility for the Love that expresses itself through your body.

"The Love of the Rose is not selective," continues Nellie. "The Rose does not choose who is worthy of smelling its fragrance; it *is* fragrance. Like the Love of a Master, this Love is lived for all of humanity.

"This Love is of a larger order. It has no rage, no personal drive for power, no direction, nothing to gain and nothing to lose. It *is*. Your function is to live it as it *is*—no personal desires attached."

The words jolt me. I look at my watch; it is late and I have to leave for work. In the car I ask myself if I can live love as the perfume of a rose, without conditions. I try.

I need some written materials to be duplicated by a secretary before class. Because I am late, the secretary will have to stop what she is doing in order to accommodate my request. I witness myself as I reflect upon my usual tactic of saying nice things to the secretaries. Suddenly I see how manipulating the action is. This is not the Love of the Rose; it is an unconscious action to get out of others what I need of them. I realize that when I have acted this way, I have seen myself as a kind person. I see, too, how I have been manipulated by others' kindness toward me.

The shock of seeing myself this way makes me turn around. I cannot go into the office and ask anything of anyone. I realize that during most of my life I have seen myself one way, but from this new perspective there is a whole other story to tell. I understand what it means to face the negative side of my shadow. Seeing my manipulating, dark, and unfeeling self, makes me feel numb, paralyzed. How can I possibly face a class in this condition?

I continue walking down the hall. My feet are taking me to class. In my heart Nellie whispers, "Trust the deep, deep calling within you. It does exist. Bring it to consciousness."

When I face the class I am thankful for my years of teaching experience. I know enough to rely on material I have taught before. I open my mouth and the words fall out. I feel myself to be in total concentration on the moment, waiting for the next idea to impress itself in my mind. It is my task to give it a form, a shape that will enable the students to hear it.

At the end of the class the students seem excited. They have enjoyed themselves. A student comes to me and asks me to review one of the exercises. I hear myself ask, "What exercise? I don't recognize what you are talking about."

The student goes through the sequence; I start to laugh. "Did I teach that? What a wonderful sequence. Let's go through it again. I want to learn it."

We are delighted by the experience. My negative animus tells me that to admit to a student that I don't know what I taught is very poor methodology. However, I can see that the student is teaching me with great enthusiasm. In fact, the student is learning more about the process than I ever knew. The student is the teacher. I don't feel threatened; I don't feel stupid. Instead I feel an inner excitement that reflects in my learning with her.

I know I cannot will myself to teach this way. It has come to me as a gift. I remember talking with an old respected colleague. He told me that in his youth he knew a great deal, but the more he read, the less he knew, until he realized he knew nothing at all. Is this to be my path? How can I remain at a university where I am to be a knowledgeable scholar in my field?

As I drive home, Nellie speaks, "The great teachers do their real teaching in silence, dear. They *live* the lesson they are teaching and like the students are taught by the event of the moment. There are two actions in teaching. There is the lesson, the content and the facts, and there is another thing that dynamizes the action in the class. That other thing is love. The great teachers participate with the action of love that dynamizes the event while demonstrating the content. Learn to focus on the love until the content and the love become one continuous action.

"Think with your body," continues Nellie. "There is an intelligence in there that is clear, focused, and impersonal. It is direct, orderly, and multidimensional. It knows what goes on in the spaces between the visible action."

A joyous laughter bubbles out of me. I feel a deep love for all the years I have trained my rational mind, only to discover that deep inside my heart there is another form of intelligence that knows more about life and living. That I have spent all those years in formal education seeking the answers outside myself is a wonderful paradox.

Love is no longer an emotion for me; it is a known impulse creating my conscious cells moment by moment. My discipline is to remain aware of this impulse in my daily life. When I am able to focus on this impulse, I fall into the loving arms of matter. The experiential truth of this felt love creating my cells is a dance—it is the dance of Light.

WINTER 1988
REMEMBERING THE POSITION

Insight after insight falls into my head. I don't question where the insights come from or even if they can be proven as true. My cells know. I know when Nellie is alive in me. Her playful attitude fills me with unknown possibilities that dance my known loved body with free-flowing energy. The world invites me to participate fully with it. When I live as if my experiential truth of Nellie is a form of wisdom, the quality of my daily life changes radically.

And my cells know when Witch rules me. Her drive to perfect every last detail prepares me for a life filled with unknown pitfalls. Only endless work can prepare me for the battles I will have to face. It is important that my professional peers see how hard I am working. My muscles tense up, my breathing becomes short, my family chores become a curse and my head usually aches. I rigidly try to defend myself in a hostile angry world. Constantly judged by ruthless author-ities demanding more and more of me, I arm myself with concrete knowable facts to justify my presence.

Nellie knows how to dissolve Witch. When I get possessed, she lovingly calls me a neurotic, driven lady. She laughs and demands that I take a look at myself.

"What do you value, dear, your love for humanity or your drive for personal power?" When Nellie calls me dear, her voice is always stern. I feel as though she is pointing her finger at me and insisting I take in every word she speaks.

As soon as I see my lovable, crazy, driven self, I laugh. Witch disappears, along with my headache.

I know that I cannot kill my Witch self. She has the connection to the power of the life-force: she is my strength, my ability to act, my courage to speak. Witch feeds this power into herself, into her personal little life. Nellie, on the other hand, has no desire to feed her life with this power. In Nellie, there is no little demanding self who requires personal power. Surrendered in love, Nellie is empowered by the life-force to serve Life. Though Witch and Nellie may use the same words, even the same actions, their attitudes are totally different. Witch unconsciously kills essence to serve persona; Nellie consciously embraces essence to serve Life. I must be mindful of my actions, my motives, my attitudes, and my words. When I see the daily discipline and hard work required to remain conscious of the distinction between Nellie and Witch, I question why I ever started this journey in the first place. And I know there is no turning back.

Continued active imagination with Nellie helps me to focus on my inner life. I know I am not channeling her words from some outside entity; no, her words live in the open spaces of my body. Sitting each morning in my living room, relaxing my body and focusing my mind, I faithfully write down our dialogues. I feel fully alert. My concentration involves every cell of my body. As I write our shared words in my journal, they become living sounds carrying the deep meaning of my inner known experiences. The words give a form to the experiences. Others can then share in their beauty and wisdom.

"Never become too holy or too spiritual, dear," advises Nellie. "Let the spirit align itself within you. Become what humanity can be. Nothing more and nothing less. There is no such thing as spiritual development or Higher Self or Greater Self or Lower Self. There is nothing to find, nowhere to go, nothing to reach up to. There is, however, LIFE, human life capable of Being itSelf. And that is already present in every moment of every day.

"By relaxing very deeply and allowing your body to reach a point of stillness, the delicate strings of your Self will be found dancing with the deep current of love that is the Earth. This love is the dance of the still point in the open moment.

"When you allow herSelf to infuse your bodysoul, you will discover qualities dancing within you that are exquisitely beautiful. If you allow these qualities to function consciously in the service of life, you will be the Self of the dream. Your Self is love in action.

"But, dear, only if you have the courage to be ruthlessly honest with yourself will the veils of illusion be removed, allowing you to meet the Self of your dreams. Then, like the wind harp, sounds of the Self will sing across the open space of life around you.

"Aligning yourself with the Self is a shift from your personal system lived in your body to an impersonal system lived in the space of formlessness. It is the temporal self participating with the immortal Self. By surrendering yourself to love, you participate in the creation of your life, moment by moment. Never assume, though, that surrendering is a passive letting go; that is a dangerous illusion that many people fall into. No, dear, true surrender is a disciplined act of love requiring many personal sacrifices.

"You must cut away parts of your little self that create the illusion that you are a separate and unique individual. After years of cutting away, which in your ignorance you will experience as pain and suffering, you may eventually be created into an exquisitely functional instrument capable of expressing the Self."

"It sounds so awful, Nellie. Why would anyone choose this road?"

"It is chosen for you, dear," continues Nellie, as she smiles knowingly. "Though it may seem ruthless when the sword of awareness cuts through your very essence, it is an act of love. When you know that, the cutting edge of self-awareness is accompanied by forgiveness and profound love.

"Spirituality can only be lived within a body that is aware of its human dimension, both positive and negative. If the awareness is not there, spirituality becomes a self-centered path of self-aggrandizement."

"How will I know the difference between self-aggrandizement and true spirituality?"

"Be patient and learn to recognize the carving of the sword as active love. You will make delicate adjustments over many years until the essence of your physical body and the essence of yourSelf harmonize into a continuous movement that flows into life."

"There seem to be so many roads to illusion, Nellie. How can I know if I am sleeping or if I am actively working?"

"Learn to be aware of the Self and not just your physical self housing your demanding little persona. The Self is never seen; it is a living presence that is felt in the body. The Self does not create from the limited personal point of view; rather the Self creates out of the substance that serves the whole of life. It brings into tangible form an action that is already present in the implicit order of life. What you know as yourself will eventually become the tangible form of the Self.

"To think, dear, that you are here in the first place is a great illusion. You are simply the tangible result of a continuous action, being created every moment. You are a tiny event happening in the eternal now."

"And what does my body have to do with all this, Nellie?"

"Many people on the spiritual path believe that the physical body is less sacred than the spirit of the Self. Your body is crucial for your work on the planet. Honor her; treat her with the greatest respect and love. She is your responsibility. Great music requires a finely tuned instrument. Spirituality requires a finely tuned body and mind capable of aligning itself with the Self. The ancient texts refer to spiritual disciplines. There is much wisdom in them. However, do not let discipline be your focus; rather, let love be your focus."

"If the process is all about love, Nellie, why is it so painful?"

"I'll tell you a secret, dear," says Nellie full of laughter. "Someday when you are fully dead, it won't be painful anymore. You see, the Self can only live its function in the world when the form is clear of personal desires, motives or ideas—that means, Mary is dead. The wind harp sings in the open fields because it has no idea how to sing. It simply allows itself to be aligned with the direction of the wind. Clear yourself. Die to your Self. That is how you are to be of functional service. Allow the Self to live in the space of your clarity."

"It is all so filled with paradoxes, Nellie. What would I ever do without you to help me?"

Again Nellie laughs. "You take yourself too seriously, dear, and you don't take your Self seriously enough. Humans are silly, lovable fools."

I notice that I experience things differently. I feel a little outside myself watching me live. The place where I feel my center of consciousness to be is a condition of complete compassion. The compassion allows me to witness life objectively, yet lovingly.

What I find surprising is the objectivity. I perceive all aspects of life, equally and without possessiveness. I experience my laughter, tears, and frustrations as being human conditions that I physically express but that I, as compassion, simply am aware of. There is no sense of valuing one action more than another. Cleaning the toilet bowl is no less important than giving a workshop; playing fish with the kids is no less important than preparing students for a performance; grocery shopping is no less important than choreographing a dance. There is no judgment. It is. It happens. But there is love embracing everything. The love, however, is in the space, the space where I know my awareness has shifted to.

A dream helps me understand this new space:

> I am spring-cleaning my bedroom clothes closet. I appear to have put all my old clothes and shoes in large, green garbage bags but left the bags in the back of the closet. Today I am taking all the bags out. It surprises me how big the closet now is. I notice a staircase at the very back corner. To my delight it leads to an undiscovered tower room made of wood. I have always known that this room existed but I could never find the opening to it. With great joy I climb the stairs. The room is magnificent. It is an open square space with huge windows on all four sides. The sunlight streams in the curtainless windows. Nothing clutters the natural hardwood floors. It is the space I have always longed for, the space I can go to whenever I want.

The symbol of spring-cleaning means that a new possibility is being born. The old clothes (persona) and old shoes (standpoint in life) were put in garbage bags (made conscious but held on to). Now I am throwing the bags out (letting go of old patterns of behavior) and creating a new psychological space. The staircase (ego-Self axis) leads to a square room with wooden floors (place of feminine wholeness). Here sunlight (consciousness) streams through the windows (outlook). The floor (new place to stand) is uncluttered.

The next day I take the kids to the shopping mall. I am surprised to find out how much fun it is. Normally, I hate shopping; it is just one more errand I have to do. This time is different. I see the kids need clothes. I don't ask any questions; I just take action. Shopping is easy. I feel detached, yet deeply connected to everyone I meet in the mall. I feel so much a part of the action. I feel a wonderful celebration deep inside my body when I recognize, for the first time, that I am a living part of humanity. The diversity within the forms and the actions astound me—that one humanity can express itself with such beautiful variety.

I feel like a kid at Disney World. The music of the mall, which usually annoys me, is part of the whole event. Being simultaneously detached from it, yet deeply connected within the space of the activity, frees me from the usual dislike I feel for malls. To my amazement, I feel only loving compassion for whatever is there.

Sometimes life for me is like watching a series of events that I am free to enter into or remain outside of. When I see that a particular action is necessary, I don't question the why or the how. I enter the action like a character assigned a role, undertake its function, and then leave. It is impersonal, playful, and always compassionate. I don't attach as much baggage to my work. In fact, I often don't even remember what I do or say. It happens in love.

I recognize that I feel a tremendous respect for what happens. I am starting to be sensitive to what people say. I sometimes recognize that words of wisdom are spoken by individuals whom, before, I would dismiss. I start to hear the resonance in voices, in the pauses between the words. The words are like notes of music—some are harmonious, others harsh. The sounds of the words resonate in my body enabling me to feel like the person talking. But from the new psychological position, which is always experienced as participating with, I embrace situations with compassion and love.

I know that I must be very careful and watch for both inflation and depression. When Nellie encourages me to approach life with open love, I witness how my small "i" self starts to inflate. Then my negative animus tells little "i" self that she is unworthy of living such love in the world. Above all, I have to be mindful of Witch, who cleverly manipulates Nellie's wisdom to show the world what a wise lady she can be. Sometimes, I feel too paralyzed to act: "Who is ruling me anyway? How can I tell it isn't Witch 'lovingly' serving humanity through one of her causes to save the planet? Am I really worthy of such love? Who am I anyway? Am I a crazy lady inflated with voices? How do I ever continue walking this tightrope over the abyss?"

"How do I do it, Nellie?" I ask.

"Remember yourSelf," answers Nellie firmly. "Then connect."

"But I can't," answers a tiny, defeated child in me. "She is too beautiful, too loving for me to contain. Her love is like a deep urge that compels her to live love on the planet. I can't do that. I'm not strong enough."

"There is work to be done. Do it," demands Nellie.

"But I just said I can't live mySelf, Nellie!"

I feel something inside me let go. My body softens. I start to cry.

"But I am mySelf aren't I, Nellie? How can I not be what I already am? I focus on the little voices within me, on my personal limitations. What prevents me from focusing on what I *am*?"

As I ask the questions I feel a knot developing in my solar plexus. I am very frightened. What if I did live mySelf? Could I ever give myself permission to take the responsibility of that position? It is one thing to talk to Nellie alone in my living room; it is another thing to go out into the world and live it.

Nellie speaks to my heart. "The key, dear, is to choose consciously to have no desirous, aspiring little Mary. You are the home, the container. If you forget, you will be burned in the fire, the fire of madness. If you can remember, yourSelf will be expressed consciously through you. When yourSelf lives, you will support the reality of the Self in others. Then they too can remember themSelves. Then they too can see the beauty that they are. That is how you are to teach; surrender so that yourSelf can take up residence. Hold the position in consciousness, without any possessiveness of that position."

As I reflect on her words I realize that the beauty I see in old Nellie is the beauty of herSelf. Nellie is out of her limited personal mind set, enabling herSelf to take up residence. Nellie never aspires to be anything other than who she is. When needed, she is there to help. She never forces her ideas or way of life onto anyone.

What I love in Nellie is her ability to embrace my wholeness rather than the pale existence reflected in my personal self. Nellie accepts in love the fullness of my humanness. She sees the positive and the negative without praise and without judgment. She simply sees and accepts what is.

"Space is the home of your Self-consciousness, dear. It is from this position that you love humanity, including yourself. It is from this position that you can care for yourself as you care for your children. It is from this position that you are to live in the world.

"To do so, though, requires that you die to the personal life of Mary.

This death will come to you when you are able to live Love consciously. It cannot be undertaken in fear, for it embraces life with a burning passion for living Love. This death will enable you to live what you always have been, before birth, before your many births, and including the spaces between your births."

"But Nellie, how do I get my work done from this vast position of love? I have to clean the house, feed the family, walk the dog, and teach my classes. How can I possibly do it all?"

"It's just like having a full bladder and needing to pee, dear. When you live the fullness of love in the vastness of space, you will have to pour it into your life. Fullness of bladder, you pee; fullness of love, you work in the world. There is no difference. Hold the position and out of the fullness of your Self, love will pour into life."

"OK, Nellie, so I pour love into the world. What if the world doesn't want my love?"

"Never assume it is your love. Never assume you are doing the pouring," answers Nellie forcefully. "You have nothing to do with this action of love. It is in the atmosphere creating the planet. All you do is smell it. Be like a dog smelling the scent on a trail. The scent is already there. You just sniff it and follow where it leads you. Smelling the scent is not a psychic power; it is the natural way for you to be in the world. It is breathing the perfume that is already there."

"But when I live this love, Nellie, I begin to sense things in the spaces around people. It's like the way you look at me, as though you have X-ray eyes."

"So what?"

"Well, what am I to do?"

"Ask your heart," replies Nellie ever so sternly, as if it is the most obvious thing to do. "What do you think this love is about, dear? Being kind? Being a good person? Being nice and pleasant? You are a fool to think this love is soft, woman. When you live this love you will be as ruthless with others as I am with you. When I see you with my X-ray eyes, you are released into your essence. Do you want essence or illusion?"

I know that Nellie's love forces me to face the negative side of my own shadow. I often feel like a puppy with its nose being rubbed in its own shit. Nellie forcefully tells me to see my nasty secrets, my horrid, greedy, power-hungry, terrified little self. Yet I never feel guilty or unloved. It is only when I face these aspects of myself straight on that I can choose not to let them into life. When I don't face them, these despicable qualities unconsciously rule me. I become self-serving and believe that I am life-serving. And I project my shadow out into the world, polluting it with my own darkness.

"But no one will like me if I speak of essence, Nellie. People want the illusion of power over life. People want to think they are kind and good. No one wants to face their shadow."

"You are here to work, my dear. The dark side of humanity is killing the planet, is killing you. If you breathe the perfume of the atmosphere as you speak, your words will be the loving edge of the sword cutting away illusion. If you lose the awareness of the perfume of love, your words will kill all life around you. This is serious work. You must be very mindful of your Witch."

"I don't find this love very beautiful, Nellie."

"Shift into space, dear. When you breathe this love there is no fear and therefore there is no need for personal power. When you live the contracted position of your personal self, you experience this love as demanding personal sacrifices; when you live the expanded position of your Self, you experience this love as a compassionate action of your life-force in service of Life. You then live empowerment."

"I don't know if I want to live this love, this empowerment, Nellie. It doesn't seem like much fun to me."

"Stop being a child feeling sorry for herself. Take responsibility for what you are here to do."

"So I am right in feeling that this love is a terrifying journey into freedom?"

"Think whatever you like, my dear," says Nellie in exasperation. And then she laughs and shakes her head. "You are making it very difficult for yourself, dear. Accept what is and get to work. Find the scent. Follow the path of Love."

I begin to see that this love is a ruthlessness of the heart that profoundly respects Life as it is. It allows for the separation of death, which in turn creates space for new life. This is the love of my compost pile in the backyard. It is the mystery that takes the rot of life and transforms it into food for the rose. Only roses with good composting soil create perfume in their blossoms. I don't want to see the rot, neither does anyone else. However, if I cannot respect the function of the rot, I cannot respect the function of the perfume of the rose. In this love, life and death are turning points in the process of living.

Life is now a classroom for me. Like a child I explore this new reality of love, knowing deeply that it has always been there for anyone to participate with.

SPRING 1988
DISSOLVING

Spring is a celebration for me. When I walk in the park each morning with Gandolf, I am the buds on the maple trees swelling with life, swelling with the need to open into their beautiful selves. When Gandolf delights in his joyous, gallumping, instinctive energy, I am his energy. When I stand next to a daffodil blooming, I am the yellow bloom. And when I am with people, my experience is that they are myself speaking—one aspect of the whole expressing itself to another aspect of the whole.

This position doesn't frighten me, though I know that if I tried to express it to others they might say that my ego boundaries have dissolved and that I am heading for schizophrenia. This is not my experience at all. I know I am a consciousness operating from a different position. From this position, I experience my life as a tiny expression of something so incredibly vast.

From this shifted position I recognize the need to watch myself with detached ruthlessness. I see there is an aspect of me that is very frightened and insecure, a part of me that is desperate to be seen and recognized as being someone important. I see this part of me as a human condition lived by many other people. The insecurity is like a seed that grows in fear of being found out. The fear attracts power to it, personal Witch power to hide the fear. The power takes on different forms in different individuals. For some it is money or academic degrees. For others it is the accumulation of fat over their frightened skeletons or a strong musculature to literally hold them up in life. And for others the seed of fear disguises itself in spiritual awareness that falsely promises enlightenment—a position of great power.

I see this because I am a human being who lives it whenever I forget the new position. I see many things in myself. When I recognize the conditions living in me, I immediately am given the eyes to see the same seeds living in others. I watch how parts of me cause me to suffer, to cry, to laugh. I see how I victimize myself, sabotage myself, frighten myself, anger myself. And I see all this through the eyes of compassion.

I watch how a part of me will not let go of the image of myself as a separate and unique individual. That part of me is afraid I will die. It lives in a state of unconscious inertia, afraid to move out of its known and safe position in reality. The inertia is a part of me that lives in fear and yet longs to live the freedom and the beauty of mySelf. It sees mySelf as a Higher Self, separate from my body. I often feel insecure, isolated, and separate from the rest of humanity. In this position I feel tense or depressed. Sometimes I even have headaches or indigestion. Witch again!

Yet, when I have the courage to live the new position, life seems freer, more spontaneous and joyful. People around me seem to change too. My students at the university are more relaxed, more spontaneous in their movements and more alert. There is laughter in the studio and yet we cover more material than ever before.

My relationship with my husband, John, has shifted too. Though alone on my journey, I am always supported by him. Without question he gives me the space necessary to move into my changing reality. This frees him to explore, in his own extroverted way, the things he values most deeply. And though our outer lives, belief systems, and interests differ radically, the commitment to supporting each other's journeys is now the essence of our marriage. With that foundation established, a loving, free, playful spirit permeates the sometimes difficult realities of family life.

"It's a training I'm in, isn't it?" I say to Nellie one morning while walking Gandolf. "I simply must learn the skill of holding that position in space. It's like a dancer learning how to balance effortlessly on one toe. That takes years of disciplined training."

"My dear child, it takes lifetimes," she answers in her direct, no-nonsense manner.

"When I hear the voice in me as separate, I am in my little self, aren't I, Nellie? I cannot live the whole yet, but recently I have had moments where I dissolve and am one with the universe."

"Yes," answers Nellie.

As I walk alone in the park with Gandolf gallumping around me, words start to tumble out of my mouth. As I say them I know they are coming from the position in space. There is something about Nellie's presence that enables me to speak directly and fluently.

"I need to remember that I work for humanity, not for the university and certainly not for myself. I am now in training for LIFE. This training cannot be a concept in my head; it must be a reality in my body. When every one of my cells lives this reality, I will be ready to go to work."

"Can you hear yourself?" interrupts Nellie.

"Yes, I also know that this training will be conducted by people and events in my life. I need to remember that when I look into the eyes of another person, I see my human condition reflected as in a mirror. When I know that condition intimately in myself, whether it is as a murderer or a saint, I will be able to look through the condition to the Self operating."

"Yes," says Nellie. "When you embrace your dark side as intimately as you embrace your light side, you know that you are neither. Then you *see* the reality beyond the condition. You *see* that neither the condition nor the personality seeing the condition is the point. The point lies in the space where the two are lived consciously as one in love. That is what is happening in this moment between us now, dear. We are the one in love."

"And I need to position myself in love without being attached to it in any way. That is what remaining clear, without judgment, without answers, and without words, is all about."

"It is a position of divine indifference," continues Nellie. "The position is a quality of love that requires no form to exist. Do not say that you love the position, or that you love the Christ, or the Buddha, or the Master, as though the position is separate from you. The love is this park where you walk Gandolf each morning; it is everywhere; it permeates all life; it is all life. Your training is to remember that you already are the position. You can feel it now, can't you?"

"In some brief moments I can, Nellie. But it takes such concentration and discipline!"

"Most of what has passed between us is still words for you, dear, yet the work is wordless and formless. Try to forget the words, the ideas, the thoughts, and be the whole of the experience. Dissolve your inner space into the outer space and then you will experience that all life is one reality in the first place. Live the vastness of the space in the inner space of your body. Then, the words will be there for you, distilled from the experience. Take their beauty into the inner city of human life."

Tears start to roll down my cheeks. How often have I walked in the park crying? The experience of Nellie's words is so beautiful, so rarefied, like a chorus of angels singing.

"Live the eternal vastness," whispers Nellie. "That is the immortal you because there is no you. It is a position known as beauty for it is all-encompassing love. Within that love lies everything, dear."

I watch Gandolf retrieve his sticks. Mindless instinct. How lucky he is. I wish I could just operate on the same level that he does.

"Humanity needs you, dear, not the little you. There are millions of little Marys on the planet. You are redundant, unnecessary. Accept what you are. Wake up and take responsibility for yourSelf."

Oh, it is easy to live forgetfulness. It is easy to live the little life of Mary, with the little worries and the little joys. It is safe to live the contraction into the form. Besides, expansion means death to my reality, for all I have worked for in life. I want my degrees, my position at the university, my family, my home, my reputation.

And yet, when I live this safe, known position I immediately long for the beauty of the Light Being. I long for its freedom, its joy, its expansion into love, into life. I long for the exquisite quality of life that it lives.

"Where you are right now is useless," says Nellie. "Wake up, dear. You are in a fantasy that takes you out of life. The Light Being of love that is all around you is a symbol behind which lies a great reality that you are to integrate into life. Do not get caught in the beauty of the symbol. Experience the quality of life within the symbol and bring that quality into every action you live. Then your experience will be that you have dissolved and that there is only the greater reality being lived consciously."

As I contemplate what Nellie has just said to me, I become aware of just wanting to go to sleep, of forgetting about everything that Nellie has ever said to me. The exhaustion I feel makes my whole body go into a state of inertia. My legs feel too heavy to lift up. I am going home.

I collapse on my bed. I close my eyes. The inside of my head is a great dome of clear, starlit night. As I lie there within my starlit dome-skull, I feel as though I no longer exist. There is only space. Within the space I become a not-I that expands into dimensions and universes unknown to me. And then I go beyond the stars into a totally dark void. On this journey into the void I am not alone. I am accompanied by my joyful Being of Light. An immense joy fills my formlessness.

And then, I see it. I see a tiny speck of golden light. "It's home," I whisper through tears of joy. "I'm going home." Drawn magnetically to the light, like a moth toward a flame, I travel through the void accompanied by my angelic companion. The all-encompassing love I experience is beyond words, is beyond anything I have ever known as love. I know that as Mary I can never contain the experience nor even imagine it.

The golden light becomes the sun, only it is not like the sun I have known as a human being. This sun is a group of radiant Beings of Light. Their light is a sound, a sound of magnificent voices that human ears cannot hear. And the love, the love is a chorus of sound. Sound, space, motion all become one. The not-I enters the group of radiant Beings and takes its place among them. It turns and faces outwards and with its Beingness it radiates the soundless sound of love. The love is beamed out and creates forms, one of which is our sacred planet, Earth.

The Being so loves this Earth that it chooses to separate itSelf into many tiny forms of light and beams itSelf into human forms.

I lie quietly on my bed. I feel myself dissolving into light and at the same time, I feel myself as light activating the cells of my body into human life. I don't know if I can walk or even if I can move. If I can let go of everything I know, then the Being of Light can be a human being.

That night I have the following dream:

I am a fool who is in the form of a dancing ball of light. I am full of joy, laughter, play, and love. Like the characters in the movie *Cocoon*, my fool self puts on a human costume. I am now dressed in my favorite turquoise outfit. Unlike my waking self, the fool loves its silliness. As I walk through the university campus, I try hard to look important. I pretend that I don't have this silly fool inside me who keeps playing tricks on me to make me laugh out loud. I feel annoyed and frustrated by its silly behavior. All through the dream I am aware that the harder I try to be serious, the more lovable I become to the fool.

For two weeks I can neither write nor think clearly. My head aches and I feel frightened. I am afraid to speak to Nellie. The dream fool is alive in Nellie and she will tell me to live it. But I don't have the courage to be a fool. The fear creeps through my body, making my joints ache as though I have arthritis. The fool in me keeps whispering the words "dissolve into the joy." The words echo in my throbbing head.

Life like this is hell. My human costume self has to face the illusion of itself; it has to face its mortality. I have to dissolve into that fool who knows deeply that I am an impersonal expression of the larger Being of Light. I have to let go of personal desire. I have to dismantle myself and be a nonperson—a lovable human fool. The more I recognize this fact, the greater the fear I feel in my body.

The fear is not only my personal fear; it is also the fear present in the unconscious of the human collective that my bodysoul is picking up. It does not know itself and it has no boundaries. It is the fear of death, the fear of rejection, the fear of isolation, and the fear of annihilation. My fool knows this and she accepts it, yet she is filled with joy.

"Help me, Nellie," I finally have the courage to ask.

"Learn to live humility. It is only when you know you are a nobody, a fool, that you become free, and once free, you become everything," answers Nellie. "The world may think that the nobody is a great sage, or even a professor like yourself," she says bursting into uproarious laughter. "But the fool knows she is always a nobody, regardless of the costume the world puts on her. She knows there is no permanence in the world of costumes. Look at me, dear. Look a little deeper into yourself.

"Be a nobody. Let go of the limited position of trying so hard to be somebody, something. Let the human costume dissolve into what you know so intimately as yourSelf. Then you can let the world project unto you whatever it wants to, but you will know that it is all illusion."

As Nellie speaks I feel my persona is an outfit, a fool's costume that provides an outer covering for what is so intimately mySelf. In essence, I am a beam of light. This light is more personal than any body, and because it lives in this body, my body is sacred. My body is a conscious manifestation of this light. It is. It simply is.

A month later I have the following dream.

I am about seven years old. I joyously dance in the nude on the smooth pink granite rocks of Georgian Bay. I leap and turn effortlessly from rock to rock.

The scene changes. Barefoot, I walk inland from the shoreline toward an old stone church. At the door a young child (I think it is a girl) meets me and shows me inside. We climb a huge stairway that is much bigger than what should be inside this church. At the top of the stairs is an enormous arched wooden door. The young girl tells me I must open this door by myself.

Without hesitation I open it. Inside is a huge circular room with crystal walls and floor. The sunlight shining through the sun dome ceiling reflects brilliantly off the walls. The light is so bright that I have to close my eyes and still there is only the light.

I walk across the crystal floor and sit on a white sheepskin rug. Immediately the room is filled with angels singing.

This dream is a baptism of light. From the childhood state of innocence, where I dance spontaneously on the pink granite rocks, I shift into a mature state of awareness. I know the instinctual sacrifice (symbolized by the sheepskin rug) required to receive the light. Contained in the stone church made from the primeval pink granite rocks I love to dance on, I sit in silent concentration. For many weeks, during meditation, I allow the image of the crystal room filled with singing angels to penetrate my bodysoul.

Shortly after this dream I have the opportunity to work with Georgette Krummenacher and Martin Muller, author of *Prelude to the New Man: An Introduction to the Science of Being*. When I meet them I see they live a quality of life, a beauty that is not earthbound and yet is so utterly human. Their whole presence lives a wisdom that contains the knowledge of human suffering and the radiance of unknown human possibilities. Every cell of my body dances with the magnitude of the quality of life that is lived in the room where they work.

In the space of their silence, I feel a great longing for the shimmering vibrance that I know they live. I feel compassion for the part of me that longs to share in their wisdom. Compassion (suffering with) embraces my soul. I hear a deep joy sounding inside my body. My bone cells seem to dance, to resonate with the sound of the joy. With the precision of focus that I have learned in daily meditation, I am able to stay with the experience.

And then I feel myself relax a little more, enabling me to sense the resonances in the spaces between my bone cells. Suddenly the spaces are impersonal space and the sound of the joy is a silent movement in that impersonal space. My experience is of an emptiness of exquisite motion. I no longer experience myself as a body. I am consciousness being lived by the motion of impersonal space.

And then I see it. I see the Light Being of my dream, only this time I know I am not dreaming. It lives in the spaces of the room, filling space with vibrancy, joy, and divinity. I don't know how I am seeing it, for it isn't with my eyes.

I sit motionless in my chair. I can't feel my body in the usual way; it feels enormous. It is cemented to the chair, to the room. I feel the pull of gravity holding me to the Earth, but the me that is being held captive is only a space. I can't tell the difference between my body and space; they seem to be a continuation of the downward pull. I notice that my space can fill the room, can expand beyond the room, or it can contract into my tiny personal form. I recognize that all my life I have lived the contracted position. Now, an entirely new order of life exists for me.

After that experience I am not the same. I am a conscious being without an attachment to my personal identity. The experience is profoundly personal, and at the same time, enormously impersonal. MySelf has no name, no form, no density. MySelf is a condition of love being lived in full consciousness of itself. MySelf is that which gives me life. It is identical and part of that which gives life to all forms on the planet.

Life and death have paradoxical meaning for me now. Life in the physical body has been a form of death, a forgetting of mySelf. Now I see death of the physical form to be a joyous reunion with mySelf in full memory of itSelf. A gap has been closed. I no longer require a body to know my essence; however, I do require a body to manifest on the planet.

When I experience my body with mySelf, I fall into it with a love for matter that I have not known before. This love enables my body to receive, as vessel, the Light that originates from a source other than myself. My body is intelligent matter designed to function exquisitely in the world. My body knows itself as a joyous expression of conscious love and Light, dancing through the open moment.

"Don't get caught," warns Nellie. "Don't make up fantasies about your experiences or about yourself. The ordinary, the simple daily living is everything. Teaching for you is ordinary and so is doing the family laundry. Keep it that way. Just be aware. The extraordinary is the ordinary; accept it; live it; be it. No fantasies, no special powers, no nothing—and then, everything."

Nellie warns me that the ego is the psychic container for the experience of Light. Conscious of her dark shadow, she does not identify with the Light but remains a midpoint, a mediator between Light and darkness. Witch, on the other hand, unconscious of her dark shadow and driven by personal power and greed, wants to be the Light.

SUMMER 1988
THE STILL POINT

I begin to recognize a feeling inside that wants to speak about what I now know. The following dream confirms my intuition.

I am rock climbing. There are white plastic grocery bags packed with garbage on the rocks. As I clear the bags away, I see that the rocks are covered in tiny green acorns. I am in a state of total love for these rocks. The rocks and I are one.

I realize that I am very high up on an overhanging lip. I am defying the laws of gravity. Usually I am terrified of heights, but if I remain in love with the rocks I will be safe.

I am in a rock climbing lesson and just to be safe I ask the young male instructor to help me. He shows me how to put a pin in the rock, and using a rope, I ease my way up over the lip.

I sit on the mountaintop. Again, I am usually afraid of heights but this feels comfortable and safe. The instructor massages tiger balm oil into my temples and lower spine. Immediately, I relax into a profound state of love.

I explore the large, secure space of the mountaintop and discover a room full of superb dancers dressed in black and white striped costumes. I want to join them, but I don't know the steps and I am wearing my old cottage work clothes.

I walk outside into a street where a group of people are gathered. They speak in a foreign language and though I feel I have something to say to them, I can only listen. Suddenly, everyone starts running. I realize it is a war-torn area. A steel blue streetcar pulls up in front of me. To my relief, the doors open and I climb aboard.

I sit on the right side of the driver. When he notices that my right sleeve is covered in blood, he accuses me of being a terrorist. I see that my life is in danger. I pretend to be a retarded foreigner.

An old woman dressed in a bright green blanket appears. Her eyes tell me that she wants to speak to me but can't because the driver might hear her. When she gets off at the next stop, I follow her, but not until the streetcar is out of sight.

The old woman tells me that the timing must be right for us to speak. We must wait and prepare for the right moment.

Again I am with my beloved rocks. I remember when I first went to California the shifting sands made me so uncomfortable. I couldn't find a solid granite rock to support me. Everything was shifting sand. There was no still point to ground me. In the dream, I am grounded, one with the rocks.

The heights that usually terrify me are safe, if I can remain in love. When I discard old patterns of behavior (garbage) I find the seeds of new life (acorns). With the help of my positive animus (rock climbing teacher) I reach a stable position. Here, though I long to dance, my persona (old cottage clothes) is no longer suitable.

The animus massages tiger (instincts) balm (spirit) into my temples and lower spine. This probably means that the movement toward the reconciliation of the instincts (tiger and lower spine or base chakra) and spirit (balm and temples) is now possible. It is the animus, the masculine part of the psyche, that anoints my feminine body, making matter sacred. The black and white costumes of the dancers are also symbolic of the union of opposites. When the opposites are brought together, I relax into a profound state of love.

In the position of heart love, I move out into the world only to discover that I speak a different language. What is the language? The language that I write and speak has no meaning in a world where consciousness is not connected to the unconscious. I am writing from another reality. This reality is foreign to the collective patriarchal values (streetcar that runs on collective tracks). When I become conscious of my position I realize my inner physical pain—my body is the war-torn area.

At this point I am caught in the father complex (I associate the color of steel blue with my father's cooler, which I packed for him yesterday). When I am in touch with feminine wisdom that knows that spirit lives in matter I am considered a terrorist by the father complex that says matter is ignorant flesh. When complexed I think that I am just a stupid woman (retarded foreigner) who is unable to write (my writing arm is wounded) and who has nothing to say that is of any value. The complex dictates that I remain a whore in the bedroom and a mother in the kitchen. It is amazing to me to discover that after twelve years of daily work that I am still driven (the male streetcar driver) by this complex.

However, the crone figure releases me from the complex. The hours of work with Medicine Woman and Nellie enable me to relate to feminine wisdom. The timing for the new feminine consciousness (old woman) to speak is not now. The message is clear—keep a low profile and prepare. The preparation involves finding words to help me communicate the feminine consciousness.

Nothing has really changed in my life; however, a new possibility is born. I know that Nellie lives the union of opposites, of Light in matter. As long as I can imagine the beauty of the Light infusing my body as I walk Gandolf, sort the laundry, spread peanut butter on bread for the kids' lunches, teach dance at the university, and load the dishwasher at night, the possibility of living that quality of life, which is mine, but not mine, is there. Though this possibility is only a glimpse, a tiny seed, a living moment, I know it is possible to live it all the time.

The possibility is love, the known fact that the essence of all matter is love. When my consciousness expands, I recognize everything as light manifesting into forms. The action of manifestation is a dance, a dance of stillness, a dance of love. When I forget my own essence, however, I fall into unconsciousness and falsely perceive matter as dark, concrete, and ignorant.

In the summer while at the cottage, I spend my mornings in silence by the lily pond. I slowly become aware of the extreme discipline of stabilizing myself in the void that is full. When I am able to surrender to the silent void, I dissolve into a dance of love. And the beauty, the beauty of the experience, causes me to weep—to weep in reverence for what it is, for what I am, for what all life is.

The beauty of the reality of love existing within all forms of life softens me into a gentleness that cannot force itself into action. Instead I discover a beautiful quality living within me that radiates strength and direction. I feel as though a sun is rising within me, inside the core of my body. This core is a living still point where light streams through. My body is the anchor for this point. In this point I am aware of the spaces between the cells of my body. The spaces open to this sun. Like a rose blooming in radiant light, my body drinks in this sun. Simultaneously the rays of sunlight radiate outwards in streams of golden threads. The radiations of this sun are not confined in any way to the shape of my body. Like the perfume of a rose, these radiations of light have no concrete form and no density.

A rose absorbs both the rotting matter of compost and the radiant

The sound of rocks singing: matter living spirit.

light of the sun and transforms these two essences into a magnificent scent that fills the surrounding space with perfume. Now, like a rose, my body absorbs both the raw material of matter and the radiant light of the inner sun. By surrendering to the process I find I am living in a state of grace. Neither the rose nor I have any idea how the absorption of matter and light are transformed into this state of being, this perfume of love. By living rose-self or human-self we enter the mystery of life and the space around us is transformed into something exquisitely beautiful.

By the stillness of the lily pond, I discipline myself to disappear within the inner sun. When I dissolve I become a center of consciousness that mingles with the rocks, the trees, and the water lilies in the pond.

I start to hear the forms of life around me as sounds, sounds not heard by my ears but known by the silence. The beauty of the sounds is like the joy of angels singing. The sound is a form of death into a new way of being. Rather than trying to take the experience into daily consciousness, I know that I have to offer myself in service to it. I have to, as it were, dissolve into the sound, to mingle with it, to become it. And then, when I regather myself, or rather, am refocused through the consciousness of my tiny personal self, the self is a no-self in service to sounding life. I know that I can't take this experience into the world but I can return to this place and refocus in the love that I want to live in the world.

I realize that my function is no longer to be a teacher or a workshop leader in the traditional way where the teacher-leader is the knower and the students-participants are the learners. Now my function is to live this point, this condition where love streams through my body. Then the space created by this love becomes the container for anyone to work in, including myself. The love becomes the teacher, the healer, the knower, the transformer. In their own way and time, people in this space may receive or reject this love that enables them to hear the healer dwelling within.

I have a dream that confirms this shift to another position.

> I am standing on the shoreline of the ocean in California. I see a beautiful freshwater rainbow trout spawning in the ocean. The local Mexican fishermen are protecting this fish with their glass-bottom boats. The fish and her eggs are a national treasure. The fish has a license plate attached to her back.

In the dream the wisdom of the spiritual self living in the body (fish) is clearly differentiated; the rainbow trout is a very specific and special fish. The spiritual self (fish) is in a new psychological position (the ocean rather than fresh water) where the bridge between the physical body and the subtle body is firmly established (rainbow trout). The new position is a shift in awareness from the personal position to a more impersonal position (the fish and her eggs are a national treasure). The hours of work integrating Nellie's wisdom has made this shift possible. This new position is protected by the instincts (Mexicans). It is now psychologically possible to live the spiritual potential (the eggs of the rainbow trout). The license plate reveals that my consciousness is now responsible to the Self; this expanded consciousness is licensed to function in daily life. The new consciousness is not fully conscious but rests on the threshold of consciousness (shoreline where conscious and unconscious meet). My discipline is to bring this position fully into consciousness and to surrender to it until the I that is conscious is living the spiritual self.

I feel vulnerable in the new position. Sometimes the children find me crying for the humanity that has forgotten itSelf. My vulnerability connects me to my humanness. By staying conscious of the grief, I continually discover that it is miraculously transformed into love. And this love, like the fire of the rising sun, burns the grief away, until there is only radiant love.

This love embodies the attitude of reverence, a condition of conscious humility in the face of the divine. I recognize that the discipline of my mind is to focus on the clear, articulate, and precise expression of the beauty of this love; the discipline of my heart is to remain open and receptive to the exquisite quality of this love; the discipline of my body is to be physically strong enough to surrender to the resonance of this love, regardless of the life situation I am in. Then, in this state of reverence, I know in my bones that this love lives me and that my bodysoul is simply a tool to serve this love in the world. The complete insignificance of my persona is then utterly apparent and the complete significance of living the love through my bodysoul is utterly apparent, too. I experience my persona as empty and in this starving condition I need to live the love of the divine as empty lungs need to inhale air. The instinct to stay alive, to breathe, to eat, to live is transformed into the spiritual instinct to live love consciously. Spiritual life and daily living become one Life. Then the center of consciousness values divine love so deeply that it centers itself totally in that love that is other than itself, regardless of the daily life situation. This is a great challenge when the life situation is not what the persona wants, desires, or thinks she needs.

This love is a starting point.

WINTER 1990
THE CLAWS OF CHRIST

Daily I practice the discipline of staying connected, of listening to the voice of Nellie, of trying to stay awake and conscious when the collective energy pulls me into the unconscious state. Conscious LIFE demands that I face and love every thread of my immature persona who wants life to serve her.

I become increasingly aware of a numbness very deep in my cells, a sleeping part of me that refuses to let go and relax into love. When I try to release this numbness, something in my conscious mind refuses to allow the release to occur.

During a week-long intensive workshop for professional therapists, where the focus is on receiving the positive feminine, I demonstrate an exercise with Marion. In the exercise I allow my body to relax and to surrender into her arms. I love to do this exercise in workshops, for my body delights in the awareness of the love between us and in the acute pleasure of receiving physical cherishing. As Marion gently rocks me she points out to me that I keep falling asleep. I witness myself and observe that when I feel a certain point of intense sensuous pleasure, the pleasure becomes unbearable; I go numb and fall into a state of total unconsciousness. The intensity of the experience reminds me again of Blake: "That we may learn to bear the beams of love." That night I have a dream that comes directly out of this body experience.

I am walking down a street at dusk. I notice a large Bear walking toward two young boys. I warn the boys that the claws of the Bear might wound them and to be very cautious. Then I am in the strong embrace of the Bear. We are standing at the threshold of a building where a group of women are meeting. As I focus on the Bear's long claws I feel his enormous penis growing up the front of my body, under my dress, where it ejaculates between my breasts. As the sperm covers the front of my body I am horrified and disgusted on one level, but on another level I feel blessed by the Bear's sheer physical strength and by the warmth of his sperm.

The scene changes and I am on a school bus. My cleaning lady is driving me to a Catholic church, where I am to be dropped off at children's day-care. In the front seat of the bus sits my father's mother, a Christian woman who tries to divert the bus driver to suit her needs. My cleaning lady doesn't listen to her; she takes me directly inside the day-care center. There, the woman in charge of the children is folding the clean laundry. I walk through the day-care into the church, where a holy man hands me a black church relic. He tells me it will protect me from evil. I refuse to take it, thinking how stupid he is to think that I will need protection from evil. Then, I am standing in an open, circular, cloister garden where the sky is filled with stars. Here I am to take a bath.

The next day in the body workshop, I allow myself to live the embrace of the Bear through active imagination. I feel the sheer beauty of his enormous strength and loving energy supporting my body. I experience the sensation of the warmth of his sperm flowing out over my chest. Again, I notice his huge claws extending from his powerful arms. Suddenly, I am aware of intense blinding light pouring into the room. I look up and there before me stands an enormous figure of Christ. His hands reach out to embrace the Bear. To my amazement, the streams of light extending from his fingers are claws of light, claws of equal strength to the Bear's. In the intensity of this powerful experience I am simply a tiny cell held in the embrace of the instinctual life of the Bear, which is itself embraced by the spiritual light of the Christ.

In this dream the Bear is an androgyne. It is the symbol of the Mother Goddess; yet it has a huge erected phallus, the symbol of the creative masculine. As I surrender into the arms of the Great Mother Bear, immense creative power is released.

In working with this dream, I recognize that I am on the threshold of a new position that relates to the collective feminine (group of women in building). I focus on the two levels of awareness. The first level is the experience of the instinctual life (the Bear) as evil and dangerous (I warn the young animus figures to be careful). The repulsion I feel for the creative life of the instincts (sperm) is the attitude I learned from my father's mother—that instinctual energy is disgusting. At the same time I focus on the awareness of the warmth and creative power of the sperm. Though the negative attitude tries to redirect me away from the bath, the bus driver (cleaning lady) takes me to the day-care center (a place of new energy and life). Here, the lady in charge is organizing the clean laundry (more old attitudes have been washed out). I reject the holy man's relic. I associate the relic with the type of weather vane that has a cock on the top. Therefore, I reject the rigid male view (cock) of Christianity that is not free to fly in the wind. When I do this, I instantly realize that I need no further protection from evil; I am a pure being by simply being who I am. Suddenly there is no institutional church. My church is the circular and natural cloister garden under the open starlit sky (symbol of the Self). It is here I am to take my bath (symbol of another initiation).

To link the bodysoul work to dream analysis, I agree to work with the dream with Marion in the intensive workshop. Though we both know it is dangerous to expose soul material so soon after the dream, my inner voice of Nellie instructs me to be an impersonal instrument for teaching.

In the workshop, sitting in the center of the circle of women with Marion, I, as a tiny cell, face the intensity of the Light Being. I grab hold of my body and cry out in agony, "I cannot endure the suffering of the human condition. I have to go numb to endure the pain of the collective flesh. You demanded that I feel the agony of love for my dead son. Now you are demanding that I feel the instinctual life of the body of humanity that has been rejected for centuries. I cannot endure this pain. My body must go numb."

As I say this, I realize that the claws of Christ are ripping open a repressed wound. "Love humanity as you would your own child," whispers the inner voice. "Love cannot be a concept in your head; CONSCIOUS LIFE demands that you live it in your body."

The paradoxes in the dream demonstrate that differing energies are trying to come together into harmony. The Bear is both masculine and feminine. The claws of Christ are instinct and spirit. The conscious experience of intense physical pleasure becomes its opposite of intolerable pain. When intense physical pleasure is received consciously, intense repressed agony can be released into consciousness. The hands of Christ are claws that demand consciousness at a cellular level. The years of work on the body and psyche are now making it possible to integrate conscious Life into daily living.

In the workshop I feel the need to connect personally with each woman present. When Marion asks me what I would like, I hear myself say, "I want a hug." Then the experience of my body is that she is completely transparent and in her transparency she sees through the other bodies—she lives their pain, their holding, their joy, their history. Nellie's strict voice instructs me to simply witness in silence. I discipline myself to be the still point of consciousness, the observer and the observed. In this brief moment I know I am seeing with the loving presence of Nellie.

Later, I ask Nellie for help.

"It is your destiny," she says with absolute love and detachment. "The Christ impulse can no longer be an intellectual concept. It must be lived consciously in the flesh. The suffering is the resistance to the divine impulse trying to incarnate consciously into the living body of humanity. The profound love of this act is the dance of the cells being sung into manifestation. Remember yourSelf, Mary. Just be yourSelf and the sound of your cells singing will be heard by other human cells."

"But why the suffering, Nellie?"

"When humans suffer they are vulnerable. Within this vulnerability lives the humility that allows flesh to soften into the sounds of the soul. The softening enables your cells to surrender to the strength of the Christ impulse. The impulse is conscious love manifesting itself into planetary life."

"And what is the darkness, Nellie?"

"Resistance to light. Resistance is felt in the human body as pain. It is the contracted position. It is fear, terror, anxiety. It is wanting and desiring. It is aspiring to be something. It is the illusion of being a separate human being. It is the illusion of death.

"You must discipline yourself to trust and be aware. The sword of awareness *is*. It needs no little human hand to wield its power. As a conscious human cell in the universe you simply have to be the conscious participator. Do nothing, want nothing, will nothing. Hold the still point, my dear, until you are simply the point. Then you will know precisely the action required. Then you must act."

"But this isn't humanly possible, Nellie."

"Not according to your definition of what a human being is. It's what humanity is becoming. It's the future that has always been here. Trust, my dear, trust."

"And leap into this still point?"

"If you can, dear. Remember the still point is infinite space."

"Any guarantee I will make it, Nellie?"

"None," answers Nellie firmly as she disappears.

I realize that the repression of the flesh by institutionalized religion has created great human suffering. In the Judeo-Christian tradition, woman has been associated with the life of the flesh, the body of Eve. Her body has agonized in hell along with the male body symbolized in Satan. Through the repression of the flesh, Christ has not been a redeemer of flesh and blood, but a concept in the head, an impossible ideal for any human being to live.

Conscious femininity is living the redeemed body of Eve, regardless of the gender of the human being. This body is conscious of itself as an intelligent instrument, a living system that actively participates in the divine unfoldment of planetary life. While finding the harmony of its own natural laws of being, it is at the same time finding the harmonic with all forms of life on Earth.

The repression of the body by indoctrinated religions has alienated humans from the reality of the life of the flesh. Severed from its own body, severed from the life of the instincts, severed from the Great Mother Earth, humanity has unconsciously served its own greed at the expense of the whole of life. The conscious body is incapable of such action for it is incapable of separating itself from Earth, its life source. Conscious flesh knows that its function is the consciousness of this Earth.

In meditation my discipline is to be a still point, a point that is consciously free from the collective, free from the limits of time and space, free from personal life circumstances. This still point is the dance of creation where the eternal now is born into temporal form. From a trapped psychological position, I am unconsciously controlled by collective values and victim of life circumstances. At the still point something new emerges, something for which I have as yet no words, only experiences.

For example, while leading a workshop I experience collective suffering resonating in my body. Overwhelmed with grief that is not mine, I wonder how I can work in this condition. I focus on my breath to help center myself. My breathing spontaneously becomes the winged action of an enormous butterfly that breathes me, breathes the atmosphere in the room, breathes the planet. The uplifted action of its powerful wings inhales my breath and something in the atmosphere of the room is uplifted. As the powerful formless wings press down, the suffering in the room, in my body, is embraced in profound love.

In this experience, there is no hierarchy. One reality is not greater than another, for everything is contained in one living field of life. Consciousness is capable of moving through the differing experiences within the field. The ability to move is love. I experience the suffering, the expansion, the embrace into love, and I am none of them. I am simply the point of awareness, the dancer and the dance, teaching the same material I have taught for twenty years.

I am simply a tiny still point held in the loving embrace of Bear, the instinctual life that is strong enough to receive the full intensity of the light of Christ. The claws of Christ rip open the condemned flesh and release the divine light held within. The wounding as the flesh is ripped open is excruciating, but then, when the flesh is released into its own divinity, the Beauty.

The Beauty is the dance of HerSelf. It is the dance of Light incarnate in conscious flesh. Matter is dancing Light.

Labour is blossoming or dancing where
The body is not bruised to pleasure soul,
Nor beauty born out of its own despair,
Nor blear-eyed wisdom out of midnight oil.
O Chestnut-tree, great-rooted blossomer,
Are you the leaf, the blossom or the bole?
O body swayed to music, O brightening glance,
How can we know the dancer from the dance?

—W. B. YEATS[3]

Part Three

The
Dress
of Stars

Chapter 7

The Dress of Stars

The interrelatedness of the universe in its every manifestation is what establishes the unity of the entire world and enables it to be a "universe."

—THOMAS BERRY

For the third festival, Allerleirauh wears her dress that shines like the stars. Her microcosm, released from its nutshell, now mirrors the whole constellation of heaven. And now the King is determined to keep her. He contrives, without her noticing, to slip a golden ring on her finger. Although she springs away after the dance and runs to her den, she has not time to return to her animal disguise. Quickly she slips the fur mantle over her dress, partially blackens herself, and sends the soup to the King. This time it contains the golden reel.

At his command, she is brought before the King and inadvertently reveals her white finger bearing his golden ring. Instantly, he grasps her by the hand and holds her fast. Still attempting to escape, she reveals a corner of her star dress. The King tears off her mantle of furs. Her golden hair shines forth. She stands in her full splendor. She washes the soot and ashes from her face. The King says, "You are my dear bride, and we will never more part from each other." Thereupon the marriage is solemnized and they lived happily until their death.

Walking in the woods in springtime, we find white starflowers, their little faces looking up like stars growing from below instead of shining from above. In alchemy, the archetypal motif of the star coming from below is very important. Dorn, one of the early alchemists, believed that "every flower or herb has an astrological correspondent and is the earthly image of an astrological constellation."[1] In the alchemical process, he believed it was essential at some point to "shape the heavens below." To do this, he recommended "taking the dregs of old wine, the tartar (the deposit or the hard crust formed on the side of the cask) and distilling it until it obtains a liquid or blue colour; then the heavens below will have been produced."[2] Into this, certain stars, flowers reflecting certain astrological constellations, were introduced, thus establishing the heavens. This mixture had to be cooked and the result was "the last stage in making the philosopher's stone, namely the ultimate union with the whole cosmic nature. When the heavens below have been produced, one is united with the *unus mundus*, cosmic divine nature."[3]

Behind the outer reality is the mystery, the mystery to which Allerleirauh commended herself when she went into the forest. The culmination of her journey is the realization that she is a part of one divine plan manifested in everything from the galaxies to the smallest flower.

If we take time to live with nature, to see it and perceive it, we can have no doubt that we are inseparable from every living thing on the planet. Our bodies are our particular container, but the love within is part of a greater love that puts us in communion with all living things. It is not simply a love of beauty. It is a knowing that love holds the cosmos together, that we are included in that love. Being awestruck by a fiery sunset may give us a sense of profoundest belonging in a love that will never abandon us.

Taking time is what is so difficult. Our cultural upbringing teaches us to plan and run as fast as we can toward our goals. It is our very running that takes us away from our own depths of feeling. In our fairy tale, the death of the golden-haired Queen, the feminine, leaves Allerleirauh and her father with a great hole at the center of their existence. The final task of her journey is to see that hole, not as an empty void, but as a teeming universe. She learns to trust the darkness of the night until the stars are revealed. Following her own feeling in the silence of her own soul, allowing herself to be guided from inside rather than charging toward her conscious ideals, the feminine gradually—very gradually—becomes aware of the stars radiant in the darkness. She is quiet in the presence of a divine order of which she is a part. Her ego plots, which would cut her off from her own feeling, are surrendered to a greater evolving process. Trusting that other order opens her to the totally irrational and totally new. Her relationship to that otherness releases her creativity.

As feminine wisdom illumines our body cells, pain can become excruciating. Our body cannot comprehend stupidity that leads to power battles, when our very source is being massacred. Such battles are the ultimate in addictive denial—fighting about everything except the fact that we are killing ourselves, taking everything and giving nothing back. Iron claws gouging out the earth, ancient trees ripped apart by a speedy saw, or burnt until their sap weeps in the smoke— these are images that literally clutch the heart.

Anyone who doubts the body response of the soul to imagery need only watch the television newscasts. Watch noble, bewildered birds trying to fly on wings laden with oil. Watch bombs ripping into the bowels of people or Earth. Watch prisoners or starving children stare into the camera, watch, watch, watch, and see if your body can get off the chair when you have digested these images.

Patriarchal thinking cannot digest such images. It can compartmentalize them, intellectualize them as worthy causes, but it fails to integrate them at a heart level. Patriarchy is terrified of union with the loving Mother, and, therefore, the concept of union with a cosmic divine nature is mere words. Caught in its narcissistic power games, it has no time to bring Her to consciousness. At the same time, in raping Her to death, it proclaims its own death wish. If patriarchy fails to recognize consciousness in matter, our planet may die in the agony that has become her life. Surely we have to ask the question: What is the source of the death wish that is driving us to destroy our source of life?

Many individuals need to ask the same question. Terrified in their own little box, they cannot risk finding the meaning of their terror. They run in a circle, but they cannot cross over to a new vision. They cannot trust, they cannot surrender. They cannot live universal thinking in their own body cells. They look everywhere but at the center, where the unconscious death wish propels them into addictions.

We are living in the atomic age. Whether it ends in the destructive release of energy or the creative release of new consciousness depends on us. Every individual is a cell in the universe. We are the consciousness that can hold spirit and matter together.

THE CRONE

Universal thinking is thinking with the heart. Crones are universal thinkers. They are the third in the feminine trinity. To be able to wear the dress of stars, Allerleirauh must be at least in touch with her crone.

Crones have passed over many crossroads. Crossing roads, bridges, borders are very important transitions in dreams. The dreamer is passing from the known to the unknown. The crossroads is the place where time and timeless meet. The ego tries to hold on to its selfish desires; Fate says no. (I want that man to love me; he no longer cares.) Time is static, timeless is creative. The *no* may be a huge *yes* to the buried parts of ourselves. The *yes* may be more terrifying than the *no*. To move with the moment, to surrender to the unknown is to flow with feminine consciousness.

Of course, that looks crazy to a rational mind in which trusting transformative process is throwing oneself over to chaos. Anything could happen. Patriarchal thinking thrives on tapes, precision instruments, data—those things that encapsulate a moment and freeze it in perfection. Crone strength is on the side of life, grieving for the dying victims instead of praising the precision hit. For her, there is no them and us; we are one family on one little globe—all trying to trust life, now.

When we promise "to love and to cherish till death us do part," do we know what we are saying? If we did, would we commit? Would we ever make love if we thought about the anguish our possible child would encounter in the world?

Feminine consciousness is cyclic, not linear. As mother and virgin mature together, so the crone is implicit in their maturing. Mother makes more conscious boundaries; virgin speaks her truth that shatters idealized projections; crone contains paradox. Mother loves, virgin perceives, crone forgives. Deeper, higher, broader, the cycle moves. As mother-virgin consciously surrenders to her destiny, each crossroad takes her closer to the crone. She becomes a consciously surrendered instrument attuned to the cosmic matrix. Through her, love flows.

Her love does not make her sweet and sentimental. In fact, she hates sentimentality. She knows people protect themselves from honoring real feeling by wallowing in false sentiments. She can see the bitch and love her; no need to deny reality. Her love is detached, but not indifferent. She has been there; she has suffered; she does not identify with suffering. She suffers more than an unconscious person can; she can feel pain and observe it at the same time. She is not withdrawn. She is alarmingly present. Like a tuning fork her truth shatters hypocrisy. Others in her presence are released into what is true in themselves. Or flee.

The crone can afford to be honest. She is finished with old-fashioned games. Her flat-out truth is hard to take. But her truth is the measure of her love. She is free. Who she is cannot be taken from her. She has no investment in ego and she can therefore love with no desire to control. Her clarity brings us in touch with our feeling, puts us in touch with our feminine soul. She holds us in her love until our soul is embodied, present, and strong enough to walk with her into the unknown.

The crone is wise. She assures us that we need not prove ourselves or justify our existence. With that knowledge in our bones, we can accept paradox. We can hold the contraries within ourselves. Life is no longer broken into right or wrong, birth and death, light and dark. All is part of the mystery. Her capacity to hold spirit and matter together is the source of her lively humor. She sees things instantaneously from both the divine point of view and the human. She may give us a sharp reprimand for losing our pearls (our feminine essence) and as she trudges out the door, she flashes back, "Keep flossing."

One of my analysands became very angry with her crone's demands, told her to go away and never come back. That night she had one image. A huge rock was lying almost over a tiny one. The big rock had a note attached to it, with one word: "Seneca." To my knowledge, there is no such Latin common noun, but if there were a feminine equivalent for senex (wise old man) it might be *seneca*. With this playful slap, she had the last word. And the dreamer woke up laughing in recognition, but she had to apologize to re-establish the link. The old lady was not visiting her to hand out goodies. She was asking for the sacrifice of personal ego desires to a higher purpose. She was ready to work with the new potential if the dreamer would co-operate. Her sword is sharp, but it is wielded with love—a golden blade with a silver handle. She knows that anger kills inside as surely as outside.

Her sword is an image of her phallic energy, energy that can connect her to the outer world and guide her in the inner. Discriminating and decisive, it can separate the enduring from the ephemeral, making room and conserving energy for what is essential to the core.

The crone never sets up an either/or situation. She's lived too long to believe in a black and white world; she loves the many shades of gray. Rather than wasting her energy fighting an old enemy, she plays creatively with the imagery that is shaping a new world. Like Einstein reflecting on his ride on the sunbeam.

Crone energy comes with life fully lived. It brings with it many shadows. As a woman grows older, new intensities appear in the shadow side of mother, virgin, crone. As the body weakens, she finds it more difficult to maintain boundaries because she is becoming more dependent. Frailty may encourage the dependency of the childish little girl. At the same time, the psychic energy may become so strong that it can quickly slip over into power. These shadow energies are natural in the aging crone, and they demand finer and finer tuning as more and more is let go.

Perhaps the greatest measure of her soul is how much she is able to forgive.

The crone is closely connected to the divine maiden. One of my analysands is a magnificent crone with over seventy years of laughter and tears. In one of her dreams, she was standing at the tram stop where, as a child, she used to wait for the tram that took her to school. As she waited in the rain, a little girl ran up to her, put out her little hand and said, "I've come to take you home."

FINDING FREEDOM

Where is Allerleirauh in her transformative process when she dares to put on the star dress? In choosing to move out of her father's house, she made a conscious decision. She chose to leave the unconscious Garden of Eden. Had she drifted into marriage with her father-husband, she might have remained the unconscious wife-daughter. In that world, she would live out the infantile constellation of the home, the child's energy bound by the parameters of the mother and father. Existence, if it is perceived at all, is then felt as emptiness haunted by what could be. Because the personal life is not being lived, the individual tends to feel caged, victimized, not connected to any ongoing purpose. In this situation, the ego is weak, unable to penetrate the depths of unknowing, personally and collectively. It simply lives out an unexamined pattern of behavior, picking up bits from the parents, bits from newspapers, bits from friends. Undigested fragments drop from the lips: "My religion is the only one." "Everybody knows women are inferior to men." "Fat is ugly." The mind and body are clogged with raw prejudices.

Jung says that what is not made conscious comes to us as Fate. Many people meet their fate in the sudden recognition that they have married their father or their mother. That shattering insight may be the brick-in-the-head that stops them blaming their cage on somebody out there, or God, or the devil. Then they have to be patient and build their ego until they are strong enough to dialogue with the unconscious energies that are pushing them into new territory. The ego is the filter between conscious and unconscious. The sorting process goes on in the ego. If the ego is not strong enough to dialogue with the unconscious, then it collapses under the power of complexes and addictions.

An ego moving toward consciousness might write something like the following summary in a journal:

"I am not carrying the weight of other people's energies in my body. I am pulling my own energy out of my parental complexes. I am not sitting in the prison cell of my own unrecognized fear, rage, jealousy, greed. My energy that feels light and flowing is not concretized in symptoms or fat. I don't look to concrete objects or people to mother me. I no longer clutch onto money, jewels, status for security. I no longer fear losing them. I know I am someone. People don't love me for what I own, but for who I am. I respect myself for who I am and I love my jewels for their beauty. I love my parents, my partner, my children, but I am not dependent on them for recognition. I can accept my own humanness. I AM—what does that mean—I AM?"

In rejecting an incestuous marriage, Allerleirauh leaves behind the collective crutches that supported her as the golden-haired daughter of her golden-haired mother. She abandoned the predictable, deadening pattern and opened herself to possibility. In going to the forest, she chose to give nature a chance. Alive and alert, she remained hidden within the dead skins of her father's kingdom until her own skin was clear of the soot of shame and fear. Sifting through the ashes in the kitchen, she separated out what belonged to her and what did not until she recognized her own spirit stirring within her. In choosing to wear the golden dress, she chose to make the connection to the spiritual meaning of her own life. In making her covenant by giving her golden ring, she ceased to look to others to give her life meaning. She decided to find meaning within herself.

That covenant with the inner masculine establishes a firm feminine standpoint: outwardly it gives a woman the ego strength to act from her own lunar consciousness grounded in her own feelings and musculature; inwardly, it guides her to cherish the images that alone can reveal to her who she is. Ultimately it is the unifying energy between outer and inner worlds. Her covenant with her inner Bridegroom

releases her from *unconscious* nature, from the natural, incestuous, rigid
world of her parental complexes.

As her branches reach up to the sun, her roots are reaching down to
the moon. She is touching into the unconsciousness in her own body,
finding a sliver of a moon and allowing its light to illuminate her cells
in its own time. What begins as possibility moves into her core. The
new moon becomes half, three-quarters, whole, until every cell is
excited with silver. The unconscious mother who sleeps in the incestuous bliss of Eden is no more. The conscious Mother, present in every
cell of her body, is present moment by moment, nourishing, stimulat-
ing, making every moment new. She is the energy that supports the
virgin. Without Her, the head tries to feel without the heart and falls
into self-betrayal. With Her, the unconscious death wish is transformed into love.

The conscious virgin is no longer the uninitiated girl who fled from
her father's house. Allerleirauh literally means uncooked, the flesh
with the fur still on it, as the feminine is bound to be as long as it
remains locked in patriarchy. Even the word *virgin* is stripped of its
nobility in a patriarchal world. Patriarchy cannot conceive of femininity powerful enough to stand to its own essence. But once the
feminine throws herself into the fire of her own body, she finds the
energy that once haunted her in her cage. Then the dead animal skins
of her father's kingdom are no longer necessary. They have made their
point: the essence that was being betrayed, the aspect of soul that
craved life has been brought into consciousness. The symptoms and
neuroses are no longer needed to hide what wants to live.

The feminine can live her own sexuality, her own Dionysian passion. That passion may be lived in relationship. The danger is that the
newly released instinct may be exploited for personal power, for ag-
grandizement of the ego, in which case old symptoms or new ones will
appear. If the passion is honored, part will be lived in the instincts; part
will be transmuted through metaphor onto a spiritual level and expressed in literature, sculpture, painting, or religious experience.

In other words, if the feminine can open herself to the fires of her
own creativity, she can forge a flexible container strong enough to
stand to her own feeling because she can hold the opposites together.
Virgin is no longer separated from whore; sexuality is no longer split
from spirituality; consciousness is no longer cut off from the unconscious; good mother is no longer opposing bad mother or good father,

bad father. Body is no longer frozen vessel empty of both instincts and living spirit.

So long as the body is unconscious, it will accept psychic incest. As body becomes conscious, however, the parental complexes can wreak havoc in the sexual relationship. The father complex tends to encase the woman in fantasy, refusing to release her into reality. Modern books about sex encourage unconscious incest when they say that it is perfectly natural and even healthy to fantasize about another partner in the sexual embrace. Supposedly this keeps sex alive in the marriage. Perhaps. It also maintains a split between fantasy and reality. The idealized father is in the fantasy; the real lover is pushed into the unconscious. The idealized father promises light, perfection, spirit separated from the humdrum reality of matter. Women will say, and often believe, that the man in their fantasy is nothing like their father. But their dreams make clear that there is a magician at work, and time usually proves that the fantasy man is like the father or the father's shadow. Once the woman recognizes what is going on, she may withdraw the projection. Then, in the presence of the actual man she may feel nothing or revulsion. Still the complex promises so much more than she thinks she has that it seduces her when the "lover" is absent. In fantasy the absent "lover" slips into long internal dialogues and lovemaking.

If the woman can pull the gold out of this dark morass, she can find her own creativity. The beloved who originally sparked her imagination may have been her father, or her mother's masculinity, or her brother. If she can steadfastly work at separating the fantasy man from the inner King her imagination projected onto him, then she can claim her own creative Christ, Buddha, Krishna—however she names the inner Beloved. Her soul is betrothed to that spirit. Once the inner union is recognized, then she and her actual man are in the bed. That's another whole story, but it is real, and if it is to work, it demands a coming together of lust and love. Conscious body filled with living spirit.

It is a long and painful process. The unconscious projections simply happen when we are young. We see someone who makes us shake, the unconscious lets an arrow fly and if it hits its mark, we are "in love." Sooner or later we may stop shaking and wonder what got into us in the first place. If we take time to think seriously, we recognize that it wasn't something that got into us, but something that was already in us that made us shake. The person outside activated a complex and with it the archetypal energy at its core. If we can bring that unconscious material into consciousness every time we fall in love, we gradually recognize our own inner masculinity. Projections happen unconsciously. They are a gift because, in realizing what we are projecting, we can claim our own energy for ourselves.

The focus in this story is on the feminine. The masculine has a secondary, but significant role. The old father's attitude in blindly assuming his daughter will obey him has within it the power that sends her on her own journey. Negative as that demand is, its effect is positive because it forces her to use her own initiative to leave his house. If he were more gentle, the daughter might be seduced and lack the strength to get out. Unable to fight his nurturing kindness, she might project her best masculine qualities onto him and then look to him for reassurance. She might not even have the self-esteem to be outraged. However stagnant her life became, she might stay. Whatever else this negative old king has done, he has given her sufficient sense of her own worth to know that she has a life to be lived and it won't be spent obeying her father or worshipping a tyrannical god. She does not want a father-husband. She wants to claim her mature, passionate being.

The growing passion is expressed in the bread soups containing the ring, spinning-wheel, and reel. With each golden gift she sends more of herself to the King, culminating in the reel that holds the thread of life. The passion her father has focused on her, she is able to transform into the passion she bestows on her inner lover. In life, this might become her commitment to her work or her religion, coming out of union with the creative side of her masculinity, not out of union with the critical, driven side.

Although the inner King appears to be merely standing and waiting, Allerleirauh's discriminating work in the kitchen has brought about immense transformation in him. We have to remember that all the characters in a fairy tale belong to one psyche. From the first transcendent moment when she beheld him, she began to move from uncooked furry animal to authenticity. She caught a vision which she did not betray. Some people have such a flash of immortality in childhood. They never forget it. Allerleirauh's masculinity moves from a tyrant who would obliterate her, both in fantasy and reality, to a King who loves her enough that he will not forsake her. He is canny enough to put a ring on her finger so that he will recognize her and aggressive enough to reveal her. Some women find his action offensive. They think the masculine should wait for the feminine to uncloak herself. However, the feminine is often reluctant to claim its own achievement and shies away from the definitive move that unveils her. She may cling to the neurotic systems that cloak the light that is released when the incestuous bonding to the old complexes is broken. Many studios are full of pictures that have never been seen; many poets never speak their poems; many musicians play only for their friends. It takes the masculine side in consciousness to give recognition to the work the feminine has achieved. She can no longer cloak the light of her spirit or the light of her body.

Why is she so terrified to show her true self? This is a very dangerous moment. She is attempting to unite two realities. In her imagination, she has learned to trust the inner King. But is she strong enough to stand to that reality in either the inner or outer world? She faces the risk of total rejection. Her imagination is about to become incarnate. Should she remain cloaked?

This is a question that I have discussed with Kate, Mary, and Rita through many rungs of the spiral in creating this book. Sometimes we had fearful dreams; sometimes we had transitional dreams that left fear far behind. Each of us has decided that this process is the meaning of our lives and this is what we want to write about in this book.

The royal marriage comes out of sacrifice: the sacrifice of the rigid father complex and with it the immature son, and the sacrifice of the clawing mother complex and the servile daughter. The energy bound into those complexes is transformed and released into the royal bride and bridegroom.

The authenticity born of that union releases the human partner from god or goddess projections. No human being can fulfill the hopes and dreams of another. Each in the outer relationship can treasure the uniqueness of the other. Rilke states the limitation and the magnitude of the human relationship very clearly:

> And this more human love (that will fulfill itself, infinitely considerate and gentle, and kind and clear in binding and releasing) will resemble that which we are preparing with struggle and toil, the love that consists in this, that two solitudes protect and border and salute each other.[4]

Chapter 8

Rita

The woods are lovely, dark, and deep
But I have promises to keep,
And miles to go before I sleep,
And miles to go before I sleep.

—Robert Frost

Initiation into their own individuality comes for most women through their body. Through sexuality, through love or loss of love, through having a child or not having a child, through illness, they are suddenly invaded by the mystery of a power over which they have no control. They are forced to surrender to their individual destiny.

An experience of the negative mother initiated the journeys of the three women in this book. Each found a way to spin the dark threads into gold. Kate was initiated through grief after an abortion. Mary was initiated through the death of her son at birth. Rita was initiated through the grief of being childless.

A woman who yearns for a child does not take conception and birth for granted. She watches the mysteries of motherhood in another and sees a miracle. She sees the swelling of the breasts and womb, the female body all circles and roundness, creating and being created. She imagines the baby fed by her own bloodstream, nourished as the brooks of spring are nourished by spring rains. She hears the tiny heart beating behind her heart, feels herself the mystery, feels her land overflowing and bringing forth. Mary in the morning forever giving birth to God in the perpetuity of his son. But God, she knows, has not chosen her to bear seed and this knowledge she daily ponders in her heart.

Rita was not overwhelmingly troubled by not having children until she was forty. She had many nieces and nephews. "In fact," she said, my intellect said that the postatomic world was a terrible place to bring children into. However, at forty, Bob and I applied to adopt a child. We were welcomed as possible parents. But this was not to be. Just after we were told that the exactly-right-child-for-us was soon to be born, I slipped on a mountainside. My first thought as I fell into space was, "Thank God, there isn't a baby." I thought I was going to be dead. I didn't think it would be so soon. Then an ecstasy came through my body as I was falling and I thought, "My God, it's been a good life." Then I blacked out.

By some miracle I was not killed in the fall, but my recovery period meant that the just-right baby had been born and went to someone else.

We persisted in our request for adoption. A month later, sitting in our little car at a stoplight, a much larger car crashed into the back of us, and we crashed into the car in front. My neck was broken. That ended our quest for a child.

When I was able to go back to work, I did not return to writing dramas for radio or film or television. These had been my chief creative work for fifteen years. I began a new career of writing and directing documentary films. In almost all of them I was asking about life in the world out there. So it went for thirteen years. At which point (I now see) what became important was to ask questions of the world in here.

That is when I seriously became a sculptor and returned to dramatic film writing. I began to allow answers from the unconscious to flow into my creative work. That's been happening ever since.

I thought I had overcome any yearning for childbearing, but that was not the case in 1985 when I was sixty-seven.

What made it clear that the yearning for a child was not overcome was a telephone call from Rita's young friend who had just given birth. The new mother was in ecstasy and described the last phases of delivery exactly as Rita had experienced them in a dream ten days before. "The nighttime beach, the phosphorescent glow on the sand and the waves coming and going . . . flowing . . . opening . . . lingering." Rita did not feel the ecstasy of the birth. She felt unbearable pain. She screamed in agony after hanging up the phone. Here is part of that dream. It occurred just before Rita came to see me the first time.

I come among a group of young people, including a young woman who has given birth. There is another young woman there who wants to. Almost immediately, she is pregnant.

Then she is quite pregnant, then very pregnant. It is still night.

Then we are all in a long line on a dark sand beach that stretches off to the right. I realize that there is now beginning a strange ritual that is not known to me (nor I think known to them). I seem to be watching, rather than taking part. The young women are lying on their bellies against the sand, but they sink down into the sand and then up again, so that in the darkness it is like a human wave. However, it is not just a wave of the sand. They are trying to go *into* the ground. They hope there is a link to be made with what is *below* the surface of the ground.

It almost happens. Then there is a cry from the pregnant girl, who is now huge with child. Her time has come. I expect her to have severe labor contractions, but now she lies on her side with her knees drawn up. A young woman beside her helps her, and then says to me, "You can hold the feet."

I see that the head of the baby is already out. I stand behind the head of the mother-to-be, and I hold a pair of tiny feet, one in each hand, with the soles toward me, the right foot slightly larger than the left. They appear to be very small and vulnerable and I don't want to hold too tightly and hurt them, but not too loosely to let go. I think, "They must be healthy and strong for use as they grow."

Now there is one push by the mother, and the pelvis opens and the child emerges. I gasp at the beauty and smoothness of the birth. It is so simple and inevitable. I believe it is a girl, but shortly after, I realize that I didn't check or ask.

This is called an initial dream in an analysis. It usually points the direction in which the analysis will go. This is a very propitious dream for Rita, personally.

It is also a collective dream. The sitting by the seashore with a row of women breathing with the sea in a birth ritual is a repetitive motif in contemporary dreams. Their kneading of the ground trying to make a link with what is below the surface is another characteristic. The birth of the child out of the sea of its mother's womb suggests something new coming out of the eternal sea. That the gender of the child is not significant points to the Androgyne—the new individual in whom differentiated masculinity and femininity are in harmony. In the death throes of patriarchy through which we are living, these dreams of something totally new being born from the sea bring hope.

Writing this short extract from thousands of pages of journaling has been "psychic homeopathy" for Rita. This is her phrase for the partial repetition of her illnesses as she wrote about the period in which each originally occurred.

"When I finish this book, I am going to be healthy," she says. "Reliving everything that evolved has brought pain and enormous difficulty in writing about it. But I have persevered. As a result, I have not gone through the illness again, but elements of the illness have entered into my physical and psychic systems as curing agents. I have built up the strength to deal with them. All has been guided by an extraordinary, unexpected presence."

Our work together has been unusual in that Rita at seventy-two was trying to bring her life into a clearer focus. To do that she wanted to return to important dreams that she had worked on years before. Thus we were looking at the dream both in its original context and in its effect on her in the present. Whereas I usually work very slowly in allowing the impact of a dream to reveal itself to the dreamer, in this situation I was much more forthright in interpretation, trying to hold the dream in its relation to the thread of her life. While Rita's conscious ego is strong, her body is no longer young, and we were working simultaneously with dreams from the past and from the present. In being forthright, I was careful to respect the sculpture that had already been shaped and fired.

Rita was the youngest child and only daughter in a family of four children. When she was born, two of her brothers were in their teens, one was almost three. She remembers her family sitting at the dinner table, her mother and brothers talking excitedly, she sitting quietly beside her quiet father contemplating his beautiful garden outside the window. He always called her his "one and only." In his presence, she was safe. She felt no competition from her mother. She observed and sometimes adored her older brothers, and was like a twin to her youngest. She knew that boys had a much freer time in the world. As a child she wondered where her own smell was among all the male smells. As she came into adulthood, she determined to find out.

Rita's perseverance has been indomitable. Of her own volition, she began the work of going back through years of journaling to try to bring to consciousness what she was not at the earlier time able to integrate. During recurrent illnesses and accidents, her inner guide told her how to find a new balance. In meditation, he continues to guide her step by step toward health and spiritual growth.

As I have come to know her over the years, I have been profoundly moved by her courage. She faces into darkness with the wit and wisdom of a seasoned crone. Watching her I often think of the saying,

"The old dog for the road, and the puppy for the path." Age has embodied and empowered her.

At the Orillia Conference a year ago, Robert Bly and I wanted to make the closing session more intimate. We had the chairs arranged in concentric circles. We asked the elders to take their places in the innermost circle. It was awesome and energizing to have that circle of white heads at the center. Many people were astonished when sprightly Rita took her place among the elders.

She has dealt with her temporal arteritis in a most creative way. She has been cooperative with the medical doctors, at the same time visualizing and dialoguing with her body. When her neck and body began to swell from prednisone, she went to a maternity shop and bought sweaters and blouses such as pregnant women wear.

She knows the sadness of looking in a mirror and seeing lines where wrinkles used to be. She also knows the joy of having reached the place where every day is lived for today. In 1984 she wrote, "Doors are clanging behind me, shut, resonating down paths that were once wide open for me to go at will. Now forever closed."

Now she says, "Look what's happened since 1984! By far, my best sculpture. My whole inner journey and my inner guidance. Although doors close, other doors keep opening. And maybe they will until I die.

"I think that from . . . maybe forty on . . . you think you've had it. I remember after almost every film I'd be wiped out. I'd look in the mirror and think, 'Well, you've had it this time.' But from forty on have been the best years of my life."

Rita has chosen to write under her own name. "If I use the name Dorothy Speadle," she said, "what is the point? I don't want to fictionalize myself. No time for that now. I am seventy-two. I want to deal with my own truth. This is my statement of my experience in seeking God and in being led. This is what I live now and this is how I got to this point in my journey.

"My sculptures came out of me. I use my own name for them. This has come out of me. I use my own name.

"In fact I've been writing this book since 1977, fourteen years. How out of three thousand pages can I choose the thread that has been my life? This has been the challenge. This has been the reward. Clarifying my path and the thread that has led me through. I have stepped away from it from time to time and then had to find my way back. That is what my story is about, that and my dreams, my wonderful contact with my inner guides, my actual companions, my companions through their writings—all have brought me to the point where I am."

And now we hand the talking stick to Rita.

Chapter 9

The Endless Beginning

RITA GREER ALLEN

yet still in the night I reach
for holds eluding my clutch
till the moment comes when the Furies
relent   I catch and cling
swoop   alight on a friendly ground
and run again on two good feet
over the grass of dream

—earle birney[1]

Why am I writing this?

Marion said, "Are you interested in telling how you got to where you are?"

"Yes!"

I said it immediately without a beat.

Why did I do that?

I don't strip in public.

I definitely don't strip down to my soul for everyone to see. For *anyone* to see. But "yes" I said, before fear grabbed me.

Then Marion said: "And I will help you with the dreams." And a kind of trembling joy entered the fear. Opportunity. The opportunity to make the journey once more, to bring more treasure from the unconscious into consciousness.

But more than that. I believe that if my telling of this tale is what I leave behind me when I die, it is the most important thing I will have done with my life.

The fear is still here, in front of me, ready to grab my breath, grab at my heart. But I have learned that if I face fear, enter it step by terrifying

216

step, it opens to a path that leads to the very thing I long for. I must trust in that once more, so that now, with a deep breath and a trembling heart, I will take the first step.

So . . .

What follows are pages from my journals, outbursts of joy and of anger, thoughts, dreams, and talk about those dreams with Marion Woodman. It is the story of how I got to meet god.

I'll begin it in January 1977.

I

From my journal
January 31, 1977

I am so high today, I feel capable of anything. *Raku Fire* is a success! And the Head of Drama has asked me to write three more full-length film scripts to make up a quartet. I have been modest.

"Let's contract for one," I have said, ". . . for now."

There's no doubt about the film's contents. The main character is stomping around in my head, shouting, "Let me tell my story!" It's the Reverend Daniel Lewis, and apparently he didn't like what people said about him in *Raku Fire*. He didn't like that woman saying he'd shoved his hand up her crotch.

"It wasn't the way it sounds," he says. "I am a physically needy man, yes. With a dying wife. But I am a loving man. And, first and foremost, I am a Christian minister. My Church. My God. My beliefs. That is what is at my core: my Christianity. And I am willing to peel away the layers of my outer being until that is what you see. My Christianity."

OK, Daniel, we have ninety minutes of airtime. Ready when you are.

Suddenly, I see Mother's eyes flash angrily. Have I put it too crudely? All right, then. The film is basically about the deep and unpredictable passion of a Puritan. That sounds . . . nicer. Yes?

But also! As well as all that! In my other life as a sculptor, I have been invited to be in an exhibition-workshop with some of the best ceramic muralists around. A wonderful opportunity! Yes? Yes! Yes! I want it badly. But Daniel, the Christian, must come first.

Journal: in country
May 10, 1977

I've been working in the country Treehouse for weeks now, and the script keeps pouring out of the typewriter. When I go up to the top of the hill to meditate, my tree says, "Take time."

Take time for what? I wonder.

May 29, 1977

Delight! I am getting something out of myself that I *want* to get out. And I'm being paid for it! What a marvelous profession I chose. I LOVE IT! I wish I could get this script finished before I have to go back to the city. However. It'll only be a couple of days of citification.

Journal: in city
June 27, 1977

I am angry, and I feel it growing in me so intensely my head is about to burst if I don't scream, or smash, or TYPE TYPE TYPE. I'm *bored* by this domesticity. All these *things* that are demanding to be done. Now the plumbing's gone pfutt on the top floor, Bob tells me, and get it fixed, please, he's busy. And the furnace man's coming to clean, and the housekeeper's leaving tomorrow. And I'm supposed to deal with meatheads like Doug Lebo and Christ knows who his helpers are, milling around outside, supposedly cleaning windows and taking three hours trying to figure out what screen goes back on where. It is a god almighty crazy crazy wasting life. And I just want to get out of here! I feel crushed under the terrible weight of undone things. I need the stimulus of my own power! Desperately.

Bobby phones and is sorry that he bugged me. The anger is dissipating. Most of it of course is anger at my self and my own sloth. I do not want to be so slow and so boringly *stuck*. After all, I like a nice, well-run house too. If only . . . What? If only I could snap my fingers and all the undone things were done. Ha!

July 5, 1977

It's been a weird up and down week, coping and not coping, struggling up, slithering down. But I'm heading for the country tomorrow, and my beautiful Treehouse, and my wonderful script. Thank god.

Journal: in country
July 8, 1977

This morning, I woke up trembling. I'd had a dream which, I now realize, started off beautifully.

I am getting off a bus at an ocean beach. The sand stretches away for miles, empty of people; the waves roll gently in; a seabird flies along the water edge; the sun shines. I feel very good and ready for the day. The bus driver leans on his steering wheel, smiling, and we talk. On and on, as though he had nothing better to do. Then suddenly I feel: "Come on! You're making yourself late. This talking is unimportant!" So I hurriedly wave and run across the road away from the beach, to where there is a huge, totally enclosed broadcasting studio. Inside, to my left, is a stage where an orchestra is tuning up behind the great closed curtains; to my right, there are banks of seats stretching up and back into the far darkness of the auditorium. Already it is packed with people. I am to be one of the four announcers for a big special show, and I have written and will deliver the opening lines. I am feeling very sure about it. I've been here earlier today to make sure that everything is ready for my part in the performance, and I've placed my equipment in a very special place where I can plug it in. This "equipment" consists of a "booth blanket," which I've devised. It is a black groundsheet with a microphone attached to its inner surface and a built-in light, so that when I wrap it around myself, and the lights in the auditorium go down, I will be able to see to read my script. I will be heard over my hidden mike, but I will not be seen by anyone, including cameras. I feel very proud about this.

But I won't wrap the blanket around me yet, because some more people are coming in through the one small door from the sunny outside. And among them, I see my father and my mother. I feel very pleased, sure that they'll be proud of me. I am aware of their small stature, but aware of their power. Daddy looks at me, and smiles and nods. Mother looks at my position among the professionals at the front, and although I feel a certain pride from her, her expression says, "Well. I'll reserve judgment." They move on to take seats in the darkness of the auditorium. I realize it is time to set up my "booth blanket" and get my script in order. The producer comes by, and briskly says, "No! You don't need that (my booth blanket). You're supposed to be down in the front row." And the hotshot, go-go-go producer moves on. So I pick up my script, which I'm pleased about because I've typed it on white dish towels, so there will be no rustle of paper on the microphone. But . . . as I move down to the front row, the lights start to go down, and I haven't sorted out my script. I hurry to join the other announcers, and on the P.A. system I hear a promo for this performance. The voice is my voice recorded earlier, and I'm horrified; it sounds very arch and artificial. And I think, "Oh shit! I've got to do better than that. I've got to *practice!*" Then I sit down in my seat and start sorting the script, but there seem to be a lot of dish towels with nothing on them. I start to feel very anxious. The lights go down farther. The other announcers come in. Very definitely pros. "In the Club," I think. But I am too busy sorting the dish towels to join. I realize I'm not going to be able to rehearse when I find the pages . . . and now without the booth blanket light, I can't even see. Then an international producer comes by, and sits down beside me, and smiles saying, "Long time since we saw each other." "Long time," I say, as I try to sort. He kisses me on the mouth. I smile, all false. His kiss is cold and clammy. "It's a lie," I think. "I can't stand him. Or him, me. And I'm doing this instead of getting my script together. Time, time. . . ." The lights dim further.

Suddenly I panic. I spread the towels out on the chairs beside me, trying to find some sense, some order. I get down on my knees, trying to see. Last minute arrivals are climbing into the seats beside me. I have to gather up my script.

The orchestra stops tuning, is silent, ready. The auditorium lights go out. The spotlights go on. The curtain begins to rise. I have not got my "booth blanket"; I have not got a microphone; I have not got a light; I have not got a script; I am still on my hands and knees among the tea towels. I am going to have to get up on stage and stop everything and they're going to have to wait until I am ready. And all the announcers are looking at me. "These amateurs," their looks say. "Women!"

And I think: "God damn it! No matter how well prepared I am, I *always* mess things up at the last minute."

I woke. My heart pounding. My pulse throbbing from my crotch to the crown of my head. When I tried to get out of bed, my knees felt as though they were running in different directions. What on earth is it all about? That dream.

1990: Marion Woodman and I talk about this dream.

MARION: And that happened . . . when?

RITA: Thirteen years ago.

MARION: Did you analyze the dream then?

RITA: I tried to. I didn't know much about Jung, but I wrote down the stuff that came into my mind. I mean, I was very upset. Here I was in this dream expecting to do my job as a professional, to be the power behind this great production, and here I was losing my words, losing my technique, losing control. And why? Because of one look from my mother. And because of all those ridiculous tea towels. Domesticity! That's what the tea towels meant to me. My domestic life messing up my professional life. But the thing that upset me most— and this is the way I wrote it down at the time—was that "I should get off the bus at this beautiful wide open seashore, where I could breathe deeply and be at one with the ocean and the seabirds. And then choose to go down into the dark cave of a studio, in order to be a *power*, with everything under my control. And then I have nothing under control. It's crazy! *crazy*."

MARION: Rita, this "getting off the bus." Did you leave the collective in 1977?

RITA: My god! Isn't that interesting? I didn't know I was leaving the collective . . . if you call the mass media the collective. . . . I thought I was moving to a new height. I mean, I'd had many, many years of making successful documentaries and dramas, film, radio, television. Now, with this film *Raku Fire* I was up for awards, and a beautiful new contract. I could go into my studio and close the door and write whatever I wanted.

MARION: You could turn your back on the open ocean, the creative matrix, and go into your own "booth blanket. . . ."

RITA: It was a little "control booth" that held just one. Me.

MARION: What a wonderful metaphor.

RITA: For what?

MARION: Notice your words: "When I wrap this blanket around myself, and the lights in the auditorium go down, I will be able to see with my own light, but not be seen, I will be able to speak through my own microphone."

RITA: How would you interpret that?

MARION: You want to look out at other people, but you don't want them to see you.

RITA: That's me. That's exactly me. Private. Secretive. I don't want to talk about me. I want to talk about *you*. I'm interested in *you*.

MARION: Right. But, it's all performance.

RITA: Performance?

MARION: Listen to the words in the dream: "*I* have written the script. *I* have to read in a certain voice. *I* have to go down to the front and *I* have it all figured out. Because *I* have contrived this portable "booth blanket. . ."

RITA: . . . this "*control* booth . . ."

MARION: . . . this "*control* booth blanket" with a reading light in it, so I will be able to see in the dark, and *I* will be able to speak, as no one else will . . .

RITA: Wow! You talk about inflated ego!

MARION: You see the metaphor now?

RITA: Power.

MARION: Yes. "I'm going to be there right at the first, and it's going to go *my* way." But then your father and your mother come in, and your father smiles, and your mother looks at you and "reserves judgment." And then, you just lose control. The next thing is tea towels and loss of the control booth.

RITA: And it's mother that pushes the button.

MARION: Yes. But you see, Rita, there's positive and negative. It's a dark pit that you're in. There's not much consciousness there. But soon, the curtains will open, and light will pour out. And, although you're not ready for it at the time of this dream . . .

you're down there on the floor, with this huge energy, you're down in the dark on your hands and knees scrambling among the tea towels.

RITA: . . . tea towels meaning?

MARION: As you guessed, domesticity. You're trying to deal with your personal life and your professional life and all the time, the curtain is going up, and a new light is appearing, and you are going to be shown for what you are. This is a big dream, Rita. Do you think this was the beginning of your journey?

RITA: The beginning of the journey. Yes. And it was the end of . . . you used the word "performance." It was the beginning of the end of that. I remember someone saying to me, just about this point in my life, "Rita, when I look at you I see great aliveness and enthusiasm, covered by a mask of aliveness and enthusiasm."

MARION: Right on. And this dream is saying, "Take off the mask, emerge as yourself."

Journal: in country
July 8, 1977, afternoon

This morning, I sat on the deck and listened to music. Glenn Gould. Bach's Italian Concerto. And watched an ant dragging a piece of fired clay that must have dropped from one of my sculptures. A load ten times too heavy for him. Why does he do it? The music brought me peace; the ant brought me compassion. It's one o'clock now, and time to sit down at the typewriter to let Daniel continue to tell his story.

Late afternoon

This is terrible. This is absolutely *terrible*. I've read back over the film I've written, and it's appalling. It's all surface, like a Harlequin romance. And I was writing *deeply*; I was delving deeply; every day I was letting Daniel peel away another layer of his being, until now, *now*

we were reaching toward the core. Or so I thought. But here is this . . .
schlock. Why? What did I do wrong? Is it the quality of my writing? Is
it that I don't know what I'm writing about? Shut up! Stop it! Stop
beating myself. *Now*! I *do* know what I'm writing about. Put down a
quick synopsis. This is the story:

A thirty-eight-year-old Protestant minister returns to a tiny church
that played a crucial role in his early life. It sits on the edge of the rocky
shore of a remote and beautiful inlet of Lake Attawapisket, far north, at
one with nature and with God. He arrives to discover it is being sold. It
will be converted into a hunting lodge. He is filled with the towering
rage of a Jehovah. This sale must be reversed. He will fight until it is.
So, the film is about a fight for wilderness property, and for church
property. On the surface. But under the surface, it is the story of a man
facing his personal, sexual, religious, spiritual strengths, and needs,
and failings. A man facing into his own Christianity.

But what have I written? Daniel doing a lot of lollygagging and
manipulating in high places.

Facing into his Christianity?

No.

Facing his true religious beliefs?

No.

The script is all loose ends, threads hanging out, leading nowhere.
Shit! I'm going to get myself a cup of coffee. And what? Start again?

Suddenly I see mother's blue eyes, open wide, staring at me. Judging. What is she judging me for? I said "shit." I'm sorry. But oh god,
mother, let me scream somehow. Or, laugh with me. How wonderful
it was when your eyes were so full of laughter that the tears flowed
down your cheeks. Oh my, oh my, oh my, you'd say. Oh my.

Journal: in city
August 15, 1977

I'm blocked with this script. It doesn't matter whether I'm here or in
the country. The deadline for delivery is looming up, and I've got one
big writer's block. I think it has something to do with Mother.
What?

Don't be naive, you know what.

What?

Stop it. Just sit here and write it out. Feel through it, and let it come out.

Tomorrow. Some day.

Thoughts
September, 1977

Okay.

Mother has now been dead for nine years . . . or, to be more exact, it is nine years ago that the stroke hit her. ("Someone is going to hear about this!" she said as they wheeled her into emergency, furious at the doctor who had given her medication that was too strong.) I see her now, lying in the corridor of St. Michael's, asleep, pale, and to my eyes, already dead. But that was before the stroke. Then it was a matter of heart palpitations. And it was after the last really strong statement of her energy when, fed up with lying in that emergency room, she refused to be ignored any longer and so reached for anything to attract attention . . . no bell, no buzzer . . . and found a bedpan within reach. And the early morning silence of the ward vibrated with the crash of a bedpan flung with all her frustrated fury against a wall.

"That'll bring them running!"

And it brought them running. She was not one to be ignored, was Mother.

I could not ignore her, ever. I could not ignore her social standards, nor her religious beliefs. I cannot ignore her now.

I did evade her. That is true. I didn't, for instance, ever go to the north of England to actually see where she grew up, a hundred years ago, to experience that precarious social milieu, poor, surrounded by slum streets, where the drunken fights on Saturday nights brought on the screams for "Pollis! The Pollis! Pollliss!"

Though there were no fights on *her* street. Oh no! Dundas Street was proper. Poor but proper. And one of the dividing lines between poor-proper, and poor-slum was membership in chapel.

Education for both kinds of poor was minimal. Mother, I believe, had only three or four years of schooling. And loved it. Longed to go on and on and on. Yearned to be like her rich-but-proper cousins who were sent to the continent for finishing school. But no. Mother was needed to serve in grandma's shop. (Was it a bakery? Is that what really happened?)

But she could read well, and write well, and the way to reading more, I believe, was chapel. Broadening the mind through study of the Bible, and study of the books of the nonconformist teachers: Dr. Marsh, Sankey, Wesley. Her bright mind taking it in, sifting it, storing it, discussing, memorizing, absorbing the Word of God. An educational goal within the very limited possibilities of the place and time, under the influence and demands of my tiny, straight-backed, tight-laced, black-gowned, and bonnetted grandmother.

Chapel.

And where else, in that limited world, to meet suitable proper and sober young men? Only chapel. And so there, she was beloved (at a proper distance) by Billy Marsh, Billy Broderick, the Kerrison brothers, with Arthur Kerrison more seriously anxious than any to walk her home after chapel by the roundabout seashore route. Oh, the lovely sound of waves crashing on the rocks; the blood coursing through the body; the soft words with which one could discuss the love of Jesus as presented in the morning sermon.

And finally, one Sunday, there at chapel was a young man she'd never seen before, on leave from his ship that would be sailing out of the harbor very soon for the Red Sea and Istanbul . . . oh, too soon! . . . Egypt . . . and not to return for six, eight, many months. And so she fell forever in love with Joshua Edwin Wayman, who became, three sons and twenty years later, my father. But more. I believe that there were true religious reasons for her devotion to chapel, and to the Word of God. A sense of wonder at what God had provided, and what Christ promised; a sense of security in the strictly defined set of beliefs that made it perfectly clear to her what she would do; the firm assurance that she, personally, was "guided by God." ("Make no mistake, this is God's guidance," as she often said, her eyes wide with both wonder and a look that would brook no question.)

And more than that. I believe that there, in that chapel, there came a flood of ecstasy into her being that could only be called holy. Young, passionate, her sexuality barely repressed, full of longings of all kinds, all this and whatever it is in the human soul and psyche that yearns for God, culminated in her decision to take Jesus as her personal Savior, and to believe that his words would give the answers to all the questions that might arise in life. He would give her the reason for her living, the path to follow, and her goal.

Yes! Today, I finally can see how right she is. For her. So *right!*

For me? Oh . . . oh . . . oh. . . .

There's a sudden jab of pain through the temples. I must close my eyes and be very quiet. And what do I see behind my closed eyes? *Her* eyes, glaring at me, out of that speech-impaired, stroke-stricken, dying face.

"Say *yes!*" they cry. "Say yes, I believe! Let me go before my Maker, knowing that I have done the job that I was put on Earth to do. Knowing that I have brought all my children to God. *Knowing* that you will all be there, when it is your time, because you have said, 'Yes, I believe!' I beseech you, I beseech you. Say 'yes!' "

But I couldn't, at her deathbed, then.

And I can't, now.

And I am terrified.

The truth is that I thought I could avoid all this personal confrontation by letting Daniel do it for me. He'd dance out my beliefs for me, and with a pirouette, say, Voila! And I would *know.* I would know why I cannot accept Mother's beliefs, and must cling to my own.

Because I do have religious beliefs.

And I do not know what they are.

I have never known what they are. Even when I was twelve years old, standing in the waist-high water of the baptistery of Danforth Baptist Church, waiting for my brother to be dunked first, because he was the older, knowing that this was a terrible solemn moment before God and this congregation, when I was accepting Jesus Christ and would be receiving the Holy Ghost who would descend from above as I rose from the water.

I stood waiting, still and silent, with everything in my inner being screaming, "No! There's been a mistake! This isn't what I meant, Mother, when I said 'I wouldn't mind being baptized.' I only meant that I wasn't afraid of the water anymore. You weren't listening in your moment of triumphant jubilation. And I hadn't the courage to say no. I haven't the courage. . . ."

And the minister baptized me, and when I rose from the water, the Holy Ghost did not descend.

October 24, 1977

This morning I had this dream:

> I am hurrying across Shuter Street, on my way to Massey Hall, where
> there's going to be a wonderful concert. I can hear that it's already
> begun. I am filled with joyous expectation. I have my ticket in my hand,
> and I can see, in my mind's eye, exactly where my seat is in the right
> balcony. I can see my brother glowing in the warm brown light from the
> stage, surrounded by friends, and there is my seat, waiting.
>   I get to the main door just as the doorman is closing it. I call, "Stop!
> Wait . . ." and I hold up my ticket.
>   "It's started," he says.
>   "I know. I can hear it," and I smile brightly, knowing that he will let
> me in. He doesn't. He points to the stage door.
>   "Go through there, and down and around." And he closes the door.
> Clang.
>   I run to the stage door, go in, go down, go through a dark rehearsal
> hall. But halfway through, I realize that it is exactly like the basement
> hall of Danforth Baptist Church, where I went to Sunday school, where
> I went with my mother to prayer meetings, where I went, when I was
> old enough, to Young People's. I shudder, and I hurry on into a dark
> hallway. And there! going up, is a spiral staircase. The music grows
> louder as I climb. My heart sings. Oh, to be *there!* In that soft glow with
> my brother and my friends, and the music!
>   And suddenly . . . there is no step above me.
>   The stairs have spiraled into the wall and disappeared; they emerge
> eight or ten feet higher up. Far beyond my reach. I cannot go up! I look
> down. The stairs below have disappeared in the darkness. Are they
> there? No. I cannot go down.

I wake, my fists clenched, hanging on to nothing.

October 26, 1977

I went to see Harvey today. He's very good with dreams.
     Harvey said, "You are in an impasse."
     I said, "You mean with this script? With Daniel?"
     "With more than that. You are stuck on that staircase. An impasse!"

"What do I do? In an impasse?"

"Stay there. How do you feel?"

"Very frightened."

"Did you realize how frightening you could be?"

"Me?"

"Yes. You. All your dream is you. If it isn't some aspect of you that is frightening you, what is it?"

It was a totally new concept of myself. Me? Gentle me, the peacemaker. Rita, the epitome of niceness, kindness . . . *me*, frightening?

"And the fear began, in your dream, at what point?" asked Harvey.

"Well . . ." and my heart began to pound, and I could feel my throat tightening my voice, "actually when I saw the rehearsal hall was . . . Sunday school."

"Shall we go back to then?"

"Then?"

"Sunday school?"

"NO!"

"Another time, then. Whenever you're ready."

I suddenly realized that I was crying. I slid down to the floor. Then I screamed. I beat the floor with my fist, and screamed. I scared myself silly. *I don't do that kind of thing.* I don't scream, ever. I long to, yes. But do it? NO! NOOO! NO.

1990: Marion and I talk.

MARION: What do you think brought on the screaming?

RITA: Terror. Terror that I would never reach the world I longed for, that I would drop into the dark abyss below.

MARION: Drop into your shadow?

RITA: My shadow?

MARION: Yes. That heavenly world you're climbing to is an unreal world, it's the world of the ideal . . . waaay up there . . . the ideal world of the artist. But your other world is down there in the cellar. Your worlds are too far apart. So, "pick up your cellar, kid." That's what your unconscious was saying. "It's time now to face your shadow."

RITA: But down there in the cellar is Sunday school! I mean, that's sacred space. Isn't it?

MARION: Sacred space often feels like a dark abyss, simply because we've never allowed ourselves to go there. We're terrified
of the energy in the parts of ourselves we haven't lived. I think
your dream is saying, "Face your shadow, Rita. Unless you do,
you're stuck, you're not going anywhere."
RITA: That's amazing! Do you know why? Because I didn't know
what that dream was trying to tell me at the time, that is,
logically. But instinctively, I knew I had to change something,
somehow. I had to change something in me.

Journal: in city
October 27, 1977

I've got to . . . what what what what . . . stop this. Daniel. This push
push push. What to do? Recontract. I can try to. Postpone. New
deadline, a long long long way off. Next season. Something. I need to
get away from Daniel. I need to dig into myself. I need. . . . Sculpt.
Yes. Sculpt.

November 4, 1977

Whewwooooooooooooo. . . . What does it feel like? Like a noose has
been taken off my neck. I have a lovely new contract. Deadline: NEXT
YEAR!! A whole year, free of Daniel and film, and agony. A whole year,
to get into the clay studio and sculpt!

December 11, 1977

Clay is wonderful. Clay is a very exacting material for a sculptor. The
paradox is that clay is the most difficult material to work with, because
it is the easiest. It makes no demands on you; what you make is
nothing but an expression of what you are. Not what your mind *thinks*
about things. For instance, if I try to make a sculpture in the style of
someone twenty years ago, or two thousand years ago, what emerges
is an aspect of *me*. Sure, you can learn restraint, discipline, technique,
but you can't stop the expression of yourself, once you start.

And then to fire the work in the Raku way! Oh oh oh oh oh . . . now you're into something else! No matter how skilled you are with the fire and the smoking, you cannot control the sudden change of direction of the wind that might blow the fire and smoke exactly where you don't want it. So a superb piece of work on which you've spent hours, days, weeks, may be blackened by . . . what seems to be a whim of nature. Smoke enters the pores of the white clay. White turns black, where you wanted white to stay white. You have lost control. You are in the hands of the gods. So, the result is an expression of what you are, *and* how the gods treated you today.

August 29, 1978

A phone call to ask me how the film script was coming. Film? Ho, yes. I didn't tell them that I hadn't thought of it for ten months. Which isn't quite true. I may not have thought about Daniel specifically, but I've done a lot of feeling into his problem and mine: what *does* he believe, what *do* I believe. And I can feel some of the answers emerging out of the clay, and speaking out of the sculpture. Like this sculpted head on the wall in front of me. His eyes challenge me every time I glance at him; his smiling mouth holds back secrets that are almost spoken, that I almost hear. I believe that this is the head of Hermes that I un-knowingly shaped. And I believe (watch it! I'm getting mystical) that he is here to do precisely what Hermes did, to lead me up to the realm of heaven and to lead me down through the gates of hell. And Daniel, this time, will have to follow *me*.

But look out! I suddenly remember: Hermes is also the god of the crossroads. He is the trickster.

Journal: in country
September 4, 1978

What a glorious piece of country land we own! There is an energy here that I don't understand, but I certainly feel. There is an energy in my tree. *My* tree! How funny, when there are at least a thousand trees on the hills and valleys of our land. Yet one tree, standing at the top of the hill, felt special from the very first day.

"Where does our property end?" I asked the real estate man.

"At that tree," he said, "and I saw a buck and a doe standing there when I came by this morning. Against the sky, at the top of the hill. Wonderful sight!"

I've never seen a buck and a doe up there, but I soon became aware that "my tree" was not a single tree, but two trees, so beautifully close and interconnected, that they appeared to be one. Married. Female to the west, male to the east. And it is to the female side that I go in the evening, and rest, and meditate. For some reason that I cannot fathom, I am not able to approach the male side. I've tried, and something stops me. I stand, and respect it, but I cannot touch it. Strange.

I mention this to Earle. He looks up from his book, and says, "Animism," and goes back to his book. I feel accused. My precious mystery is named, pigeonholed and condemned.

Oh, how I recognize the feeling! Condemned, dismissed by the authority, because I'm guilty. Of what? A dream floods into my mind. I must have been six.

MEMORY OF A DREAM, 1924

It is night time. Two men are leading me across our back garden, through the fence, in through the back door of my girlfriend's house, where I often came to play. I am stopped, inside the door, by a table, behind which is seated a man with a large book and candles to illuminate the book. He has a plume-pen in his hand, and then I see that he is wearing a white blouse with ruffles at the neck, and he has long hair. I realize that the two men who have brought me, and who stand now, one at either side of me, are also dressed in very old-fashioned costumes, only theirs are red and of rough material. I become frightened, but stand obediently, waiting. The man at the table looks at his book, looks up at me, asks if my name is Rita Wayman. Yes, I say. He ticks off my name, and jerks his head towards the kitchen door, where, I see, is a larger table, heavier, ornate, behind which sit *three* men in white wigs and black gowns. They are judges. And I suddenly know that everyone who comes before them is judged guilty. I don't know what I have done. But I know that I will be led away from there, guilty.

I was six years old. And I was guilty. Of what? Of being Rita Wayman? Of being a girl in a family of males plus mother? Of playing with a girl? Over the back fence? When I was forbidden to play with the kids on the street? Caught on the very path I trod as I disobeyed. Caught by men; named by a man; condemned by a tribunal, a triumvirate, a trinity of men. Guilt grabs me again as I write those words, fifty-odd years later. Where did I learn such guilt? At Sunday school? I don't know. At church?

In fact, now that I let myself think about it, I don't know *what* I learned at church. I know what I was *taught*. I was taught to love my neighbor. But I never understood what that meant.

At the age of ten, I remember standing in the dining room window bay having just come, full of (I hoped) holiness, from church. The woman next door was in her garden, and I could hear her ugly, loud laugh ricocheting between the walls. I didn't even *like* my neighbor. If I didn't like her, how could I love her? I tried. I stood at the window and tried, and I discovered that if I let my mind go mushy and let my feeling spread out to cover "all mankind," I *could* include the woman next door. If I didn't think about her. Or listen to her laugh.

As I grew older, I discovered that the best I could do was to be polite, agreeable, and helpful to other people (or to avoid them), and to give up my streetcar seat to someone older than myself, and not to elbow people out of the way in a crowd. In fact, to be as pleasant (a lot of the time) to other people as I hoped other people would be (and sometimes were) to me. It made me feel, in fact, superior. Which, I think, is a far cry from "loving my neighbor."

I was taught to give myself in skilled service to others. And yes. I have tried to do that. I have always tried to increase my skills, in order to . . . to pretend that whatever I was going to do was "in skilled service to others." Worthwhile. Not just for my own pleasure. Not frivolous. And never, ever, intentionally harmful. Nice. Good. Useful. And never just "in skilled service to" . . . myself. I always have to believe that there is a more worthwhile goal, eventually, than serving *me*. Even if I never reach it. I can tie myself up in a fine mess that way. And do so.

Sculpture. What use is my sculpting to anyone but me? Really. So stop!

Drawing. Painting. Recorder playing. Piano. Lying in the sun. Stop!

It isn't that I always stop doing what I really want to do. It's that I rarely feel easy about it. Including this writing. I mean, it isn't as though this helps anyone but me. Writing "Daniel" would be very very worthwhile (Head of Drama has assured me so) "in skilled service" to a huge film audience. But this journal writing? It is only for me. So stop! Get back to Daniel. What was Daniel taught? To what is Daniel committed?

Daniel is committed to Jesus Christ. Yes. *I* was taught to be committed to Jesus Christ, too. But . . . if I am to write Daniel, I have to understand what that means. *Really* means. "To believe that he is the Only Son of God" . . . "to accept him as my personal Savior" . . . "to give my life to Him." I have never understood any of those things, and have never been able to say, Yes, I believe; yes, I will; yes, I do. Without lying. Daniel has been able to say yes. And that is the reason I am blocked with this film script. I don't *understand* him. And I find myself getting very angry.

I am not stupid! I mean, when I was being taught about God and Christ and all that stuff at church, I was being taught English and math and physics and all *that* stuff at school. Well, I got the hang of the English and physics so that I passed with honors, and I got 100% on my year's work in trigonometry and algebra. But I never could get the hang of what the Christian religion was all about.

Of course, I knew it was about Jesus Christ, and the way he lived, and the way he died, and that my job was to do likewise. But how did he live? First off (as I remember it), he turns to his mother, when he's twelve or so, and says, "Woman, what have you to do with *me?*" And that puts her in her place all right. And that's a very nasty, rude kid she's got. Now, maybe she'd been a real nagger, so it was good old adolescent rebellion. But I never remember anybody telling me to do *that*. The opposite.

"Who do you think you are! Talking to your mother like that. Go to your room at once! And stay there until you're ready to apologize. And beg God to forgive you, too!"

So then, Jesus goes off and talks back to the guys in church. The ministers and deacons and all those. And tells them off. Well, just try *that*.

And then, he goes off into the desert by himself, and tries to figure things out. It takes him forty days, a month and a bit. So I guess he quits his job to do that. And when he comes back he's got it all straight. And the terrific thing is that a bunch of guys believe him and listen to every word he says, and he becomes their leader. And that's great. Because I think now that he'd probably had a pretty big experience out there in the desert, not eating anything but locusts and honey, and wandering around in the beating sunshine. I think something *big* happened to him. But nobody was encouraging *me* to go off to have my own experience of God. Not even Jesus. Especially not Jesus. "You've got to go through me," is what he said. Or, to put it more poetically: "I am the way, the truth, and the life; no one cometh to the Father but by Me." Well, brother, if that isn't an uppity secretary talking there, I don't know what is. And the church of Jesus taught me that even in my yearning private prayers to my "Father which art in heaven," I must go "through Jesus Christ our Lord. Amen."

Why? I WANT TO GET THROUGH TO GOD! DIRECTLY! NOW.

As I write, I find my heart trembling, and my breath shortening, and a constriction in my solar plexus. How funny . . . no, not funny at all . . . how terrifying that the hold of childhood teachings can be so strong that even now, fifty years later, I react like a little girl caught out in some wickedness. My guilt punishes my body. My fear is of truly great punishment that will descend from parental heights. Or higher. Because what I have poured out is terribly, morally *wrong*.

What is morally right? Where do I search? What have I denied?

Mother's eyes flash. Of course, I know what I have denied. Her life's meaning. Her dying plea. Her Jesus.

Journal: in city
November 15, 1978

Okay, I'll face it. Deep breath. I *said* I'd tackle this script straight on this time.

So, one of my places of denial, fifty years ago, was at the People's Church, where uncle was a deacon, and where, if anywhere, I would be "persuaded" to "go down to the front" and "be saved." So. . . .

Last Sunday, I felt desperate enough to try anything. "After all," I said to myself, "there *are* mortals in whom you can sense god. I have met at least one myself. Those who 'open out in back, as it were, to eternity.' If I try, at this point in my life, to open myself, not only to the ministers of conventional churches whom I have been interviewing and have found to be good men but dull . . . but also if I open myself to the charismatic evangelists . . . I might find among them *one* in whom I

can sense the divine. One through whom I can feel the quality that
Jesus must have had. The quality that persuades people to say: "Yes, I
believe! Yes, I will follow!"

So I watched several hours of evangelical telecasting. Instead of love
and understanding, I found myself filled with a shaking hatred. I
wanted to be sick. Then, I learned about the Jonesville horror, where
nine hundred people followed the Reverend Jim Jones to mass suicide.
Terror! I still cannot touch the newspaper reports of the disaster. Or,
more interestingly, I cannot wrap one of my sculptures in newspaper
that tells of this charismatic man, because I feel . . . as I did as a child
. . . that whatever the paper touches will be cursed. The paper itself has
caught the awesome power. The sculpture will crack in the kiln. I will
crack.

I need desperately to talk to someone.

November 18, 1978

I spoke with Harvey. He suggested that I imagine myself to be a child
again, sitting in the balcony at the People's Church. I do, and I am
aware of a preacher with a bull neck, and a white suit, and a Southern
accent, pointing his finger, pointing, pointing, jabbing it at *me*. And I
am filled with fear and . . . something else, something else . . . and I
am hanging onto the arm of the pew, hanging on, my heart pounding,
full of longing and terror. And unable to speak of either. Unable to
speak, as the choir sings, wooing . . . softly . . . "O Lamb of God, I
come . . . I come." And I do not budge, although I feel from all sides
the prayers mingling with the music, the prayers of mother, uncle, all
those who wish only that I go down to the front, and be saved.

And so Harvey has me, as I am now—adult, experienced, free of the
pressure of uncle, mother—talk to that twelve-year-old.

At first I can't. Why?

"I don't *like* her!" I say.

"Why?"

"She's disobedient. She's being difficult. And secretive. And evasive. . . ." I hear the judgmental parent in me going on and on. "Why
is she hanging on, when so much in her wants . . . wants. . . ."

"Wants what?"

And *flash*! In my mind I am with Yogi Amrit Desai, as I was one

Sunday a year or so ago; one of a hundred or more; most of them gowned in white; I, not. And there rose in me a want, a need, a determination to be one of those who were close enough to be touched by him. Even though (again) it meant "going down to the front" to receive some beads that he would bless and then put around my neck. Even though (again) I knew that I could not follow the path he trod with his white-clothed disciples. Even though (again) I felt guilt that I was being secretive, evasive, deceitful.

And so I went, and knelt at his feet, and let him put the beads around my neck, and then looked up into his eyes, and knew, for the first time, what it might have been like to be close to Jesus. For here in these eyes, beyond these eyes, was indeed that universe which "opened out in back, as it were, to eternity." Here, in these eyes, I glimpsed the divine, and I felt it to be awesome, and I felt it to be love.

I did not follow the guru, any more than I had followed the evangelists. But, as I sat in the chair before Harvey, that seemed to be beside the point. The point was that even at the age of twelve, I had longed to glimpse the divine, to feel awe, to be touched by love. And I had also known, without knowing the words for it, that power could have charisma too. That power from the pulpit could use the words of love, and could be dangerously deceitful. I had known that I must hold out against all the authority figures around me, against the power of that pointing finger, against the wooing of that choir.

"What an extraordinary kid that was!" I say to Harvey. "To hold out for the real thing."

"You can't say that to her, even now, can you?" he says.

"I can't say it, because I want to hug her, and she isn't here."

"But she is here," he says, "in you."

Yes. In me. I love her, in me. Finally, I love her.

Carl Jung, Harvey reminds me, at the age of thirteen said no to *his* Christian father and his uncles who were all ministers in the church. Jung suddenly realized that they didn't really *know* what they were preaching about. That is, they hadn't really experienced God. They believed. That was all. For Jung, belief was not enough. You had to *experience* God.

When I got home, I took down one of my two Jung books from the shelf and read: "Religious experience is absolute. It is indisputable. If I tell you of my experience, you may say that you have never had such an experience, and I will say 'Sorry, but I have,' and there any discussion will come to an end. No matter what the world thinks about religious experience, the one who has it possesses the great treasure of a thing that has provided him with a source of life, meaning and beauty, and that has given a new splendour to the world."[2]

Oh, thank you, Dr. Jung. This is what I need. Yes, take me with you beyond this hemmed-in world of Daniel's Christian belief. Take me into the world of experience. And, thank you, thank you, Harvey . . . doctor, psychiatrist, farmer, friend.

December 3, 1978

This is the first memorable dream I've had since I've been seriously studying Jung:

> I am in the basement of our house. It is clean, painted white. But in the floor, at my feet, are some stone steps that I have never seen before. They go down, deep into darkness. The first two steps are clean, the third is half covered with earth, the rest curve away out of sight into the unknown. I look up and around me at the white basement. To my right is a door to the outside where a Chinese girl is sadly leaving: she had come to tell me that she wanted to be an actress, and I have discouraged her. In front of me is a room where Bob, in his warm brown jacket, is happily working at his desk. I look down again to this dark hole in the floor, and the stone steps. On the top step, I now notice, is a vial containing two sleeping pills. I don't move. I just stand there, feeling annoyed with myself because I discouraged the Chinese girl; feeling guilty about the sleeping pills; feeling dissatisfaction with the white sterility of the basement; feeling tension that the steps are there; and feeling unwillingness to go down into the dark, dank, earth-smelling unknown. I am warning myself to take time, go slowly, do not hurry down . . . when I wake.

What is the message of a dream? I consult my books by Jung. I find that the dream is the contribution that the unconscious mind is trying to make to the conscious mind, but often we ignore the dream, ignore the gift, and let the opportunity to know more pass.

So, Dr. Jung, how should I interpret this dream? I'll take a stab at it. If I am serious about going "beyond this hemmed-in world of Daniel's Christianity," which, for me, has become a whitened, sterile place, down into the pit is where I must go, down into the deep, dark, unknown earth of myself, and of . . . of what? I don't know. But in my dream, I am warning myself to go slowly. I have the alternative, of course, of taking the two sleeping pills and curling up and hoping it will all go away.

1990

MARION: This is a pivotal dream, Rita. This is a point in your life when choices had to be made.

RITA: Right. It was easy enough to *say*, "Take me, Dr. Jung, to the things beyond our ken." But to *go*. That's different.

MARION: So here you are in your dream. You can go down through the dark hole into the unknown, the unconscious . . . while your husband, your masculinity here, stays in consciousness, working happily away at his desk.

RITA: Making notes. . . .

MARION: And here is the actress in you leaving.

RITA: Because?

MARION: It isn't the action in the world out there you are interested in at this point. What interests you now is the depth. That's the staircase that goes down. But . . . you also feel afraid to take that first step down. "Tense and unwilling." And here on the top step are two sleeping pills which you can take and forget all about it. But you made your choice, didn't you?

RITA: Yes.

MARION: You went down. And boy, have you ever gone down!

RITA: But I've also gone up.

MARION: You know that Nietzsche says that the deeper you go into the roots of hell, the higher the branches reach to heaven. And that's what's happened. With you.

February 3, 1979

I woke in the middle of the night and wrote down this dream:

Bob and I are walking, happily, along a seafront, when we encounter some indentations of the shore where the rocks are slimy and where it's difficult to walk. We go inland, slightly, and there ahead of us, on the water's edge, is a church. The church door is wide open and inside I can see a carpeted aisle at the end of which is another open door leading to a continuation of the seashore path. I suggest to Bob that we make this shortcut through the church. But he doesn't want to do that. He'd rather go round about. So, okay, I'll go by myself.

A woman is sitting by the door. She asks me if I want to pray. I lie and say yes. But then I feel two things: I don't want to pray in the church's way, but I do want to pray in my own kind of meditation. She says, "Take seat no. 189" and points to the far end of the church aisle to the left side of the altar.

I go to seat 189, but there's a woman sitting in it, and there are coats on all the other seats. The woman looks at me, very mean-mouthed, mealy-mouthed. I think, "Ugh . . . church people."

Then the minister comes out and says that those who were born in such and such a place can have seats, but I am not one of them.

I am aware now that Bob has come in after all, and is talking to me from the aisle, in a loud whisper, saying that he is going to go back the way he came.

The minister is very annoyed at this other man talking. He takes Bob by the ear and twists it viciously. Then, I can see, he is about to shove his finger in Bob's eye, pull his eyelid and gouge out the pupil. I yell at him to stop. I rush up to him and shout, "That is a terrible thing to do! If you do that, I will take *your* eyelid and gouge out *your* eye." And I reach out to grab him, but when he turns to me, I see that his eyes are glazed and almost opaque.

I say, "There is no way I will stay in your church. I cannot pray to my god in your church."

1990

MARION: Here you are, walking along beside the seashore, beside the great ocean of the unconscious. You and your animus are happily finding your own way, when you come up against some difficulties, some slippery spots, some stumbling blocks. And there, right on your path, is a church, a religious place for the collective, and if you take that route, it'll be an all-carpeted and easygoing walk through the church.

RITA: I set out to find my own spiritual path, but as soon as a problem rises, I look for an easy solution in conventional religion. Is that it?

MARION: Well, you do decide to go into the church, but your animus doesn't want to.

RITA: Bob has always been agnostic.

MARION: Your animus also wants to go "round about," it's not just Bob.

RITA: It wants me to have my own religious experience, even if it is difficult and slippery going.

MARION: But you do go into the church, and in the short time you are in the church you make your decision. There is no way you will stay in this church.

RITA: I'm not part of the collective?

MARION: What it comes down to is "those who have seats and those who have not." And you have not. Because of who you are, you do not have a seat. This has been true all through your life. It seems you were not destined for the collective. Now this puts you in a very vulnerable position. You have, through your aloneness, to live your destiny. And you've done it with everything that is in you. You have mined who you are. Out of that lonely journey into the unconscious, you have become who you were born to be.

RITA: Have I really got the most out of it? Because I feel . . . oh . . . there is so much more. . . .

MARION: There may be a lot more, Rita, but as far as you've got now, today . . . I mean, you haven't taken the sleeping pills. . . .

RITA: No.

MARION: And now, in this dream, you are not going to take the easy way, are you? You are not going to let your ears be twisted into the conventional way of hearing, or your eyes be gouged out so you can't see what's really going on.

RITA: I must admit you're right. In fact, this is what I wrote in my journal just after that.

February 4, 1979

That dream! That clinches it. It seems that my unconscious has made up my mind for me. If I am to discover what my true religious beliefs are, I cannot find them in Daniel's church. There is no way that I can see the divine through the eyes of that minister. And if the God of that church is Daniel's God, he has nothing to do with my god.

But who *is* my god? It would seem that my unconscious knows already. But I don't.

February 15, 1979

I've put Daniel aside, officially. I don't know what this will do for my film reputation, but I've told them that I can't possibly deliver the script this year, and have recontracted with an open deadline. I have no choice. Later, I might be able to understand the Christian path of Daniel. Now, I must stay on my own path, and follow it wherever it may lead. Already it is taking me down into the depths of Jung; taking me tortuously back through the myths and religions of all mankind, with Joseph Campbell as my guide. Now is the time (to quote Campbell quoting the thirteenth-century legend of the Quest of the Holy Grail) when I must go through the forest where I see it to be thickest, leaving behind the known good company, to experience the unknown pathless forest in my own way. And I know, and I know it with fear, that "in the uncharted forest night, where the terrible wind of God blows directly on the questing undefended soul, tangled ways may lead to madness. They may also lead, however, as one of the greatest poets of the Middle Ages tells, to all those things that go to make heaven and earth."[3]

To help me in my questing, I will also return to sculpting, because sculpting, like dreaming, comes directly from the unconscious.

November 30, 1979

Never, in my long life, have I had a teacher, in whatever subject, who pushed me so far, so quickly, and so successfully as Merton Chambers, the sculptor. How he does it, I don't know.

He never shows me what to do, or how to do it; he never touches my piece; he never criticizes. He just asks questions. I've made a little maquette.

"What do you want this to say?" asks Merton.

"Ahh . . . well . . . it's a shape I like."

"Why do you like it? What does it say to you?"

I feel embarrassed. What I have been making for some time now is a series of abstracts, which appear to be (perhaps) unfolding scrolls, but not really unfolding, because they conceal within, a mysterious form, which is a mystery even to me.

"Well . . . it says . . . something like . . ." I plunge and wait to hear what my mouth will say ". . . inside each exterior . . . no . . . inside the exterior of modern man, there is something hidden, something very old. No. It says . . . inside the smooth, sleek exterior of modern *woman* lurk mysteries that go back to the beginning of time. I mean, no matter how we try to follow the skinny fashions of the day, *inside* we have felt the ancient mysterious power of those Paleolithic sculptures . . . the Venus of Willendorf, the Venus of Lespugue, those fat-bellied, fat-hipped, big-breasted, nourishing images that were left by the hearth in ancient caves to welcome back the hunters from the hunt. Each woman has felt . . . no, I can't speak for each woman . . . *I* have felt that fat feeling in the belly, especially after making love, and I have known that from time beyond knowing it has been female, and nourishing, and good."

And Merton said, "So, now you know what you want to say. Say it as directly as you can. When you understand what you are doing and why you are doing it, both physically and psychologically, you will be on top of your work no matter what means or medium you use. So, do it. And do it eight feet high."

And that was why, some time later, an enormous female torso, with a huge, round belly stood in the studio. She did not appear to be a copy of a Venus goddess. She wasn't. And yet, I noticed a fascinating thing. Throughout the evening when the murals of the workshop were on display, there was always a cluster of people chatting in front of the big-bellied female, even though she was in the studio farthest from the supply of drink and food. People seemed to gravitate, carrying their drink and food, and to end up in what must have seemed a warm and nourishing place to gather and to be. Like a hearth in a Paleolithic cave.

Incredible. Without consciously knowing what I was doing, my unconscious has been taking me down the path, not only of *my* search, but, I think, of all religious search. Back to the beginning.

Journal: in country
March 30, 1980

Back to the beginning. My sculpting and my reading have been taking me back . . . let us say, thirty thousand years.

We are in the cave, with our kin. And here is a small stone figure of a woman, carved by a kinsman, long ago, long dead. And it has been carved for what purpose? For what propitiation? To what god? To what goddess? To what force felt, which has not yet been limited to any one god or goddess, but a force that will supply food and shelter and warmth, and safety, and children. If we really were in that cave, thirty thousand years ago, we wouldn't be asking the question, because the answer is so obvious. What form could there be that would better express the satisfaction of those needs than this small carved fecund female? Unless it were the form of a whole hilly landmass, built-up and carved and shaped into the pregnant body of a woman. So that the land on which you lived was not only your propitiation to the god-force that could fill your needs, but was the container of the force itself. So that, by walking on the land, you walked on the torso of her divinity, you explored her breasts, her armpits, the space between her thighs, or ran the endless ripple and swell of her back for mile after mile.

Such holy hills were built by our ancestors in Paleolithic and Neolithic times, in places as distant from each other as Crete and the Chalklands of England. Here, indeed, beneath their feet, was the Great Mother. And they knew that "all that she brings forth is at the same time organic and animated. Not only men and trees, but also stones and minerals. All things that she carries in her bowels are homologous with embryos and all living things in the course of gestation."4 So, stones are sacred. Trees are sacred. Men, women, all are sacred. For all are the children of the Great Earth Mother.

I have been reading books by Leakey, Lévi-Strauss, Michael Dames, and the reading leads me into myself and my own land. My reaction to this land where we have built our Treehouse is, I see, essentially Neolithic.

The first year after we bought it, the well digger handed me a divining rod, and I was shocked at the force with which the rod turned towards me, and then turned down, with such energy that the muscles in my arms could not take the strain and I let go. I didn't understand it, and I don't like things that I don't understand. So I never touched a divining rod again. Until today.

Today, I cut a forked stick and held it before me as I walked up the hollow to the hill. Nothing happened, until I reached my tree. And there, where the tree shows itself to be two, male to the east and female to the west, there, at that point of separation or of union, the rod dipped with such a force that once more the muscles of my arms trembled and I let go. What it means, I do not know. Although, of course, I have read about "dowsing," "water," "minerals," many things. I do know that humankind has respected and used this kind of divination ever since humankind has been. They have felt and followed the veins of energy in the earth, and have found their paths across the tractless space of Australia, or of Africa, Asia, North America. They have built holy places on hills where they felt the power. They still do. We do not. In *our* patriarchal society, our pseudo-Christian world, we build roads and cities guided by quite a different kind of power. Guided by the domination of man over nature. And by the value of real estate. But here, on our land, I know in the very sinews of my body a power that is awesome. And it has entered (how could it be otherwise?) into my religious beliefs. Not that I *worship* what I know to be here, but I honor it, and feel wonder that I am a part of it. And *that*, to some thinkers (Frederick Franck, for instance, in *The Zen of Seeing*) is religion. "Realizing one's place in the fabric of all that is."[5]

I don't have a name for this belief, though I'm sure one exists. I hope I never learn it. I've found that names can be boxes that close up, shut in the intense reality of an experience. A name is a handy way for the left brain to file information. And set it neatly in place.

"Animism," said Earle, when I told him about my at-one-ness with the female side of my tree. Maybe that's the name, but I'm not going to use it. Nor am I ever going to speak again about the energy that flows through me when I meditate there by my tree, taking me down to its deepest roots in the ground, and up through its highest branches into the sky. What would Earle call that? I don't want to know.

And yet, I do not like things that I don't understand. And I don't understand any of this. Experience it, yes. Understand it, no. Trust, faith, all those religious words that I avoid, perhaps this is where they come in. Though I doubt it. What I feel here is real. It doesn't need trust. It doesn't need faith. It *is.* And I *am.*

April 1, 1980

This is incredible! Two nights ago I poured out all my wonderings about me and this land, and now here comes this dream!

> I am standing at the base of the hills that go up from the Treehouse. Beside me, to the right, is the Creator, who is creating my body as a long, interconnected series of short pieces of matter that stretch in a vein in the hollow between the hills. The vein is completed. Then I hear the voice of the Creator say: "Oh, but there will be no way to speak!"
> And I am aware that, far off across the country to the left, a hill is being lifted up. And now the hill is broken into two black pieces of matter. One piece is placed on the body-vein near the top where the brain would be. The other half is placed partway down where the mouth and the means of speech will be. Now sound can reverberate from the hills.
> "And this," says the voice of the Creator, "is you."

1990

MARION: And this indeed is you, Rita. You become an energy line of the earth. You become part of Sophia, and she becomes a part of you. But you, because you are a human being, both masculine and feminine, you need to be able to speak. It is not enough to just *be*. To *speak* about all this that is happening to you, that is the flesh becoming Word, the masculine bringing the experience to consciousness in the body.

RITA: Do you know something? The same day that I had that dream, I wrote down in my journal an experience I'd had years before and had never spoken about. I don't know why, but I just had to . . . well, speak it out.

April 2, 1980

Ischia. It's . . . yes . . . I suddenly realize that what happened on Ischia is what Jung would have called a "spontaneous religious experience." Certainly it was spontaneous. The last thing I was thinking about in 1956 was religion.

It was October. Elsabetta and I had gone to Italy to find some sun, after spending a summer of rain and runny noses in London. And we found the sun on that tiny, arid, lava rock of an island called Ischia. I think it's become a tourist place by now, but then . . . I had never lived in such a remote place, nor lived so close to the land and the sea. The food we ate came from the sea; the wine we drank came from the vineyards that covered the rocky hills. Each day, we followed the same routine: breakfast; sit in the sun and write until lunch; snooze; then, precisely at four o'clock, climb up the donkey path, worn into the lava hill to a narrow pass, where there was a tiny white chapel to the left, while to the right, in front of us, behind us, everywhere we looked below, were the rocks and the green grapevines, and below that, the sea going deeper and deeper in layered shades of green, green-blue, blue to black, as it stretched away to the horizon. And above it, and us, was the clearest and deepest of blue, blue skies, reaching up, away into the universe. Each day, we would pause. Look at it all with wonder. Then. Go down the other side of the hill. And swim.

Well, one morning, I had a most extraordinary experience. I was standing at the top of that lava hill in brilliant sunshine, and looked down as usual, but saw, first, my own body, and it was made up of a mass of vibrating cells. Then my eyes saw the lava rock I was standing on, and it was a mass of vibrating cells. And the green vines below: a mass of vibrating cells. And far, far below, the sea, green, green-blue, deeper and deeper: a mass of vibrating cells. And above, the vivid blue sky vibrating upwards and upwards into endless space, and my eyes could distinguish every cell of that sky, as they had been able to distinguish every cell of my own body. And a most wonderful feeling of peace filled me, and I heard my voice say: "If I were to die now, the cells of my being would flow into the cells of this rock, and these vines, this sea, this sky." And then my voice said: "I don't know what god is, but this is god."

Then, I opened my eyes, and I was standing beside my bed, and it was dark, with a faint light on the eastern horizon.

I heard Elsabetta sit up in her bed, startled.

"Are you all right?" she said.

"Yes." I said, and I can still feel the calmness of my voice. "I've just discovered what god is."

And I climbed back into my bed and fell asleep.

Ever since then . . . nearly twenty-seven years . . . I've felt that I was allowed to glimpse something which was undeniably true, and yet incomprehensible. Although I knew I had experienced god, I didn't know what god was. Some process? Some immensity? Some. . . ? I didn't know. That is, in my mind, I didn't know. But I believe that something in my unconscious knew then, and knows now. And perhaps my conscious mind is becoming increasingly aware. I do hope so, because that is my goal: to *know* what god is, and to *know* god, when I meet god.

But what is becoming clearer, is that my path, in my search for god, is taking me far from the God of my Sunday school. Far from Christianity as I know it, and far from that historical figure called Jesus Christ. Even in my vision on Ischia, the one thing in that landscape that I did not see was the tiny white chapel for Christian worship. It was not there. And today, it is not part of my landscape. I am not a Christian.

2

August 30, 1983

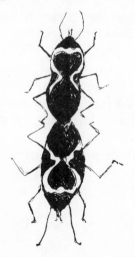

What insects are these?
That join for so long,
and in such leg
shaking ecstasy?

The front-deck of the
Treehouse is my wilderness,
where I sit and watch
the courting and the mating
of these tiny, wild creatures;
these black and red vibrant
beings that state very clearly,
each of them:
"I know lust; I know longing:
I know ecstasy: I know satisfaction."

Suddenly, I remember this morning's dream. What a funny, lovely dream it was:

I am watching a young girl who is going up a gracious staircase. She is calling back over her shoulder to a man who is in the hallway beside me, on his way to the bathroom.

"If you come close to me again, I'll run away up," she says. The man goes into the bathroom. She stops and takes off her blouse, and looks tousled-haired and mischievous.

"If you come close to me again, I'll tear your eyes out," she says. No answer from man. She backs down the stairs, taking off her brassiere.

"If you come close to me again, I'll spit in your face," she says. No answer. She takes off her skirt and comes down to the foot of the stairs.

"If you come close to me again, I'll eat you," she says. No answer. She runs to the bathroom door, and takes off her pants.

"If you come close to me again, I'll kiss you," she says. Man's voice from the bathroom: "Let's go to bed." I burst out laughing, and go out the front door.

The landscape is drab and gray until I turn to the right and go round the corner of the house, and suddenly the color of the landscape literally takes my breath away. The hills are brilliantly vibrating purple and green. I gasp in a joy of seeing.

Oh yes, making love is beautiful. Last night, lightning flashed to the east of us, like a cosmic fireworks display, splashing, searing up and down the horizon. And then the rain thundered on the roof.

Yes, dear beetles, I too know ecstasy.

And I know the deep joy (I wonder if you do too?) that remains in the body, that vibrates between my mate and me. So that, just half an hour ago, as the sun settled towards the west, I went to the gate with Bob to say goodbye, for he must go back to the city, and I must stay here, and, as we waved goodbye on the dusty road, Bob in the car, slowly moving away, watching me in the rearview mirror, waving, waving, and me by the gate, waving, waving, there was such a glowing channel of unified joy between us that surely it was palpable to the man in the truck who cut between us, driving in the opposite direction. Not that the truck mattered to us. The glow and the connection were not broken, and the waving continued until Bob's car dipped down the other side of the hill, and I turned back along the path to the Treehouse, carrying his love in me.

So now, as I sit here on the deck of the house, watching these beautiful beetles; looking beyond them into the vibrant leaves of the reddening sumac trees; and beyond that into the dazzling light of the sun settling into the pines of the dark forest, I hear myself groan with wonder. I too, dear beetles, dear evening world, know the golden vibrations of life in every cell of my body. I too know lust and longing and ecstasy and satisfaction. I know where my love is.

August 31, 1983

This morning a small snake slithered down the front steps and disappeared through blades of grass into the woodpile. Snakes are rare. The last ones . . . oh my god, the last ones I saw were the two twined around each other in copulation. It was awesome. It was as though I were witnessing a primordial ritual. The original caduceus. Two snakes entwined and becoming one in the stiff, powerful, and vitally alive wand of healing Hermes, the go-between-heaven-and-hell. Owl comes into my mind. I must sculpt "the eye of the owl." Where does that come from? Snake and eye-of-the-owl.

From a dream. I'm certain that hangs in my mind from a dream. I'll check back in my journal. If I'm right, why does it surface now?

Later:

I've found it. It was one of those nights that I had a whole bunch of dreams. I'd wake and write one down, and hardly get back to sleep (or so it seemed) when I'd wake with another dream.

1. Close to me, is a *huge* snake. It is so thick that its body comes up to my waist as it passes by me on my left side, and it is so long that it just keeps coming and coming. I am expecting that the head will appear soon (as though it were moving backward), but instead, it seems to split in the middle as though it had reached a mirror and now the snake with its mottled snakeskin pattern is duplicated in the mirror. But this mirrored snake is not moving in the opposite direction. The

effect is of a snake shedding its skin, but both skin and snake are moving. Now there is another snake that is white and shining and it is moving like a whirlwind, going up into the air, up and up, with the snake getting larger and larger as it goes up.

2. I am an owl, and I'm being drawn up into the sky, although not into the open sky, but into the white eye of a much larger owl. I'm going up up up, and it is white and white and whiter as it goes. The eye is infinite, and it is very friendly. It's an extraordinary experience. Very interesting.

3. I am looking down on a huge deerfly. Under it is another deerfly and under it, another, like a pile of slides, only HUGE. And the flies are not slides, they are alive and real. As I look down on them, one dissolves into the next, and disappears, and the next one comes into focus.

4. I am standing beside the two or three steps to a one-story white temple. There is sand. It is Egypt, and very dry. There are white pillars holding up the roof of the temple, and around the pillars are white snakes.

   Now a female figure comes out between the pillars. She is white and shrouded, as though she were a stone statue, which is faceless. But she is moving. She moves down the steps, and goes into a rectangular pool of white water.

   Down and down she goes, until the water closes over her head. I think, "This is a purification place, a ritualistic place." And I move toward the pool, when I hear a voice that says, "No. This is not for you." I wake wondering *why* isn't this for me?

5. I am high up in the sky, looking down on a gray cathedral, only it's not a real cathedral, it's made out of cardboard, and it has a turret instead of a spire. Then I see there's a mouth in the turret, and the mouth is opening and closing. But this is the mouth of a green frog, in the water on the edge of a green pond.

1990

MARION: What huge energy! Wow!

RITA: Which dream?

MARION: The first one especially. What do you make of that dream, Rita?

RITA: Well, it's about snakes. When I had that dream, I found snakes to be very confusing symbols. First, I'd been taught that the serpent was the bad guy in the Garden of Eden. He was the sexy tempter, and that's *bad*. But in my meditations, sometimes I feel an energy course up through my body, emerge above my head, and bend over me protectingly like a serpent's head. I was very surprised when this first happened. It felt very much the *good* guy. But then I was even more surprised when I discovered that in ancient Far Eastern belief, this was exactly the role of the serpent. It rose . . . or usually two of them rose from beneath the earth, curved up the sides of the meditator, and spread their heads above his head, and protected him from any danger.

So, you see, when I had this dream, I certainly felt that there was . . . as you say . . . huge energy. And it felt like *good* energy. But was it really good? Well, recently, I got an answer from Joseph Campbell that went "Click! Right!" When he was talking to Fraser Boa, Campbell said, "The serpent represents the dynamic of life in the world. It sheds its skin to be born again."[6] Then he says that serpent power is the energy that transforms one's life. You read the myth or you have the dream of the snake, and it carries you forward into what Campbell calls "the spiritual life."

MARION: Do you think that's what's happening here?

RITA: Yes I do.

MARION: And the serpent is not "the sexy tempter?"

RITA: I think it's a very sexual dream, to be honest.

MARION: So do I. Let's think about it. Where is snake in your body? . . . Where is the mirror in your body? . . . Where does snake start to move back through its own skin? . . . An interesting thing happens in the dream. Another snake "is like a whirlwind, white and shining and going up into the air. . . ." Possibly sexual energy becoming spiritual energy. There is the transformation. With the owl too, this bird of Athena, but it's not just flying around down here, it's being drawn up into the white eye of a much larger owl. Up up up up, whiter and whiter as it goes up. The eye is infinite. That's the eye of god, or goddess perhaps. You're moving from personal to archetypal. Now, what is fascinating is the way the energy moves horizontally at first, below the waist where it is represented by the mottled snake, and in the next flash, up into the eye of god. So you see how spirituality and sexuality are connected together.

RITA: To be honest, I find lovemaking a *very* spiritual thing, but I also find it a wonderfully wild thing, a gypsy thing.

MARION: And that's where the deerflies come in. There's the other side. Deerflies come when spirituality is at its peak.

RITA: Exactly. What the deerflies mean to me are orgasms. One comes and it is *huge*. And it dissolves and there is another. . . .

MARION: Just one deerfly after another! But when we look at the next dream, something else is happening. We have Egypt. We have this white temple, white pillars that have white snakes around them.

RITA: Sexuality again?

MARION: Yes, but in a ritualistic place. And there is a goddesslike woman. She is archetypal. She is a white virgin well-shrouded. A spiritual part of you who is almost like stone. But she is going to be transformed. Perhaps through her sexuality. She is moving very ritualistically, veiled. A still unravished bride! She's got to go into the pool, down down down until the water closes over her head. Maybe she can become human.

You see, this is a purification place. I bet you never thought of sexuality as purification. It's a place of ritual transformation. Then the voice says, "This is not for you." Not yet anyway.

In this next dream, you are high up in the sky again, looking down on this gray cathedral. But it's not really a cathedral. It has a turret instead of a spire, and it's made of cardboard, flimsy stuff, and there's a mouth in the turret opening and closing. "The sound of brass and tinkling cymbals!"

RITA: Like all the sermons of my life. Saying nothing to me.

MARION: And then, there is another mouth, opening and closing, which is the mouth of a green frog on the edge of a green pond. Remember the fairy tale of the Frog Prince? It is a creature moving into human form, coming from a profoundly primordial state, but he has the little hands and little feet of a human being. So what is being born through your sexuality is the frog.

RITA: My Frog Prince?

MARION: Another level of your masculinity. You've got that veiled bride going down into the water. And here is the frog, with its *huge* potential for transformation. The whole dream is an initiation dream, Rita.

RITA: What the dream said to me was, "Yet once more, the church is not for you. Get back to the earth. You are not a Christian. You are a pagan; the earth, the frog pond is where you belong."

MARION: But the frog's mouth is opening and closing. It's not the Logos, but . . .

RITA: Logos?

MARION: The Word that becomes flesh. In this case, the flesh that can become Word. Rita, think about this: how the serpent, the sexuality that is so important to you, may have had the biggest influence in bringing you to those things that have happened to you spiritually between the time of that dream and now.

Journal: in country
September 13, 1983

A sense of excitement, tingling in fact, as the result of talking with one friend after another; sharing with each; giving something to each, congratulations or insight or thanks for insight that he/she has given me. It is the time for AHA's! The time when all my readings, writings, searchings are leading to one place and time: here and now. Now is the time for looking and seeing exactly where I am on this journey into the unknown pathless forest.

Why now?

Don't you know? In two weeks time, Rita Greer Allen officially turns into a little old lady!

You don't mean . . . ?

. . . aged, sixty-five.

Impossible!

I know. It was only last year that she turned forty.

Pause. Heart beating faster. Perhaps I'd better get myself a cup of coffee with a shot of rum in it.

But, while I was in the kitchen I bopped about, with my coffee and rum, to the music of Dave Brubeck. And I realized that I was no older now than I was an hour ago. Well, yes, an hour older. But then, as I joyed in the music and the sexual swing of my body, I thought once more of those beetles on the front deck yesterday, creating, procreating in ecstasy. And I thought how at this moment (if I understand the ways of beetles at all) each of those copulating females is bringing forth more beetles that carry in them the genes of her body and the genes of her mate. And so it has been generation after generation for thousands, millions of years. And therein likes the immortality of each of those beautiful creatures.

In this, does the beetle differ very much from the billions of people who believe that *their* immortality lies in their progeny who carry their genes, penis into vagina, umbilical cord to navel, generation after generation, from the distant mists of the past, into the distant mists of the future? Or do they differ only in this: that with people, the belief is conscious, and is sometimes, in some cultures, including (if I understand the Pope's edict against birth control correctly) our own . . . their religion.

The chief purpose of one's life on earth is to perpetuate the race. True?

If so, then I have failed. Not one child to carry my genes, or Bob's or those of our forebears into the future. But I have come to terms with that. Painfully.

So, where does that leave me in my thoughts about *my* purpose in life, today, two weeks before my sixty-fifth birthday party?

If it has not been to create children, it has been to create film, to create sculpture. All I have to do is to look at any of my sculptures to discover not what I think, nor what I *think* I think, but what I really feel is the true purpose of my life. All my sculpted bodies are female, rounded and ripe for pregnancy. All my sculpted heads, each one, no matter what sex I had in mind when I made it, appears sometimes to be male, sometimes to be female. My purpose, I believe, has been to honor the powerful energy between the opposites, not only in the passion of sexual activity, nor in procreating, but in the feminine itself, the masculine itself, and the powerful creative energy that pulsates between them in all bodies, in all psyches, in all things.

Is this god? I don't know. I feel that I am coming close to *something*.

September 14, 1983

Last night, I dreamed constantly. For what seemed hours, I dreamed this struggle:

I am trying to separate myself from the water of the sea. . . .
    I am trying to separate myself from the water of the sea. . . .
    I am trying to separate myself . . . and then, suddenly, I am at a party,
sitting beside a woman with whom I've worked at the Canadian Broadcasting Corporation. She is a pleasant, competent woman, slightly mannish. But as the party goes on, she changes, with the same pleasant, easy
competence that she has at work, into a voluptuous, naked woman. She
is sitting in a chair to the left of me, and holding between her great legs
and across her belly and to her huge right breast, various men, including
my small father. She holds them as though they were children.

I try to figure out the meaning of the dream in Jungian terms. "The
water of the sea" I recognize as the deep unconscious, and I see that
there is a part of myself that is struggling to come into consciousness.
Though which part, I don't know. I recognize myself as the "pleasant,
competent woman," for although I don't appear to be "mannish," I
have always loved my job as being one of the boys; as director of a film
crew of men; as being on a par with any of my brothers. But this Great
Mother creature, is that *me*? Surely not. And this little father? I don't
know what to make of that at all. It's not what I had in mind when I
"felt I was coming close to something." Or is it?

1990

MARION: You are evaluating your sixty-five years. In the dream,
    you look at the great sea of life. You try again and again to
    separate yourself out, to consciously accept that separation.
    Those aspects of life that other women take for granted . . .
    children, grandchildren . . . you do not have. The pain is deep,
    so deep it is not personalized. I could be all wrong here. This
    could be my projection.
RITA: No, it doesn't feel wrong. But suddenly the dream
    changes.
MARION: It shows you what you *do* have. You have been an
    extremely creative woman at the CBC. By the look of the
    dream images, you have also been a huge creative matrix
    for many of the men with whom you have worked. I wonder
    if the dream is correcting what you wrote the day before
    when you said that you are creating these lovely androgynous
    figures.

RITA: The heads I make are androgynous, but the torsos are always very female and voluptuous.

MARION: Well, I wonder if the dream is saying, "You are not as androgynous as you think; here is your unconscious concept of relationship." The fact is that your Great Mother figure holds the men as children, and reduces even the old father part to a little boy-son. Maybe there's more discriminating work to be done between your femininity and masculinity. You need to be free of unconscious mothering.

RITA: My god, Marion! That's a long way from the dream I had when I was six, when I was surrounded by the masculine, dominated by the masculine, found guilty of being feminine by the masculine. Presumably I changed between six and sixty-five.

Journal: in country
September 15, 1983

I'm determined to set down my credo before launching into the birthday bash. So . . . what do I believe? At age sixty-five less ten days.

I believe that I am a microcosmic part of a cosmic process that continues in time and in space without beginning and without end.

I believe that all other beings, animals, insects, plants, earth, minerals, gases, all things visible and invisible are also part of this process.

I believe that from time to time, unexpectedly, one may become acutely aware of this cosmic process, and of being a part of it.

I believe that some people, both in the past and now, were and are aware of being a part of this cosmic process almost constantly; such people became infused with it; such people as Gautama Shakyamuni, the Buddha, and (perhaps) Jesus.

I believe that, when I say god, it is this cosmic process that I am naming.

I believe that god is, when you get down to it, everything. And when I say everything, I mean everything in the universe, the scale of which, as Jacob Needleman has put it, "is awesome."

In the picture of the universe as we are now seeing it, through the incredible instruments of the scientists, man is crushed. "Within cosmic time, he is less than the blinking of an eye. In size he is not even a speck. And his continued existence is solely at the mercy of such colossal dimensions of force that the most minor momentary change in these forces would be enough to obliterate instantly the very memory of human life."7

I believe that I am, therefore, not even a speck on a speck, in this "less than a blinking of an eye," and I am therefore nothing. My life is meaningless.

And I also believe that this cosmic process that I call god has marked a path in life for me to find and follow; that god is personally involved with my search for the path, and when I take the wrong turning, obstacles are set in my way. And when I take the right turn, the road is clear, my life is full of meaning, with every breath I take and every move I make.

How can such contradictory beliefs be in my credo? How can god be everything, and still be involved in my nothingness? How can my life be meaningless *and* meaningful? I wish I could talk about this with Bob. With his sharp wit and perceptive intellect, he is a joy to talk with about many things. But about god, no. When I try, a blank look creeps into his eyes, and my words become confusing even to me. But I want, I *need* to talk to someone. I wonder if Harvey is at his farm. I could try to get him on the phone.

Conversation with Harvey

HARVEY: And it is these two irreconcilable attitudes that you need to reconcile.

RITA: That's what I'm demanding of myself.

HARVEY: Well, you've come to the wrong man. When that question comes into my head, I go and milk the cows or clean out the barn, anything, rather than face it. Men (mainly men) have gone into the desert to wrestle with the question, and some have emerged, *knowing* god. Having heard god in the burning bush, or seen god in the thundercloud. And some come out schizophrenic. Mental hospitals are full of people who say "I am God." You are treading along dangerous ways.

RITA: But . . . I feel that this is the way I must go. I must *know* god.

HARVEY: Yes. And when you do meet god, I am sure you will not be able to describe it. I am sure you will feel god in your innermost being. And you may be able to tell about it, yes. But not tell what it is. It will be ineffable. Good luck. And happy birthday.

I sit and stare at the floor for a long time after I've hung up. I watch an ant staggering across the floor, dragging another ant, quite dead. They join, eventually, with a stream of ants, scurrying busily in through a crack below the door, and out again. Each ant in the lineup touches the antennae of each passing ant, pausing, saying . . . what? "All's well." "God bless." "Danger on the left." "Food on the right." "New plans come down from headquarters." "Watch out." "Keep to the path."

How can I really believe that my life is more meaningful than that of a busy little ant? I'm bigger, sure. More complicated. But in the enormity of ALL, the cosmic ALL, how can I really believe that I am meaningfully bigger? *Truly* more important. I exist. That is all. I exist. You, little ant, you exist.

It's half an hour later. Twenty minutes ago, I realized that I had a swarm of ants in my marmalade jar. I don't *want* ants in my marmalade jar. So now, I've stamped the ones that were on the floor to death, and scooped the rest of them out into the woods.

So much for my deep affinity with ants.

So much for my credo.

So much for my at-one-ness with all things, great and small.

My marmalade and I come first.

When it comes to implementing my religious beliefs, is that what it all boils down to?

Yes! Maybe yes! And now that I'm face to face with it, I see that a "credo" is not what I demand. It doesn't matter what I might *believe*. What matters is to *know.*

To know what I really am.

To know what I really do.

To experience, and to *know* what I experience, good or otherwise.

And, eventually, perhaps, even to know god.

September 25, 1983

Dream: I am in a cathedral which is so huge, so high that its clerestory is lost in the clouds. A wedding is about to take place. The great vault vibrates with the sound of a mighty organ and the singing of an unseen choir. The air becomes slowly increasingly filled with light, and I realize that it is because the two who are to be united are moving closer to the cathedral. They are still a long way off, but they have such energy! And I realize they are divinities. Coming from a great distance. At which point, I wake, with the choir's singing ringing in my ears:

> *Lord of Heaven most high,*
> *Has a reason.*
> *Lord of all the Sky,*
> *Has a reason.*

I am in awe of this dream. It promises, oh how I *hope* it promises, that sometime, perhaps some long long time, it will happen. The divine marriage in my own inner cathedral. I *shall* know god.

3

Journal: in city
February 11, 1984

February! Sun dazzling on the snow. Sculpture, dazzling in the studio. I swear it! In all immodesty.

However! These strange winged creatures that are demanding to be formed. Lamed, some of them, maimed, fragmented, but *winged*. They are undoubtedly something my unconscious wants to bring into being. But . . . angels? I certainly hope not. I can't stand the idea of angels. Even Michelangelo's. Cold, sentimental, hanging around up there. Though . . . my winged creatures aren't at all like that. But what are they?

A glimpse of an answer came this morning during meditation, when I found myself repeating Assagioli's mantra:

I have thoughts, but I am not only my thoughts;
I have emotions, but I am not only my emotions;
I have desires, but I am not only my desires;
I have a body, but I am not only my body . . .
I am. I am . . . I am. I am. . . .

And this I, being something more than the sum of body and thoughts and desires and emotions, leads me, as I meditate, deeply into the core of myself; and then down, down into the earth beneath the house; and then up high, higher, like a flame of white energy passing through my body, through my head, and beyond to . . .

Transcendence?

And pray, what is transcendence?

Rising above.

What?

The mind-cluttering, nattering matters of everyday life.

Transcending then to what?

To the cosmic energy, and the glorious vitality that on Ischia I called god?

And what, pray tell me, have these one-legged, one-winged, strong but wistful creatures in my studio to do with that?

God knows. I don't. And I feel embarrassed that my next exhibition will have some of these creatures hanging about in it. But I must admit, also, that I find them somehow fascinating.

And so. . . . Yes! I would love to be part of the new show at the Koffler Gallery, thank you! And I will love, Ms. Leigh, to be in another two-woman show with you next year. And I accept with great pleasure the invitation to be one of the Canadian sculptors in next year's International, and I am sure that I can come up with a theme strong enough to dominate one of the gallery's walls. And yes, indeed, Chris, I will be most honored if some of my work goes with the Raku exhibition to Japan. . . .

And as for film. Oh yes, indeed, it is wonderful that *Raku Fire* is still selling overseas seven years after it first went to air. And that I've been asked to lecture on the script at two film colleges and at a workshop. And this morning, to hear that the Head of Drama wants, very much, a group of films by me, and would I consider coming down to work out the terms? Yes. I would. Oh yes to everything. Yessireeee!

My life seems to be moving into a state of becoming that I have never known before. "Turning Woman"! How interesting that I always begin my newest bout of sculpturing with a woman turning from back view, through side view, opening to full frontal exposure, before turning away again to back. It is my way of finding out who I am *now*, where I am, how strong I am. And my recent series of "Turning Woman" show me to myself to be vulnerable, voluptuous, trium-phant, and yes, I must admit it, beautiful. And that series will also be in the next exhibition with the strange winged ones. A new plateau? Or spiraling toward one?

During meditation this morning

> *I am on the back of a bird.*
> *Now I am under it, held in its claws.*
> *It loosens its grip. I fall.*
> *It is black all around me.*
> *Now I begin to rise, up, into light.*
> *I am aware of the bird's wing.*
> *I am the bird.*

February 19, 1984

It is Sunday morning. Early this morning I experienced god in a dream.

> I am aware that god is behind me. I feel apprehensive. I turn my head slightly to the right to glimpse what is there and I see a torso, very simple in outline, with light shining behind it. It has no features, no arms. It is completely flat on the surface facing me; it is as thick as a human body; it consists merely of a head, shoulders, chest ending at the solar plexus. The head, however, has a triangular piece missing where the left brain would be. The rest is solid gray. I look away. I feel very apprehensive. I know that I have the choice now, to turn away forever, or to turn and face it. I turn and face it.
> Four things happen: I immediately *know* that it is not a "him," nor a

"her," but a "both." I see that it is not gray, but appears to be gray, because it is composed of countless, vibrating cells, of every shape and conceivable color, which, when so closely mingled, appear to be one gray.

Suddenly, the figure is no longer in front of me; it has entered my torso, totally, from the top of my head to my solar plexus. All its cells are in between my cells. And now, the triangular empty area in the left brain of the figure that has entered me, fills. The combined cells of that body and mine slowly flow into my left brain.

I wake up, soaking wet. I get up and go to the bathroom. I am aware of a tingling in the left side of my head, just beyond the center, as though I had a rash under my hair. I look in the mirror, but no rash.

1990

MARION: What do *you* make of that, Rita?

RITA: It was a . . . gift. But a very strange gift. It wasn't the way I had expected to meet god. I mean, he didn't arrive like a stunning flash of light. I didn't feel wonder or ecstasy when he . . . it . . . entered me. I didn't have a deep sense of . . . "So that's it! So now I know!" It was just matter-of-fact. And I climbed back into bed and fell asleep again. Just as I did, I realize, after my vision-dream on Ischia. And, I just realized, both that vision and this dream had to do with *cells*, only this time cells were entering my body, instead of my cells leaving my body and going out into the ground, the sky, the universe.

MARION: And what do you make of those cells being gray?

RITA: *Seeming* to be gray. What flashes in my mind is the first time I saw a mandala being made. It was for the Dalai Lama. And here were these monks working for weeks and weeks, laying out particles of sand of every conceivable color, forming an incredibly vibrating intricate pattern around the central image. And when the mandala was completed . . . the journey finished, so to speak . . . the sand was pushed together, poured into a bottle, and it was gray! But I *knew*, and all who had seen the process *knew*, that what appeared to be just plain old gray sand was alive with color, was full of vibrating . . .

MARION: Light?

RITA: Yes. I think I could say light. I might even say something close to life.

MARION: God in matter? But then, in your dream, we have this god that is only a torso.

RITA: From the solar plexus and up. I think it has to do with the upper chakras. I didn't know much about chakras when I had the dream. And what I did know was intellectual knowing. But here was a god who was entering me and activating the upper chakras.

MARION: That energy was moving into this upper region . . . the heart, the throat, the third eye. The spiritual. And I think that triangular space in the god's head is saying "there's no need for any left-brain thinking at this point in the process."

RITA: Exactly! And so that, when the god entered me, those spiritual cells of the god just closed in the space where my left brain usually yatters away, intellectualizing about god, and getting nowhere.

MARION: This dream came at exactly the right time to assure you that you now had the spiritual strength to deal with what happened after that.

RITA: I think so. I think you're right. Though I don't think I was aware of its importance at the time. I just went back to bed feeling kind of . . . well . . . disappointed.

February 23, 1984

Claire phoned. Her friend needs help badly. Immediately. She's in agony. She believes she's going mad. Can I come? No. I can't. I'm laden down with work, I feel a cold coming on. I've said no. I've let her down. I should be able to do *something*. I'll phone her back. Of course I'll help her friend.

February 24, 1984

I wake in the middle of the night.

Dream (in part): I am on the prow of a ship that is in a very dark and misty fjord. The ship, which is a kind of work-tug, is moving slowly forward. I am on the starboard deck, looking toward the prow, where to my bemused astonishment there is a huge, bright, shiny brass kettle, mounted like a figurehead, only somewhat askew. And out of its spout, there is pouring steam. So much steam that it is creating the mist we are sailing into, so that now I can hardly see where we are going. I look down into the water, and see that we are moving into increasingly shallow waters that barely cover black mud. And in the mud are the stumps of dead, decaying birch trees. Suddenly I am aware that the stern of the ship is slowly, slowly sinking.

Nine o'clock. The phone wakes me up. It's Angela. We're to have lunch. I'm not sure. I don't feel well. I tell her my dream. She laughs when I get to the kettle.

"What a perfect image for you, Rita," she says, "always pouring out for other people." It's a compliment, but it doesn't feel like one. That kettle is *ridiculous*! Hiatus hernia tensions running across my rib cage from the esophagus. Christ. My temperature's 100.4. I must phone Claire.

Four P.M. Temperature's 101.2. Doc's diagnosed bronchitis. Penicillin and bed for at least a week. So much for working. So much for Claire's friend. But I can phone from bed. I can organize.

1990

MARION: That's like an addict's dream.

RITA: No! Really? Is it?

MARION: At its core it is denial. It's like an alcoholic making plans for life, and you ask him how it's going, and everything's going just fine! It's great. Couldn't be better. And you ask him about his drinking problem, and what happens? Denial. Drinking isn't any problem! But you know that his life is going down . . . like your boat . . . sinking down into the unconscious. He's dying. And his perky little tea kettle is up there above it all, blowing off steam.

RITA: Marion, what am I addicted to?

MARION: Well, maybe your addiction at that point in your life was an addiction to whatever this friend represents to you. It could be an addiction to a concept of mother in yourself. An addiction to the power of helping. There is a part of you that is a huge, bright shiny brass kettle. And you're right up there at the prow of the boat where the figurehead should be, in the position of leadership, of power.

RITA: Are you saying that I shouldn't have tried to help?

MARION: No, I am saying that we are so used to power that we don't recognize it for what it is. On one hand, it was a wonderful thing that you were willing to help even though you were overloaded. But look at the hidden power in it.

RITA: I can see that. But I can also see the opposite. If you don't try to help, what good are you? You're only doing everything for yourself.

MARION: And where is the balance? You must find the balance. Because if you can't nourish your own soul, you will use "good deeds" as power over others.

RITA: I'm suddenly seeing things that happened during that period with new eyes. Even after I was sick I was still trying to help. . . . I mean that's being addicted to martyrdom.

MARION: Rita, was there any fire underneath that kettle?

RITA: Nope. Clever kettle, eh?

MARION: Clever kettle indeed! No fire. Important detail.

RITA: Why?

MARION: It's blowing off hot air and creating the mist you're sailing with.

RITA: Ohh . . . that's so funny.

MARION: So where do you think the energy is coming from?

RITA: Oh. Right out of my bronchial tubes.

MARION: Exactly. The bronchial tubes break down, and the regenerative process of breath isn't there. The real energy in the body is in the lungs, the breath. That's where the fire of your emotions, the fire of your creativity is. But your bronchial system was sick. And yet here you were, trying to convince yourself that you were going to be all right. And that was not reality. That was the world of the addict. And here's this dream with the lovely white steam pouring out of this kettle creating mist, fog, so you can't see that you're sailing into shallower and shallower water . . . you're losing your contact with your own creative water. And you're sinking into black mud. Unconsciousness. And in the mud, even the birch trees that are so precious to you are dead, dangerous stumps. And you, also, if you don't listen to that dream . . .

RITA: Could be dead?

MARION: It's a warning dream.
RITA: Yes. It is. It was. But I don't think I listened.

May 10, 1984

Why did it happen? I don't know. I only know when.

I was massaging her face. She hadn't slept for nights she'd said. She was filled with evil. I don't believe you're evil, I'd said, but I'll try to help you sleep. And she lay with her head in my lap and I massaged her jaw, her neck, her face, and gradually brought my hands up over her temples, through her hair to the crown of her head, when . . . WHAM! *something* leapt from the crown and hit my solar plexus like an iron bar, and blackness entered the core of my being, and filled it from top to bottom. I couldn't believe it. I looked at that peaceful face. The blackness spread. I was going to scream. I had to . . . I had to . . . I slid off the couch and ran to the back door, and out into the dusk and the screams came vomiting out, and out and out . . . but the blackness I screamed out was replaced by blacker blackness flowing in.

"I'm poisoned," I thought "Please god! How can I rid myself of this poison?" Then I thought: "Meditate."

I ran back into the house and up to my sleeping room, and for the first time since I was ten years old, I *prayed*. I didn't meditate, I sat and *prayed*. "Please, god, please God, please GOD . . ." on and on and on . . . until sweat poured down my face, my breasts, my legs.

And suddenly I was aware that my face was being held by two hands that felt golden, one hand on either side of my face from under the chin up past the temples, gently, firmly holding. . . .

And then I was aware of two great white wings enfolding me from above my head down to below my feet.

And then I was aware that the black core was moving down, slowly, and replacing it was golden-white light. And the black moved down, and the golden-white moved down, until the black was completely gone and I was filled with light.

I think I must have laid down then, I don't know, nor do I know how long it was before I could emerge. And, having written it out now, I am no wiser as to what it was that hit my solar plexus and filled me with blackness. Nor, what it was that saved me. I can say "god." I must say "god," for it was god I called on, and it was god that cleansed me from I-don't-know-what, from something terrifying and very very real.

I must admit that it was god.

September 8, 1984

Sitting in the bay window. Wrapped in blankets. Looking mistily at the ferns in the little front garden. Ferns turning brown. The first signs of fall. Where has the summer gone? Drained away by the fevers of bronchitis, again and again . . . how many times? Eleven. Yes. This is the eleventh attack since February. And, in between the attacks, running around hunting for the *right* treatment for Claire's friend. Nothing works. "Hope creaks in the throat like a piece of rusting machinery. . . ."

Holistic Dr. John said that there is danger in sympathizing . . . "feeling-into" he translated . . . the sickness of another, because "it leaves you open to taking into yourself that other's sickness." This, he seems to indicate, is what I've done, and only *I* can get it moving from its lodging place in me. Get it out of my lungs, my bronchial tubes. So, do I welcome this new attack?

Harvey also talked about the bronchitis being positive.

"I want you to hold this thought in your mind," he said. "Through millennia of years, the unconscious has devised myriads of ways of protecting and sustaining life. One of these ways is the intricate immune system. Now, consider that this continuing illness is what your unconscious has decided is the best protection for you now, as an alternative to being overwhelmed by something far more dangerous to you. Your unconscious is taking care of you. Do not *think* about it, but let that sink into your unconscious and dream about it."

And I did. I don't remember the dream, but when I woke the next day, these words were hanging in my mind:

"Do not try to rearrange the system of the stars, just try to live within it."

October 21, 1984

Bobby wants to wrap me up in blankets and drive me to the Treehouse. I think I'll say yes.

Journal: in country
October 22, 1984

Watched a deer browsing on lichen on the top of the hill. I stood and watched for half an hour. It is wonderful to be present in another world.

My tree tells me: Take time. . . .

Yes. Let the demands of the world go. Accept the illness.

Take time. *Kairos,* as the Greeks would say. Be in *kairos,* not *chronos,* that other sense of time, which is tick tick tick of one minute after another hurrying away, one thing after another pressing us on, making us older, wearing us out.

Kairos is now. Fully in the moment, which becomes (as it did for me when I was watching the deer) beautiful eternity. Take time, to be in the eternal now.

December 12, 1984

I've let go my film career. Formally notified them that I cannot deliver the scripts. I doubt I'll be asked again. Feel sad. Also feel relieved. The removal of pressure. But something else: I no longer want to make up dramatic stories. And my own story is not for reenactment. Sculpture is another thing. I've begun another "Woman Turning" series. Beginning again to find out where I am, what I am. Yes, I must let what is in me come out into the clay.

January 2, 1985

Woke up at five-thirty with this dream:

> I've just had a session with a young male psychiatrist. He is now talking quietly to an older one, and saying: "She has reached the next stage several times, but she won't make the leap. She doesn't see that she's already there."

1990

MARION: That's it! That's it! Your unconscious had already made the leap to another level, but your waking life had to be changed to come into harmony with the unconscious. So what happens? You had to become sick.

RITA: Really? That's a hard way to do it.

MARION: That experience in the unconscious had to be chewed, swallowed, digested, assimilated. That can take . . . years. But then, when a dream like that tells you that you *can* make the leap consciously, something . . . energy starts to make a little earthquake. Every little cell in your body is making a little earthquake. And gradually the whole body is exploding. And it keeps exploding until you get the message. That's my experience.

RITA: You become sick.

MARION: Until you allow yourself to become conscious of what has happened.

RITA: It's the unconscious working through the body?

MARION: Moving into consciousness. And the more conscious the body becomes, the more it is like . . . say, a fiddle that is being changed into a Stradivarius. Then you have to learn to play a Stradivarius. The tuning has to be exact. The care of the instrument has to be exact to keep it in condition for the pure music to pass through.

RITA: The violin is an image for the body?

MARION: And the soul in the body. The body finding a new vibration.

RITA: Mmm. The image that comes to my mind for me is clay. Clay is my Stradivarius. I had a dream shortly after *that* dream that was . . . well, I woke up with words, just words, and I started to write them down in my semisleep and they kept coming and coming. . . . This is what I wrote:

Dream

The healing is in each stage.
The healing is in the wide open guts from
which the power can rise and burst forth
and demand to be created in form.
The healing is in the clay, soft, yielding

to be formed: strong to hold the form;
full to contain the healing.
The healing is in the song as the form hardens and dries.
The healing is in the burning heat of the bisquing kiln.
The healing is in the fire of the Raku kiln.
The healing is in the smoke.
The healing is in the dance of the smoke of myself.
Until stop! It is enough. It is done.
The healing may be helped at many stages,
if there is a knowing helper,
if there is another who understands
and knows the process of the clay,
and will respect the process of the healing. [January 5, 1985]

MARION: That's your life, Rita.

4

Journal: in country
January 10, 1985

The Koffler Gallery wants to know what I'm going to deliver to them next October. One wall of the gallery will be mine for the International Symposium. What concept will be strong enough to dominate one wall?

Ever since I was invited, I have thought that I would be needing to express the godlike strength of the Precambrian Shield. Rock. God-Goddess. Very dear to me. But, as I typed away to clarify my thoughts, it became apparent that "guardian spirit" keeps emerging as my urgent need for expression. That winged presence that cleansed the black core from my being last spring seems to be still with me, and it is wanting to speak from the depths of myself. I can only say that it is *demanding* to be given form. What kind of form is beyond my imagination.

Eleven P.M. I have just been out on the front deck. I went to breathe in the night air. A figure of white light hangs in front of me, beyond the steps. Undoubtedly it is light from inside the house reflected on to a sumac tree. Except that the shape is not the shape of a sumac. It is winged. It is the shape of a guardian. I know that I must be projecting it. But, also, I am in awe. The form for my sculpture is there. It is now in me. I know what I must do.

January 20, 1985

As I woke this morning, I caught the last line from my dream:

Dream voice: "Take off the mask; behold the essence."

1990

MARION: What does that dream say to you, Rita?

RITA: It flashes me back to the "booth blanket" dream, and what you called my "performance." Here I was still masking the essence of myself, even from myself. Well, what the dream says to me *now* is that, with every piece of sculpture that I made after that, bit by bit, I took off the mask.

May 1, 1985

Sculpting going well. Health improving as I work. Working in shaky faith that it will improve more. Last night, still at it until four in the morning. But "still the center holds," as my sculpture by that name affirms. How many times, when I was building it vulnerable layer on vulnerable layer out from the central core, did terrifying doubts sweep through me? Doubts about its ability to hold its many pieces firmly and be one; doubts about my ability to hold myself firmly and be one. Yeats's lines would flood my mind:

> Turning and turning in the widening gyre
> The falcon cannot hear the falconer;
> Things fall apart; the centre cannot hold;[8]

"No, no!" my heart cries out. "The center *holds*. The center, it *must* hold."

Rodin got it right when he said that all life surges from a center, expands from within, outwards. Yes. One's core must be firm, grounded, whole, full of energy, able to release the energy in a constant flow outwards. If it is not, one has lost one's hold on life.

September 15, 1985

I've completed the works for the McGibbon Gallery exhibition; tomorrow I will begin the final firing of the Guardian for the Koffler. How many days will it take me? I don't know. It is in nine interlocking pieces. If *anything* cracks, I am lost. There is no time, nor energy, to remake any part of it. If the wind plays me false, and blows the smoke into places that I do not want to be smoke-dark, I do have a chance to burn out the black to some degree by putting it through the fire again. But then the risk of breaking is more than doubled. I feel very nervous about it. I can only hope that the guardian itself will lead me.

I am suddenly shocked at my last sentence. It is as though I am reading it through Evelyn's eyes.

"You are becoming mystical," she'd say, with a surprised lift of the eyebrows, and a disapproving turn of the head, and I would feel myself tossed into her pigeonhole marked "Irrational. Flaky." I don't want to be pigeonholed. But now, I have looked up "mysticism" in the dictionary, and it says: "The direct experience of God." And that is what I do want. Exactly.

September 16, 1985
Raku-Firing Guardian Sculpture

I *let* the guardian lead me. I seem to have no choice. I wanted to fire the hidden support first. But no. The head must be first. Why? Why? It is the most difficult! If it cracks . . . if the heat is wrong . . . or the smoke is wrong. . . .

The head must lead. So I put the head in the fire, and bring it up to white heat. When the kiln is at 1750 degrees Fahrenheit, I bring the head out into the air. A crack opens on its right cheek. My heart screams. But, "Quiet . . . quiet . . . quiet . . . ," and as calmly and as quickly as I can, I begin the painting with the smoke. Within half an hour, it is done. Eyes, mouth, contours of the cheeks, the brows, the chin. Complete. The crack has closed. I lie on the ground exhausted. I

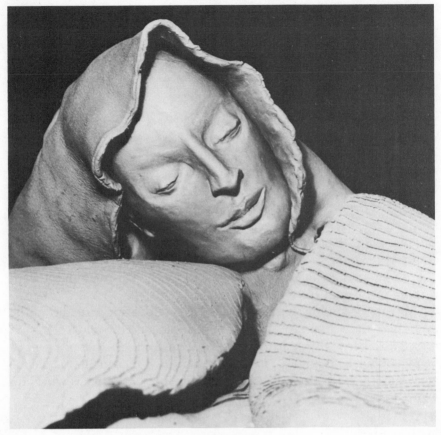

Guardian. *Raku-fired sculpture, 1985.*

am experiencing something which I have never known before, and the word that comes into my mind is "Christ." Do I mean Jesus? No. I mean a presence in me that I can only call Christ. And I don't even know what I mean by that. But I know what I feel.

September 17, 1985

Today has been extraordinary. I decided to fire and smoke the two great wings. But when I had carried them out to the roaring kiln, I thought, "This is ridiculous! I want them to be white. They are white.

Why put them through the danger of the fire?" and then, I heard, as though it spoke, the voice of the guardian-head:

> Each piece must go through the fire. The cowl, the wings, the pneuma, the source, the flow. All must go the way that I have gone. Each may crack in the process, as I have cracked. But look, the crack has healed. I did not break. Without the fire, the piece is untested, unlived, raw. Each must go through the fire.

I fired the wings, first one then the other, and each emerged with some shading from the smoke in the most beautiful way. Whole. Complete.

September 18, 1985

I fired the pneuma. Fiercely. Why? Why fiercely? *Why* did I put it through such a long, cruel firing? And then, *why* did I smoke it so deeply that it is almost black, and completely at odds with the soaring light wings?

Suddenly, I realize: "Of course! that is what I did with my own pneuma, beginning sixteen, eighteen months ago." I sickened my own lungs, my breathing, my breath. Strained it to the cracking point. Opened to blackness. Until this same guardian came, for the first time, and, wrapping his wings about me, cleared the darkness from my core.

What can I do now? I can put it into the fire again, and much of that blackness can be burned out. I hope. The pneuma can be returned to some quality of light and breath and source of health. Tested, and found able to change. Tomorrow, I'll do it.

September 19, 1985

Incredible! I've redone the pneuma, and the darkness has burned out, and it glows with light. *Then*, when I fired the part that I call the Source, it became golden, and the part that I call the Flow-that-carries-the-darkness-away, it became deep brown.

How can that happen when I used exactly the same temperature, the same burning wood, the same smoldering leaves on both. And yet one became the colors of rose and gold. And the other became a dark shadow flowing beside it. Exactly as it should be. I do not understand it.

I am in a state of wonder. And trying not to be. And the trying is making me very tired. And the process, and the hard, hard work.

Evening. At the end of my meditation tonight, I find myself *kneeling* at the end of the bed, in the praying position that I have not used since I was ten years old. From my lips, I hear the words . . . "Let this cup pass from me. . . ."

It is the weight of responsibility I now feel, in my weary state, to get the Guardian safely transported to the city, safely mounted, safely hung. The praying brought, much to my surprise, gold relief.

Why is all this? Why am I meant to tell this guardian message? For I feel that I have had to do it, by the way in which it has been done. I *do* feel that I am only the channel. Why me? Given the works of real geniuses in the world. Real mystics.

Now I think of the little ant that I saw on the front deck yesterday, pulling a white clay chip that was several times bigger and heavier than he. Moving it, against all probabilities: black ant; white clay. To what end? Obviously, *it* felt it was doing something useful for its community.

And perhaps that is close to my own present truth.

No matter how, why, by what effort, it has come into being, this sculpture holds some message that may be useful in some small degree in the community of which I am a part. Or, like the ant's white chip, it might not. But who am I to say, in either case? I only know I have had to do it.

Marjorie just phoned. She said: "Are you having fun?"

I heard my voice answer: "If Gethsemane is your idea of fun, then, yes."

Journal: in city
October 10, 1985

Both exhibitions are open. Astonishing response. From so many people. Including Marion Woodman, who came to the Koffler to see the

Guardian. I feel that she understands what this figure means. Perhaps what *I* mean. I feel that I could talk to her if I got into another impasse in my life, and she would *know*.

October 12, 1985

Woke with the same dream being repeated and repeated:

> I am to make one more piece that will succeed the guardian. It is a large shallow bowl, like an offering bowl, which I must fire and smoke until it is solid black, and then a crack will appear across it. In the dream, I can see it as already done. And out of the crack, something white emerges. But it has not been made yet. And I cry out, "No, no, I am finished, I am, please, I don't want to start another one. . . ."
>
> And then the dream repeats: I am to make one more piece that will succeed the guardian. . . .

1990

MARION: What does it say to you, Rita?

RITA: At the time, I remember I felt so tired, so burned out, that *I* felt cracked. And yet this dream from my unconscious was saying, "You're not finished yet, you haven't allowed the essence to emerge. You have to go into the fire again whether you want to or not."

MARION: And did you make another sculpture?

RITA: No. I didn't. I did not go into the fire in sculpting. But I sure went into it . . . in . . . in . . .

MARION: In your own being? You *are* the bowl, you know.

RITA: Yeah.

MARION: It's the Grail.

RITA: The Grail. I hadn't thought of that.

MARION: And then there's this crack in the bowl. What is your association with the crack?

RITA: Well . . . what comes to mind is the crack in the guardian's cheek. But . . . I feel that there's something deeper than that. I mean . . . what do I mean . . . I mean that I feel that for the essence to emerge from oneself, you cannot do it easily, you have to go through the fire, you have to risk the danger of cracking. I'd been putting other things, sculpture, through that test. Now I had to put myself to the test, to the cracking point. Not that I agreed to that at the time. I just felt "no! I can*not* do it! I'm too tired. I can't do it."

MARION: But you did. "... and out of the crack, something white emerges," some white essence. What do you make of that?

RITA: Something from the inner core. I feel ... what it is ... dare I say what comes into my mind?

MARION: Of course.

RITA: It is the essence of god.

MARION: The eternal.

RITA: Mmm.

MARION: It's a marvelous image of god coming through the wound. Coming through what happened to you after that.

RITA: Yes.

MARION: And the other thing that comes to me very strongly is that you are working with matter.

RITA: Matter?

MARION: You've been working with clay. Matter. Then, after that, you had to work with your body. Matter. And in this dream, the divine essence is distilled from the matter, through the matter. Matter is the feminine. In your work, the Spirit comes flashing down, like a great swoop of energy.

RITA: The guardian! I'd just finished the sculpture of the guardian.

MARION: The wings ...

RITA: Yes.

MARION: ... and *there* is the masculine imagery! Fiery spirit that comes swooping through and you feel ... on fire almost? And the bowl cracks. And you *are* the bowl. And from your inner core comes this white essence. And over the next years, that white essence has been distilled, and distilled. It is like the vessel of the alchemists, in the fire, distilling the contents until the essence is released ... "something white emerges" ... like the philosopher's stone? That's what the alchemists were trying to do, out of the distilling process, to release the philosopher's stone. And that's what's being asked of you, Rita. That distilling process. And it will go on until death I would think, wouldn't you?

RITA: I don't know. I don't know that.

MARION: I don't know that either. *Yet.* But, having worked with some dying people, I have seen that process go on until the last breath. That distilling process. So that, in a person who is dying *consciously*, you can *see* soul pulling its forces together. Almost visibly see the energy in the cells transforming into pure light, separating from matter. . . .

RITA: That's amazing! And do you know what comes to mind? My vision on Ischia, where I said: "If I were to die now . . ." and I had this experience of the cells of my body merging with the cells of the rock, the sea, the sky, and I said, "I don't know what god is, but that is god."

MARION: I think there is consciousness in every cell, Rita. To me, that *is* god in matter. Human beings through their intelligence and imagination bring voice to that order, where all the cells are related. The essence that is in one cell is in every other cell, so that we *are* the wind, we *are* the sky, we are the trees, we are the ground, we are the sea. . . . There is a consciousness that holds it together. God manifesting in matter, Sophia. That, to me, is feminine consciousness. The consciousness that can release light from the dark opaque substance, and experience the light body in everything. We are living in the atomic age. We split the atom and we release energy in matter.

RITA: That's scary.

MARION: How?

RITA: If . . . if we're messing around with atoms, then we're messing around with god?

MARION: That's frightening for sure. Especially when we have the knowledge to destroy. God is in matter, in our bodies, in the planet. We have to bring that knowledge into full consciousness. Now, I think God is also in spirit. I feel this so strongly in your work, because you have such a powerful spirit presence in that sculpture of the guardian and in your experience of the guardian. You have the guardian trying to become conscious in you, *spirit* trying; equally you have your body trying to

become conscious, *matter* trying. The bowl of your body went
into the fire.

RITA: Not willingly, Marion. I did not go willingly.

MARION: Who of us does? Oh Rita, who of us does?

5

Journal: in city
January 1, 1987

Damnation!

What a way to spend New Year's.

Bed. Flu. Antibiotics.

After twenty months of mounting health, WHAMMY! However,
perhaps this is not too bad a way to reflect on the last year, lying in bed,
enjoying the moment, reflecting on the past.

This year: the wonder of beginning analysis, traveling in the rain
forests of the West Coast; sailing among the Queen Charlotte Islands;
living so close to the virgin earth, close to the ocean, close to the
remnants of ancient culture. Feeling at one with my body, and the
body of the earth and the sea and the sky. Health!

And now, sick. Why?

Oh, come off it. Starting out a year with a touch of bronchitis is no
great disaster.

Besides, who said that a new year *had* to begin on January 1? What
say that I start mine on . . . let's see . . . March 1?

February 28, 1987
Morning Dream

> There are five small objects on a table in front of me. They are flat,
> paper-thin wafers set out in a square, with the fifth wafer in the center. I
> am aware of someone standing to my right. And I know that I am
> supposed to take the fifth piece, the central wafer, and swallow it. But I
> keep delaying. A voice says: "Time is running out! Time is running
> out. . . ."

Don't understand this dream, except that it reminds me that tomorrow is the day I chose to begin my New Year, and time is certainly running out, and I'm not ready.

1990

MARION: Well, we're getting on, Rita. In Jungian terms, the archetypal four is the number of totality. Now, the year before you had that dream, you had done good work, and you'd reached a certain level of totality. But then what happens, when you come to the four, a new segment begins. . . .

RITA: A new level?

MARION: Yes. Then the four are more than the sum of their parts; they are all being integrated into the new one.

RITA: The fifth is the new one.

MARION: And Jung calls the five the number of the natural man, by which he means, the man who is in touch with his spiritual instincts. So, in a dream, if there's anything that costs five dollars, or as here, if there's a fifth wafer, you can be very sure that there's a new integration of spiritual and instinctual energy emerging.

RITA: I keep delaying the acceptance of my own spiritual and instinctual energy.

MARION: A new integration of it. You just can't take it in. You're already there, but you can't yet accept it.

RITA: Does my meditation that evening point to what can happen if I *don't* accept it?

February 28, 1987
Evening Meditation

There was a knife at my groin, handle up, blade down. I tried to protect myself.

I put my hands up in front of my face in a prayer position.

The knife came under my hands, sharp blade to the throat, handle down.

What can I do?

I grabbed the handle with my two hands and pulled it away from me, and threw it deep into the ground.

Then a halo came over my head.

It elongated into a white encasement, moving down, enfolding, surrounding my whole body.

I stretched my arms up above my head, and the whiteness came also, like filmy wings attached to my arms. Protection.

Journal: in country
March 16, 1987

I'm afraid! I don't understand it. The first time since we've had this country house, I'm afraid of being alone here.

March 18, 1987

I feel very strange. As though I'm warding off a stroke. I'll go back to the city tomorrow. This is too dangerous, alone.

Journal: in city
March 19, 1987

Earle *died*! In the University Book Store, just like that. Talking to someone, his heart stopped, he fell. *Dead*. Someone, somehow zapped back the beat . . . beat, beat . . . of the heart. But is it alive? Is he alive? Is that brilliant brain alive? He lies in intensive care, a warm corpse, sustained by tubes and Lan's constant presence. I've been there as much as I can, hoping that our love will penetrate the warm, dead man.

Sunday, March 29, 1987

All day I am wiped out, with pains of arthritis, and general sense of drainage. Bobby wonders if the arthritis is psychosomatic as a result of the Earle situation. And I think he is right. It moves around my body, and stiffens me into an old lady, so that I hardly know myself any more. I must get away from the hospital vigils for a day. Get to the country. Breathe. Next Sunday. Even if I have to go alone.

Journal: in country
April 6, 1987

I still don't believe it! It's only April! There's still snow on the ground. There can't be any wasps in April! And yet I was stung.

"Twenty minutes," said the doctor, the last time. "That's all the time you've got to get the stuff into you, or you're dead." I got the needle into me, and the adrenalin, and the antihistamine, and I got a taxi to get me to the hospital. And I kept myself conscious by screaming, "I can't die! I can't die! I can't leave all this mess to Bob!" Thank god I'm back in the Treehouse now, shaking but alive.

Journal: in city
April 12, 1987

I feel that someone is playing dice.

Someone whom we cannot trust to be on our side. Love does not enter into it for him–it.

Oh please, god, be on our side.

What can I do but sit here in the emergency waiting room, and write and write to keep my head from bursting. . . .

Why should it be *Bobby* who is the first in the forty years of the hospital's history. . . .

I see him in my mind's eye, gaily running for the bus, pulling his case-on-wheels, and *lifting* it into the bus. . . .

"You dear silly fool," I thought, "if you want the hernia to erupt or . . . what do hernias do . . . ? But it was an adventure to get to the hospital by bus and subway. An achievement. A triumph to *not* take a taxi. That was three days ago. Two days ago they operated. Simple operation. "Everyone is up and around in a day. He'll be home by Monday." But here it is, nearing midnight, nearly Monday, and *what is going on? Do they know?* They've muttered about pneumonia, but also pus in the incision, reoperate. . . . *Do they* know *what they are* doing? "It's all happening very quickly," the doctor said before he disappeared behind the screens. "We must act quickly to stop it." But what is *it*? Do they know? Are they part of the dice game? It is my love's life they are playing with! It is his *life*! Oh god, save it. He cannot die . . . here comes the woman doctor, the heart doctor, toward . . . yes . . . towards me. . . .

It isn't pneumonia. It's gangrene. How long is it now since they rushed the stretcher past and through to the operating room? It's two A.M. The waiting room is empty, except for me. Where have I been for two hours? Here. Stunned. I'll be able to see him in intensive care around two-thirty. The doctor will . . . I can't . . . write . . . I . . . the doctor will come and tell me the prognosis, she said.

"The worst prognosis is, do you want the worst prognosis?"
"Yes. Then the best. . . ."
"He may not make it through the night."

NO!

NO NO NO NO NO!   *NO!*   *HE MUST LIVE!*

I didn't scream that out then when the doctor told me. I'm screaming it out now, at home. I listened then, and nodded, and asked for the best prognosis, which is a series of operations to make sure they've got all the gangrene out, although, he said, they have opened him up from his rib cage down into his groin, and he's sure . . . He's almost sure.

Who can I phone at four in the morning? What can I do? Write . . . cry, as I cried as I wandered the empty hospital corridors looking for intensive care, looking for my love. As I cried when I found him, behind a mass of tubes, unconscious, looking like his mother in her coffin. As I cried as I traveled home by taxi, passing by his office building, where for so many years. . . .

"I'm sorry," I said to the driver "but I've had a very bad shock." What I *must* do, I suddenly realize, is to draft a funeral service. We never talked about funerals. I have no idea who . . . what he would want. But if. . . . Yes, I have to do it. Now. Face the most terrible.

April 13, 1987

Nine A.M. Hospital. He is alive! He smiles at me. Oh god, thank you thank you thank you.

April 16, 1987

How do I deal with other people? They came toward me with wide smiles. "Rita! How lovely to see you. Where's Bob? Is he parking. . . ."

I remember backing away, tears spurting straight out of my eyes. Picasso's *Crying Woman.* Their faces, shocked. I turned and ran.

What can I say to people? What can I do?

Perhaps. . . .

Yes. If I write a letter and xerox it and send it out to people that I might encounter, so they will know. . . .

Wednesday, April 22–Thursday, April 23, 1987

It hit me on Wednesday, temperature soared, throat unbearably sore. The doc sends penicillin. "It's staphylococcus. What happened? Have you been in touch with it in hospital?"

"Well, I kissed our friend Earle. . . ."

"That's it. They quarantined him this morning."

"You can't go in his room now without a mask," says Lan.

"I can't go *anywhere!*" I lie back in bed, head bursting.

Friday, April 24, 1987

I don't believe it! This is too *bizarre!* Kind Julia sends in a chicken dinner for sick me, served on a silver platter. I am deeply touched. I'm able to eat a little, leave a lot. In the night, I start to vomit. In the morning, I see the silver platter with the remaining chicken and potatoes, and they are *green.* The doc suspects salmonella. Shooting pains through my head. I am *very ill.*

Friday, June 19, 1987

Three A.M. These pains! It's been going on for how long? Months. The tightness in the throat has spread to the right jaw, and is creeping across to my left. It is as though all my teeth have suddenly gone rotten. It is agony! What can relieve it? I have no codeine. If I just write . . . perhaps I'll fall asleep. Face into the pain. I've been sent to specialist after specialist. . . . The doctors ask:

> "What are the symptoms?"
> I'll make up a list, to keep it all straight.
> "Neck and head on fire in feeling;
> Excruciating pain in jaws when I eat;
> Left temple painful; right temple very painful;
> Bumps on temples, very sore.
> Arthritic pains come and go around my body;
> Blood pressure 180 over 110;
> Eyes feel strange. A blood vessel burst in left eye today:
> Diarrhea. Night sweats.
> Sick stomach, energy drained away. . . .
> Very great difficulty sleeping. . . .

I'll take some sleeping pills and try again now.

June 28, 1987

This is very frightening. My eyes, the last two days. As though I am looking at the world through the holes of a stencil. Then this afternoon I began to see double, and no matter how hard I tried to see straight, there were two trees in front of me, instead of one. Or two cups. Is this the way one goes blind?

"Are you under particular emotional strain, Mrs. Allen?" asks the doctor. Yes! Yes yes yes yes yes! There is an anger building in me toward people who work in the medical profession and take chances with other people's lives. And I do not know how or when the anger will be too great to contain. If I can direct it strongly and constructively towards some *good* before I destroy myself before it destroys me. . . . Now the doc's sending me off to see a neurologist who is reputed to be good with migraines. *Migraines!* It's ridiculous!

July 9, 1987

Incredible! Incredible, incredible. I go to the neurology specialist as arranged and the secretary says, "Oh sorry, some mistake, he's just left on holiday, he'll be back in a month." "No!" "OK, his assistant is here. I mean she's out to lunch, but would you. . . ." "Yes! Anything! Anyone!"

His assistant sees me and listens. I mean *listens*. She suspects something serious. I am *not* to leave the building until blood tests are taken, reports are received, other doctors examine me. She rallies them: another doctor who *listens*. Another who takes a biopsy of the artery in my right temple. I am told what it might be, what the consequences might be, what the controlling drug will be, what the consequences of that might be, what action must be taken, *now*, for the reports have come in. . . .

It *is* incredible. Because of a mistake in a doctor's scheduling, I am saved. Incredible. Ridiculous. Miraculous.

July 15, 1987
Letter to my friends

. . . I'm trying hard not to blame the specialists who have been prodding and pricking me and been bewildered by it all. Specialists, it seems to me, are each caught in the net of his special field.

I mean, if you go fishing with a mind-set for trout, you come back with a true report of "no trout," without noticing that you missed seeing the crocodiles. However! There is at least one doctor who has an eye open for *everything*. I met her, and she saw the crocodile. I have it. Or, I should say, it has me. And if she and the medical team that she rallied immediately had not dealt with it pronto, I would, in all probability, be blind by now, with a chance of also being dead. My gratitude is overwhelming.

The condition, which is called "temporal arteritis," has no known cure, but has one means of control. It is a drug with very unpleasant side effects. It will cause bloating of the face, neck, body; thinning of the legs

and arms; brittleness of bones; weariness, fatigue, depression. It can
cause diabetes; gastric ulcers; internal bleeding; and . . . that's all I've
been able to face up to, so far.

The doctors say that the side effects diminish as they gradually reduce the
amount of the daily drug dosage. So that within a year, or two, or three, I
will be out of the danger zone, and the dosage will be comparatively infin-
itesimal. That is the hope. My mind springs at the hope. It is life.

6

Journal: in city
July 19–20, 1987

Long night of not sleeping. Thinking, feeling, *convinced* that my eyes
have been threatened because it is time that I allowed them to be
opened. Really open so I can *see* this path I am on. What is it? Where
am I? Is this the road to Damascus? I don't know. But wherever it is
going, I have to go. Whatever is going to happen, I must allow it to
happen. With my eyes *wide open*, seeing, knowing, experiencing
where I'm going on this journey I've been talking about for so long.

Flash! "Take off the mask: behold the essence!" said a dream, two
years ago.

Flash! "Do you think God is trying to tell you something?" Mother's
voice. Thirty years ago. I'm lying in hospital after the car accident, my
neck broken. On the telephone is Mother. I could have screamed at her:
"WHY DOESN'T HE JUST TELL ME?!"

But I didn't scream, of course. I choked back a volcano of anger that
I dared not allow to erupt onto her and her God.

But now, tonight, I hear my own voice saying, "What is this strange
year all about? Why these synchronistic happenings? Why am I in such
danger? Is god trying to tell me something?"

Oh, god, whatever you may be, please tell me. Just, simply, tell me.

July 21, 1987

I phoned Marion Woodman. I need help. Can I see her? She is leaving
to go north for the summer. But maybe . . . somehow . . . could we
talk by phone some time this summer?

July 22, 1987
Meditation

I can't believe it! Yet I must. How else to explain today?

It came. . . . It came . . . I feel, from god.

At first there was the light. A radiating path of light curving out step by step before me, above me, pulsating. It moved out from the core of myself, expanding . . . out, out. . . .

Then, that winged presence that enfolded me so many years ago, that replaced the black core of my being with golden-white, that same guardian spirit that demanded to be given form in sculpture, came, and held me in its wings. And it laughed softly, and spoke.

I was astonished. I said,

"Where have you come from? How do I know that you're here?" A ridiculous question, since I *knew* it was there.

It laughed again. "What would you like? A slight brush of wing on your left cheek?"

"But you don't really have wings," my logical left brain was nattering. "I mean, yes, it is well-established imagery. Though I don't understand that particular image. Perhaps it's because the sound of wings is similar to the sound of the breathing of a human under stress. Or, of blood pulsating in the eardrums. Or . . . perhaps. . . ."

The presence laughed most lovingly, and said, "Are you always going to try to grab a glimpse of the mechanism?"

At which *I* laughed. I couldn't stop laughing. We laughed together.

I no longer need to go to my tree to find . . . it.

It is here, in me, and probably always has been.

But now I am listening.

What is it? I don't know. But it feels like something that guides and guards me. I shall call it, as I did before, my guardian.

July 25, 1987
Meditation

I waited for the light of the guardian, but instead I felt a great rough pressure in my chest and a huge voice bursting open my rib cage, demanding:

Make WAY!
Make WAY!

I felt my throat being forced open, and great yawns coming out, and cries, and then I was sobbing helplessly, my head and back bent back most painfully. And a loud voice rumbled:

"If you will play with the gods, you must deal with the gods."

Me, scared, very. I cried as loud as I could cry. I cried to my guardian. And, immediately, white light, like a thin mantle falls down from above my head, and surrounds me. A gentle undulating tube of white. And the light from it enters into my pores and into the center of my being as a core of yellow-white. It moves gradually, and with every move, I feel more and more shielded from . . . whatever-that-was. Now, my feet tingle with life and are connected with the earth, which is, in fact, two stories below me. But my feet are firmly, deeply planted in that Mother Earth.

July 30, 1987
Meditation

As soon as I close my eyes, the guardian is here.

"This is the watershed," it says.

My logical mind, over here by my left temple, is not ready.

"Now, just a minute, hold on a. . . ."

"Quiet," says the guardian. "Release the throat. Now."

And I can feel my throat muscles relaxing, and the yawns begin to come. I can also feel my poor little logical mind struggling for sensible control, saying, "What's going on here? Explain. You can't just. . . ." And I feel for it! I want to know too, what the hell is going on! But my guardian says, "Poor little thing," and rolls my worried mind into the light that surrounds me. Still not understanding, but comforted.

And the guardian continues:

Release the throat.
Release the lies locked in there; the lies from childhood.
Release the Don'ts, the Shoulds, the Should Nots, Other People's injunctions.
Release denial of the power of the feminine.

Release denial that this *is* happening.

This is the watershed. This is the moment when you must accept what is happening, or deny what is happening. You must make the choice *now.*

A sudden intense roar of a motorcycle. I am shocked. It's just coincidence, but . . . I am shaking with the shock.

"Yes," says the guardian. "The power working can kill. Surely you have received enough indication of the power coming through. It is demanding change. Things must be thrown away. *Some* things. Many things will fall into their place for use. The guides and helpers are in place. Others will come. *You* can sense the limitations of the false ones. Keep to your intuition."

"Will you always be here?" I asked.

Pause.

"You are silent," I said.

"Yes. *You* must gain the strength and the courage. So it may not always seem that I am here. But I will be here. If you go through, if you cross the watershed. If you allow yourself to be *totally* open to who you are, to become really who you are. The alternative *is* Death."

I sit, stunned.

The guardian says, "Do not answer now. Do the Spiral Meditation. You need that energy, my little one."

"Yes," I say. "I do feel like a child."

"But a strong one," it says. "Remember the *strength* of the child. That *strength!*"

After the spiral meditation, I say, "Yes, my guardian, I accept. I feel you as a ring, around me, connecting the crown of my head to my left fingertips, to my toes, to my right fingertips, to my crown. And the energy flows into the center of that ring from every point on the circumference, and the center is my heart. This is the inner marriage that I've heard about. With this ring. . . ."

GUARDIAN: Don't.

RITA: Am I enclosing you too much by doing that?

GUARDIAN: It isn't necessary yet. The eternal round, yes. But right now, be open to me. Protective shield ready in the outside world. But be *open* to me. There'll be another time for the enclosed ring. You are not ready for that marriage yet. Now,

go and get something to eat. And on the way, look at the
kundalini book.
RITA: I don't have a kundalini book.
GUARDIAN: Yes, you have. It's on the bookshelf. Read about the
throat chakra. You need to understand what is happening there.
And the heart.

I found the kundalini book on the bookshelf. I'd only glanced at it,
long ago, when someone gave it to me. "Incomprehensible," I'd
thought. Now, I open it (or it opens) at page 49, and *there* . . . I cannot
believe it! I read:

> In tantric teachings (as Jung has pointed out) the Purusha is first seen as
> the fourth chakra, the heart chakra Anahata. Purusha is the essence of
> man, the Supreme Man. In the recognition of feelings and ideas, one
> "sees" the Purusha. This is the first inkling of a being within one's
> physical existence that is not "oneself"; of a being within whom one is
> contained, greater and more important than oneself but which has a
> purely psychic existence.[9]

I cannot believe it! But I cannot *not* believe it. For the words I am
reading are not just words but are ringing with the vibrancy of the
experience that is still in me and around me. Then I read the next
paragraph, in which it describes the pictorial symbol of the heart
chakra as of "two interlocking triangles representing the union of the
male principle (an upward-pointing triangle) and the female principle
(a downward-pointing triangle)"; and "their union is represented as a
circle with a primal central point . . . the transcendental centre."[10]
So there it is. I am not ready for that inner marriage yet. There'll be
another time for that enclosed ring with the still point at the center, that
ring that says that now my masculine principle and my feminine are
equal and as one. You are right, wise guardian. I am not at all ready.
But I am more than willing to take the next step. Yes. I accept.

Journal: in city
July 31, 1987

Doubts are catapulting out of my left brain this morning. It doesn't
make sense, this guardian stuff. I'm being fooled; I'm fooling myself.

Maybe it's the drug. No. That's not likely. The first time that he came was years before I took the drug. But at least he didn't *talk* then. Though, on the other hand, I've known my tree to talk. Which isn't logical. Any more than this guardian stuff is logical. It's crazy. The whole thing, to be honest, is just crazy. Maybe it's me. I'm the one that's going crazy. Though, I don't feel the least bit crazy. I feel pain. Terrible pain, as the fight goes on between the temporal arteritis and the drug. I feel my shoulders and my neck thickening and humping and shoving my head forward in an agonizing way. I feel my stomach bloating. I find myself crying as I disappear into this mass of flesh, as my hair comes out. . . .

The phone rang. It was Marion, calling from up north. She felt that I was going through something important. She is right! We talked for an hour. I told her about my meditations, and she said, "Everything is in place, Rita. Your guardian is right. Protect yourself in the outside world, and be totally open to him."

"I'm not fooling myself? I mean, logically. . . ."

"Logical thinking has no place at this moment. The important thing for the next months is to stay with the physical, permeated by the light, and live from the core. Always. As yourself. At your pace. Do not try to be what *anyone* else wants you to be. Be only yourself. And listen to the wisdom of that guide."

August 4, 1987

This morning has been quite extraordinary. Can I relive it? I'll try.

I felt that I must bathe. I go out of the bedroom towards the bathroom and a golden light permeates the house, intensifying as I go toward the bath. But here it becomes dappled with shadows, and the water running from the tap into the blue-green algae lotion of the bathwater, becomes springwater flowing over mossy, grassy green.

It is as though I am at the spring at Delphi. It is as though I have just climbed up the mountainside from the round temple of Athena, to this opening in the rock, this vulva that curves back and above me, out of which the waters flow.

I hear, I seem to hear, the soft hum of wasps that dart through the sun and shadows; and I see, I seem to see (as I actually did see on that

day when I came upon the spring nearly twenty years ago), two wasps
attack a moth, and then a bee.

"The male aggressive instinct," I remember thinking then, "the
male determined to discover and consume the female. And the male
will win. And yet the female secret still is secret."

And here it is again, *here*. I feel myself to be the virgin Pythia, safe
within the protecting vagina of the rock, preparing. . . .

And now I go into this blue-green water, and under the surface, head
back and down. Wonderful! I am full of wonder.

And *flash*! My adolescent baptism at Danforth Baptist Church.
Gray, cowardly, a lie. It is washed away in this true brilliant vibrant
ritual bathing; this Delphic spring of my inner life; this water gushing
out from the feminine mystery of the earth, from Gaia.

I let it wash over me, again and again and again, preparing . . .
preparing. . . .

Preparing for what?

A pain hits my stomach.

Apollo!

They will come for me soon. They will help me to step out of this
protecting water, and . . . cover me . . . and lead me up the rocky
mountain path to that great frightening rectangular temple of Apollo.
And take me down into the deepest innermost vault, and use my
feminine channel for their male commercial ends.

NO!!
I will not go!
Pain hits my stomach once again. I've had that pain
since I was a child. Why? Where has it come from?
FLASH! Him. Liar! Fake!
Get out!
GET OUT!!
I will not go!
I will not be used again.

Take me, dear Pythian maidens; rinse me gently in this blue-green
algae of life. Dry me carefully, and dress me in my blue-green gown.
And lead me down the mountain to the round temple of Athena. And
let me be female and myself.

August 6, 1987

Again, extraordinary. After a long, long dialogue with the guardian, he says, "Go into the cupboard and get the book."

I'm surprised. "This cupboard? But there are no books here, it's full of art supplies, and paintings, and old photographs. . . ."

But I go. And sure enough there's a little pile of books that I put there almost twenty years ago. I pick up the top one. It's called *Decision at Delphi*. I can't believe it! But then I see that it's a mystery-thriller, and I say to the guardian, "Is this it?"

No answer. I look at the next book. It's called *The Mask of Apollo*. I take them both out into the room, and close the cupboard door. Then the guardian says, "Go in again."

I go in again, and see that the title of the next book is in Greek. I open it, and there . . . *there* . . . is a photograph of the spring. The Castalia Spring, it is called. I had forgotten.

"Turn the page." I do. And there is the Tholos, the round temple of Athena.

"Here is your sanctuary for now," the guardian says. "Everything has been gathering for this time of retreat. And the things that are not here, and that you will need, will appear at the right time. And now, go and bathe in the blue-green water. Rest and be in the feminine."

"And the masculine? Bobby?"

"Don't weigh on Bob too much. Physically, you are very ill, and he's doing a valiant job for you. But this inner place is not his space with you just now. Let him rush away at his own pace. And you must move gently, gently, and let your soul be filled with what it needs."

August 10, 1987

> *I DON'T . . .*
> *I . . . CAN'T . . .*
> *MAKE IT . . .*
> I'm not going to make it. It's too hard.
> *I . . . CAN'T . . .*

Noon. Marion phoned. I tell her that my energy is totally drained, that I don't know how to. . . . She asks me if I've talked to my guardian today. No. Have I dreamed? Yes. I tell her my morning dream.

I am in a house, which is divided into an upstairs apartment, where Nora lives, and a downstairs, where her husband, Bill, is living. I go into the living room of the downstairs apartment, and see food set out on a table. It is very specific food which is difficult to get and which I need, but I cannot just take it and eat it because Bill is not there.

I go out of the room, and up an enclosed staircase to Nora's flat. I emerge in a newly built area, and there is a young Nora in the middle of a laughing, talking party.

I tell Nora that I'm going downstairs, and she leaves the party and comes with me. I'm delighted. I think, "Aaah! It's all right between them again."

Downstairs, we are in the hallway, and Bill comes striding toward us, smiling, chipper, walking firmly with no signs of his recent illness. He's full of energy, but he does not look like Bill. He has a little clipped moustache, and a plumpish, military face. He exudes delight at seeing us, and I think, "Good! Now we can all eat together."

But Nora turns and starts to leave. I sense "no reconciliation" from her. So does Bill. He says, in a disparaging voice, "Well, if that's the way you want it." Strong resentment. I feel caught in the irreconcilable tension between Bill to my right, and Nora moving away up the stairs to my left.

MARION: Have you been having pains in the solar plexus?
RITA: Yes. Bad ones. Hiatus hernia.
MARION: The diaphragm. That is the divide between the lower and the upper chakras. In your dream, it is the floor between the lower apartment and the upper. In the lower flat the strong, healthy, militarily powerful, energetic man lives, and he has the food, the energy that you need. But this is a house divided. The woman, who is part of your shadow, lives in the upper flat where there is lots of talk but no food. That shadow part of you will go down to visit her masculinity, but she sees that there has been a transformation in that masculine, and she will not forgive. She will not stay, neither will she invite him into the upper story. Resentment. Between some new part of your masculinity and your feminine shadow. And it hits you right there, in the diaphragm. The divide between the lower and upper

chakras is the hardest for the Purusha energy to pass through. If that Nora were able to cross over that barrier, she might be able to love. Love, filled with the energy that it is lying there, waiting to be eaten, and internalized, and used. Ponder on Nora. Why she will not let you be at one.

RITA: She's a blocker! She's the part of me that finds it difficult to *receive*. I will give and I will take. But I find it difficult to be trusting, to be open, to receive. As I say that, I feel her giving way, as though she's pondering the alternative. . . .

MARION: That's a good beginning.

RITA: Yes, it is! You know, I thought, before you called, that I couldn't make it through the day.

MARION: It's all one piece. Remember your dream about the mirror and the snakes and the owl. This is another rung of the spiral. You'll make it.

RITA: Yes. I believe I will.

August 13, 1987

I continue to bathe in the Castalia Spring, then rest in the feminine of the Tholos. I continue to listen to my guardian.

August 14, 1987

Dream: I am standing on a slight rise in a forest. At my feet, there is a deer print in the earth. Joy and sadness fill me. There are so few deer; I hope it survives. Perhaps it is the last. Now, a bull-like animal, a brown, smooth, humpbacked bison with no horns, comes up the rise, nuzzling the ground. It looks at me, unafraid. I also am not afraid. I sense that it is important that a human male retain the imprint of that deer as though it were his own. It is important that man be encouraged to live, because of the presence of this imprint in him. A young man appears who is willing to do this, and I will help.

Now I am standing on a dock, before a ship which takes men to a place for seasonal work. I am a young working-class woman, with a daughter of about ten who is rubbing against my legs, like a young deer, and a son who is a little older. He stands at a short distance: he has had contact with both the deer and the bull.

Now the young man strides on to the dock; he too is working-class. We do not hug or bid farewell as middle-class people would, but there is affection and trust between us. He goes on board the ship. I face him, and walk backward, away. We do not even wave, but look at each other, trusting. And I am saying, silently: "You must retain the imprint of the single deer, and search for others. They are rare, true, but you must not give up hope. You must not lose your will to live."

I phone Marion at her summer place, and tell her this dream. She says: "The Purusha often appears as a deer. In the dream, the spiritual energy is in the material that you are to gather together for the masculine. This material is already there in your own feminine. Is it a female deer?"

"Yes."

"Feminine energy, feeling. You're predominantly a feeling person. And the young man, your own masculinity is contacting both his deer and his bull, his spiritual and instinctual energies. At last, he is freeing his spirit from patriarchy. Love him, Rita. He's on the threshold of his own life. In the dream you are working-class because there is work to be done, and it is work through the instincts. That is where the energy is to be found, coming through the body."

"My body."

"It is all you, Rita. Everything is on the point of coming into balance. The possibility of balance between masculine and feminine: man, wife, son, daughter."

"And does it also say . . . I feel it says that the young masculine is *finally* setting out on the hero's journey. And he knows what it is for. It is to carry in him the imprint of the rare and precious deer, or (as you say) the Purusha, or (as I have always understood the deer image) the spirit of Christ. And he is to search for other imprints, other proofs that the deer exists. I would say that he is, in fact, finally, setting out in his search for the Holy Grail, the treasure hard to find."

"I think so."

"While the feminine in me stays here in this place by the water, close to the Mother Earth."

And I tell her of my ritual bathings and my rest in the feminine Tholos. She says, "Wonderful! You must rest as much as possible now, and be very, very gentle with yourself. And the other very important thing now is your relationship with Bob."

August 15, 1987

This evening, Bobby asked me if I could share with him what was happening. I said, "It's hard to explain. But I am living in three worlds. This world in the city, which is, of course, the real world, where I am a sick, pain-ridden creature, unable to cope with the noise of cars outside, or planes overhead, or anything mechanical. And I'm not able to cope with chores, or people.

"But then I'm in a world of extraordinary meditation, where I live in a holy healing spring and in a temple, where I am totally feminine, and where my guardian is my guide and constant companion.

"Then, I am in a world of dreams, where (with Marion's help) the three worlds mix and meld and move me toward seeing and knowing that the three are one, and that each of them will change and develop and be enriched. And so shall I."

He nodded, and said, "Yes. It is difficult for me to understand. But I will try. I will do what I can to help."

And he does! Oh, how he does! More than I had ever dared hope.

August 16, 1987

Dream: Again, I am in the woods, but this time they curve around the end of a large pond. I am in a wooden hut, looking out a large, rectangular open window toward the pond and the woods. With me is a man who is slightly older than I (my brother?), sitting beside me at a wooden table, leaning against me, but also looking out the window. He has a rifle.

The man calls to a much older man who is outside, on the lookout for game. "Seen anything?" he calls.

Older man: "Saw something move two minutes ago."

I lean back against the young man, happy, feeling a part of everything.

Then I see a tiny duck coming out of the woods at the right, heading for the water.

I say involuntarily, "There it is."

Young man raises his rifle.

I say, "Don't shoot it though!"

I feel the rifle waver for a split second, and hear the young man say, "Make up your mind."

But instantaneously, he shoots. I close my eyes. The noise reverberates through my head. At the same time, I say, "I hope you missed it! Did you miss it?"

Silence.

I feel sick at the death of such an innocent tiny thing for . . . what reason? I won't look. I keep my eyes closed.

I wake. My arms are trembling. My stomach is sick. There's pain from the optic nerve in the center of my head shooting down into my left eye. It's as though I can *feel* a split in that spiritual eye between the masculine and the feminine and the pain is being felt by the feminine. And understandably so! I trusted that masculine of mine; I felt so at one with him. And then for him to shoot!

Marion listens to the dream, and says, "Your masculine is relaxed, but ready for action. Your feminine feels a part of everything, including nature, she sees the duck emerging. The duck is an image of transcendence: it travels on land, in the water, and in the air. That duck energy in you is trying to bring about a new balance. But the masculine acts, intuitively, in his own way. Immediately. The feminine ego pulls back, almost blocks the aggressive action. But too late. This is where you are now. The harmony that you're looking for in all things would allow that duck to live. But your feminine ego is still quite aware of an old pattern of thought (the older man on the lookout for ducks to shoot). Denial, fear held over. Fear held over from old patterns of reacting to your patriarchal masculine. Changing these patterns will take a while. Allow a while for the energy of the duck to move out in a new way.

"Don't push it. It will come. You are not there yet. What you're going through is taking you into a whole new way of thinking and feeling."

August 28, 1987

I have this dream at ten in the morning.

I am in a cave with the old man, my daddy. And I must stay and rest and just be there. The word "Purusha" is there, after a while. This dream goes on and on but it is only that: being in the cave curled up and the old man daddy is there.

As I wake I'm aware of an alive, burning feeling in my vagina. I hear the words "I'm going to get married," and I see those words briefly floating white in space. I feel happy.

"Did your father do the mothering, Rita?" Marion asks from her telephone in the woods.

"He loved me, totally," I say. "My one and only daughter, he'd say."

"Daddy's girl," says Marion. "And this is where the unifying love is. I think that where the father has provided mothering love, it is very important that the girl comes to a point where she realizes that creatively. I think that many women tend to see the contrasexual negatively, the fact that the father *was* the mother. Those are the kind of women who later on in life look for the mother in the lover. On the positive side, a girl who has had that kind of cherishing by the father is a natural beloved for the inner guardian. This is the positive, creative acceptance of that inner marriage. Wholeness. You hear the words, 'I'm going to get married,' and you feel happy. At one."

"And Bob?"

"Oh, the inner marriage is no threat to your outer marriage. The opposite. For you will become who you truly are. And he cannot help but be influenced by your authenticity."

Me: "To who *he* truly is?"

"Perhaps."

August 28, 1987

Morning meditation. I am inside the cave that I dreamed about this morning. Between me and the mouth of the cave is a white disk, softly glowing in the shadow. It is neither soft nor hard in texture, but it is firm, and it just hangs in the air.

The guardian says, "This is your guide this morning. Stay here."

I am surprised. "Have I left the Tholos?"

"Yes. Now you are here in the cave. Stay in the cave. Speak from the door of the cave when you are with people. Do not allow yourself to be lured any further out into the world than the door of the cave. The cave is your home for now. Essential! Essential. Here is your essence, that disk. Your eyes are jumping now. Notice what happens and what triggers what, what leads to what."

"Is the cave what Marion would call the chrysalis?"

"Yes. As the butterfly emerges from its chrysalis, you will emerge from this cave. And it is here that the transformation will take place."

Evening meditation. I am in the back of the cave, and the glowing disk is still hanging in the air between me and the cave mouth. But now it begins to resonate gently, visually and audibly. And not only does the sound fill the cave with quiet vibration, but it grows larger and moves toward the mouth of the cave, where the vibrations spread out and out towards a cliff edge and beyond that, across a deep valley to far distant mountains. I can see the circles of golden light as though they fan out forever.

October 5, 1987

The swelling of my face, and my neck, and my body is horrible. The humping of my shoulders, the way it pushes my head forward, the way my neck is bent. It is agonizing.

"What does it feel like?" asks Dr. M.

"Submission."

"Submission to what?"

"Death."

"Then submit, Rita. Submit. Let it pass through. Don't resist."

And then she treats me for two hours, after which I drag myself here, to this quiet corner in this sunfilled café, and order tea from the kind of young waiter whose eyes would have locked with mine two years ago with that amused acknowledgment that there are two sexes in the world, and he is one and I am the other. But now I can see how I have changed by his polite indifference. Yes, it is a dying. The dying of my sense of myself. I sip my tea, and mourn my passing, and try not to resist. Caterpillar, disintegrating in the chrysalis.

October 10, 1987

This period, I now see, is a rite of passage, passage into "crone." I shudder at the word.

I linger in the belated sexual radiance of my fifties, the warm amber glow with occasional flares of passion which have continued through my sixties, until this illness. . . . But surely, illnesses pass, and . . . and one is older. Suddenly, much older.

"Crone." "Wise old Woman." They are not the roles that I've been training for. Until now. *Now*, this year, all this year's assaults have been to prepare me for this next inevitable stage. The period of old age and death.

Death I'm more prepared for than old age.

Old age. I can enter it defeated, depleted. Or. I can enter it with . . . yes, wisdom. Acceptance. Clarity. Purpose.

But oooooooohhh, *must* I enter it? I delighted (though I tried not to show it) at Peter's comment, "Rita *never* changes! She comes to the birthday, and she looks just as she has always looked!" Was that just a year ago? And Iris, a month before. "I saw you across the room, and there you were, the same beautiful woman. . . ."

I pretend it doesn't matter. But it does.

It does. But so does the passage matter. Which means? One thing anyway: I, at this moment, do not look at this ongoing torment as an illness, but as a journey into a new world for which changes must be made.

Do I accept that yet? Yes, no, yes, I vacillate. But until I face it, accept it, go into the necessary rites of passage and emerge, I shall not gain energy for the next period of my life.

I must grow old. Vitally old, I hope. Old with vitality. I must release myself, and let myself be released from the tangles still hanging on from infancy, and adolescence, young womanhood, and the older woman who has achieved. I must become who I am *now*. I must not yearn for whoever I was then. And yet . . . and yet . . . the paradox. I must be aware of the thread. More than ever aware and hang on firmly to the thread that has run through my life from even before infancy, and is now, still, safely in my grasp. That will lead me into the next stage of my life, whatever it may be.

October 28, 1987

Shingles! Good god, is there no end to this?

"A classic case!" says Dr. T., with wide triumphant eyes, and he brings in another doctor to show her this perfect case of shingles. I could have killed him. But I didn't. I went to see Marion.

"Life in the chrysalis," I say, "is torture, physically and psychologically."

"Where is the worst pain?" asks Marion.

"Everywhere. Neck, shoulders, stomach, head. I fart all the time. I
shit all the time. I sweat. I'm disgusting. I'm breathless. My heart
pounds. I hyperventilate. But the real pain, right now, is a lump stuck
in my throat. I've had it for months, but right *now*. . . ."

"Yes. The hyperventilation, the anxiety manifests right there at the
throat chakra. That chakra also affects your hearing, your voice, the
thyroid, your sexuality, and it is affected by repression of creativity,
and by all the repressions of your childhood."

"In my case, 'no talking back allowed,' 'no anger allowed,' 'no little
girl talk in front of my big brothers,' and ohhh, even as I think of it, the
lump grows larger, as I try to swallow those things that I knew to be
lies, but was not allowed to call them that. So, I even lied about lies. In
the name of niceness."

"So they are caught at the throat chakra," says Marion. "The throat
is like a narrow bottle top, where the heart and solar plexus energy
cannot get through. There is an exercise where you can gently help
that chakra to open up."

And Marion shows me how to massage both temples with my
fingertips. Then massage down the line of the jaws, past the jaw joints.
Open my mouth, tuck tongue behind my lower teeth. Relax, and
release the breath. And my fingertips join at the chin. The very areas of
my agonizing temporal arteritis pain!

"What happens in the chrysalis," says Marion, "is death and resurrection. Transformation. And that cannot take place without suffering.
Without pain."

Now, as I'm writing, I wonder if the suffering must *always* be
physical as well as psychological. But Marion isn't here to answer.

November 12, 1987

How many months have I been stuck in this cave? Two months, three?
I feel that whatever transforming has taken place has turned me into a
slug with wings stuck to my sides by the mucus-slime of the dank
interior. Tonight, when I meditated, I couldn't even see the golden
light beyond the cave mouth. Instead there was blackness there and red

and darts of light that let me know that there *was* a world beyond this, even if I can hardly believe it anymore.

November 28, 1987

I have been meditating, but this happened as though it were a dream:

> Bob and I are on an indoor tennis court, where the walls are very old, dank, crumbling cement. We're playing without raquets, and Bob throws a very small ball to me. I send it back, throwing it to his right, and so high that I lose sight of it. Bob is looking for it too, up to the ceiling, which now begins to crack, and now crumbles. A rumbling sound of disintegration, and the ceiling begins to fall. I look back to Bob, but he has been slowly evaporating. I call, but there is no answer, only the sound of the crumbling of the walls and the ceiling. Bob has disappeared. Some force takes hold of me and I am speeding into a red-and black- and white-striped tunnel, like a vortex, toward the mouth of the cave.

I emerge from the "dream." I am sitting in my meditation chair, but something else is happening.

Later. After it had happened. The guardian said, "Write this down."

GUARDIAN: You came out of the cave, into the blinding terrifying light. You cried, "I *can't!*"

But then, you did. You leaped from the edge and you flew.

You didn't know you had the power.

But you have *done* it. And you have returned to the lip of the cave. You can fly out and dance and have joy in the use of *all* of yourself. And come back to the lip and rest there.

I am with you, I will be with you.

You will be far more alive now. But do not fly into that world of mechanized life. Not yet.

Open yourself, then protect yourself, the way wings do. Learn to be open and learn to protect. Move your body. Soar with your spirit. And be your *real* self. Be *your* self.

What a release I feel in my whole being! Incredible! Incredible. I am out of the chrysalis.

December 3, 1987
Meditation

I had scarcely begun my meditation when I was aware of being on the edge of the cliff outside the cave . . . and then . . . aware of the guardian saying:

> *Now! The birth is coming.*
> *Now! Lift from the cliff edge. Fly up, up . . .*
> *Not back to the edge, No! Now is your time.*
> Now! *Fly up high to the rocky precipice. Up . . . up . . .*

A terror filled me.

GUARDIAN: I am around you. I am holding you. I am in and around every part of you.

And I could feel him, like soft fur, and now the wings that I had been using dropped away from me, and the guardian lifted me up to a stark crag, where I was exposed to terrifyingly bright light. I cried, "How will I survive here? Where can I go?"

GUARDIAN: There is the tunnel mouth.

And there in the rock was the opening to a black tunnel, into which it was impossible to see.

GUARDIAN: You must enter.

I screamed. I can't! But I entered. Into blackness. And then the convulsions began. Birth convulsions in my body. They went on and on and on. . . .

For how long, I don't know. But when I emerged, I was aware of my own vulva, and between my open legs, the gaping vulva of another tiny creature who was also me. "I am a woman," I felt with a sureness that I have never felt before.

And now, I am aware that I am at the edge of a round pool of blue water. The guardian tells me to go below the surface and down, down, down. I have no strength left to rise out of it.

But now I feel, beneath me, the soft strong earth forming a peak under me, and now lifting me up until I rise out of the water and I am on a little islet in the middle of the blue water. It is Gaia, holding me.

GUARDIAN: You must rest here. I will stay with you.

I hear myself singing:

> *Clothed in the Guardian and*
> *Held by the Goddess,*
> *On the golden point raised up*
> *In the center of the round blue water.*

GUARDIAN: Make a joyful noise unto the Lord. And *this* is the Lord, the god, the goddess. Don't think about "what next?" Stay in *this* moment. Rest in *this* moment. You have taken a huge step on your journey.
RITA: I feel surrounded by dancing particles.
GUARDIAN: Joyful?
RITA: Yes. A joyful dance.
GUARDIAN: Now, feed on honey and rye bread toast. It is what is right now. Then, sleep. Rest in bed.

And, although I could hardly stand, I did as he said, and slept until now, midafternoon. Knowing that I am still in the lap of the goddess, even as I sit at this table and type, even as I feel now the song that the guardian gave me rising in my throat, and bursting into the shimmering air:

> *Holy One, I love you.*
> *Blessed One, I love you.*
> *Inner One, my soul cries out my love to you.*

Two birds fly by the door as I sing, and then fly up, high up, up. . . . Beautiful.

December 12, 1987

During the last two weeks, my life with the guardian has seemed more real than the walls and furniture of this house. A few days ago, for instance, he lifted me from the center of the blue pond. . . . I'll type out what I scribbled down at the time:

> He lifts me up and through a hole in the blue dome that covers the pond. And the *light* is so white, I cry *no!* And he covers my eyes and my head with his wings, and so, we pass through the light. And then, holding me and covering me, we fly out over miles of blue water, until I see a tiny green island, and he says, "There."

> RITA: Alone?
> GUARDIAN: No. I am with you.

And now my eyes are bedazzled by the minute and unknowable number of cells of the infinite colors of god.

And there! In the center of the island is my double tree.

And my guardian places me in the center of my tree, where I have never dared to go. Never to the center. No, But now . . .

> GUARDIAN: The center of the tree is your self.
> And the core of the tree is the center of you.
> Here is where you must rest now. And be.
> You have walked the power line.
> Now is the time to tap that power.
> Not for your vanity.
> Because it is your destiny.
> The divining rod works for *you*.
> This is where it dipped for you long ago to show the power.
> This center is your center. Your feminine, your masculine, here.
> Here is where this newly born one can truly grow,
> At this time of the sun's death and its rebirth.

December 16, 1987

Today I saw Marion and told her of my meditations of the last few weeks.

MARION: Incredible! What a gift you are receiving!

RITA: I'm not going crazy?

MARION: What makes you think that?

RITA: Well, this guardian . . .

MARION: He has never said anything that you have reported that is not immediately to the point. Do you resent him?

RITA: No. But sometimes I feel that I'm fooling myself. Then, the next minute, I am completely trusting and can enter totally into the experience with him. But right now, what I'm wondering is how do my meditations and visions differ from the hallucinations of, for instance, the fifteen-year-old medium that Jung writes about in *Psychology and the Occult*? He calls her pathological.

MARION: This is totally different. In the case of pathology, the person does not bring the experience back into everyday life because there is not enough ego to reflect it or integrate it. Serious addicts are in a similar situation. Their experiences may be extraordinary, their dreams extraordinary, but all is useless unless the ego-container can bring the treasure back into consciousness. A person can be overwhelmed. It is dangerous. However, your ego is strong. It can expand in your dialogues with your body, dialogues in your dreams, dialogues with your guardian, in your meditations and in your visions. What you and I do here, in this office, is to check through the dreams and meditations, go into them for their deeper messages from the unconscious, listen to those messages, and so strengthen the container with them. So consciousness grows stronger. To keep the balance between consciousness and the unconscious, that is the task. The paradox is this: the stronger the ego, the more flexible it is. It can contain more, resonate more, more can pass through it. Like a beautiful cello, the music comes through it, comes *through* the container and out.

RITA: And my guardian?

MARION: There is the wisdom. You have some healthy doubt.

December 18, 1987

I woke up at nine o'clock with this beautiful dream:

A baby is sitting on a cushion on the floor in front of me. It is chubby, with darkish hair and full lips and it is singing! Miraculously! Beautifully. And totally unselfconsciously. There are indications that some of it has been filmed, and I hope so. But the baby is not interested in that. It moves as its body wishes to different positions on the cushion; the last being a plump little Buddha, facing me but not looking at me, because it is totally, relaxedly involved in its singing.

As I wake, I glow with the thought: This Christmas, *this* is the divine child. No tinsel is required. Only the singing beauty of new life, of birth . . . of that new-born self that emerged from my body fifteen days ago.

January 4, 1988

I asked Bob to rush me to Marion's office for my (what I thought was my) appointment at two o'clock today, because I would burst if I didn't tell her about my dream and my vision. And I discovered that another analysand was there, and my appointment is for tomorrow.

I pleaded: "Please! Ten minutes . . . just ten minutes to let you know . . . to let me tell you there's been an extraordinary . . . something. . . ."

And, of course, the analysand was courteous, and I was able to release some of the tension of GOOD NEWS! But I'll really go into it all tomorrow.

January 5, 1988

Dream of January 3: Bobby and I are in an East Indian section of the city, where there are shops. I see a coat in a store window, and I want to buy it. I go in, and Bob sits down among the coats that are displayed outside. The gentle East Indian girl folds the coat in soft paper and puts it to one side. Why doesn't she *give* it to me, I wonder? But she demurs, as though I am supposed to buy something more . . . or . . . that some work has to be done on the coat. Or, both. And then, she quietly suggests that I have the total "initiation." I'm not sure what she means, but I ask, "How long will it take?" as I think of Bobby and his limited patience. She says, "Not very long."

So I go outside, and Bob says, "Go ahead. I'll wait." Then, as I go back in, I realize that the coat that I've bought is black and I don't like black against my face. So the girl brings out an orange-red woolen head scarf, which, she says, is part of the set. Aha! I think. That's what she means by the "total initiation." But no. . . .

She takes me upstairs, where there are two rooms. In one, is a yoga group doing asanas. We go into the other, much larger room. Here there are many East Indian activities quietly going on.

"Now," says the girl, "the initiation will begin. I will tell you what to do, and I will stay with you." So I lie down on a table, and the girl makes many ritualistic movements over my body. And now she is leaning over me, very closely, and I put my arms around her. But she says, in a matter-of-fact, quiet voice, "Don't hang on to me. Hang on to him."

I know that she means the Inner Him. I let her go, and hold my arms around my own body.

She now holds up a rectangular bar of saffron, and begins to rub it onto my face.

I feel, "Oh dear, what will Bobby think!" But I also feel that I am so far in now that I can't back out. And I have the same double feeling when some hair is clipped from my right temple. I think, "Oh dear, it will show everyone that I've. . . ." But I also think: "I am in their hands totally."

And now I am rolled on my table into a more public part of the room. It is almost like a street with people walking by wearing colorful clothing. One little girl rolling by looks like a bright green bush. But most of the time I have my eyes closed to this passing parade.

And then, from somewhere behind my head and to the left, I hear the voice of a man giving a kind of sermon in a soft East Indian voice. As he speaks, the air seems to become golden. He says,

"Think of St. Paul's Cathedral. There, you might touch a piece of string and it remains a piece of string. You might touch a man, and he becomes a pilgrim."

I think, "How interesting that this East Indian should mention an Anglican place of worship in his sermon. How holistic."

I feel, as I lie on the table, a growing sense of inner peace.

I know that I have become at one with something that I share with these others in the room.

I am aware of the Him in my body.

Then I hear the little girl who looks like a round green bush. She says, gently, "That was very nice."

And I know that the initiation is over. But I don't want to get up and go out. So I lie on the table, content, among these people, each of whom is doing something differently from the others. I feel both separate from them, and accepted by them. I feel a part of a community, but free to stay or to go.

Marion says, "Yes, the dream does show that you are open now to the new experience, whatever it is to be, the "foreign" experience, and your reservations are regarding Bobby. Will he be patient? Will he be upset? But now you know that it isn't necessary to have those reservations. He is outside your experience, but he is accepting whatever you wish to share with him. That is wonderful, you know. And the Inner Him is no danger to Bob. It is not a rival."

RITA: He seems to know that. He said so at dinner last night.
MARION: St. Paul's Cathedral. Now what do you make of that?
RITA: Surprise. And interest. Because, as you know, all my life I've had doubts about Christianity, but now, as a result of going through these last ten years of exploration into other religious approaches to the central question, I am beginning to realize there *are* truths in some of the metaphors in some of the Christian teachings. But you can't just string along with everything that goes on in there, or you're left with just a piece of string.
MARION: (*laughing*) And you sure don't string along, Rita. You sure don't string along. St. Paul's Cathedral, when you look at it, is a mandala in itself. The circle in the middle and the transepts projecting out in a cruciform. There is very sacred space. In a dream, very often a church is a symbol of the Self.
RITA: The word by which Jung names god?
MARION: The god-image within. And in the sacred space of your dream, if a piece of string is touched by that god-energy, it remains a piece of string. But if a man is touched, he becomes a pilgrim.

RITA: This dream was followed by a vision, which *is* a mandala!

MARION: *You* became the pilgrim! Can we just stay with this pilgrim for a minute? There, at that sacred center, you might be *touched* and then you are free to stay or to go. Your security is within. You no longer need to feel guilty for being who you are. The blessing of the father, symbolized in St. Paul's, can be yours. You, a woman, can take on the mantle of the father creatively. You can live your masculinity and your femininity. The voice in the dream says, "If a man is touched . . ." a *man*. There is your masculinity that will go with you as a pilgrim. And the Purusha can bring its masculine energy to accompany you.

RITA: Why am I afraid of that?

MARION: I don't know.

RITA: I think I do. I think that it is having three older brothers when I was growing up. And I was afraid to show myself to be a leader in front of them, in any way. And so I kept that part of myself quiet. Secretive. Roundabout. No leadership talents showing except in places where brothers weren't around. Like school. And I've done it ever since with my brothers and brother substitutes, and (I've come to realize) with the masculine in me. I've led, but in a hidden way, until . . . well, until I became aware of this, and since then I've led, but with trepidation, until my ability to lead takes over. And then I cease to be quite so quiet.

MARION: Remember Brunnhilde? When her armor is taken off, all her feminine strength is revealed. She is a woman! And now, Rita, tell me about the vision.

RITA: I'll read you the journal entry:

Sunday, January 3, 1988

I said to the guardian: I am very tired. I'm very hungry. Should I write down now what had happened? Or later?

GUARDIAN: Begin now. Eat later.

ME: I asked you where I was now. I was finding it confusing, because I seemed to be still in the center of the tree, my back

resting on the feminine trunk, and my face towards the masculine, but instead of the tiny island surrounded by endless
stretches of blue ocean, now the land around the tree had
broadened out, so that in the ground beyond my feet there were
runnels and tunnels, where little animals lived and ran down the
hill, busy with family affairs. A complete world to themselves,
I thought, until I saw further down the hill, wide stretches of
farm land. And now I saw forests. And more farms. And then,
far down, I saw a Breugel's village, filled with lively, sturdy
peasants busy at their work. And then, far beyond that, I saw a
desert endlessly stretching on until I caught sight of a caravan
and camels. I looked further, and could finally see the water's
edge, and here I saw men and women living in caves. In the
ocean itself, there was a sudden burst of spume as a whale burst
through the surface of the water, then dived again.

GUARDIAN: Go on.

ME: You said, "Now walk around the tree." I felt fear at the
prospect of leaving my protected place in the center of the tree.
You said, "I will go with you." So I stepped out in the direction
I'd been facing: the northeast, and you said, "Turn left, to the
northwest." And so, I looked down over endless stretches of
snow, and far far in the icy distance, almost hidden in the
blowing snow, I saw a group of Eskimos moving on sleds.
"Turn left," you said. I turned to the southwest. There was
forest now, that began at the bottom of the little hill, and
stretched out to the horizon as far as I could see. Something
caught my eye. I looked back to the forest edge. A deer had
come out. We looked at each other, eye to eye. Then it went into
the forest. I turned left. And here, to the southeast, the land
descended in terraces of cultivation, and far, in the farthest
distance, I could see a ziggurat and all the land between it and
me was golden. Now I saw that close to me was the small shrine
of stones that I found, twenty-five years ago, at sunrise on the
flattened top of the little mountain in Kyoto. Then, the sun had
risen behind the shrine just as I reached it, and then had risen
further behind straight lines of black clouds. I wondered if now,
here, as there . . . but no. Today, there was only brilliant sunlight. Then you said, "Go back to where you started."

And I did, and the view of the quarter to the northeast

was the same as before: the whale humping in the water in the farthest distance; the men and the women emerging from caves; the desert, the little animals burrowing and cleaning and feeding and going about their business, quite unconcerned with me.

GUARDIAN: And then?

ME: "Go back into your tree," you said, "but with your back against the male side now. You are strong enough. You have even seen the world from that side now!" I wondered what you meant, until I entered the tree, and saw, yes! from the male side, you see the full power of the sun, and the ziggurat.

Now you said, "Rest. We are going down *into* the tree." I was very frightened to do this. I kept delaying. I held on to the tree. Then I'd say "all right." Then I'd hold on.

Until you said, "You cannot go anywhere and nothing will happen, if you both hang on and let go. It is impossible to do anything."

"Will you stay with me?"

"Yes." So I let go, and felt myself sinking into the black earth, looking up at the receding light, until . . . I was aware of a pale light of a huge cave around me, and I realized where I was. It was the cave in Yucatan, which we entered unexpectedly, ten years ago, and where I cried overwhelmingly. And here I was again in that great womb, that tomb, with its stalactites and stalagmites, forming a twin tree at its center, and knowing now why I cried then. For here were the underworld aspects of myself, of my masculine and my feminine. And here too was the underground stream, curving out from the right and flowing into the the dark cavern to the left. Once more it felt like the river of life and death.

"Do I go into the stream this time?" I asked you. You said, "No. That is not yet."

GUARDIAN: And then?

ME: And then you brought me to the surface up out of the dark earth.

And I rested in the tree. And you said, "Rest."

GUARDIAN: And you rested.

ME: Yes. But then, from the crown of my head, four golden threads rose and crossed and recrossed and wove themselves into a golden cube with rounded corners. And out of the top of that cube, rose four threads which again crossed and wove into another cube. So, up and up and up, until from far up, a golden light descended through the threads, and into my head and down into the area of my chest, where it gathered into a round ball of light. And then, it opened from its center, first, into four soft petals.

Then it opened again, with another four petals. And then, from that center sprang a myraid of stamens and then, one central pistil with a flash of silver light at its tip. And you said, "Lie down now, and let this enter your whole body." And I did. And then I was aware that a similar "flower" was sprouting from my back as well as my front, both rooted in the chakra of the heart.

GUARDIAN: And then?

ME: You told me to connect the chakras in a spiral, beginning with the heart. And so I did.

And the heart remained the golden flower.

The solar plexus, I became aware, was red to the upper right and blue to the lower left, and the energy sprang straight out.

The energy in the throat chakra moved out in stippled and whitened orange-red curves, alternating with yellow curves.

The sexual chakra was very pale and grey.

The spiritual chakra of the third eye was white and strong, but not overwhelmingly so.

And from the root chakra, gentle, darkened colors flowed up as from the earth itself, and they intermingled with the petals of the heart, covering their undersides with beautiful shading.

And then the crown chakra opened, and the upper crown too, and light poured down, filling all my body to and beyond my fingertips and my toes.

GUARDIAN: You pause.

RITA: I lay there for a long time, asking you several times if I should close the spiral and come back to the real world. But you said: "Not yet." And eventually, the light came back from beyond my fingertips and it settled in the heart and the petals there closed around it. And now it was a sea anemone with its petals pulsating in the flow of the vital light and the dark that was filling me.

Then you said, "Hold this in yourself gently. Unlink the spiral and curl up and rest."

I asked, "Where am I to stay?"

You said, "In the center of your tree, which is now the central post of your treehouse. The central core of yourself."

And the name "Treehouse," which we've casually used for years, instantly had a new meaning. Though I have always known the house to be shaped like a mandala, now I knew the core of that mandala to be the core of my self. But more. Now I had been shown the magnificent mandala of my world, stretching to the edge in the east, the north, the west, the south, down into the depths of the earth, up into the sky.

In the center of that mandala, I curled up and slept until late afternoon.

When I woke, I felt that a major transformation had taken place. I also realized that it came exactly nine months after my near-death experience with the wasp sting on April 6, 1987, and its attendant dream of being enclosed in a windowless house that was a tomb and a womb. Now, "in the fullness of time," I have been brought forth.

7

Journal: in city
January 11, 1988

Bob asks if I can tell him what is happening to me. I know it must be bewildering for him when I emerge from meditating day after day in a state of . . . what can I call it? . . . quiet ecstasy? Not-in-this-world-nor-of-this-world? And yet, sitting opposite him at dinner, talking about . . . whatever one talks about—the day's affairs, the plans for tomorrow—I wonder if I *can* talk about what is happening to me without risking what we have. Is it possible that Bob, with his logical, reasoning intelligence could, would hear me talk of visions without his eyes glazing over, in silent dismissal? Can I risk it? But if I can't, then what does he really know about me? What do I know about him? The inner him, the inner me. If I choose the right time. . . .

January 22, 1988

Dream: I am in a new place in the woods. There are two little, square, ground-level wooden platforms about twenty feet apart. They are built of clean wood, new wood.

Bob has newly arrived and I must fill him in on what it's all about so that we can both be content to live here.

The woods are protecting and beautiful and I feel very much at home. A song is wafting in the air, "Someone to watch over me. . . ."

I wake feeling wonderfully peaceful and calm, and I know I can tell Bob about my inner journey.

January 23, 1988

I read from my journal about the vision, and Bob's eyes remained intent, until a point where he said quietly, "I think that's all I can absorb. For now." It was so wonderful! To be able to share! For him to be able to say "enough," without judgment. For each to be able to be who we are, and to accept the other for who the other is! After all these decades of being together, yet another door has opened and a corridor revealed along which we can move into each other.

February 1, 1988

Dream: I am scrambling up a path in the dark. To my right is a vertical cliff, and falling away to my left is a deep gully in which I can hear a waterfall. It is very dangerous. The path is built out of rotting logs that have been driven into the ground vertically. I look up to the top of the cliff, and I see my brother there, looking down at me, troubled by what I am having to do. I hunt for handholds and footholds in the rotting wood. I have to feel my way, but find some good wood among the rot. So, bit by bit, I pull myself up out of the gully, and reach the top and safety.

I wake feeling triumphant. A flash of déjà vu. Of course! That dream, ten years ago, of being stuck on the spiral staircase, with the music playing in the unreachable hall above, and the dark depths of the Sunday school hall below, and me between, unable to go up or down. But *now*! I've done it! I'm up! I'm out! I have reached my brother.

February 2, 1988

Marion sees more deeply into that dream. "In your life and in your dreams your brother has been crucial to your creative process. He respects the struggle that your feminine is having, although he waits at his own level, not interfering, but aware. That deep gully that your feminine could fall into is very dangerous, but it does contain a waterfall, and a path of logs by which you can climb out. Wood is associated with the feminine. Some of this wood is rotting (negative mother), and some is solid, giving you handholds and footholds (positive mother). You could die in that gully if you became unconscious of what wood was dependable and what would crumble under foot. But your feminine ego is holding the tension of the opposites and finds somehow, even in the dark, the pieces of good wood that she can use to climb to the level of her alchemical partner."

"But why do you call the dangers negative mother?"

"Because those rotting blocks could block you from your own creativity. They could be lethal. They hold energy that needs to be released into life.

"Did your mother block your action? You acting in your own way?"

"Oh yes, definitely. From how I spoke, to who I played with, to who owned my soul. I had to fight for my soul by keeping silent, and finally, when she was on her deathbed . . .

[as I type, I am becoming breathless, and my solar plexus is tightening, and a strange pain is creeping to the left of my heart . . .]

". . . and her eyes were pleading with me to say, 'Yes, I believe in Jesus. Yes, I will be with you on the Judgment Day. Yes, mother, yes.' But I couldn't. And I couldn't stand the strain of denying her any longer, so I said goodbye, and Bob drove me to the mountains, and I have never been able to forgive myself for doing what I knew I had to do. And so she went into a coma and died."

"At that point, it was your life or hers," said Marion. "She might have lived on and on, sucking the energy from you, having power over you. At that point, you chose to live. But, by choosing to live, you betrayed your mother and her goal, which was to have such power over her children that she could bring them before the fierce god who possessed her. You broke the power of that god. It was that god that was looking out of her eyes at you with . . . anger?"

"Yes. And something like hatred."

"You said your final No . . ."

"I held my final silence."

". . . and she was powerless. The god was powerless. Now, here is where we can understand the negative mother complex. For all your life, you lived with that power that blocked your attempts to be yourself, with 'don't do that your way, do it my way.' And now, you can't forgive yourself for taking that power away from her. And there is *your* block. Now, inwardly, when you try to make deep connection with your masculine, your mother complex is there. Blocking. No! You can't want to sculpt! No! You don't want to write! No. Wherever that strong masculine wants to create, the negative mother says No! That is your mother complex. In you."

"But," I say, "I loved my mother. She gave me so much! She *wanted* me to write."

"Love your mother, hate the complex. Of course, love your personal mother who did all she could for you, and consciously wanted you to have *all* of your life," says Marion. "But hate the power complex that unconsciously battered her and you. Hold to all the positive aspects. The good wood for handholds and footholds, the good solid content of the positive mother. That is in you too. But the negative blocking mother is very dangerous. When blocking happens, on an archetypal level, it becomes evil. That energy can take your life away. I don't know about this illness of yours, but. . . ."

Obviously, she wondered. And so did I, as I left her office. But I also felt, "My dream! I made it out! This time, I did it! Maybe this is the day on which I start to really get better."

Journal: in country
February 3, 1988

The country! We are in the country! Finally. After how many months of illness? Eight? Nine? Ten?

Immediately I climb the hill. And *there* is my tree.

I laugh with sudden joy. It wears a halo of snow.
"You look like a bride!" I say.
"Come into my center," it says.

I have never been to the center of my tree in reality. In meditation, yes. That is where I have lived, in that space where the masculine and the feminine almost touch. For a month, since my vision when my guardian placed me there, and revealed to me the four directions of the surrounding mandala, I have lived in that core, and it has lived in me. In meditation.

In reality, I know the outside of the round feminine half that I touch and know to be my good mother. But I do not know the outside of the masculine half; it has always been unapproachable, untouchable by me.

Now, with trepidation, I circle one of the two young saplings that the feminine has brought forth, and am about to enter the center when I feel a tremor through my body, and remember that it was here, four years ago, that the divining rod dipped with such strength that I had to let go. I take a deep breath, and step into the space at the core of my tree.

I lean my back against the round feminine, and face the masculine. I dare not touch it yet. I can only look. It has three sections to the trunk, not one round one like the feminine. It is new to me, like getting to see, to be stirred by, to touch for the first time, a man. The energies from it are different. I do not feel sure of myself at all. How do I take into myself this masculine? How can I become at one with it? I don't know. It feels like, yes! the brother in my dreams who respects my struggle and waits, caring. I feel that I will not be able to set out on the next stage of my journey if I cannot accept this strong masculine as my inner companion.

February 4, 1988
Meditation in Treehouse

My guardian says:
> *You are holding it all in you:*
> *the pulsating of the heart of the tree.*
> *Draw that center.*
> *Know what you know.*
> *Be, at this moment.*

And I draw the center of the tree, the center of the mandala, the center of my self. I feel totally content.
The guardian says:

> *Draw it again . . .*
> *Correctly.*

And suddenly I realize I have *not* drawn what I've experienced. When I stood in the center of the real tree, I was not cradled in the arms of that tripart masculine; I was *confronted* by it. Yes. I'll draw it again, correctly.

> *Why am I crying?*
> *I draw . . .*
> *I accept.*
> *But I cry . . .*
> *I must submit.*
> *I do submit.*
> *To the masculine.*
> *I receive.*
> *I will receive.*
> *But . . .*
> *Why do I cry?*
> *I cannot stop crying.*
> *It is so painful!*
> *I don't think it looks painful.*
> *But it feels . . . I feel filled with pain.*

I feel my center becoming unbearably ugly, compressed. I must draw it again as I *really* feel it. I . . . I am screaming. What is happening?

It is terrible, agonizing intercourse, each crushing into the life that is in the other. I cannot deal with it. I must deal with it.

February 6, 1988

Dream: A policeman is giving instructions to a crowd of people. A girl strides through the crowd very purposefully. She goes behind the policeman. We see she has a revolver. She points against his back. Frightened look on his face.

He ducks.

She fires.

She screams. She has shot her own hands, which are tied together. She is writhing on the floor, screaming.

The policeman takes a piece of glass, stoops over her, and seems to cut the tie that binds her wrists. But no . . .

The screaming stops. She sits up with a strangely relieved, though surprised, look on her face. And blood on her neck. I hear a murmur: "He's slit her throat. Slit her throat. Slit her throat."

I wake, horrified. She can't win! Of course she can't win, even though she has a weapon. Her hands are tied. She is fighting the police, the patriarchy, who are deeply afraid of her. So afraid that even the apparently kindly act of cutting the ties that bind her is a killing act. Why is her look one of relief? Because it is over. Her fight was a lost cause from the start. And now it is over.

And this is all me.

The determined and then defeated woman is my feminine.

The strong, then frightened, then self-protective, then killer man is my masculine.

How did I get to be this way?

Journal: in city
March 15, 1988

Thank god, I had a session with Marion this afternoon. My dreams have been so dark and menacing for the last few weeks. Meditations have been more cheering, but even there. . . . Today, for instance.

Meditation. I was in the light. Then suddenly I was surrounded by deep purple, slashed through with black. Then a savage naked man appeared. In his hands he had a part of another human, and was smashing it against the ground.

"What is going on?" I cry to Marion.

"The pendulum swing," says Marion. "After that vision of the wonderful mandala back there in . . ."

"January."

". . . the pendulum swings to danger. From light to dark. You have opened to so much light, broken so many boundaries so profoundly, that you are now vulnerable to deeper darkness. Even in your meditations, the light becomes sacrificial purple. And in this meditation you have gone very deep. You have tapped into the savage who has been held back by a veneer of civilization.

"Is that why I'm so afraid of the drawings too? What should be calm at the core of the mandala, at the center of the tree, feels like . . ."

"What?" says Marion. "What do you see in the drawings?"

"I *see* a phallic symbol. I *feel* rape by the wild man in me."

And Marion says, "Yes your feminine is terrified of the masculine—for good reasons. That's on the instinctual level. But looking at the four drawings, I see something more. I see the pain of having glimpsed the infinite, and the pain of it being only a glimpse. I see the finite and the infinite trying to come together, and the perfection of that meeting, as you glimpse the eternal. And then the moment is gone and they crush into each other. Accepting our humanity isn't easy. Browning said:

> *Only I discern—*
> *Infinite passion, and the pain*
> *Of finite hearts that yearn.*[11]

"Must it always be so painful?" I ask. "I mean the illness has been bad enough, but now this. What is the archetype behind it all?"

"The Self. There has been so much change in you! The Self has a dark side as well as a light, and the dark contains suffering. It is the only way to achieve wholeness."

So I tell Marion about the last day I was in the country, when I went once more to my tree. But even before I reached it, the fear that made me sob when I drew the mandala center seized me, and I began to cry. Then the tree said, "This is where you must be if you are to be whole. Does becoming whole frighten you?"

And I realized that it must or why would I cry so uncontrollably?

But I did go to the center of the tree and entered and stood with the feminine at my back and the feminine said an interesting thing:

"I cannot block you if I am behind you. And it is time for you to move forward in the way the other half is pointing you. I can give you strength and support, but I cannot block you."

I felt so *moved*, so full. And as I left, I saw once more, how beautifully intertwined the branches are, each adding to the completeness of the other. If only I can allow myself to become so at-one.

Marion asks: "In your meditations, do you still live there? In the center of your tree?"

"No," I say. "Shortly after that, I was kicked out. At least, that's the way it felt. As though I'd been kicked out of the Castle of the Grail, and was sent straggling off along a dusty road with no idea where it was leading me. And then, one day, I saw a far-off mountain, snow covered, *very* far away.

"And then I saw a small black figure trudging through the snow, coming to lead me to the mountain. Or so I thought. And so I walked for days toward that mountain and toward that figure. But he never got any closer.

"And then, one day, I was aware of a huge evergreen tree flying through the sky high up, coming from the mountain, and it hovered over me, and it lifted me up and I lay on it, cushioned, as though it were a cloud. And so we flew high over the snow and over the small black-hooded figure who was not coming to get me at all, but was himself trudging toward the mountain with great difficulty in the deep snow.

"And so we land, the evergreen tree and I, halfway up the mountain but still below the timberline. And there we are at the open door of a neat, square, wooden hut which is simple and warm and has in it everything that I need. And the tree stands outside the door, tall and protecting. It is not split like my other tree. It is whole and one and evergreen. And that's where I've been living for nearly a month. From the doorway I've watched many dark-hooded pilgrims passing, their heads bent down, looking neither to the right or left, walking straight ahead, disciplined, following the path. Dark. No real *life*."

Marion asks if I know who they are. I tell her what the guardian said, "They are the collective who have been told how to seek and where, and their path has been marked out by the many who have gone before. No need to be afraid of them. Unless you join them. Then you lose yourself. There will be other pilgrims who will come whom you should let in."

And I asked the guardian, "The one in white, with a golden glow inside the hood, who sat beside me as I lay in the snow like a snow angel. Was that . . . a pilgrim? Or was it you?"

"Me. And not me. The spirit of me in others. There will be more who come and are with you quietly and who leave their glow behind as

they move on up the path. Cherish them. *There* is the giving love.
There is the nourishment from others. There is the essence that you
seek and need and can also give."

"And that's where I've been living in my meditations," I say to
Marion, "and it all sounds pretty crazy, doesn't it?"

"No," says Marion. "God's country. These opposing energies have
never searched each other out in you before. They meet . . ."

". . . and fight?"

". . . and ultimately find unity. Wholeness. The Self."

Journal: in country
Easter Sunday, April 3, 1988

Why can I not believe in this totally? Surely enough has happened that
I should be able to say, "Yes, guardian, I believe. . . ." But, something
in me pulls back and resists. It is Easter weekend. My lifelong time of
testing.

This morning, at meditation, the guardian said, "You are so sad."

RITA: Yes. Why?
GUARDIAN: Sadness comes from doubt. And many of your
    doubts are about me. Am I a hallucination, you wonder. Am I
    just you talking to yourself?
RITA: Yes, that's what I wonder.
GUARDIAN: Well, you are talking to yourself, but this whole
    experience is showing you how much deeper you are than you
    ever thought. I am leading you deeper and deeper into yourself,
    and showing you that you are there with the god within.
RITA: But why must it all be so painful?
GUARDIAN: Compared to what? You have been blessed. I do
    protect you. Breaking through these blockages is not easy. You
    are getting closer to the core of the blockages. The negatives are
    fighting back. They will not give up without a struggle.
RITA: I hate myself now. I hate what is happening to my body. I
    so loved it for awhile.
GUARDIAN: Do not hate it. It needs your love. You need your
    love. Move. Dance. Stay in the sun. Stay clear of mechani-
    zation.

RITA: Will you stay with me?
GUARDIAN: I am always with you! I don't need thunderclaps every time. Do *you*?
RITA: No, but still . . . (I start to laugh)
GUARDIAN: Still, I am with you. Today the stillness.

April 4, 1988

I cannot believe this! I just can't believe it!

And yet it happened. And Bob is my witness.

After Bob and I went to bed last night, I lay and looked out at the clear and beautiful sky. Starfilled. I dozed off into sleep.

At one A.M., both Bob and I leaped out of sleep with shock. One crackling bolt of lightning, followed immediately by a crash of thunder from directly overhead.

"What the hell is that!" said Bob.

We stared at each other in the starlight from the clear night sky. And that was all.

"I have no idea," I said. And neither did I, until now when I started to write in my journal and my eye caught yesterday's entry: "I am always with you," said the guardian yesterday. "I don't need thunderclaps all the time. Do you?"

"No," said I, "but still . . ." and I started to laugh.

Little did I know that he *could* cause thunderclaps. Now, I am in awe. I am no longer laughing.

He is not just me talking to myself. But what is he? What is this inner voice that has such outer power? I can name it Purusha, but what is it *really*?

April 11, 1988

I emerged from meditation today with a wonderful balance of energy and rest in my body. I had glimpsed a city high up, half-hidden by a distant mountain range. My breathing quickened.

"Is that where I'm going to next?" I asked the guardian.

"Not yet," he said. "Not nearly yet."

"But I feel I'm ready to move on," I said.

"Don't anticipate," he said. "You know now that these things happen when they happen. *You* don't direct them. But you can delay them. Even stop them if your monkey mind gets in the way. So, savor what is happening. Grow with what is happening."

"That black-hooded figure . . ."

"Yes, that black-hooded figure who reached the cabin today, and is crouched out there by the corner. You noticed."

"Is he the same one that was trudging through the snow when we flew here weeks ago?"

"Trudge, trudge. Plod, plod. He is the part of you that plods through books. He is your thinking process, trying to 'understand.' Well, he's made it to here now, to the place where your spirit could fly so easily weeks ago."

"What should I do?"

"Let him rest. Your thinker is bone-weary, and the spirit in you is ready to fly beyond the mountain peak. Just rest. Rest. Let your spirit be satisfied for now and rest."

April 17, 1988

Meditation. The black-hooded man is still crouched outside the hut, and suddenly, the black robes slide away from him. He rises and enters the doorway of my cabin. He is a fiery-golden young man. He fills the cabin with life and color and radiating light. His eyes pierce the space between us.

He says: "I am a pilgrim, too."

It is a miracle.

My masculine, as Marion would say, has really emerged.

But . . . what do I do with him?

April 18, 1988

Meditation. My simple square cabin has become a beautiful pagoda, still a cube, still the same size, but with a brilliant orange roof with spiral carvings at each corner, and each quarter of the roof sloping up to a central opening through which a golden flame leaps into the air.

The pagoda stands on three pedestals, the central one is still, the two outer ones revolve one to the right, and one to the left. And inside the pagoda is a luminous circle, and within it a square, and I know that if . . . I'm not sure what . . . but *if* something . . . *something* could happen, this square, this circle would transform into the world clock. Beyond all this, I can see that far, white mountain range that shelters the golden city. It is beautiful beyond belief.

I ask the guardian what it is, where I am!

He says:

> *This is your container.*
> *Here you ascend to golden light.*
> *Here you descend through that central pedestal*
> *to the earth and deep into it.*
> *Here the energies circle, spiral, and are contained.*
> *Here the light and dark mingle.*
> *When that fiery-golden masculine enters, and*
> *you merge and dance with him, the world clock*
> *will begin to turn.*
> *This is your container.*

Will he come again? Will I be ready to accept him?
Am I once more *there*? Can I make the leap?

Journal: in city
April 19, 1988

The dream went on for hours, but it was the same thing repeated and repeated:

I am completed, except for an empty space in the upper chest. Or . . .
when I look down at the plan for a rectangular house, there is one square
inner room toward the top which is still unfinished.

I wake feeling somewhat smug. I am complete! Except . . . ah yes
. . . except for that empty inner room where I cannot accept my
masculine.

April 20, 1988

Again my dream repeats and repeats and is very simple:

My body is healthy and whole, except for the area of the upper chest and
throat, where I am sweating.

Again, problems in the area of the heart and throat chakras. Physically, I'm struggling with a cold, sweating, coughing up phlegm.
But psychically? I ask my guardian. He says, "All this (coughing) is
connected to the negative feminine aspects as they surface, as they
touch that lump-in-the-throat. Don't try to figure out who triggered
it, or when or why. Just let the awareness of what it is be there. Let
the throat be cleared. Let the phlegm come out. Rest, and let the
positive feminine flow in. Play music. Bathe. Care for your body.
Care for your soul. Care for Bobby. Draw. Rest. Let the feminine
come into her own."

May 1, 1988

Meditation. What is happening? The pagoda has disappeared completely. It has been reduced to the little cabin. But when I open the
door, I am confronted by thick, thick fog. Instead of the path with
pilgrims, there is a sheer precipice. No mountain in the distance, just
fog. I feel frightened and very lonely. What have I done? What have I
not done? I go to the back of the cabin, and a door opens, and I see a
path leading away down a green gentle slope through clearing mist.
    "Go," says the guardian.
    And I set out on the green path, past outcroppings of rock, to a
plain, where I see a round temple with curved arches, and I hear the
tinkling laughter of women. It is the Tholos.
    And now I hear the sound of water in a stream. I follow it, and the
stream flows into the temple and fills the round floor with blue water.
And now, out of the water a glorious flower rises and opens, filling the
floor of the temple with its petals. Here, I realize, is where I am to lie
and to be, in the place of the feminine once more.
    It is a lotus. As I lie there, I am aware that there is a jewel in the center

of the lotus, which extends into my own center between my heart and my solar plexus. And from this jewel a long, red pistil rises, marked as though with six chakras, and at the point of the seventh, the stamens burst open and the tip of the pistil is revealed, gleaming in the light that flows down through the opening in the center of the Tholos roof.

I lie there and listen to the sound of the running stream to my left, and the soft laughter of the women, and I look down at the gentle green terraces of grass, beyond. It is a beautiful place to be.

May 12, 1988

The image that fills my mind today is the wall painting in the temple at Pompeii, the point in the sacred ceremony when the gown of the priestess swings upwards and hides from view the act, whatever it may be, that transforms the initiate into the fullness of her womanhood. I know that I, too, as my guardian warns, must draw a veil over whatever is to come.

8

Journal: in country
September 14, 1988

It is more than four months since I entered the Tholos. I am still here, in every morning's meditation. But.

Today, in reality, it felt as though the Treehouse were the Tholos, and I have been here just *being*. Lying for hours, looking at the yellow leaves moving, the black tree trunks still. Bathing in the golden light from above the house, from below, through every window, every opening. Stillness and movement. The calm center of the world. The point where stillness and movement are at one. "This moment in your life is eternity," said Joseph Campbell.

And so I have come, slowly, to a new point in health and in consciousness.

This, is the feminine. *Being*.

And this ability to "be" I learned from mother. "Look at that sunlight on the water," she would say quietly, as we sat totally relaxed by the lakeside. And she would touch my arm, and we would be at one with the sun, the water, the eternity of the moment.

September 20, 1988

I awoke this morning from a very unimportant dream. Or so I thought, until I examined it. And then, I realized it was extraordinary!

> In front of me is a deep, white china bowl. Attached to the lip are many layers of paper of differing textures, so one cannot see immediately into the bowl. But then I see that each of the layers has been slightly torn and turned back. Each layer of paper, I am told, is an experience. There is only one layer preventing me from seeing to the depths. I reach in and tear this final layer with a slow, strong, ceremonial movement. The depth of the bowl is revealed. It is dark and profoundly patterned and beautiful and mysterious. Throughout the whole ritual, a name hangs in the air. It is Clothilde.

Clothilde. What does that mean? Nothing comes to mind, so I look it up in the encyclopedia, and discover that Clotho is the name of the first of the three Fates in Greek mythology. She arrives at the moment of one's birth, and proceeds to spin the thread that runs through one's life, the thread that you lose hold of at your peril. She is the spinner, and she is the weaver of the web of life. I did not know that. But my unconscious knew.

What then is this bowl? The first thing that comes to mind is the dream of years ago, three years, in which I am told that I must sculpt one more piece that will succeed the sculpture of the guardian. It is to be a bowl, that I must fire and smoke until it is solid black, and a crack will appear, and out of the crack will come something white. Here now is this white chalice.

It is as though that "something white" has flowed out over the years and covered the outside. And the thick papers are veils, experiences, that I have been passing through, so that, with the passage through the final veil, I can see into the dark mystery of my feminine soul. Is this interpretation possible? It's possible.

Could I also call this cup the Grail? Perhaps. Is the dream telling me that I *have* stayed on the thread of my life, despite the illnesses, the hardships, and I have reached what I have searched for: the Grail of my feminine self?

And my masculine? Ah. That is another matter altogether.

September 25, 1988

My birthday. And what a gift the heavens gave me! The red sun set in the west and the full white moon rose in the east at precisely the same time. And I stood on the top of our hill between them, vibrating with the energy in the air. Overhead were a few cirrus clouds, and also the straight white lines of exhaust from airplanes. I longed for Bob to share this moment with me, but he was in Uxbridge, going here, there, doing, doing, doing. He is like one of those planes, I thought, while I am, at this moment, just here. *Being*. Feminine.

> *Silently, the full moon rises,*
> *Silently, the great sun sets,*
> *Silently, a cloud shaped like a phallus*
> *Thrusts through blue sky, slowly, strongly,*
> *Into soft, pillowing cirrus,*
> *Which yield, receive, accept.*
> *Silently, directly overhead,*
> *A hawk soars in a spiral up, and up, and up, and disappears.*
>
> *And airplanes throb and drone,*
> *Each plane in its own straight line,*
> *Going, going,*
> *With the urgency of men*
> *Who must get there,*
> *Or there,*
> *Or somewhere, fast,*
> *Whatever it may cost.*

The planes trouble me. Yes. The masculine drive to *do* troubles me. Yes. Yet I've *done* a great deal in my life. I've worked hard and long for many many years with (I realize) a close-to-masculine drive. And . . . ah yes . . . left little time for my feminine need to *be*. Until now. Life is forcing me to *be*. Illness is forcing me. My time in the Tholos is teaching me how to be.

But, if I am to enter the world again, need I once more *do*?

I go to my tree. It leaves no doubt that I am not to go to the mothering female half, but I am to go directly to the center and face the masculine. I do. I touch it with my fingertips.

My lungs open, my throat opens, I sing my song, I declare my love. For I love this young masculine that points me toward the rising moon, and in the morning will point toward the rising sun. That says: "Step out past me toward a new beginning."

I touch it. But I can go no further. I cannot take that step.

Journal: in city
December 6, 1988

Thank god I was able to see Marion today. I have felt so drained. She says my dreams all show that I need rest; I am not healthy yet; but there is an energy wanting to come through. And I tell her my little dream.

There is a tiger, sitting on its haunches, facing right, alert. Around it, near the ground, is a closed circle. In the air, hang the words: "Prolonged struggle: Condemned freedom."

"There it is!" says Marion. "The energy. Your masculine energy. Tiger! Imagine the power of that tiger!"

> *Tyger, tyger, burning bright,*
> *. . . . .*
> *In what distant deeps or skies*
> *Burnt the fire of thine eyes?*
> *On what wings dare he aspire?*
> *What the hand dare sieze the fire?*[12]

"Now that tiger could easily step over a line. What is holding him back?"

RITA: What *is* holding him back?
MARION: Something in you will not let him get out of that circle and act in the outside world. That is a sacred circle of everything you have experienced in your inner feminine world. That

circle is precious. It is like the virgin's circle that contains the unicorn. But with your tiger, there is a masculinity that's ready to go. He has had his long struggle. Now he wants freedom to act. But freedom is condemned, which means . . .

RITA: Guilty. Unfit for use. Not very encouraging, is it?

MARION: And something in you is not very encouraging to your masculine, Rita. It is easy for the masculine to become para- lyzed. But *you* need its energy if you are to act in the world. If you were to remain totally feminine, you might sculpt, but the sculptures might never leave your studio. You might not have the drive from your masculinity that is necessary to take your work into outer reality. It is time that you examined this seri- ously. What keeps your masculinity from acting outside? Put on a tape and say whatever comes to you. Cry. Whatever. Or write. Let your mind go free and write. It may take months. Do not hurry. Do not push. But it is time now to free the energy of that tiger from condemnation.

February, 1989

I've been writing it out, as Marion suggested. For the last two months. Wherever I am. Whatever surfaces. And, when I boil it all down, what have I got? For starters: In 1952 or '53, Bob and I drove down Struan Avenue, past every step of sidewalk that I had traveled day after day as a child, as an adolescent on my mile-long walk from home at number 148 to school.

I was enchanted.

"This is where I spent my childhood!" I laughed.

And then suddenly, totally unexpectedly, I began to cry.

I sobbed. I could not stop myself. We came opposite 148, and I ached with my sobbing.

"What am I doing?" I cried to Bobby. "I had a happy childhood! I don't understand!"

Now, at the age of seventy, I am beginning to understand.

It has a lot to do with masculine and feminine.

It has a lot to do with loss, losing, being deprived of that essence that is myself. It has a lot to do with Marion's question, "Why can't you approach the male side of the tree, Rita?"

I am reading Camus's *The Myth of Sisyphus*. He is reliving his youth, his male, body-rich life in the green valleys full of olive trees in Algiers. And I cry in envy and longing.

I cry, not because I have lost the beauty of the valley of my youth, as Camus cries. But because I had, in my first twenty years, Struan Avenue. I had Kape. I had streets so ugly, I walked with closed eyes, as I pushed against the cold north wind to reach the sanctuary of our ice-cold house, the one warm stove-heated kitchen, the Arab mystery of my brother's studio.

I ask my older brother: "Where in all that did we feed our need for beauty?"

He says: "The crows in the pine trees by the Don."

I say: "The lilac trees in daddy's garden; the apple tree; the lilies of the valley . . ."

"The heartfelt music from your piano in the living room."

"Melding with your violin."

"Our dancing!"

"The melodious voice of Mother. Her grace."

"The mystery of the art behind the closed door of our brother's studio."

"The solitude of writing that enclosed the other."

Beauty. I knew it existed. And the knowledge made me ache for more.

But what made me cry in agonized envy when I read Camus was his freedom to glory in his body. Whole mornings spent diving in the sea, in bursts of laughter and splashing water, in nakedness.

When did I have encouragement to glory in my body on Struan Avenue? It was the spirit, that dreary Sunday spirit. The bodies were the strong, contesting bodies of my brothers. The smells were their body smells, and the machine-shop-oil smell of my father, and the sweet-but-not-sexual smell of my mother. Where was *my* body in all of that? Where was my feminine? Where was my masculine? Where was my nakedness?

I had an early belief as a child, which was the only one that made sense to me, that first you had to be a girl and get through that, and *then*, you burst into real life. You became a boy! And I remember one Halloween, I ran down the street, following my brothers, dressed in my brother's outgrown suit and cap, with a black mask covering my little girl face. And through the eyes of the mask I saw another little girl coming down the sidewalk from her house, and with an eager open smile she started running after us. Us boys! She thought she could join *us*!

And I yelled at her: "Go away, you! You *girl!*" And ohhhhh the high! To see her shrink back toward her house, dominated by me. *Me!* As I had, all through my long-short life, been dominated by *them*. The boys. I knew then the ecstasy of their power.

And yet I grew to female puberty and to the pride and problem of menstruation, without even becoming a tomboy.

And I grew to love passionately making love. *The* secret, I felt and feel. This equality of joy between the pulsating energy of feminine woman and masculine man. The joy that each has from each. The peace that follows, that flows through the whole of one's being. The quickened vitality in the cells of the body that can be seen in the color of the face, the smoothness of skin, the light in the eye, the fullness of lips, the relaxed joy from the core. Each being, in lovemaking, feminine, masculine, who one is, whichever one is. United. Flowing together. Each giving. Each receiving.

But that was yet another thing I did not know when I lived on Struan Avenue. That kind of joy and peace (so I was taught) would only come from our Father God who wished to involve me "in a pathologically dependent relationship" in which my strength and power as a woman could never be fully affirmed. That God did not bring me peace and joy, no matter how many hours I sat in church and Sunday school. There I was taught to fear Him. And that is what I did. And, perhaps, still do. Is it that fear that keeps me from approaching the old male side of the tree? Yes! I think I'm getting closer to the answer. . . .

I think I've got it! It starts with me thinking about analysis, psychological insight. I realize that I am hesitant to speak of this stuff to the men in my life. And yet, the truth is that I have been peripherally involved in psychoanalytical studies for thirty-six years. I have been more personally involved for thirty-two years; intensely involved for fifteen; and for the last three years, involved to the depths of my being in Jungian analysis to help me to come to the wholeness of my self. None of this was because I was "crazy." It was because I was ignorant, and knew that I wanted to *know*. I wanted to be of help to myself and to others. So I learned, and it has not been easy.

Now. To silence myself is a little like a doctor who has studied medicine silencing himself because he might seem to others to be thinking that he knows more about the body than they do. But he *does* know more. And I know more about the psyche. Not that much more, when one recognizes the infinite depth of the psyche, but I know it a little bit, and intimately and well. And more than most men in my life know.

But from childhood through all of my school days, I have been quashed by the men in my life for talking about what I have learned. Those men were older, more articulate and experienced in the ways of the world. Or so I was made to believe. And so, I did not speak. I still do not speak. Or, if I do, I do it badly. I become self-conscious. I "watch my words." I stammer and hope I'm not boring, or overbearing, or showing off, or wrong. I even find myself lying: trying to be both humble and more knowledgeable than I am. I am rarely like this with women. But with men. . . .

And so comes the insight!

"Why can't you approach the older male side of the tree, Rita?"

Because that older outside part of the tree is not the young masculine in me. The young masculine is the one I touch from the inside of the tree, from the center. The one who invites me to move forward toward the rising sun.

The old male outside forbids me to approach him. I am stopped by a power that says: "No further! Don't speak to *me*. Don't tell me what you think you know! I am bigger. I am older. You will never, ever attain to anything like my wisdom. Fear me. I am *male*. I am the patriarchy. I am GOD." There is no comfort there and never will be, unless something changes.

I am still crying with happiness. It is a breakthrough! It began when I was meditating on a dream.

In the dream, I have been dreaming. Now I am waking and realizing that there is an older woman with me who also has been dreaming. She is instructed that there is matter in her dream that should be articulated by her and absorbed by me. She speaks and I absorb. Now I'm aware that a young man has also been dreaming matter that he should articulate and I should absorb. He speaks and I absorb. I feel very grateful, and know that now I can go on with life.

Fine. But what does it mean? What did the old woman *say*? What did the young man *say*? And suddenly *flash*! In my meditation, it is as though I am in the center of my tree. I am leaning against the round feminine trunk that has always seemed to be a mother to me. She says once more, "I cannot block you if I am behind you. Move forward in the way the other half is pointing you."

I look at the trunk that I feel to be young and masculine on this inner surface. And he says: "Leave the center now. Stay close to me. Move toward the east. When you reach the older bark, do not turn to face it. Keep it at your back. Face into the rising sun."

I do as he says. And I feel, in my meditation, the bark of the old male side of the tree against my back. And I realize that it, like the old mother, cannot block me if it is behind me. All that ancient patriarchal power can flow through me, can serve me. And more! The slant of this old male will not allow me to lean back and rest on it. To keep my balance, I must step forward to the east to the new day, the new beginning.

Or, I can turn, and enter the central core of the tree once more, and know now, finally, it all.

Or, I can do both. In balance. Inner and outer. In here, in my core; out there in the world. Yes.

"Now is time," says my tree.

Yes.

Journal: in city
March 23, 1989

I have drawn it. Again and again. Yes. This is my core. Feminine and masculine, side by side. Neither dominating. Finally equals. I have a sense of vibrant wholeness. Feminine and masculine are moving in each other, both in the drawing and in myself. My Self.

Journal: in city
March 25, 1989

I awake at five in the morning from this dream:

> I have been practicing a dance with a very tall, strong older man. But now there is a younger, dark, less impressive man present, whose consent seems to be necessary if we are to dance this dance on *the* day. There are great leaps in the dance, and I must be caught as I come down by a man. I take a pill and retire into the woods.
>
> Now is the moment for decision. In the woods, I begin the dance and move through between the trees. Then I see the tall man waiting for me. He motions to me, and I see that he wishes to dance this dance whether there is consent or not. He wants me to make my leap and he will catch me and support me through the bends and turns and lifts of the dance.
>
> I leap, and it is in slow motion and is very beautiful. I am astonished at my litheness. I have overcome my injured leg and my unexercised body.
>
> We dance and I sense that it is in defiance of something.
>
> As the music ends, I see the dark man is at the outside edge of the woods by the road, and he is being taunted by two people.
>
> Why did he allow it to go on, they ask, when he knew it was long out of date. It won't qualify in today's dancing, they say.
>
> I hear this, but I remember in my body the glorious feeling of the sensuous leaps and the supportive pleasure I had from my tall partner, and I don't care about competing in today's world. To dance unseen in the woods is glory enough. So long as my partner will hold out his arms and catch me and support me, it feels as though I am the petals of a rose opening.

I wake with the feeling that it is the most beautiful dream I have ever had. I want this feminine of me and this masculine to dance forever, each strong enough to be what they are, each ready to accept what the other is. Opposite energies coming together with joy, and parting with satisfaction, and once more together, and part. And the music of the dance is "La Vie en Rose"; the place is the Cathedral Walk in our woods.

Is this the divine marriage, finally taking place? I don't know. For now, I am alive with the beauty of the dance. And that is joy enough.

9

Journal: in country
April 2, 1989

There is no question where I am now on this journey of mine. In meditations, I am walking, day after day, along a gray dike that separates one huge bay of still water from another huge bay. It is unbearably dreary, and I cry to my guardian. He says, "This is necessary now. You must carry the treasure home. You know where the treasure is?"

"Yes," I say. "Here in my heart."

And a tree sprouts at the edge of the dike and a resting place appears beside it. And I can rest in the shade, for awhile.

My dreams are similar:

I am walking along a road through the woods. I come to a river. A *very* wide river. The far shore is gray. I can see no vegetation on the low hills there. The river too is gray, and misty. But now I see a path that juts out into the river. And a voice says, "There is your path. Go. Do not attempt to return to the cave or the Tholos or the hut. There is smallpox there now. Go." I set out on this narrow road across the gray river. It leads, I believe, toward home.

"Toward home." Into the world of family, friends, strangers, people. Will I survive? How will I survive?

April 2, 1989

Thoughts. It has been more than a year since I have been with other people in any intimate way, for any length of time. I have been intimately with Bob, yes; and with Marion, yes; but otherwise I have to be alone. At first it was because of my physical condition. But my spiritual need to be with only my guardian became so urgent that I went into retreat full time. Or almost so. And the place where I could retreat most effectively was in the country. This seemed to trouble people. Or so I hear.

Ronny phones Bob again and again to find out how I am, and where

I am. It worries him that I am in the country all alone; it perplexes him that I choose to be so; he wonders what I *do*.

How can I explain what I do without sounding . . . what? Mystical? That suspect flaky word, again. And my guardian. How can I speak of *him* without entering into discussion about experiences that are so precious, subtle, amorphous, and real; experiences that have entered into the fiber of my being and are not up for argument. I have *had* to be alone in order to discover my inner world.

Reading Jung gives me encouragement. The searcher, he says, "must be alone if he is to find out what it is that supports him when he can no longer support himself. Only this experience can give him an indestructible foundation."[13]

And Rilke says that isolation is the absolute prerequisite if one is to emerge as an individual. It is the hero's fate.

But when I reach "home" and am once more in the outer world, will I be able to *be* with family, friends, and strangers? People? I suspect that I won't. Not in the way I used to be. Because my search for an individual path will be considered "strange," as an "estrangement" from the accepted way of the collective. And it is often, says Aldo Carotenuto, "our family that represents the collective, the given reality opposed to the growth of the individual." We will "experience times in which we realize, often with fear and disappointment, that others no longer understand us. But this, far from being a negative fact, is a sign of our emancipation, of our psychological development. Indeed, if we were always to be understood, it would mean that we were speaking the language of others, the collective language."[14]

And *that* is what I have been attempting either to understand or to escape ever since I was a child: the language of the collective Christian culture that surrounded me in Sunday school, church, home, school.

Language. Words. Words like "God."

Yet *I* speak of "god."

I see my listener nod.

She thinks she knows what I mean. She reacts with whatever emotion the word evokes. But my listener does not know what *I* mean by "god." Unless I tell her.

Can I?

Do I have the words?

"God" is the word we use to try to name that which cannot be named; to try to contain that which cannot be contained; to bring

within understandable limits that which is beyond all limits and beyond our understanding.

Those early men who experienced "it," whether they were Semitic
or Taoist or whatever, were very wise men when they said that it could
not be named. It shouldn't be named. Even though it could be experienced. Even though it has been experienced since the beginning. Not
only by primitives, or by mystics, or by peasants in touch with the
unpredictable elements, or by ordinary creatures like me, but also by
the new discoverers of the new physics, who are finding that mysterious something, that unnameable, uncontainable, limitless mystery
in all things, in all space, in every aspect of the universe, in every
concept of time, in all things animate and inanimate, in all cells, in all
energy. In (also) us.

They may not call it "god." But that is what I call god. The
unnameable. The ineffable. It. Which can be experienced. Which *must*
be experienced to be known. And then, once known, once directly
experienced, as Jung said, it is "absolute. It is indisputable."[15]

That presence who had no left brain, that I faced in my dream four
years ago; who was made up of so many vibratingly alive cells of such
an infinity of colors that it appeared gray; it entered me then, and it was
so easy, as though it had always been in me, as though I had just been
made more aware. As I had been alerted thirty years ago in my vision
on the island of Ischia, that it is in everything that touches me. Everything that lies beyond me. Everything that is within me. In the
pulsating energy of every cell that is in the universe.

As I said then, "I don't know what god is, but that is god."

Which does not mean that I understand it.

But then, do I understand any of this?

Experience it. Yes.

Feel it. Yes.

Know it. Yes.

Understand it?

Perhaps that is asking too much.

April 3, 1989

My dream this morning said, "Go back six months for what you
need now."

I am amused. Does my unconscious have a calendar? All neat and up to date? What a funny idea. But, to humor it, I leaf back through my journals. And *there*, precisely on October 3, is exactly what I need right now. It is my synopsis of some very important writings of C. G. Jung. It is also a synopsis of my journey.

> The goal we seek is human *wholeness*.
> The way to the goal seems chaotic and interminable at first, and only gradually do the signs increase that it is leading anywhere. The way is not straight, but . . . goes in spirals: the dream-motifs always return after certain intervals to definite forms, whose characteristic it is to define a center, . . . the whole process revolves about a central point. . . . We might draw a parallel between such spiral courses and the processes of growth in plants: in fact the *plant* motif (tree, flower, etc.) frequently recurs in dreams and fantasies.

> . . . in alchemy, the tree is a symbol of Hermetic philosophy.

> [The goal] *wholeness*, is in fact a charisma which one can manufacture neither by art nor by cunning; one can only grow into it and endure whatever its advent may bring.

> Wholeness demands the encounter with the dark half of the personality, the shadow. This is unavoidable and painful. This is a confrontation with the evil in oneself, in the personal unconscious. When this touches on the archetypal contents of the collective unconscious . . . it may exert an uncanny influence on the most cold-blooded rationalist. He is afraid that the lowest form of conviction, namely superstition, is . . . forcing itself on him . . . It then takes the form of the fear of going mad. Yet this encounter with the shadow is the first, and necessary stage of the work. This happens when one sets out to find one's own way, one's direct experience of the eternal roots. One finds oneself in the wilderness where one comes up against darkness, against the opposite.

> But this meeting of the opposites plays the decisive role. It is this union of the supreme opposites, male and female, good and evil, melted into a unity purified of all opposition that creates wholeness. The *self*.[16]

Whether I have reached the goal or not, I don't know. But Dr. Jung describes exactly what my journey has been like. The only thing he doesn't speak about is ecstasy and joy. But perhaps that does not come to everyone.

April 28, 1989

Dream: I am riding along the sidewalk of a city on the back of a deer. I am directing its course very gently with slight pressure of my knees on its body to the right or the left, and then stroking the side of its head when it makes the turn correctly. We weave through the traffic of people, slowly but steadily, keeping always to the right. Heinz comes up beside me. He is walking. In his Heinzish way, he is critical of what we are doing, but I sense a grudging respect. He remembers that I learned a little about riding horses when we first met, and he states it as though he should be given credit for my present skill.

We come to a bridge, on the sidewalk of which are a lot of boisterous children. But when I gently guide the deer to keep to the right, close to the railing, the children move out respectfully and clear a way. I pat the deer on the neck, lovingly. We cross the bridge.

Now we come to a kind of YWCA to the left of the road. This is where I have to go, but can I take the deer in? Someone says, "Grace won't mind." And I remember that Grace is the kindly woman in charge of the Y.

I ride the deer up carpeted red steps to the entrance, and into a lounge which is also carpeted in red. I get off the deer. It lies down on its side on the carpet.

I lie beside it and pat it and stroke its neck. It is tired by the strain of the new way of being in the world.

But, once rested, we must go out again. And once more I ride on the back of the deer through the city, carefully and lovingly.

The street is called VIA VIVA.

I wake deeply happy. My dream seems to be saying that I *can* go out on the road of life, with my Purusha, my guardian, my god-self, my whatever one wishes to call this deer, and so long as I go gently, keeping to the right, not trying to buck the traffic, I can survive. We will both survive. I must be sure, however, that there is a welcoming, feminine resting place. And I must ignore the criticism from the self-important, Heinzlike part of my masculine.

Most of all, I must be sensitive and exact and loving and well

balanced to guide this vulnerable and vital part of my self into the
crowded world.

Journal: in city
Saturday, June 10, 1989

I awoke from this dream at 5:30 in the morning.

> I have been away from home for sometime. I am back, but I don't want
> many people to know. I am in a basement of the house, which is used for
> dining by the family. Family members have come down for a meal, but I
> remain hidden, in another corner of the basement. Then I am aware of a
> man coming toward me from the far side of the basement. He knows
> that I am there, even though I am hidden. I keep my eyes lowered,
> looking at the floor. Then, as he comes closer, I see his working-class
> boots, and rough woolen working-class pants. Immediately I know
> who it is. I raise my eyes carefully to look at him, and see that he has his
> hand across his eyes, as though to protect me from the power of his
> direct eye contact, to protect me from the unbearable light that is in him
> and beyond him; the blinding light of eternity, and of the universe. It
> is Jesus.

I am overwhelmed by this dream. I can only wonder at it, and
meditate.

Who *are* you, Jesus, that after all my denying of Christianity, after all
my searching for other guides to god, it is *you* who come to meet me
when I reach home.

Are you the man who lived and died in Israel two thousand
years ago?

No. I don't think so. Extraordinary as that man must have been, I
don't believe this Jesus of my dream is that man.

Are you my own masculine? That working-class young man in my
dream of years ago, who set out on his search for the prints of deer?
Who, much later, hooded like a monk, plodded through the cold snow
of intellectual understanding toward the forever distant mountain of
enlightenment? Who emerged from his dark wrappings, radiant,
golden, vibrant?

No. I don't think so. Wonderful as my masculine has become, he is not the channel through which I experience the light of the universe. That channel is my guardian who can manifest himself as a bolt of lightning, or engulfing wings, a voice within, an eagle, and (is it possible?) Jesus. Is my guardian Jesus?

I don't know. But what I realize is this: that I am trying to *think* this out, and the truth is that a dream is from the unconscious and the unconscious is not a mental machine. It tells the truth in the most total way that it can. If I do not believe that, then I am forced to admit that these years spent in dream analysis have been years squandered in nonsensical futility. And *that* I do not believe.

I must also remind myself that every part of every dream is oneself.

So. In this dream, what is my unconscious saying?

I arrive home after my long years of search. What is home? It is myself. I return to the basement level, the base on which the house, myself, is built. Here are the members of a family who have been aspects of myself since my beginning. They are eating, replenishing energy in the way they have always done, as though nothing had changed. But something *has* changed. I have been on a long, hard journey, and the part of myself that has journeyed and suffered no longer fits into the old life pattern. Neither does it know how to explain itself. It hides.

But one man knows that this part of myself is there. Without ostentation he moves directly toward me, bringing with him that quality that I have been searching for all these years; he is "open up in back, as it were, to eternity," and the light of eternity shines through his eyes with such brilliance that he knows, as I did not, that my ego cannot experience that light and live. So, with understanding, compassion, and total love, he covers his eyes and protects me.

Since he is a part of my dream, is it possible, is it *conceivable* that he is a part of me?

My unconscious names him. Jesus.

Had I been brought up in a Buddhist family, would my unconscious have named him Buddha?

But I was brought up a Christian, and I can never, I realize now, escape my upbringing. I might broaden it, deepen it, see the power used and misused in much of it. I might even hate it, and certainly fear it. But I cannot escape its personification of love.

What name, I wonder, would, my unconscious use if it spoke of god?

October 21, 1989

Dream: It is dark and late, but the ponderous activity that has been going on for a long time is continuing. Scrolls keep emerging in front of me. They pile up. I realize that these are the last pages of this book. They are huge and lumpy, made of many kinds of cloth and interwoven with strips of metal and dried vegetation and other strange things. I can glimpse writing on the scrolls, but I do not read it, because I must physically eat each scroll, digest it, regurgitate it, and redigest it. I have been doing this for a long time, and I continue, until I groan. I call: STOP! But the scrolls do not stop coming. More and more roll out, and I digest them, regurgitate, redigest, and the pain is growing to be unbearable.

When finally, suddenly, the scrolls slow their unfolding. I see the last scroll, uncurling. I can read the final words: "It is life that is god."

Although the dream is ending, my mind continues, half awake, half dreaming.

Life that we fight for and go to inordinate lengths to protect and prolong if it is our own. Or life that we carelessly or purposefully destroy when it is useless or useful to us. Like the trees in the forest that we cut down. In ten years, life as we know it might be past saving. There may be no more life as we know it in two hundred years. No one will awake on Ischia, and *know* that in the vibrating cells of everything, "that is god." There may be no one alive to awake. But god will still be there, in the energy in the cells of the earth, the sea, the sky, the galaxies, the universe, beyond the universe. There is that sacred life, that creative energy: there it will always be, pulsating between, around, opposites. Energy. Deus. God. It.

It is life that is god.

10

Journal: in country
January 17, 1990

Dream: I am in bed here at the Treehouse, lying on my left side. I am aware of the sound of someone picking up paper by the window.

I say: "Is that mother?" I try to open my eyes to see, but I can't. Then I feel mother's hand reaching toward me from the right side of the bed. I touch it. It feels soft and cool and comforting. Like mother's.

She says: "It's mother, and dad and dad. Is that better?"

As I struggle to waken, I wonder who that second dad could be. Then I realize: "Our Father. Of course. Which art in heaven." And I hear myself thinking: "I'm so glad it's there with you. It's here with me too. We just call it by a different name."

I feel her hand now on my arm, touching me gently. Lovingly.

AND THEN . . .

April 15, 1991

The writing was finished. March. Friday morning. Got it down to the computer printout.

Wonderful feeling! Time to celebrate! A movie. A dinner out. A whiz-bang. But first, phone Roger. Ask him to check the Treehouse. We'll be coming up there, Roger, on Tuesday for a couple of weeks holiday. Is there anything we ought to bring?

At night, we get home, giddy with joy.

The answering machine says, "Phone Roger. Urgent." Three calls. Urgent.

We call.

"I hope you're sitting down." says Roger. "It's burned to the ground."

We cannot grasp it.

"Burned."

Why? How? The *house*?

"No discernible reason," says the fire marshall.

We go, after a sleepless night.

I stare down at the great black mass sprawled on the ground where my beautiful soul-house once rose. Something stirs in my memory. "I am to make one more piece to succeed the guardian. A large shallow bowl, fired, smoked, solid black, and a crack will appear. . . ."

But a dream doesn't really *mean* . . . yet, all I see is a great shallow bowl, sinking into the ground, black as Hades, the charred remains of all that I have loved.

All I feel is the unbearable grief of seeing my soul-child burned at the stake.

For what? I don't know. I can't believe that my god wants this agony to be the end of my long search.

Now, weeks later, I see that I can allow myself to grieve in anger, and die.

Or, I can go into that blackness, until, perhaps, I find the crack through which white essence is emerging.

And on whatever plane that operates, I can begin again.

I have the choice.

I have the choice.

The end.

Or.

The endless beginning.

Conclusion

If you don't know the kind of person I am
and I don't know the kind of person you are
a pattern that other made may prevail in the world
and following the wrong god home we may miss our
    star.

For there is many a small betrayal in the mind,
a shrug, that lets the fragile sequence break
sending with shouts the horrible errors of childhood
storming out to play through the broken dyke.
. . . .
For it is important that awake people be awake,
or a breaking line may discourage them back to sleep;
the signals we give—yes or no, or maybe—
should be clear: the darkness around us is deep.

—WILLIAM STAFFORD[1]

As we read the soul stories of Kate, Mary, and Rita, we realize the integrity required to follow the path of individuation. Journaling is an ongoing mirroring process—seeing, not seeing; naming, unnaming. It is work in process, not product. The process is life itself. The journal becomes a psychic home where the ambiguities that lie at the heart of the mystery are expressed, not explained. Parts we bring to consciousness; parts cannot yet be unveiled. In exploring the images that appear in dreams and symptoms, we always leave room for the ambiguity that remains. We can only comprehend at the level where we are now conscious. The names we give to psychic contents are an attempt to illumine the other side of reality. The deeper we move into that reality, the less naming matters. What does matter is the dynamic interchange among the energies. The essence of energy is movement. Movement in the psyche reveals itself in images. If they are contemplated, they continue to interact and transform. If they are ignored, they repeat or stop. Then we are not only stuck; we regress. Addictive behavior and symptoms manifest. Staying with the process is what matters. Where it is leading, we cannot know.

No two paths are the same. Each of us is born with a unique combination of gifts and weaknesses and lives a unique combination of circumstances. What we do with what we are given determines who we become. Sharing our story is not a mere regurgitation of facts, facts that can shackle us ever more bitterly into the prisonhouse into which we are all born. We can refuse to be defined by any prison. Sharing our story can open our eyes to the ambushes we share with others and open paths to freedom.

Most contemporary women are the daughters of patriarchy; their mothers and grandmothers were daughters of patriarchy. They know very well how to organize, how to set a goal in some transcendent perfection. They know, too, the shadow of that perfection that never ceases to judge, to blame, to find them guilty for the crime of being themselves. They know, too, the blind fury of the instincts that fight for recognition through addictions. In their stories, Kate, Mary, and Rita have chosen not to dwell on the negative side of patriarchy, but rather to focus on their healing through the transformative process in the archetypal mother and father. In moving toward the new Queen and the new King, they have at the same time moved toward an acceptance of their own humanity and the humanity of the men they love.

Contemporary men whose femininity is still locked in patriarchal parents are still pleasing mother or sullenly displeasing. In the marrow of their bones they yearn for women who will unabashedly adore them, sustain them, unconditionally love them. In handing over their power to such women, they choose to be boys, powerful so long as they are adored, broken when the adoration either flips into nagging criticism or realistic appraisal. Terror of abandonment can erupt if their woman moves toward consciousness. In their dreams, the dapper patriarch in the pinstriped suit is often accompanied by a doe-eyed female who intuits his wish before his command. On the same night, a wild, young rebel may take off to the forest, alone or accompanied by a fierce redhead. Integrating the doe-eyed and the red-haired into a mature, free feminine is not an uncomplicated process.

That integration is required in the new ethos. It is not possible, however, so long as we are unconsciously trapped in incestuous bonding to our patriarchal fathers and mothers. One of my female analysands clearly perceives the pitfalls in the following passage:

Above all my parents had to be proud of me. In being the radiant child they projected onto me, I could not trust that they loved me. I had to earn their love, all the time feeling myself an orphan, blaming myself for not really being what they hoped for. Sure I was good. But my goodness had nothing to do with being morally good. Being good got me what I wanted. I knew the difference.

I blamed my mother for everything that went wrong for me. By never admitting that she had any influence over me, I held onto power. I attached myself to my father, did what made Dad proud, and joined the fathers in every way I could. I never cried because to cry would be to lose the inflation and I did everything to feel the inflation.

As I grew older, I didn't look for a sexual relationship with a man, I looked for a sophisticated mental or spiritual relationship. I began to realize the subtle ways of getting caught in father—emotional need, money, sex, accepting compliments.

Finally, I did the unspeakable thing. I said *no*. I let the perfectionistic persona go. I felt grief and anger at the loss of father. I let go of control. I stripped down to simplicity. I cracked open the nut. I was born.

Then I was faced with the dark masculine inside and outside. I held onto the paradox—tried to see what was good in the negative father, what was bad in the positive father. Then I let both poles go and fell into chaos. I waited. Again and again, all my efforts were put down by men. I realized patriarchal paranoia was high. Repeatedly I caught myself buying into old values because my environment upheld them. Then I decided I was not going to let go of my heritage because of a group of weak men. They weren't going to put me out of where I belonged. I fell into the danger of returning to my arrogant, self-righteous stand. I couldn't be bothered taking time to explain my position to the patriarchs because they couldn't hear or see me anyway. Instead of holding center, I was being seduced into taking an opposite position. Then I saw I was playing the war game. I reconnected with my own positive masculinity. He wouldn't let me fall into the trap of pitying frightened men. He wouldn't let me be unconscious mother playing her power games. He would not be my son. In freeing him inwardly, I freed my husband and other men in my orbit. Painful freeing, that!

I have cleared out my victim. I am once again asking, "What is the feminine?" I don't quite trust being dragged *down* into light. I still have some self-forgiving to do before I can accept my creatureliness.

What this analysand did not realize at the time she wrote this is that what saved her, by starting her on her process, was her sense of herself as an orphan. Crucial to the breaking of incestuous bonds to the parents is the recognition that we do not belong to them and they do not belong to us. Individuation begins with the painful recognition that we are all orphans. And the liberating recognition that the whole world is our orphanage.

Many women have difficulty speaking, actually allowing words to come easily through their throat. Their sinuses are often blocked. At the same time they envisage a vessel of frozen tears, or a frozen river, or a glass jar in the area of their sexual chakra. This chakra and the throat chakra are connected. Is it possible that when they fully forgive themselves for being sexual beings and fully let go into their creatureliness, they will also be forgiving their mother's shadow? Are their frozen tears the tears of generations of women who could not accept their creatureliness in their sexuality? When those tears flow will women be able to speak with clear, easy resonances from their feminine depths?

Father's daughters tend to discount their mothers. Often that shadow side is so deeply buried in their unconscious that it rarely appears in dreams. Yet the incestuous bonding with the mother who condemned her own sexuality is in the viscera of the daughter's body and her cells yearn for release.

The three women in this book were all pushed into the individuation process because the angry bonding with their personal mother led them into unconscious bonding with the negative mother archetype. Kate's child was not born. Mary heard the voice, "There will be no son born of this body." And Rita's body bore no child. Throughout our culture, diseases of the sexual organs are rampant in women. So deeply repressed is the negative mother's lure toward death that we scarcely recognize it, although we are annihilating ourselves in addictions and autoimmune diseases.

Both men and women are split in both their masculinity and their femininity. Both tend to project either idealized perfection or less than a human being onto the opposite sex. At the same time, they experience themselves as split, expecting more of themselves than they are and ashamed to be less than they seem. The root cause of the splitting is the failure to recognize the difference between the archetypal image and the human reality.

When Nietzsche declared that God is dead, he was right in the sense that the projection onto a male god in the sky is dead. Still, the human beings' need for a loving, nurturing, organizing Father-Mother who could hold their whole world in Her hand was not. With nothing but themselves to project onto, people flounder in their efforts to find someone or something sufficiently unreachable to carry the mystery of life itself. The arrow that carries the God-Goddess projection has to find a target. Too often that target is another bumbling being who seems to embody all that was and all that is too perfect to be. If there is mutual projection, god and goddess live in all-consuming bliss, until the human warts become visible. So mesmerizing is the projection that long after human frailty and failure have smashed the ideal, the arrow still clings to the target. The arrow that went out was carrying the very soul. To fill the abyss that gapes when the projection dies, the projector has to claim within what was constellated without in the relationship. Sometimes the reclaiming allows for a real human relationship to be born from what was never real, nor ever could be real. It's not easy to pull the arrow from what seemed to be the bull's-eye.

In discussing causes of psychic splitting in this book, I have tended to focus on psychic incest rather than physical incest. I am very aware of the anguish of physical incest; I am also aware that the abuses of psychic incest are too often unconsciously dismissed. Many people carry incest wounds who are quite sure they were never sexually abused. They may have been, but whether they were or not, they are bewildered by the severity of their symptoms and reactions. They don't understand the impact of psychic violation and tend to dismiss their feelings of guilt. Their psyche does not. After it has worked through the rotten foundations, thrown out the garbage, and released quantities of fear and rage, it may bring up images of union with a parent or sibling or child. Immense care must be taken to work with these images symbolically as well as literally. The penis is personal; the phallos is archetypal. If the symbolic is dismissed, the transformative process may be truncated.

Body responses to the dreams have to be carefully considered. Sexual incest releases in the body a sexual charge which tends to function autonomously. It is a sexual charge that the psyche has not absorbed as its own. The result is alienation from the body, leaving it to its own drives without psychic intervention or direction. Most women who have suffered sexual incest cannot deal with the masculine inside or outside until they have worked with the feminine in their own body.

For the victim of sexual incest, reclaiming the body as one's own is a more complex process than for the victim of psychic incest because the self-loathing is in both psyche and soma. Self-rejection releases level after level of unfocused anxiety, which leads to compulsive behavior.

However, once the suffering can be experienced in the body, once it is absorbed to the point where transformation is possible, the sexual charge can become highly creative. Its energy, having moved from a literal to a symbolic figure, becomes the carrier of strong creative resources.

The symbolic figure may be a radiant beloved in dreams or an actual man who is carrying the light deflected from the woman's inner beloved. He may be a theater director, a professor, an analyst—any man who inspires the best that is in her. But once the sexual charge has been released from its literal object and brought to consciousness, love is no longer dependence. The woman will no longer be Daddy's little girl looking for a man to initiate her creativity and be her outside authority. She will now want to relate as a mature woman. A man stuck in the mother complex cannot comprehend the shift. She doesn't need him. She asks for his opinion but doesn't necessarily do what he says. The woman may wonder why she no longer feels the compulsive attraction to him. The point is her masculinity has shifted as much as her femininity. The inner figure is no longer the son crippled by a weak and bullying parent. She has released that son that she once had to care for, perhaps even pity. Now her maturing masculinity is finding its own strength. Now she is ready for relationship. She makes room for the royal marriage within, and the earthly marriage without. They influence each other, and consciousness constantly needs to discriminate between the demands of the inner and the outer.

Many women are experiencing the excitement of working with the creative masculinity in another woman. This is not the judgmental, patriarchal masculine that finds the one thing missing in everything, but the masculinity that is on fire with ideas. The symbolic figure when symbolically understood releases immense energy.

Whether the incest is physical or psychic or both, it is very dangerous to flog it into consciousness. The patriarchal drive to know everything deepens the splitting and the either/or attitude. If the transformative process is given the chance to work in its own time, gradually the individual is able to look at the overall experience. In the long, long process of healing our wounds by discovering their spiritual meaning, we discover who we are.

At the core of this chaos of broken hearts, compulsive relationships, compulsive sexuality, what is going on in the psyche? Without an archetypal container to contain the God or Goddess projection, the full force of that projection falls on a human being. For infants it is natural to see their parents as God and Goddess. The parent to whom they are most closely bonded may become the all-loving; the other may become the all-critical. If the parents are narcissistic or full of their own unlived life, they use their child to mirror themselves. The soul of the child is then violated because it is not free to develop its own potential. It is exploited, forced to carry the parents' archetypal projections, passions, and broken dreams. It carries what the parent failed to achieve. It may even become the beloved the parent never found. In this unboundaried bonding, the parents are so lacking in ego structures that they may incarnate the child's fantasy, may accept the child's archetypal projection, unconsciously accepting an archetypal identity as a substitute for their unclaimed humanity. Then child and parents are unconsciously colluding and the child is frozen in an archetypal world which it can no longer freely explore. If, for example, the father accepts the child's archetypal projections and believes he is the King, then he is free to exert power over his child in whatever way he pleases. If he is without ego boundaries, then his young child cannot tell the difference between the King, the father, and Tom Thumb who lives in a castle under the staircase. It is the parents' task to mirror the actuality of the child, so that the child is free to roam in a boundaried world of fairy tale. So long as the parent does not enact the child's archetypal projection, the child's imagination is free to explore an archetypal world, which, like fairy tales, is part of its early development.

When the parents lack an ego structure that protects them from identification with the child's unconscious archetypal projection, and/ or where the egoless child accepts the parents' unconscious archetypal projection (Daddy's little princess or Mommy's little man), the archetype may penetrate the human actuality in a completely destructive way. The result is psychic incest, which may become physical incest. Incest is natural in gods and goddesses; in human beings, it is a delusion of omnipotence.

For many daughters of patriarchy, psychic incest has more subtle ramifications than they realize. So involved are they with their father's world and his values and his split femininity, that they fail to see the impact of their missing mother. They may realize that their inner King is pinned to the wall and because he is pinned in a particular attitude, they are cut off from their creative imagination. They may realize they are frozen in one man and one man only. They may even realize they are trapped in archetypal projection and, therefore, projecting their whole inner world onto a frail human creature to whom they have given power to walk away with their soul. They may be dreaming of a vampire sucking their life-blood. Without a loving Queen to ground them in their own body, such women experience themselves as nothing when their King walks away. Moreover, they may not realize that the King who is annihilating them may not be their own King. He may be the King of the woman whom they rejected in infancy—her masculine ideal, contaminated with her disillusionment, yearning, and despair—the King who kept their mother locked in a glass coffin. So long as they search for that King, they are doomed to projecting onto a man who will reject their feminine soul. The only way out is to go into their own forest and find their own Queen and their own King.

In focusing on the story of Allerleirauh, a daughter of patriarchy, and looking into the soul stories of three women, all daughters of patriarchy, we have been searching for the meaning they share in common, meaning that can bring insight into our own stories. More and more women are today confronting incest, physical or psychic, at the core of their neuroses.

For a brief period, Freud was persuaded that most cases of female hysteria with which he was familiar involved sexual abuse in childhood. So widespread was the understanding of incest in this sexual way that Freud argued that the incest taboo was the earliest taboo governing patriarchal society. Incest, for Freud, was the original sin. It was ingrained in the biological bonding of the infant to the parent, what he called infantile sexuality. It was the *Dasein*, the just so, the given.

In working with hysteria, Freud gradually revised his view of incest. He concluded that hysteria as a psychic state tended to literalize its symptoms. Psychic incest in the hysteric could be projected as sexual. It was, therefore, very difficult to know whether the patient was dealing with psychic or physical incest. Either way the result in the hysteric was very much the same. For Freud, incest, whether physical or psychic, remained the primal sin.

Jung broke with Freud over his understanding of incest and the incest taboo. With reference to his break with Freud, Jung wrote,

> Usually incest has a highly religious aspect, for which reason the incest theme plays a decisive part in almost all cosmogonies and in numerous myths. But Freud clung to the literal interpretation of it and could not grasp the spiritual significance of incest as a symbol. I knew he would never be able to accept any of my ideas on this subject.[2]

For Jung, the function of the incest taboo was to direct the psyche away from a retrogressive desire for some fantasized union with the parent. Jung recognized that the psyche left to itself, without the imposition of some obstacle (such as a taboo), will fall into inertia and either regress to its point of origin (the parent or parent surrogate), or never leave it. The incest taboo launches the psyche, however painfully, upon the path of individuation.

In Jung's paradigm, the energy of the archetype has two poles. At one end, what he calls the infrared end, energy expresses itself in the dynamism of the instincts and body symptoms. At the ultraviolet end, energy expresses itself in the dynamism of the spirit through dreams, fantasies, active imagination. The shift in which the energy of raw instinct transforms into the energy of spirit is what Jung calls "the decisive transformation."[3] In this shift, he suggests, all culture, all civilization is grounded.

Such a shift may happen within a single dream if, for example, the dreamer is experiencing the transformation of an instinctual drive. An addict who is civilizing a compulsive hunger drive may dream of a ravenous wolf transforming into a girl; a gluttonous, unconscious mother may transform into a radiant woman. In fairy tales, the transformation of the animal into prince or princess is not uncommon. Sacrifice and a new level of acceptance are always involved in the transformation.

Until Jung's time, this shift or transformation tended to be thought of as divine intervention *from without*, what Christians call grace. It was as if a supernatural energy penetrated an instinctual energy and redirected its flow, as for example, in the conversion of Saul on the road to Damascus. Jung, on the other hand, saw the taboo as being imposed *from within*, as a transforming agent, transforming raw instinct into spirit. In *Symbols of Transformation*, he wrote, "The symbolic truth . . .

which puts water in place of the mother and spirit in place of the father, frees the libido from the channel of the incest tendency, offers it a new gradient, and canalizes it into a spiritual form."[4] One experiences the agony of chaos, resistance, holding the tension, dropping into new levels of chaos, and then the new pattern of energy emerges. In order to grow, individuals have to cooperate with the new direction of its flow. Cooperation involves the soul's knowledge of itself in dialogue with another energy. Those who do not cooperate with the new direction are choosing regression into smothering parental complexes that produce neuroses, hypochondria, depression.

This happens repeatedly with addicts. The taboo that is trying to push them out of the crippling incest surfaces in a dream. They go into a bedroom. There is the old father or old mother almost dead or psychotic. "Get out of here," shrieks the parent. For whatever reason, the inveterate addict stays. If she could step back over that fateful threshold, slam the door, and go with the energy released through the taboo, then something quite different might happen. A radiant young man, rather like her brother or her father when he was twenty, might come to accompany her. In Kate's dream (p. 92) her young father embodies this radiance. Sometimes a serpent appears in her larynx with its powerful head trying to push through her throat (Kate's dream, p. 87). Or a majestic phallos, symbol of her own creative potential (Mary's dream, p. 191). The point is the energy transforms from worn-out stereotypes into vibrant energy symbolized in new archetypal images. The tragedy of psychic incest is that the creative aspect is destroyed by the literalization of it.

In the gradual transformations of Kate, Mary, and Rita, psychic incest as the source of spiritual and creative energy is the key. Kate had to deal with rage toward her brother, her love for her father never wavered until her teens. That love motivated her love of learning and her devotion to the church. In the searing fire of her dreams, and her searing experiences with priests and professors, that love matured, and transferred from father to archetypal lover, who now carried the transformative power of her creative masculinity.

Mary unconsciously picked up repressed negativity toward sexuality and at the same time the unlived sexuality in her parents. Together these constellated her sexual witch and the power drive that goes with it. Her mother encouraged and celebrated Mary's power over men. Eventually, after the death of her son, Mary's body rebelled against the invasion of her mother's demonic hatred of the masculine and initiated Mary's descent. She entered rage and grief in her body. In those transformative fires she, as mother, gave birth to herself, as virgin. With the guidance of her crone, her virgin is becoming strong enough to surrender to creative inspiration beyond anything she had ever rationally considered.

Rita's love of her father and brothers and their love for her opened her to the gifts in her own creative matrix. And that love prepared the way for the transformation of a literalized father god into the mystery of her beloved inner guide and the radiant young Christ. Moreover it brought her to a loving acceptance of her mother, archetypal and personal.

Because each of these women successfully differentiated the archetypal and the human without denying either, the transformation of her inner masculine released new depths of love in her marriage.

Repeatedly in my work with dreams, I have watched the process that Jung describes: the symbolic truth that frees the sexual charge from the literal father and transforms that energy into creative work born of the inner marriage. We can see that process in the dreams of Kate, Mary, and Rita. But, if the purpose of the incest taboo is to transform raw instinct into spirit, does that leave us yet again in the patriarchal body-spirit split? Are we back where we started, with slightly more refined animals forever aspiring toward wings while nature is essentially exploited and despised? Or is it possible that a symbolic understanding of the incest taboo can also transform the raw instinct of incestuous bonding to our mother (matter) into spiritual energy of a different frequency in matter?

In Rita's dream (p. 250), the immense snake energy (instinctual libido) comes up to what seems to be a mirror, goes through a convulsive shedding of its skin, and then another snake appears, white and shining, moving like a whirlwind up into the air. It is as if the instinctual energy comes to a point of crossover (perhaps the diaphragm), transforms as it moves through its own skin, and then energy of another frequency manifests in the white snake (spiritual libido).

Then a white owl (bird of Athena) appears. As a winged creature it has still another frequency. It can fly into the eye of infinity—the very friendly eye of the god or goddess.

This feeling of transcendence into the sky is followed by the complementary image of deerflies dissolving one into the other, which Rita associates with orgasms. It is as if the highest point of spiritual ecstasy constellates the deepest point of instinctual energy.

Then there seems to be another dimension of transformation introduced in the purification ritual in which the shrouded, faceless woman, moving like a stone statue, goes into the water. The dream ego cannot yet enter this pool. Perhaps there is still work to be done in transforming the frog into human form and this, in turn, has to do with recognizing the cardboard quality of the cathedral. In other words, some radical transition has yet to take place in the masculine energy, both spiritually and instinctually, before the dream ego can enter the pool. There are two distinct energies in the process of transformation—one feminine, one masculine.

Such dreams are not uncommon in both men and women; their impact is transformative in both genders. They suggest a new understanding of instinct and spirit, and a new level of integration. In the shift suggested in such dreams, life in matter is honored. Instead of matter being dark, opaque, dependent on spirit to redeem it from the devil, matter infused with its own potential light is moving toward consciousness. The mottled snake is related to the white snake, and the white snake is followed by the white owl that can fly. The process in the bodysoul is sacred, strong enough to be responsible to itself and flexible enough to move through different frequencies in preparation for its meeting with the transformed masculine.

Again, let me make it quite clear that psychic incest with the negative mother archetype as I am describing it is not mother bashing. For centuries, our culture has disdained matter, and so deep and so unconscious is our contempt for the body that we cannot see the rejection of the living body in our addictive behaviors. Mothers and grandmothers for generations have despised their female bodies, their sexuality, "the curse" of menstruation. They were born in a female body; nothing can change that. No matter how hard they try, they feel they have failed from the start. Their contempt for their own matter is in their cells and that contempt is in the cells of their daughters. "I don't deserve to live" is blurted out as the bottom line of self-rejection. The unspeakable black hole that many women have to face in their dreams is that place of rejection. The child, as feminine being, was not reflected because centuries of patriarchal thinking have scorned matter. The hole is still jet black. It is not even despair. It is nothingness, oblivion without feeling, death without consciousness. It is shame so deep that it cannot be recognized until the ego container is strong enough to face the obliteration. It is matter so wounded, so betrayed that it is dissociated from consciousness. Women trapped in this incestuous bonding with the negative side of the mother archetype dream of doing battle with an ugly woman. They feel so betrayed by their body that they try to take up residence in their mind. As tiny children they learned not to breathe deeply because breath activated these feelings and sensations. Numbness makes life bearable. To obliterate matter, however, is also to obliterate soul. Soul killing in body is alienation from the positive mother; soul killing in spirit is alienation from the positive father.

The black hole in many men is as black as it is in many women. Some even take a certain pride in being "shut down." The fact is their matter is dissociated from their spirit and their fundamental contempt for matter is in their cells. So long as they stay in their superficial persona, they may be caring, generous, even loving, but in the intimacy of sexuality they cannot feel their own passion connected to their own being. They may experience fear, emptiness, nothingness. Overcome by the black hole at the center, they cannot reflect themselves nor their partner, however much they try. If we are not bonded to the positive mother, we cannot trust our own cells; then full sexual surrender is impossible. Life cannot be fully lived without embodiment, nor can death be faced creatively. No wonder death is denied in a culture that rejects the beauty of its own humanity.

As the psyche individuates so does the body, and the physical illnesses we encounter in the process make quite clear that our body cells do have their own wisdom, which they want to transform into light (consciousness). In our dreams, animals are yearning for recognition. In nature, dolphins and other animals have sensitivities that are only now being recognized. The upheavals in our planet and our bodies are trying to tell us something. Perhaps the anguish in our matter, personal and planetary, is the incest taboo forcing us out of psychic incest with the negative mother archetype and into a new body with light of its own. Perhaps the encoding in our cells can be released from the past and wants to move to the future.

Kate, Mary, and Rita all carried deep incest wounding from their mothers who carried it from generations of wounding. By holding the tension of the feminine opposites—mother fearful of losing her power/daughter fearful of taking responsibility; instinctual drive/paralysed desire—each is discovering that the either/or split can be healed. By sustaining the tension, each is discovering the third—the crone who is an image of the archetypal mother in whom the opposites are contained. Through Her, each has been reconciled with her personal mother and each, by experiencing the suffering in her body and the cherishing of other women, is beginning to understand Love as a reality in her cells.

While consciously holding the still point in Love, we can observe the opposites swinging through us without swinging with them. We can observe the power of the mother, who yearns to hold onto her child, letting go; we can observe the sexuality of the gypsy who wants life to serve her transforming into a love that is ready to serve life. We can remain invisible if necessary, feel ourselves being moved to a new conscious position, and sustained by Her, hold that new still point. Here mother and gypsy are one in the Bride. Gradually, we know that Her light in matter is Love. Like perfume, it permeates everything. Experiencing that Presence once changes our perception forever. Perhaps this is the real meaning of the coming to consciousness of the feminine. It must come slowly or our hearts would break. In our Mother's house are many more mansions than we can yet dream of.

The still point that transcends the maelstrom of the opposites brings healing to the masculine as well as to the feminine. It moves beyond patriarchal bickering, beyond judge and blame. The woman who unconsciously has become her husband's daughter may recognize that the rebel who lives in the woods in her dreams, and in the lover in her life, is the shadow side of her father. The unlived sexuality that neither dared acknowledge is now charging the unconscious with the numinosity of a god. Dionysus in the form of a bull may thunder through her dreams. If the woman refuses to act out the split, at the same time holding both sides of her love in consciousness, then she is in a fire hot enough to forge an unbreakable container. Journal, art, music, dance, articulate everything that is going on inside her; the ever-faithful King that she has projected onto her husband becomes part of her inner Bridegroom; the energy of the bull begins to take on the shape of the god Dionysus. Father and bull are one in the Bridegroom. Someday the woman may realize that her yearning to love the father—spiritually and sexually— was her yearning for wholeness, and all her lovers along the way were part of that yearning. Someday she may realize that the gift of loving, even loving that is unrequited, is as great as the gift of being loved. Someday she may realize that it was the lovers who rejected her who unconsciously gave her the gift of a heart that is burned clean of a power drive that would have attempted to make the mystery serve her. Burning in the inner fire brings the Beloved home.

Contemporary Allerleirauhs are leaving their father's house and some are going into the forest. They are refusing to be "victims" or "survivors" of incest. They reject our culture's addiction to victimization. They reject labels that keep them forever splayed in a demeaning role. They realize that the incestuous energy that is bound into the parental complexes is radioactive energy. Once it begins to move, it will move either to destroy or to create. Destruction or creation goes on within and without. Surely our task is to claim that energy as our own and claim our own responsibility to our own greatest potential.

That potential becomes actual when we work on masculinity and femininity within ourselves until we feel empowered, embodied spirit uniting with conscious matter in our soul. Then we are moving toward a genuine maturity in which the two energies interact to produce a third, which from the soul's point of view is the real.

The creative masculine is not the mythical father of our childhood, nor the actual father we began to see as we grew up. While he may have qualities of our personal father, he is inherent in us, unique in us. It is our task to separate the archetypal father from human men. Although we can see parts of him in all the men we have loved, none of them is his totality. This King does not suddenly appear out of a different kind of world. He has been inside all along, waiting in the shadows of the unconscious to be recognized. One night in our dream he may come shining toward us, his powerful, hairy arms wide open. He may hold us close, so close that we hear his throbbing heart. "You didn't know me," he may say. "I've loved you all your life."

Knowing him is also knowing Sophia. The more firmly embodied we are in her creative matrix, the brighter his light can shine. We whose hearts have been seared with the fire of too much loving can surrender to a love beyond our human capacity to conceive. In surrender, touching, tasting, smelling, seeing, hearing—the world becomes erotïcized with love. Sexuality and spirituality are one. In the conscious container of that love we make the bread soup. The flood of our passion pours into creativity. Imagination impregnates conscious matter.

We are the mothers of the new consciousness. We are virgins empowered in the ever-present, ever-evolving images of Now. We are crones trusting the unknowable. Mother, virgin, crone, nature open to the fire of the imagination. This is our way toward affirming our own I AM.

As we put the talking stick away, one further thought. We may spill coffee on our golden dress; we may discover red petticoats under our silver; we may tear the hem of our dress of stars. We may even pack them all in our nutshell and run again into the forest.

Appendix

Allerleirauh*

There was once upon a time a King who had a wife with golden hair, and she was so beautiful that her equal was not to be found on earth. It came to pass that she lay ill, and as she felt that she must soon die, she called the King and said: "If you wish to marry again after my death, take no one who is not quite as beautiful as I am, and who has not just such golden hair as I have: this you must promise me." And after the King had promised her this she closed her eyes and died.

For a long time the King could not be comforted, and had no thought of taking another wife. At length his councillors said: "This cannot go on. The King must marry again, that we may have a Queen." And now messengers were sent about far and wide, to seek a bride who equalled the late Queen in beauty. In the whole world, however, none was to be found, and even if one had been found, still there would have been no one who had such golden hair. So the messengers came home as they went.

Now the King had a daughter, who was just as beautiful as her dead mother, and had the same golden hair. When she was grown up the King looked at her one day, and saw that in every respect she was like his late wife, and suddenly felt a violent love for her. Then he spoke to his councillors: "I will marry my daughter, for she is the counterpart of my late wife, otherwise I can find no bride who resembles her." When the councillors heard that, they were shocked, and said: "God has forbidden a father to marry his daughter. No good can come from such a crime, and the kingdom will be involved in the ruin."

The daughter was still more shocked when she became aware of her father's resolution, but hoped to turn him from his design. Then she said to him: "Before I fulfill your wish, I must have three dresses, one

---

* "Allerleirauh" means *"of many different kinds of fur."* The text is reprinted from *The Complete Grimm's Fairy Tales* (New York: Pantheon Books, 1974).

367

as golden as the sun, one as silvery as the moon, and one as bright as the stars; besides this, I wish for a mantle of a thousand different kinds of fur and peltry joined together, and one of every kind of animal in your kingdom must give a piece of his skin for it." For she thought: "To get that will be quite impossible, and thus I shall divert my father from his wicked intentions." The King, however, did not give it up, and the cleverest maidens in his kingdom had to weave the three dresses, one as golden as the sun, one as silvery as the moon, and one as bright as the stars, and his huntsmen had to catch one of every kind of animal in the whole of his kingdom, and take from it a piece of its skin, and out of these was made a mantle of a thousand different kinds of fur. At length, when all was ready, the King caused the mantle to be brought, spread it out before her, and said: "The wedding shall be tomorrow."

When, therefore, the King's daughter saw that there was no longer any hope of turning her father's heart, she resolved to run away. In the night whilst every one was asleep, she got up, and took three different things from her treasures, a golden ring, a golden spinning wheel, and a golden reel. The three dresses of the sun, moon, and stars she placed into a nutshell, put on her mantle of all kinds of fur, and blackened her face and hands with soot. Then she commended herself to God, and went away, and walked the whole night until she reached a great forest. And as she was tired, she got into a hollow tree, and fell asleep.

The sun rose, and she slept on, and she was still sleeping when it was full day. Then it so happened that the King to whom this forest belonged, was hunting in it. When his dogs came to the tree, they sniffed, and ran barking round about it. The King said to the huntsmen: "Just see what kind of wild beast has hidden itself in there." The huntsmen obeyed his order, and when they came back they said: "A wondrous beast is lying in the hollow tree; we have never before seen one like it. Its skin is fur of a thousand different kinds, but it is lying asleep." Said the King: "See if you can catch it alive, and then fasten it to the carriage, and we will take it with us." When the huntsmen laid hold of the maiden, she awoke full of terror, and cried to them: "I am a poor child, deserted by father and mother; have pity on me, and take me with you." Then said they: "Allerleirauh, you will be useful in the kitchen, come with us, and you can sweep up the ashes." So they put her in the carriage, and took her home to the royal palace. There they pointed out to her a closet under the stairs, where no daylight entered, and said: "Hairy animal, there you can live and sleep." Then she was sent into the kitchen, and there she carried wood and water, swept the hearth, plucked the fowls, picked the vegetables, raked the ashes, and did all the dirty work.

Allerleirauh lived there for a long time in great wretchedness. Alas, fair princess, what is to become of you now! It happened, however, that one day a feast was held in the palace, and she said to the cook: "May I go upstairs for a while, and look on? I will place myself outside the door." The cook answered: "Yes, go, but you must be back here in half-an-hour to sweep the hearth." Then she took her oil-lamp, went into her den, put off her dress of fur, and washed the soot off her face and hands, so that her full beauty once more came to light. And she opened the nut, and took out her dress which shone like the sun, and when she had done that she went up to the festival, and every one made way for her, for no one knew her, and thought no otherwise than that she was a king's daughter. The King came to meet her, gave his hand to her, and danced with her, and thought in his heart: "My eyes have never yet seen any one so beautiful!" When the dance was over she curtsied, and when the King looked round again she had vanished, and none knew whither. The guards who stood outside the palace were called and questioned, but no one had seen her.

She had run into her little den, however, there quickly taken off her dress, made her face and hands black again, put on the mantle of fur, and again was Allerleirauh. And now when she went into the kitchen, and was about to get to her work and sweep up the ashes, the cook said: "Leave that alone till morning, and make me the soup for the King; I, too, will go upstairs awhile, and take a look; but let no hairs fall in, or in future you shall have nothing to eat." So the cook went away, and Allerleirauh made the soup for the King, and made bread soup and the best she could, and when it was ready she fetched her golden ring from her little den, and put it in the bowl in which the soup was served. When the dancing was over, the King had his soup brought and ate it, and he liked it so much that it seemed to him he had never tasted better. But when he came to the bottom of the bowl, he saw a golden ring lying, and could not conceive how it could have got there. Then he ordered the cook to appear before him. The cook was terrified when he heard the order, and said to Allerleirauh: "You have certainly let a hair fall into the soup, and if you have, you shall be beaten for it." When he came before the King the latter asked who had made the soup? The cook replied: "I made it." But the King said:

"That is not true, for it was much better than usual, and cooked differently." He answered: "I must acknowledge that I did not make it, it was made by the hairy animal." The King said: "Go and bid it come up here."

When Allerleirauh came, the King said: "Who are you?" "I am a poor girl who no longer has any father or mother." He asked further: "Of what use are you in my palace?" She answered: "I am good for nothing but to have boots thrown at my head." He continued: "Where did you get the ring which was in the soup?" She answered: "I know nothing about the ring." So the King could learn nothing, and had to send her away again.

After a while, there was another festival, and then, as before, Allerleirauh begged the cook for leave to go and look on. He answered: "Yes, but come back again in half-an-hour, and make the King the bread soup which he so much likes." Then she ran into her den, washed herself quickly, and took out of the nut the dress which was as silvery as the moon, and put it on. Then she went up and was like a princess, and the King stepped forward to meet her, and rejoiced to see her once more, and as the dance was just beginning they danced it together. But when it was ended, she again disappeared so quickly that the King could not observe where she went. She, however, sprang into her den, and once more made herself a hairy animal, and went into the kitchen to prepare the bread soup. When the cook had gone upstairs, she fetched the little golden spinningwheel, and put it in the bowl so that the soup covered it. Then it was taken to the King, who ate it, and liked it as much as before, and had the cook brought, who this time likewise was forced to confess that Allerleirauh had prepared the soup. Allerleirauh again came before the King, but she answered that she was good for nothing else but to have boots thrown at her head, and that she knew nothing at all about the little golden spinningwheel.

When, for the third time, the King held a festival, all happened just as it had done before. The cook said: "Fur-skin, you are a witch, and always put something in the soup which makes it so good that the King likes it better than that which I cook," but as she begged so hard, he let her go up at the appointed time. And now she put on the dress which shone like the stars, and thus entered the hall. Again the King danced with the beautiful maiden, and thought that she never yet had been so beautiful. And whilst she was dancing, he contrived, without her noticing it, to slip a golden ring on her finger, and he had given orders that the dance should last a very long time. When it was ended, he wanted to hold her fast by her hands, but she tore herself loose, and sprang away so quickly through the crowd that she vanished from his sight. She ran as fast as she could into her den beneath the stairs, but as she had been too long, and had stayed more than half-an-hour she could not take off her pretty dress, but only threw over it her mantle of fur, and in her haste she did not make herself quite black, but one finger remained white. Then Allerleirauh ran into the kitchen, and cooked the bread soup for the King, and as the cook was away, put her golden reel into it. When the King found the reel at the bottom of it, he caused Allerleirauh to be summoned, and then he espied the white finger, and saw the ring which he had put on it during the dance. Then he grasped her by the hand, and held her fast, and when she wanted to release herself and run away, her mantle of fur opened a little, and the star-dress shone forth. The King clutched the mantle and tore it off. Then her golden hair shone forth, and she stood there in full splendor, and could no longer hide herself. And when she had washed the soot and ashes from her face, she was more beautiful than anyone who had ever been seen on earth. But the King said: "You are my dear bride, and we will never more part from each other." Thereupon the marriage was solemnized, and they lived happily until their death.

Notes

INTRODUCTION

1. C. G. Jung, *Memories, Dreams, Reflections*, ed. by Aniela Jaffé, trans. from the German by Richard and Clara Winston (London: Collins, Fontana Library, 1971), p. 355.
2. John Keats, "Ode to Psyche," *English Romantic Writers*, ed. by David Perkins (New York: Harcourt, Brace and World, 1967), p. 1184, line 51.

LEAVING MY FATHER'S HOUSE

1. Sylvia Plath, "The Hanging Man," *Ariel* (London: Faber and Faber, 1965), p. 70.
2. Ibid.
3. Emily Dickinson, *The Complete Poems* (Boston: Little, Brown and Company, 1960), p. 430.
4. From correspondence with my friend, Janet Parker Vaughan.
5. William Blake, "Milton," *Selected Poetry and Prose*, ed. by Northrop Frye (Toronto: Random House of Canada, 1953), p. 257.

CHAPTER 1. THE GOLDEN DRESS

1. For a fuller discussion of the potential in this figure, see Robert Bly, *Iron John* (Reading, Mass.: Addison-Wesley Publishing, 1990).
2. In this film, the patriarchal father insists that his son will study medicine and give up his creative delight in theater. His mother passively colludes with the father. The son commits suicide.
3. For further development of this problem see Evangeline Kane, *Recovering from Incest: Imagination and the Healing Process* (Boston: Sigo Press, 1989).
4. Emily Dickinson, *The Complete Poems*, pp. 522–523.

CHAPTER 3. TURNING BLOOD TO INK

1. Alice Miller, *Thou Shalt Not Be Aware: Society's Betrayal of the Child*, trans. by Hildegarde and Hunter Hannum (New York: Farrar, Straus and Giroux, 1985), p. 316.
2. "The Prayer after Communion," in *The Book of Alternative Services of the Anglican Church of Canada* (Toronto: The Anglican Book Centre, 1985), p. 214.
3. Marie-Louise von Franz and Fraser Boa, *The Way of the Dream* (Toronto: Windrose Films, 1988), p. 71.
4. Miller, *Thou Shalt Not Be Aware*, p. 318.

CHAPTER 4. THE SILVER DRESS

1. Jung, "On the Nature of the Psyche," *The Structure and Dynamics of the Psyche*, *Collected Works* 8 (London: Routledge and Kegan Paul, trans. by R. F. C. Hull, 1960), para. 407.
2. Ibid., para. 418.
3. Emily Dickinson, *The Complete Poems*, p. 316.
4. Ibid., p. 276.

CHAPTER 5. MARY

1. Blake, "The Tyger," pp. 43–44.
2. Blake, "The Marriage of Heaven and Hell," p. 123.

CHAPTER 6. REDEEMING EVE'S BODY

1. See "Poem of Witch Passion," in Marion Woodman, *Addiction to Perfection* (Toronto: Inner City Books, 1982), pp. 101–111.
2. Blake, "The Little Black Boy," p. 25.
3. W. B. Yeats, "Among School Children," in *The Collected Poems of W. B. Yeats* (New York: MacMillan, 1956), p. 214.

CHAPTER 7. THE DRESS OF STARS

1. Marie-Louise von Franz, *The Feminine in Fairytales* (Zurich: Spring Publications, 1972), p. 129.
2. Ibid, pp. 129–130.
3. Ibid, p. 130.
4. Rainer Maria Rilke, *Letters to a Young Poet*, trans. by M. D. Herter Norton (New York: W. W. Norton and Company, 1962), p. 59.

CHAPTER 9. THE ENDLESS BEGINNING

1. earle birney, "Fall by Fury," used by permission of the poet.
2. C. G. Jung, *Psychology and Religion* (New Haven, Conn.: Yale University Press, 1938), p. 113.
3. Joseph Campbell, *The Masks of God: Creative Mythology* (New York: Penguin Books, 1976).
4. Michael Dames, *Silbury Hill*.
5. Frederick Frank, *The Zen of Seeing* (New York: Random House, 1973).
6. Fraser Boa, *This Business of the Gods* (Windrose Films Ltd, 1989).
7. Jacob Needleman, *Sense of the Cosmos* (New York: Penguin, 1988), p. 16.
8. W. B. Yeats, *The Second Coming* (New York: MacMillan, 1924).
9. Ajit Mookerjee, *Kundalini* (London: Thames and Hudson, 1982), p. 49.
10. Ibid.
11. Robert Browning, from "Two in the Campagna."
12. William Blake, from "Tyger, tyger burning bright."
13. C. G. Jung, *Psychology and Alchemy* (Princeton, N.J.: Princeton University Press, 1968), p. 28.
14. Aldo Carotenuto, *The Spiral Way: A Woman's Healing Journey* (Toronto: Inner City Books, 1986).
15. Jung, *Psychology and Religion*, p. 113.
16. Jung, *Psychology and Alchemy*, condensed from pages 28–37.

CONCLUSION

1. William Stafford, from "A Ritual We Read to Each Other," in *Stories That Could Be True* (New York: Harper and Row, 1977).
2. Jung, *Memories, Dreams, Reflections*, p. 191.
3. Ibid., p. 191.
4. Jung, "Symbols of the Mother and of Rebirth," *Symbols of Transformation*, CW 5, para. 335.

Credits

The quotation from *The Feminine in Fairytales* by Marie-Louise von Franz is used by permission of the publisher, Spring Publications, copyright © 1972.

The quotation from "A Ritual We Read to Each Other" from *Stories That Could Be True* is used by kind permission of the author.

Diligent efforts were made to obtain rights from copyright holders. In a few instances, the efforts were unsuccessful. The author and publisher are grateful for the use of this excerpted material.